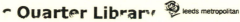

Islam, Secularism, and Nationalism in Modern Turkey

Common wisdom argues that in the interwar period, Kemalist secularism was very successful in eliminating religion from the public sphere in Turkey, leaving Turkish national identity devoid of religious content. However, *Islam, Secularism, and Nationalism in Modern Turkey* reaches another conclusion through an investigation of the impact of the Ottoman millet system on Turkish and Balkan nationalism. It demonstrates that even though Mustafa Kemal Atatürk successfully secularized Turkey's political structure in the interwar period, the legacy of the Ottoman millet system, which divided the Ottoman population into religious compartments called millets, shaped Turkey's understanding of nationalism in the same era.

This book analyzes this subject through investigating topics including:

- Turkish nationalism
- Nationalism in Eastern Europe in the interwar period
- The Ottoman legacy
- Kemalist citizenship policies and immigration
- Kurds, Ottoman Muslims, Greeks, Armenians, Jews, and the ethno-religious limits of Turkishness.

Islam, Secularism, and Nationalism in Modern Turkey is essential reading for scholars and students with research interests in Turkey, Turkish Nationalism, Balkans, and Middle Eastern History.

Soner Cagaptay is senior fellow and director of the Turkish Research Program at the Washington Institute for Near East Policy, a Washington-based think tank. Dr Cagaptay is also chair of Turkey Advanced Area Program at the US State Department's Foreign Service Institute. His research interests include US–Turkish relations and modern Turkish history.

Routledge Studies in Middle Eastern History

Islam, Secularism, and Nationalism in Modern Turkey

Who is a Turk?

Soner Cagaptay

Routledge
Taylor & Francis Group

LONDON AND NEW YORK

First published 2006
by Routledge
2 Park Square, Milton Park, Abingdon, Oxon OX14 4RN

Simultaneously published in the USA and Canada
by Routledge
270 Madison Ave, New York, NY 10016

Transferred to Digital Printing 2006

Routledge is an imprint of the Taylor & Francis Group, an informa business

© 2006 Soner Cagaptay

Typeset in Baskerville by
Newgen Imaging Systems (P) Ltd, Chennai, India
Printed and bound in Great Britain by
Biddles Ltd, King's Lynn

British Library Cataloguing in Publication Data
A catalogue record for this book is available
from the British Library

Library of Congress Cataloging in Publication Data
A catalog record for this book has been requested

ISBN10: 0–415–38458–3
ISBN13: 978–0–415–38458–2

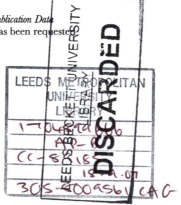

*Sultan ve Mehmet Çağaptay'ın aziz
hatıraları için...*

Contents

**Conclusion: understanding Turkish nationalism in
modern Turkey—the Kemalist legacy**   156

Illustrations

Figures

Maps

Acknowledgments

This book is based on my doctoral dissertation that I wrote in the History Department at Yale University between 1996 and 2002. I am deeply grateful to my supervisor and mentor, Professor Ivo Banac at Yale University, for his indispensable guidance at Yale. I would also like to extend my gratitude to my readers, Professors Abbas Amanat and Ben Kiernan, for the valuable support they have offered me at Yale.

Furthermore, I would like to thank Professor Ayhan Aktar of Marmara University, Istanbul, for his encouragement during the writing stages of this project. I am also indebted to Professor Şükrü Hanioğlu of Princeton University, Professor Reşat Kasaba of the University of Washington, and Professor Hakan Yavuz of the University of Utah for reading drafts of various parts of this research.

I would also like to express gratitude to my editor Cathy Shufro of the Berkeley College at Yale for her excellent editing work on this dissertation. In addition, I would like to thank my assistants Nuray Nazlı Inal and Düden Yeğenoğlu for helping me edit the dissertation into its current format.

The hardworking people of the Interlibrary Loan Service at Yale's Sterling Library provided me with many books that were so essential to the completion of this project. Other library staff, including Circulation, Microfilm Collection, and Borrow Direct personnel, made available much needed material for this work. In this regard, my special thanks goes to Abraham Parrish and Michael Funaro of the Map Room who created the highly successful maps in this dissertation.

I also would like to express gratitude to various institutions within Yale University that have bestowed many generous grants toward the completion of this project. Additionally, I would like to thank Florence Thomas, the graduate registrar of the History Department, who took care of so many important details during my tenure at Yale.

I carried out a very significant part of my research toward this work at the British Public Record Office (PRO), the Turkish Prime Minister's Republic Archives (Başbakanlık Cumhuriyet Arşivleri—BCA), and the archives of the Turkish Ministry of Interior (Dahiliye Vekâleti—İçişleri Bakanlığı). I also worked at the National Library (Milli Kütüphane), as well as the libraries of the Turkish Historical Society (Türk Tarih Kurumu) and the Turkish Grand National Assembly (Türkiye

Büyük Millet Meclisi—TBMM) in Ankara. I would like to extend my appreciation to these institutions and their staff for allowing me the opportunity to take advantage of their research facilities.

Finally, I would like to thank my family, especially my sisters Hatice Çağaptay and Suna Çağaptay-Arıkan, for their support.

Note on names

Throughout this work, I have used the contemporary Turkish spelling for all towns and provinces in Turkey. The only exceptions to this rule are for Istanbul and Izmir. I have used the common English spelling of these names, instead of Turkish İstanbul and İzmir. Where the name of a city or a province has changed since the 1920s, except for variations in spelling, I have given the former name of that province in brackets and then used the contemporary name throughout the study. The only exception to this rule is Dersim, whose name became Tunceli in 1936. In the early 1930s, much of the history of this province focused on its name (see Chapter 7); hence, I refer to this province as Dersim until 1937, and as Tunceli after that. Additionally, I have used the English version of the names for rivers, mountains, and other geographical features.

Notes on personal names, translations, and archival sources

Personal names

Throughout this study, I have used the Turkish spelling for all personal names. New last names were adopted in Turkey in 1934 (see Chapter 4). Hence, if I mention people before this year, I give the last name they adopted in 1934 in brackets. Then, I refer to them with their adopted last name throughout the rest of the study. There were quite a few people in interwar Turkey who had last names prior to 1934, and who used their last names first and first names second, as was the practice then, hence for example, Saraçoğlu Şükrü. Most of these people kept their last names after 1934, simply changing the order of the first and last names. In initial references to such people, I use both formats of their last names, hence Saraçoğlu Şükrü (Saraçoğlu).

Translations

Unless otherwise noted, all translations in the manuscript are mine.

Archival sources

In completing this dissertation, I had access to a number of very significant archives, whose collections provided me with valuable insight. Although I did everything I could to corroborate evidence from one archive with documents from other archives or secondary sources, this was not always the case. I am aware that this may be a shortcoming. Hence, I only hope that my work paves the way for further studies that make more complete use of archival sources.

Prologue

[…]
Çeşmelerde abdest alınmaz oldu
Camilerde namaz kılınmaz oldu
Ma'mur olan yerler hep harap oldu
Aldı Nemse bizum nazlı Budini

Budinun içinde uzun çarşısı
Orta yerinde Sultan Ahmet camisi
Ka'be suretine benzer yapısı
Aldı Nemse bizum nazlı Budini

Budinun içinde serdar kızıyım
Anamun babamun iki kuziyim
Kafesde beslı kınalı kuzıyım
Aldı Nemse bizum nazlı Budini

Cebhane tutuşdı aklımız şaşdı
Selatin camiler yandı tutuşdı
Hep sabi sibyanlar ateşe düşdi
Aldı Nemse bizum nazlı Budini
[…]

No more ritual ablutions at the fountains
No more prayers at the mosques
Thriving places turned into ruins
Austria (Nemse) has taken our cherished Budin [Buda]

The long market inside Budin
With the Mosque of Sultan Ahmet in its middle
With its structure like an image of Ka'ba
Austria has taken our cherished Budin

I am the daughter of the Ottoman commander in Budin
To my mother and my father, the apple of their eyes
Their henna-tinted lamb, nurtured behind shuttered windows
Austria has taken our cherished Budin

The powder house caught on fire, our minds were numbed
The sultans' mosques burnt in flames
All the young men and children were thrown into fire
Austria has taken our cherished Budin
[...]

My adaptation of Andras Riedlmayer's translation of a Turkish folk ballad, lamenting the fall of Buda in 1686, collected at Ada Kale, an Ottoman-Turkish island enclave at the Iron Gates on the Danube. (Ada Kale, home to Turkish Muslims from Hungary, who had fled there in the late seventeenth century, was engulfed by the Iron Gates dam in 1968.) Turkish text of the poem in Ignacz Kunos, *Türk Halk Edebiyatı* (Turkish folk literature) (Istanbul, 1925), 19–20.

Introduction

Turkish nationalism today

> The Minorities are rapidly disappearing as entities. This program of Minorities is essentially the latest phase of a conflict between the radically opposed political ideals; Ottomanism or federation of the heterogeneous, and Turkish or homogenous nationalism. The idea of nationalism and the idea of the race are the ideas of new Turkey.
>
> (From a US diplomatic memorandum dispatched from Istanbul, December 1938)

The use of the term Turk in modern Turkey is a puzzling phenomenon. People in the country see all Muslims as Turks, regardless of their ethnicity or language. In view of this, not only ethnic Turks, but also others such as Kurds, Circassians, and Bosnians are regarded as Turks, while the non-Muslims (including Armenians and Jews) are not, even when they speak Turkish. This is not simply a matter of semantics: in Turkey, being a Turk has tangible benefits. Since only Turks are full members of the nation and considered loyal citizens, this perception is key to joining the mainstream society of the country. On the other hand, not being regarded as a Turk leads to the stigma of being an imperfect citizen.

This explains the marginalization of Jews and of Christians, including Armenians and Greeks, from the Turkish nation. Despite the fact that the contemporary Turkish Constitution of 1980 defines all inhabitants of the country as Turks, in real terms non-Muslims, especially Christians, are not viewed as Turks.[1] For instance, they are barred from becoming diplomats or army officers. Furthermore, public antagonism toward Christianity is not uncommon. An example of this was the recent controversy involving Turkish-Protestant churches. News appeared in the press between 1999 and 2001 (and lately in 2004) that small grassroot churches had sprung up in the major cities. There was an immediate nationalist public backlash against this. The fact that these churches were mostly started by Turkish Muslims who had converted to Christianity was ignored. The public blamed Christian proselytizing by foreign missionaries. Christianity was seen as unfit for Muslim Turks, who would not have converted if it were not for Christian missionaries.[2] This illustrates that Christianity is viewed as alien by the larger Turkish society, a painful situation for the country's small Christian communities.

Although the use of the word Turk excludes some groups from the nation, it includes some others. Today, most people in Turkey regard all Muslims in the country as Turks. Consequently, when some people among them, such as the Kurds, do not see themselves as Turks, most people in Turkey resent this. In the early 1980s, the terrorist Kurdish nationalist Kurdistan Workers Party (Partiya Karkeran Kürdistan—PKK) launched a violent separatist movement against Turkey. The PKK forcefully claimed that the Kurds were not members of the Turkish nation. They were a separate national community. Accordingly, the PKK wanted to carve a homeland for the Kurds in Turkey. The government reacted to this. Various segments of the society, including some Kurds, rallied to Ankara's support. On the other hand, while some Kurds threw their support behind the PKK, others remained aloof from the organization.

The ensuing struggle between Ankara and the PKK has had an immense toll: between 1983 and 2000, the country suffered 38,000 casualties and an estimated $250 billion in material costs and damages. Today, Turkey seems to have militarily defeated the PKK after much fighting as well as a 1998 *tour de force* against Syria, which provided a safe haven for the PKK.[3] Although the fight seems to be mostly over, Ankara's tenacity against Kurdish separatism should still be accounted for. Popular support for the government in this regard, despite the huge social and economic losses of the struggle against the PKK, ought to be understood too. Moreover, why have so many Kurds remained aloof to the Kurdish nationalist cause?

In order to explain these dilemmas of modern Turkey, one would need to clarify what constitutes Turkishness. This requires an analysis of Turkish nationalism, beginning with a study of the birth and entrenchment of the notion of Turkishness in the first half of the twentieth century, when modern Turkey emerged as a nation-state. Some of Turkey's contemporary nationality-related dilemmas seem embedded in this period and even earlier. Turkish nationalism materialized during the last decades of the Ottoman Empire. At this time, when the Ottoman millet system fell apart, with its religious compartments (millets) yielding to different nationalist programs, Turkish nationalism emerged as a powerful political force within the Muslim millet. It became an increasingly dominant ideology between the Constitutional Revolution of 1908, and the Empire's end in 1922. The speedy dismemberment of the Ottoman state in this period was followed by the establishment of the Turkish republic by Mustafa Kemal Atatürk in 1923. Then, together with secularism and Westernization, nationalism became one leg of the ideological tripod of young Turkey. Defying the Ottoman past, Atatürk and the ruling Republican People's Party (Cumhuriyet Halk Partisi—CHP) attacked the Ottoman legacy. They spent much of the 1920s rebuilding the country after the huge material destruction of the earlier decade of warfare. They also reformed Turkey into a secular nation-state based on the Western model.

However, it was really in the 1930s, a decade of authoritarian nationalism, that Ankara concentrated its energy on state-sponsored nationalism, defining what constituted Turkishness. Between the CHP's Third General Congress in spring 1931, and Atatürk's death in the fall of 1938, this idea was incorporated into the constitution as a principle of the Turkish state, where it still remains. Besides, the institutions and ideology of modern Turkey were firmly established in this decade. A specific understanding of what constitutes Turkishness became legally enforced and publicly accepted in this era. The 1930s were a decade of authoritarian nationalisms all over eastern Europe, including Turkey. This presented many opportunities for nationalisms. Turkey and other eastern European states were constrained by relatively few barriers and had many means available to them to impose specific nationalist ideologies on the larger societies. Since the 1930s, Ankara's understanding of what constitutes Turkishness, enforced through many state practices in this decade, has dominated the relations between Ankara and its citizens, especially the non-Muslim and non-Turkish communities, such as the Christians and the Kurds. Hence, it seems that in order to understand the aforementioned nationality-related dilemmas of contemporary Turkey, one would need to examine nationalism in Turkey in this decade with an emphasis on the relations between the state and its minorities. This endeavor would not only highlight Turkey's nationality-related predicaments but also offer possible solutions to them.

1 From the Muslim millet to the Turkish nation

The Ottoman legacy

> When a nation experiences a great disaster or when it is confronted with grave danger...in such times it is only the national personality who lives in the soul of the individual.
>
> (From Ziya Gökalp's work, *The Principles of Turkism*)

From ethnicities to nations

In his groundbreaking work on nationalism, *Nations and Nationalism in the Global Era*, Anthony Smith argues, "modern nations owe much to *ethnies*."[1] Smith defines the *ethnie* as a pre-modern ethno-religious community "that possesses a common ancestry, myths and historical memories, a shared culture, a link to a historic territory and some measure of solidarity."[2] The modern nation arises when this ethno-religious community is transformed in a process that usually begins when the *ethnie* faces an external threat.[3] The "mythomoteur," the constitutive myth of the *ethnie*, reacts to this threat by mobilizing the community.[4] The political activation of ethno-religious community leads to its "cultural revival," as well as "territorial and genealogical restoration."[5] Memory, myths, and symbols play an important role in this process, which results in the birth of the modern nation.[6] This model of nationalism sheds light on the ascent of Turkish nationalism before, during, and after the First World War, when the Ottoman Empire fell and the modern Turkish nation arose.

The fall of the Ottoman Empire: from the Ottoman Muslims to the Turkish nation

The fall of the Ottoman Empire was marked by its territorial decline. The Empire's weakening, which started in the late seventeenth century, accelerated throughout the eighteenth and the nineteenth centuries. Then, the Ottoman Government (Sublime Porte) lost its Central European territories in the Vojvodina, Hungary, Croatia, and Dalmatia to the Habsburgs, and later, its northern Black Sea and Caucasus possessions to the Russians. These events were followed by the persecution of the Ottoman Muslims in the lost territories.[7] Respectively, Hungarian and Slavic Muslims in Central Europe,[8] Tatars in the

Crimea and the Steppe, Circassians, Abkhazes, Chechens, Daghestanis, and other Turks and Muslims in the northern Caucasus faced extermination by the Habsburgs and the Russians. Those who survived often emigrated to the remaining Ottoman territories.

This territorial decline accelerated in the nineteenth century with the emergence of the new Balkan states. The rise of nationalism among the Balkan Christians produced devastating results for the Muslims (and the Jews)[9] on the peninsula because nationalisms in the Balkans, like nationalist movements elsewhere, aimed for homogenous national entities, each "with its own political roof."[10] Most Balkan national movements established this idea of homogeneity based on religious affiliation. The first Greek constitution, adopted in 1822, defines the citizens of the new Greek state as the "*autochthonous* inhabitants of the realm of Greece who believe in Christ."[11]

Ironically, this nationalization-through-religion that contributed to the decline of the Empire was rooted in the Ottoman millet system. During the pre-modern era, this system had divided the Ottoman population into strict religious compartments, called millets. Over centuries, it had merged the ethnic identities of the Ottoman peoples into religious ones, making the millet identity dominant among many Ottoman subjects. Accordingly, when the Balkan Christians turned to nationalism in the nineteenth century, their idea of ethnicity would be shaped by the millet system. At this time, the pre-modern (ethnic) identities of the Balkan Christian communities reemerged under the aegis of the millet system. Then, religion became the principal venue of nationalization in the Balkans. Accordingly, Christian Ottoman millets in the Balkans developed into religio-national communities during the last phases of the Empire.[12] These people saw the Balkan Muslims as their non-nationals, even though the latter shared their language.

The ensuing political chasm between Christians and Muslims was aggravated by the fact that the Christians in the Balkans had resisted (Muslim) Ottoman rule through an emphasis on their (Christian) faith.[13] Accordingly, the Muslims' presence in their prospective homelands became an anathema for the Christian nations. This produced dramatic results for the Muslims: Balkan nationalisms aimed to annihilate the Muslims in order to achieve ethnically homogenous national homelands. For that reason, following the establishment of Greek, Serbian, and Bulgarian states during the nineteenth century, many Ottoman Muslims, including Turks, but also Greek, Serbian, Macedonian, Bosnian, Bulgarian (Pomak), Albanian, and Roma Muslims faced either extermination at the hands of the newly independent states, or were expelled to the shrinking Ottoman possessions in Europe or to Anatolia.[14] The demographic aspect of these events was of epic dimensions: Justin McCarthy writes that between 1821 and 1922 alone, more than 5 million Ottoman Muslims were driven away from their homes, while another 5.5 million died in wars or due to starvation and disease.[15] Even more were displaced. Kemal Karpat notes that between 1856 and 1914, more than 7 million immigrants came to Anatolia from various parts of the Ottoman Empire.[16]

The series of events produced significant results in establishing national identity. The first was in the realm of self-identification. Karpat argues that before the expulsions, Islam had been a passive political identity among the Ottoman-Turkish Muslims. After the massacres and evictions, however, the fact that they had been persecuted due to their religion encouraged surviving Ottoman-Turkish Muslims to embrace religion as an active identity.[17] They started to see religion as a political marker in due course.[18] The subsequent political genesis was catalyzed by the penetration of the capitalist economy into the Ottoman state during the late nineteenth century, a development that promoted social mobility among the Turkish Muslims. Moreover, mass literacy, introduction of the printing press, newspapers, and a universal army service kindled group awareness among the Turkish-Muslim community. These events led to increased physical and cultural contacts between this community's previously isolated segments.[19] They fostered the growth of a political-communal identity and led to a growth of national sentiments among the Ottoman Muslims.[20]

A second repercussion of the expulsion of the Ottoman-Turkish Muslims was that once in Anatolia, the immigrants focused on the peninsula as their homeland (*vatan*).[21] Incidentally, at this time, *vatan* emerged as a popular theme in the Ottoman literary genre.[22] For instance, poet and playwright Namık Kemal (1840–88) produced many popular works based on this idea.[23] In his highly emotional plays, among them "*Vatan yahut Silistre*" (The Homeland or Silistre), Kemal focused on the love for the homeland as a virtue above all.[24]

A third impact of the immigration of Ottoman Muslims to Anatolia was the enhancement of the peninsula's Muslim and Turkish demographic base at the expense of its Christian communities.[25] During the nineteenth century, Anatolia was about one-third Christian. By 1913, the incoming Muslim populations had diminished the Christians' demographic weight to around one-fourth.[26]

The speedy dismemberment of the Ottomans had other ramifications: the Empire's decline generated a real perception of an external threat among the Turkish-Muslim community. This feeling was exacerbated by the self-serving diplomatic maneuvers of the European powers to which the Ottomans were subjugated in a humiliating way. In the eyes of the Turkish-Muslim community, the Empire was weak. At this point, both the (mostly Turkish) émigré as well as the (heavily Turkish) native Anatolian Muslims identified common dangers awaiting them. Now, more than ever, these people bonded as a political community.[27]

The perception of vulnerability among the Turkish Muslims climaxed during the Balkan Wars of 1912–13. Then, in a matter of a few months, the Empire lost 69 percent of its population and 83 percent of its territory in Europe.[28] The apogee of these losses was Rumelia, a large swath of territory in the central and southern Balkans that the Ottomans had considered an inalienable part of the Empire since the fourteenth century.[29] With Rumelia gone, Istanbul's European possessions were reduced to a bare enclave in Eastern Thrace. The Ottoman Empire, which had been part of Europe since its establishment, was now nearly driven out of the continent. The human dimension of the Ottoman defeat was catastrophic: the territorial losses of the Balkan Wars were accompanied by the mass persecution of the Ottoman Muslims.[30] The following excerpt from the 1913 Carnegie Endowment report on the Balkan Wars illustrates this:

> Evidence of Rahni Efendi, of Strumnitsa.
> The Bulgarian Army arrived on Monday, November 4, 1912. With the two Bishops and two other notables I went out to negotiate the surrender of our town with the commandant... The procedure was as follows: The Servian commandant would inquire: 'What kind of a man is this? The answer was simply "good" or "bad"... When sentence was pronounced the prisoner was stripped of his outer clothes and bound, and his money was taken by the Servian commander. I was pronounced "good," and so perhaps were one-tenth of the prisoners. Those sentenced were bound together by threes, and then taken to the slaughter house; their ears and noses were often cut off before they were killed. The slaughter went on for a month; I believe that from three to four thousand Moslems were killed in the town and the neighboring villages.
>
> (Carnegie Endowment, *The Other Balkan Wars*, 277)

The loss in 1912 of Salonika, the largest Ottoman city in the Balkans, with a predominant population of Muslims (and Jews), was another psychological trauma for the Ottoman-Turkish Muslims. (Almost two decades after this catastrophe, in 1931, Yunus Nadi (Abalıoğlu) (1880–1945), then a staunchly Turkish nationalist journalist, noted this trauma: "When they told me that we lost Salonika, my imagination could not bear this."[31]) For the surviving Balkan Muslims, who saw themselves as the heart and the mind of the Empire, the events were a genuine shock. Thus, the upsetting experiences of the Balkan Wars boosted a wave of nationalism among the Ottoman-Turkish Muslims.[32] The ruling elite of the Empire lost their faith in a multi-ethnic and multi-religious Empire.[33] These intellectuals, army officers, and bureaucrats, mostly from the Balkans, started to focus on the Turks' place in the Ottoman realm.[34] They defined Turkishness as including the Turks and Muslims in Anatolia (and Thrace). Eventually, a nationalist historiography emerged to propagate this position.[35] This genre focused on Anatolia as a final refuge as well as the immutable homeland of Turks and other Ottoman Muslims.[36] It also glorified the Turks as an ancient and civilizing people of Anatolia. Now, Turkishness emerged as an umbrella identity for the Ottoman Muslims in Anatolia,[37] while Turkish nationalism rose as a political force.[38]

The rise of the Committee of Union and Progress (CUP) and the fight for Anatolia

The events surrounding the Balkan Wars had immediate ramifications. At a critical turning point in 1913, the Committee of Union and Progress (İttihat ve Terâkki Komitesi), the Young Turk party, which had orchestrated the 1908 Constitutional Revolution overthrowing the absolute monarchy of Sultan

Abdulhamid II, carried out a *coup d'état* and seized power in Istanbul. So far, the CUP had shied away from adopting Turkish nationalism as an exclusive ideology. However, following the Balkan Wars, it took over Turkish nationalism,[39] *vis-à-vis* the non-Turks of the Empire.[40] In 1913, the CUP government declared Turkish as the only medium of education in the Empire's high schools.[41] Next, it installed Turkish as a compulsory subject in the community schools of the non-Muslims.[42]

The CUP took further steps against the non-Muslims, including demographic and economic Turkification, with which it aimed to achieve Turkey's homogenization.[43] For instance, in 1913, Istanbul signed a treaty with Sophia to exchange Bulgars living in Thrace with Turks and Muslims from Bulgaria.[44] Another agreement for action, one that was not carried out, was signed with Greece to facilitate the exchange of the Greeks who lived along the Aegean littoral with the Muslims of Macedonia.[45] Next, the CUP passed laws to favor Turks and Muslims in commerce and industry. This helped increase the Turkification of the Empire's economy by forcing the Christians to the margins of Ottoman economic life.[46]

The rise of Turkish nationalism continued into the First World War. The Empire's collapse beneath the military might of the Allies during the war increased the perception of vulnerability among the Turkish-Muslim community. Ziya Gökalp (1877–1924), the founding father of Turkish nationalism, writes that in times of great political disasters, national feeling gains utmost ascendancy.[47] As the Ottoman Empire fell apart, the Turkish *mythomoteur*, the feeling that the Turks were a distinct people, became a decisive force.[48] Turkish nationalism "discovered Turkishness," and the notion that the Turks shared a common past and territory (Anatolia and Thrace) spread among the Turkish-Muslim *ethnie* of the Empire.[49]

As the war advanced, Anatolia became especially important.[50] After the loss of the Balkans, the Ottoman Empire had become essentially a Near Eastern state, with its territories stretching from Anatolia down to the Arabian Peninsula. During the First World War, however, with the help of the British, the Arab subjects of the Empire engaged in a separatist rebellion against Istanbul. Now, the Turkish-Muslim community of Anatolia (and Thrace) was convinced that Turkey was its only homeland.[51] (The evolution of Gökalp's thinking envisioning a multi-national Ottoman state run by Turks, to a Turco-Arab state, and finally, to a Turkish state, illustrates this shift on an intellectual level.[52]) Now Turkish nationalism focused its energy, exclusively, on Turkey.[53] This resulted in what Anthony Smith calls the "territorialization of the *ethnie*."[54]

While territory was at the core of the Turkish national movement, a challenge loomed in the horizon: Armenian nationalism already coveted parts of Eastern Turkey. This put Armenian nationalism at odds with Turkish nationalism and created resentment among the Anatolian Turks/Muslims against the Armenians. The animosity *vis-à-vis* the (Christian) Armenians was sharpened by the fact that the Muslim immigrants from the Balkans and the Caucasus came to Anatolia feeling frustration toward Christianity. The immigrants identified this faith as the cause of their upheaval from their homelands.[55] Besides, since they had experienced merciless deportation and extermination, the expellee Ottoman Muslims felt justified to resort to antagonism toward Anatolia's non-Muslim population in order to secure the peninsula as the "Turkish homeland."[56] Turkish nationalism turned increasingly hostile toward Anatolia's non-Muslims.[57] With the beginning of the First World War, for instance, there was government antagonism against the coastal Greek populations of Western Anatolia. Citing security reasons, the CUP deported some Ionian and Marmara Greeks into the Asia Minor hinterland.[58] Moreover, it pacified the male Greeks of the area by conscripting them into the labor battalions of the Ottoman army. Because of such pressure, many Greeks of the Aegean littoral started to flee to Greece.[59]

However, the CUP had even more drastic steps *vis-à-vis* the Armenians. Anatolian Armenians lived predominantly in eastern Anatolia and Cilicia, where they formed a large religious minority among Turks, Kurds, and other Muslims.[60] The CUP used wartime circumstances as an "opportunity structure"[61] to initiate the Armenians' removal from these areas. With a perceived risk that those Armenians in eastern Anatolia could act as a fifth column for the advancing Russian armies,[62] the government made plans to expel all the Anatolian Armenians to Syria and lower Mesopotamia. Deportations started in 1915. Disease and famine decimated the Armenian populations. The fighting in eastern Anatolia between the Ottomans and the Russians only added to the chaos. Atrocities against the Armenian civilians added to the catastrophe. A variety of actors, including the Ottoman-Kurdish para-militaries and the secret, nationalist cadres of the CUP carried out mass killings. Hence, during the course of 1915, most of the 1.2 to 1.5 million Anatolian Armenians either died or were expelled or fled from Anatolia. The people who survived the ordeal ended up in Ottoman Syria and Mesopotamia. Some others took refuge in Greece, Bulgaria, Russian Armenia, Cyprus, and Egypt, as well as Western Europe and the United States.[63] By the end of the war, the total number of Armenians remaining in Turkey was under 100,000.

The deportation of the Greeks and the Armenians was part of the CUP policy of Anatolia's ethnic reconfiguration.[64] In accordance with this, the Committee had plans with regard to all non-Turks. For instance, after the disaster of the Balkan Wars, Muslim refugees, including not only Turks, but also Bosnians, Pomaks, Albanians, and Roma, had inundated Anatolia. The CUP resettled them in accordance with a plan to render Anatolia as ethnically Turkish as possible. Non-Turks were dispersed among the Turks in central Anatolia. For instance, Albanians were banned from settling in Turkish Thrace,[65] or western Anatolia.[66] Together with the Bosnians, they were relocated into the heavily Turkish central Anatolia.[67] The CUP made sure that these people would not make up more than 10 percent of the local population where they were transferred.[68]

The Russian occupation of eastern Anatolia in 1915–16 created another wave of Muslim refugees. Turks, Kurds, Georgians, Lazes, Azeris, and Circassians fled the Russian onslaught into the Anatolian interior. The CUP shuffled these refugee populations, too. It aimed at their demographic dilution among the Turks,[69] resettling them away from their ethnic kin and in the midst of Turkish populations. For instance, Georgians and Lazes were relocated far from their homes, to northwestern Anatolia, while the Kurds were transferred *en masse* to central Turkey.[70] Following the fall of the Russian Empire, and the end of the First World War, when the Ottomans lost the war, the subsequent Armenian occupation of large tracts of eastern Anatolia exacerbated the plight of the region's Muslims. Armenian armies moved through eastern Anatolia, along Upper Euphrates and around Lake Van, massacring and deporting local Muslims. Many people, including a large number of Kurds, fled ahead of the Armenian armies, into inner Anatolia.[71]

At the end of the First World War in 1918, the CUP cadres fled the country. Although the Ottoman state disappeared, it left behind an important legacy. First, a politically active Turkish-Muslim community had been consolidated in Anatolia. Second, Turkish nationalism had emerged as a force to be reckoned with.[72] Third, the population of Turkey had been transformed dramatically, with a sharp drop in the number of Christians. In the interim, large groups of non-Turkish Muslims had been dispersed among ethnic Turks, where they could be assimilated. Finally, Anatolia was less Christian and more Turkish now than before.[73]

2 Secularism, Kemalist nationalism, Turkishness, and the minorities in the 1920s

Anatolian Muslims rally to liberate Turkey

The Greek-led Allied invasion of Turkey at the end of the Great War, the Armenian incursion into eastern Anatolia, and the French-coordinated Armenian foray into Cilicia all aimed to decapitate Turkey, but in vain. These assaults only added to the intensity of Turkish nationalism. They furthered the amalgamation of the Turkish-Muslim ethnie into a national community. While Armenian armies grabbed large parts of eastern Anatolia in 1918, French-led Armenian legions from Syria occupied the major cities of Cilicia in 1919. The Greek occupation, which started on the Aegean Coast in 1919, soon expanded into the Anatolian interior (Map 1). This put the peninsula, the centerpiece of the Turkish nationalist movement, at risk.[1] In reaction, on January 28, 1920, the Ottoman parliament adopted the "Misâk-ı Milli" (National Pact). This dictated that those areas of the Empire that were within the Mudros Armistice line of October 30, 1918 and "inhabited by the Ottoman-Muslim majority" were an "indivisible whole."[2] In retaliation, the Allies occupied Istanbul on March 16, 1920. Then, Mustafa Kemal (Atatürk) and the nationalist cadres, who had fled to the Anatolian interior, started organizing a nationalist campaign. The bulk of the upper echelons of the imperial military joined the Kemalist struggle.[3] The leadership rallied the Anatolian-Turkish Muslims by emphasizing their common religion, shared history, and joint territory.[4] Now, the aforementioned aspects of ethnic mobilization, such as territorial and genealogical restoration, as well as cultural revival, became the guiding principles of the Turkish struggle.[5] The Kemalist appeal proved successful: the Anatolian Muslims united *en masse* behind Ankara to redeem Anatolia.[6]

The Turkish nationalist forces first dealt with Armenia. Between 1919 and 1921, Turkish armies in the East pushed the Armenian troops across the Aras (Araxes) river into the Caucasus, while nationalist militia captured the occupied Cilician cities. Then, after a successful series of battles against the Greeks between 1920 and 1922, the Kemalist campaign drove the Greek army out of Anatolia. Most western Anatolian Greeks fled. Because segments of this population had supported Athens' campaign for Asia Minor, fear of reprisals caused them to escape to Greece. The flight of the Ionian Greeks accelerated as chaos prevailed

LEEDS METROPOLITAN UNIVERSITY LIBRARY

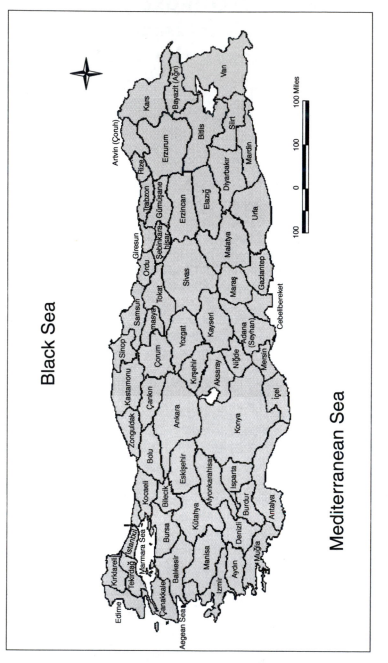

Black Sea

Mediterranean Sea

Map 1 Provinces of Turkey (1927) (Administrative divisions—boundaries approximate).

Source: Büyük Atlas (1939).

in western Anatolia: the retreating Greek armies burned the cities, and the advancing Turkish armies secured them ferociously. During the summer of 1922, most western Anatolian Greeks, including the prosperous Greek community of Izmir, left the country.[7]

The few Greeks who remained following the end of the Turco-Greek War would leave soon. Following the establishment of the Turkish republic on October 29, 1923, one of the first acts of new Turkey was the removal of rump Greek population. The Turco-Greek population exchange treaty, signed on January 30, 1923, stipulated the transfer of the remaining Anatolian Greeks to Greece in return for Muslim-Turkish community there. Asia Minor's rump Greek-Orthodox community, including the Karamanlıs[8] of central Turkey and the Pontic Greeks of the Black Sea, left for Greece. Only the Greek-Orthodox communities of Istanbul and the Aegean islands of Gökçeada (Imbros) and Bozcaada (Tenedos) were exempted from the exchange. (Greece reciprocated by allowing the Turkish-Muslim community of Western Thrace to stay.) The completion of the population exchange in 1924 marked the end of the Anatolian-Greek community.[9]

Secularization: the ascent of nominal Islam as a marker of Turkishness

By 1925, compared to its Ottoman predecessor, the Turkish republic was ethnically more homogenous. It was also a more secular state. The first sign of this was the abolishment of the caliphate on November 2, 1924.[10] This act was the first of a series of reforms which would secularize Turkey during the 1920s under the rule of the CHP.[11] Other secularizing reforms[12] began on January 2, 1924, when the Muslim sabbath, Friday, was dropped in favor of Sunday. Henceforth, Saturday and Sunday would be the weekend, according to the new calendar.[13] Then, on March 2, the ministry for Islamic law (Shariat) and pious foundations (vakıfs) was abolished. This move stripped Islam of state backing. In addition, religious seminaries (madrassa) were shut down,[14] while religious high schools were put under the authority of the Ministry of Education.[15] These institutions had been the core of Koranic instruction in the country, and their closure was a serious blow to religious education. On November 30, 1925, Sufi dervish lodges were closed.[16] Finally, in a symbolic act that epitomized the breaking of links with the Ottoman past, the fez, a must-wear accessory for all adult Muslim men in the country, was declared illegal. A new law required all men to wear western-style hats.[17] Next, in another emblematic move, Turkey dropped its lunar calendar and clock, and switched over to the Gregorian calendar and solar clock.[18]

A major step toward further secularization came a few months later (on February 17, 1926), when the Turkish Grand National Assembly (Türkiye Büyük Millet Meclisi—TBMM) approved a secular civil code to regulate matters of marriage, inheritance, divorce, and adoption.[19] Next, on October 4, 1926, the government annulled the Shariat courts, declaring Islamic law null and void.

Finally, on April 10, 1928, the parliament eliminated from the constitution the declaration of Islam as Turkey's state religion.[20] Soon after this, on November 1, 1928, Ankara announced that Turkey would drop the Arabic alphabet, and switch over to a new, Latin-based alphabet effective from January 1, 1929.[21] This was a drastic step: the Turks would no longer learn to write in Arabic, the alphabet of the Koran.[22]

Secularization required a dramatic shift on the rationale for Turkish nationalism.[23] So far, Islam had united the Anatolian-Turkish Muslims. After 1924, Kemalism dropped references to this from its definition of the nation. Secularization pushed the Islamic faith out of the public domain. Kemalism needed to fill this void. Given that Atatürk envisioned Turkey as a modern nation-state of citizens, the regime targeted a new, national, and all-inclusive identity for the country's inhabitants. So far, besides Islam, Kemalism had resorted to Anatolian territory and Turkishness to appeal to the Anatolian-Turkish Muslim community.[24] Now, having turned its back on Islam, Ankara promoted a varied definition of the nation.[25] First, avoiding irredentism,[26] Kemalism emphasized Turkish territory (Anatolia and Thrace) as the base of the nation. Atatürk declared: "the people of Turkey, who have established the Turkish state, are called the Turkish nation."[27] Second, Atatürk stressed a shared past, and interests and the desire to live together as the common denominators of the nation.[28] Gradually the official definition of the nation also focused on a voluntaristic formula.[29] Accordingly, for instance, Article 5 of CHP's new by-laws adopted at the party's Second Congress, held in Ankara during October 15–22, 1927, stipulated that one of "the strongest links" among the citizens was "unity in feelings and unity in ideas."[30]

The third leg of Kemalism's notion of Turkishness in the 1920s was language. If all the citizens spoke Turkish, then Turkish citizenship and nationality would be the same.[31] The party's 1927 by-laws cited "unity in language" as one of the strongest links among the citizens.[32] This dictated the Turkish language and the desire to be Turkish as the prerequisites for being a citizen. While territory, voluntarism, and language emerged as markers of Turkishness, the question was the viability of these notions *vis-à-vis* the country's ethnic and religious diversity. In 1927, Turkish was far from being everybody's language in Turkey. In this year, in a country with a population of 13,542,795, 86.42 percent of the people spoke Turkish, and 13.58 percent spoke other languages.[33]

A dilemma for Kemalism: Turkish citizenship vs Turkish nationality

This pointed to a problem: territorial nationality suggested by Anatolia, and ethnic nationality indicated by the Turkish language did not overlap: in other words, political membership of the state and ethnic membership of the nation were not the same. This phenomenon became apparent with Turkey's 1924 constitution.[34] When this was discussed in the TBMM, heavy debates took place around its Article Eighty-Eight, which defined the inhabitants of Turkey.

While a few members of the parliament argued that the constitution should declare all people in Turkey as Turks-by-nationality, a majority of the MPs objected to this. The latter camp, led by the nationalist poet Hamdullah Suphi (Tanrıöver) (1885–1966), asserted that although they could be citizens, it was not possible to acknowledge Armenians and Jews as Turks unless they abandoned "their languages, as well as Armenianness and Jewishness."[35] The constitution needed to recognize Armenians, Jews, and other non-Muslims as Turks-by-citizenship and not as Turks-by-nationality. The TBMM acknowledged this notion. The final version of Article Eighty-Eight said, "The People of Turkey, regardless of religion and race, are Turks as regards citizenship."[36] With this, Ankara made a distinction between citizenship and ethnicity. First, it recognized all those in Turkey as Turks-by-citizenship. (Later on, Mahmut Esat Bozkurt (1892–1943), Turkey's Minister of Justice between November 1924 and September 1930, would use the term, "Kanun Türkü" [Turks-by-law] to refer to this category.[37]) Second, Ankara asserted that only some citizens were members of the Turkish nation. This institutionalized a gap between Turks-by-citizenship and Turks-by-nationality.

Another challenge to the idea of all-inclusive Turkishness was rooted in the notion of Turkish culture. This was demonstrated in the CHP's documents. The party's 1923 statute dictated that "every Turk and those who come from abroad and have accepted Turkish citizenship and culture" could become the party's members.[38] The 1927 statute added that the promotion of "Turkish language and culture" was the party's main principle.[39] Only those citizens who have "*accepted the Turkish culture* and the Party's principles" were eligible for membership to the party.[40] It was Ziya Gökalp who inspired the Kemalists in their usage of the word culture or "hars." According to him, the nation was a community of individuals united by a shared culture, based on common education, morality, socialization, and aesthetics.[41] Gökalp defined the nation through collective values.[42] Hence, the word culture in the CHP documents referred to the common past and mores (i.e. Islam) of the Ottoman-Turkish Muslims in Anatolia as well as their education and socialization in Turkish.

The role that Gökalp ascribes to Islam ought to be clarified. Islam is not only a faith: in its nominal form it is also a particular set of belief systems and mores which dictate the routines of daily life and socialization for the Muslims. Accordingly, Islam can serve also as a culture, as well as an identity (and in modern times even as an ideology) for the Muslims. Until Kemalism, Islam had united the Anatolian-Turkish Muslims around a joint faith, a collective culture, a shared identity, and a common political goal. And when secularism pushed the faith dimension of the religion to the margins of the society, nominal Islam remained central to Turkish society as its culture and identity. Notwithstanding its secularism, Kemalism was compelled to sanction such nominal Islam as a marker of Turkishness. An analysis of the relations between the state and minorities in the 1920s demonstrates that despite its commitment to secularism as well as territorial-voluntaristic-linguistic forms of citizenship, to a large extent, Kemalist nationalism was still molded by Islam.

Turkey during the 1920s: a multi-ethnic Muslim nation

By 1927, there were still non-Turkish speakers in the country: 13.58 percent of the population (totaling 1,764,985 people) used languages other than Turkish,[43] including 1,184,446 speakers of Kurdish; 134,273 speakers of Arabic; 119,822 speakers of Greek; 95,901 speakers of Circassian; 68,900 speakers of Judeo–Spanish;[44] 64,745 speakers of Armenian; 21,774 speakers of Albanian; 20,554 speakers of Bulgarian; 11,465 speakers of (Crimean) Tatar; speakers of 8,456 French; and 7,248 Italian speakers, among others.[45] These non-Turkish-speaking populations were concentrated in certain provinces of the country, including the predominantly Kurdish East (Map 2).

On the other hand, Turkey was less diverse in religious terms. In 1927, 97.36 percent (totaling 13,269,606 people) of the population was Muslim, and only 2.64 percent was non-Muslim.[46] Among them were 109,905 Orthodox Christians; 77,433 (Gregorian) Armenians; 81,872 Jews; 39,511 Catholics; 24,307 Christians (including various Eastern Christians); 6,658 Protestants; and 20,196 people of other religions, of unknown religion, or without religion.[47] Although the non-Muslim population was numerically insignificant, it was concentrated in certain provinces. This gave it a strategic importance in the government's eyes (Map 3).

With this demography, the Kemalist state of the 1920s welcomed the non-Turkish Muslims. Ankara believed that a merger of the Muslims into the Turkish nation was a historical necessity. The non-Turkish-Anatolian Muslims shared a joint history with the Turks such as the recent Independence War, in which they had allied with the Turks. The legacy of the Ottoman-Turkish Muslim *ethnie* united the Anatolian Muslims. Ziya Gökalp, who saw the Turkish nation as a community of the Turks and other Anatolian Muslims, had argued that all the latter could become Turkish if they assimilated.[48] To achieve this, they needed to be assimilated into the Turkish culture and learn Turkish.[49] With this in mind, Ankara launched policies in the 1920s, including a Turkish-only education system and a ban on ethnic identification to facilitate the amalgamation of Anatolian Muslims into the Turkish nation.[50]

In fact, integration had already made inroads, especially among the immigrant Muslims. The passage of these people into the Turkish nation had been eased by the fact that they had abandoned their cultural and social institutions in the Caucasus and the Balkans, around the Black Sea and the Aegean. Being among Turkish-speaking Muslims had provided them with the elements of "assimilability under the Turkish language and Muslim religion."[51] These immigrants had merged into Anatolia's Turkish majority through an experience of joint socialization and shared institutions.[52] Consequently, by the 1920s very few still spoke their native languages.[53]

The Kemalists somewhat incorrectly expected that the autochthonous Anatolian Muslims such as the Kurds, Arabs, Lazes, and most of the Georgians would also assimilate quickly, since like the immigrants, these, too, had a common history with the Turks. They, too, descended from the Ottoman Muslim millet. In a speech to the parliament in 1920, Atatürk had pointed at this, by stating that

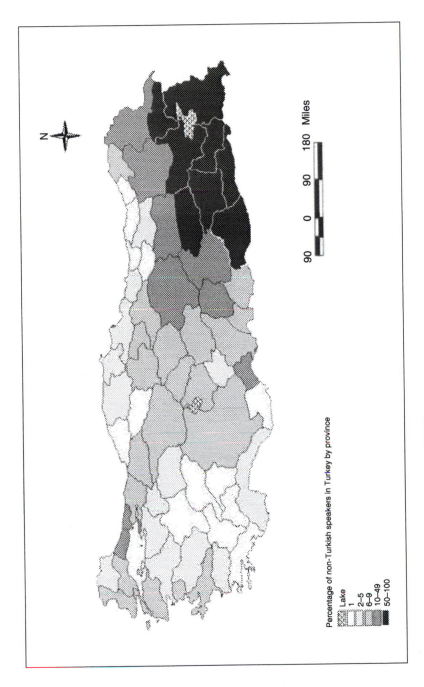

Percentage of non-Turkish speakers in Turkey by province

Lake
1
2–5
6–9
10–49
50–100

90   0   90   180   Miles

Map 2 Distribution of non-Turkish speakers in Turkey (1927).

Source: Büyük Atlas (1939). Data: Statistics Yearbook, Vol. 2 (1929).

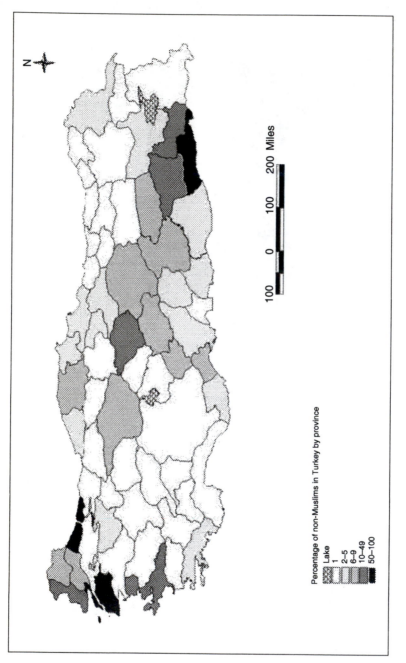

Map 3 Distribution of non-Muslims in Turkey (1927).

Source: Büyük Atlas (1939). Data: Instanbul Cumhurry el Matbaas (1929).

"You, the members of the high parliament, are not only Turks, or only Circassians, or only Kurds, or only Lazes: but the Islamic elements made up of all them."[54] Ziya Gökalp, himself of Kurdish origin, also promoted the assimilation of the Kurds by arguing that the National Pact "delineated an ethnographic boundary," shared by the Turks and the Kurds.[55] However, the autochthonous Muslims did not have the same reasons as the immigrants to merge into the Turkish nation.[56] The native Muslims had neither been uprooted from their homelands, nor lost their cultural and social structures due to expulsion. Among them, the Kurds were especially unique. Of all the non-Turkish groups, they were least likely to be absorbed into the Turkish nation.

Kurds in the 1920s: the role of religion in assimilation

A comparison of the Kurds with the other Muslims reveals their uncompromising position with regard to assimilation. First, in 1927, the 1,184,446 Kurdish speakers were the largest non-Turkish nationality in Turkey's population of 13,542,795.[57] Next to the Kurds, the other Muslims were demographically insignificant. The next largest groups among them, Arabs and Circassians constituted less than 1 percent of the population each. The rest of the communities were even smaller.[58]

Second, in contrast to the other Muslim groups, which were mostly dispersed, the Kurds inhabited a large, contiguous territory in Southeastern Turkey, where they were an overwhelming majority. According to the 1927 census, they comprised a plurality in seven provinces in the Southeast including Van, Muş, Siirt, Diyarbakır, Mardin, Ağrı, and Elazığ (Map 4). In Van, for instance, they constituted 79.1 percent of the population. In addition, they were a significant minority in seven other provinces in the east, including Urfa, Malatya, Erzincan, Kars, Maraş, Erzurum, and Sivas.[59] Hence, nearly 90 percent of Turkey's Kurds lived in fourteen adjoining provinces, containing "a third of Turkish territory but only a fifth of her people."[60]

Third, the Kurds differed from other Muslims in Turkey because they did not identify so strongly with the Turkish-Muslim *ethnie* of the Ottoman Empire. Throughout the Ottoman era, the Kurds had lived in Kurdistan, a rugged, autonomous area, which had been considered part of the Ottoman fringe. They had not generally associated with the Ottoman state or the Turkish-Muslim *ethnie*.[61] Traditionally, the Kurds had been subsidiary to this community. During the nineteenth century, Tanzimat reforms and the centralizing measures of Sultan Abdülhamid II had brought them under direct Ottoman rule. Additionally, *fin-de-siècle* Armenian nationalism had moved the Kurds to ally with the Turkish-Muslim *ethnie* of the Empire. However, even then, the Kurds had remained on the periphery of the Turkish-Muslim community.[62] Accordingly, the Kurds, who had not seen themselves as Ottomans in the past, now faced problems in their passage to Turkishness.[63] Of all the Muslim groups, Kurds, whom British diplomats described as a group that stood "apart from the other minorities, partly because

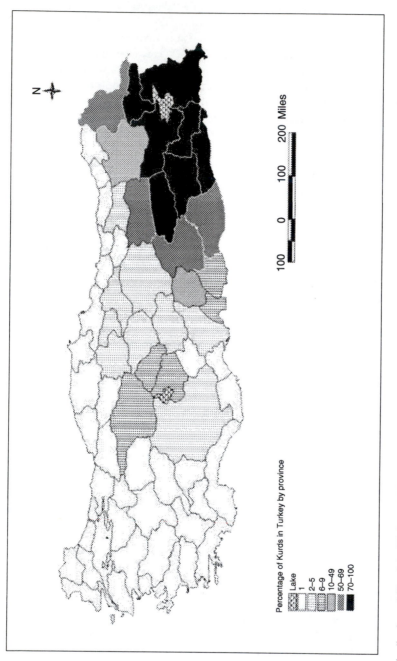

Map 4 Distribution of Kurds in Turkey (1927).

Source: Büyük Atlas (1939). Data: Statistics Yearbook Vol. 2 (1929).

of their compactness and partly because of their warlike nature,"[64] were the least likely to assimilate.[65]

Nevertheless, Kemalism had the same expectations of the Kurds as it had of other Muslim groups. A Turkish dictionary, which described the Kurds as "a *population* living around the Iranian border,"[66] summarized the gist of these anticipations. The Kurds were not to nurture a separate ethnic identity. They were to assimilate.[67] The Kemalists saw the Turkish language as the basis of this. In their view, the Kurds did not speak a distinct language, but a dialect of bastardized Turkish, which had evolved while these individuals had lived on the mountains, isolated from the Turks, and mixed with the Arabs and Persians.[68] The Kurds needed to return to the Turkish culture. Now, they could confirm their Turkishness by learning Turkish. The Kurds reacted to this with a number of uprisings.[69] A book published by the Turkish Army Staff Headquarters lists thirteen disturbances in Turkey between May 1925 and November 1930.[70] All took place in the predominantly Kurdish areas, and some were more than local flare-ups. In the Sason region, for instance, there was constant military activity against the local Kurdish tribes from 1925 until 1937. Between 1926 and 1930 alone, there were three uprisings in the Ağrı province, near Mt Ararat: the first in May–June 1926, the second in September 1927, and the third during the summer of 1930.

The most significant Kurdish unrest during the 1920s was the Şeyh Said uprising. This insurrection started in February 1925, in Diyarbakır and Elazığ provinces. Şeyh Said and his men, inspired by a blend of Kurdish nationalism and Islam, garnered significant local support toward this rebellion. They captured the towns of Elazığ and Palu, and established control over a large swath of territory. The government led by Prime Minister Fethi (Okyar) (1880–1943) was unable to cope with the sheer power of this challenge. On March 2, 1925, the cabinet fell following a vote of no confidence in the TBMM. On March 4, İsmet (İnönü) (1884–1973), who would remain in power until November 1, 1937 took office. The very same day, İnönü passed the "Takrir-i Sükun Kanunu" (The Law for the Maintenance of Order) through the TBMM.[71] This suspended political liberties, gave the government wide military powers, and declared martial law in the Kurdish provinces.[72]

The İnönü government used its extraordinary powers first to shut down various critical newspapers. Next, it acted against the opposing Progressive Republican Party (Terakkiperver Cumhuriyet Fırkası—TpCF). The party, which had been established on November 17, 1924, had become a gathering place for the Turkish opposition. Some of Atatürk's closest military and political associates from the Independence War, who had grown wary of his leadership, or had been alarmed by secularization, had banded around the TpCF.[73] Among the party's members were prominent commanders of the army, including Ali Fuat Paşa (Cebesoy) (1882–1968), Cafer Tayyar Paşa (Eğilmez) (1879–1958), Rauf Bey (Orbay) (1881–1967), Refet Paşa (Bele) (1881–1963), and Kâzım Paşa (Karabekir) (1882–1948). Famous politicians and scholars, including Dr Adnan Bey (Adıvar) (1882–1955), Mehmet Rahmi Bey (Eyüboğlu) (1877–1952), and İsmail Canbulat (1880–1926), had also joined it.[74]

İnönü aimed to get rid of the TpCF. He used the İstiklâl Tribunals to achieve this. These courts had been created in accordance with the Law for the Maintenance of Order. They had special powers and no appeals.[75] The Tribunals brought forth a number of cases against the TpCF and its members, which led to the party's closure on June 3, 1925. That effectively ended all political opposition to Kemalism.

In the meantime, İnönü had turned to the Şeyh Said uprising. After much effort and a huge military campaign, he managed to wrest control of the region in April 1925. Şeyh Said and his men were captured on April 15 and executed immediately after trial in the İstiklâl Tribunals. The government pursued a harsh policy of retaliation,[76] which included deportation of the rebels' families to western Turkey. Next, on September 1926, Ankara issued a ban "on entry of foreigners into provinces east of the Euphrates."[77] With this, it made sure that foreign observation would be prevented while it carried mop-up operations in the Southeast. In the interim, the breadth of the uprising remained a source of distress for the government.[78] It signaled to Ankara how many Kurds were willing to take up arms against it. Hence, after the pacification of the Southeast, the government turned to different means to address the Kurdish issue. The Minister of Interior Affairs, Şükrü Kaya (1883–1959) noted then, that Ankara had realized the

> foolishness of endeavouring to tame this mountainous and virile people by wiping out their leaders, burning their villages and closing the passes leading to their grazing grounds in the hope that once more the problem of a dissentient minority could be resolved.
>
> (Foreign Office—Great Britain
> (hereafter FO), 424/268/E129)

Soon, the government acted in this direction. "Şark Islahat Raporu" (Report on Reform in the East), an official report drawn up by the Minister of Interior Cemil (Ubaydın) (1883–1957), Minister of Justice Mahmut Esat Bozkurt, the Speaker of TBMM Mustafa Abdülhâlik (Renda) (1881–1948) (Çankırı), and General Kâzım (Orbay) (1886–1964), addressed the major problems of eastern Turkey with these concerns in mind. The report first pointed at the preponderance of Kurds in the provinces to the east of the Euphrates, as well as in Malatya, to the west. Areas that had mixed Turkish-Kurdish populations needed to be gradually Turkified and assimilated. Ankara had to prevent the Turks' absorption into Kurdish culture, and facilitate the reverse assimilation of those who had merged into the Kurdish tribes.[79] The report laid out a five-step strategy toward this end. First, it asked that Ankara ban the public use of Kurdish in those areas of the country with mixed Turkish and Kurdish populations.[80] This could help cut down on Kurdification. Second, in addressing unrest, Ankara could deport "families, which posed a risk, to Western Turkey."[81] Third, in order to maintain better control, the government needed to build new railway lines, roads, and *gendarme* stations throughout the East.[82] Fourth, Ankara was to establish an Inspectorate-General to govern eastern Turkey. Finally, the government had to set up a military regime in the East until the measures were implemented fully.[83]

Ankara acted on this by instituting a special legal regime for the East. On June 25, 1927, the TBMM passed Law Nr 1164, which created the Umumi Müfettişlik (Inspectorate–General).[84] The First Inspectorate was established on January 1, 1928, as a regional governorship with extensive powers. The mandate of this covered Diyarbakır, Elazığ, Urfa, Bitlis, Van, Hakkâri, Siirt, and Mardin. With its seat at Diyarbakır, the Inspectorate unified this restless, overwhelmingly Kurdish area, which had recently witnessed the Şeyh Said uprising. It would approach this region with a conciliatory face[85] to prevent future Kurdish rebellions there.[86]

At this time, the region was still reeling from the devastation of the Şeyh Said uprising. (The destruction of large portions of Eastern Anatolia during the First World War only aggravated this situation.)[87] Thus, the region's first Inspector-General, İbrahim Tali (Öngören) (1875–1952) had a difficult task ahead of him. Öngören used a mixed policy, including road building, education, and land reform, to tackle the region's problems. These measures were accompanied by a relaxation of military rule. On December 5, 1927, the TBMM passed Law Nr 1178. This terminated the deportation of Kurds from eastern Turkey in accordance with Law Nr 1097, which had been passed in the aftermath of the Şeyh Said rebellion.[88] Meanwhile, the transportation network of southeastern Turkey was greatly improved. For instance, a new highway was built from Elazığ to Erzincan, cutting through previously inaccessible Dersim. As roads extended eastwards, it was expected that the Kurds would come "under more constant authority, and Turkish officials on their parts will get a truer understanding of the special problems of the Kurdish districts."[89]

Öngören also used land reform, education, and military service to curb the growth of Kurdish nationalism. Breaking up large estates through land reform was designed to limit the influence of tribal chiefs and leaders, who had led most of the nationalist uprisings in the region. One British traveler noted in 1930, "the Kurdish movement, as the Turkish government always maintains, no longer exists, the Kurdish chiefs having, in fact, all been reduced to powerlessness."[90] Education, the other prong of Öngören's policy was also a means of pacification:

> İbrahim Tali Bey's policy relies upon education of all kinds, carried out through schools and Türk Ocagis.[91] As every child goes to school, so every man goes through the army, which itself has become a great school...It is clear that even ten years of this procedure will make an enormous difference in the outlook of the people which has neither priests, literature nor leaders to keep its own traditions.
>
> (State Department—United States
> of America (hereafter SD), 867.154/10)

The army was also an efficient school of Turkification. "Kurdish soldiers who were sent to western Anatolia" were "taught to read and write Turkish."[92] Accordingly, these people were being "turned into good Turks.[93]

By 1928, the Inspectorate's "carrot and stick" policy had improved the security situation in the East. A good indicator of this was, that, during the summer of

1928, the government softened its attitude toward the region. Kurdish families that had been deported to Western Turkey in 1926 were allowed to return to their homes.[94] In addition, martial law that had been in effect since 1925 was lifted and an amnesty was offered to rebels who turned themselves in.[95] "Another indication of a better state of things was the tour which İbrahim Tali Bey, the Inspector-General, made as far north as Van and Bitlis in September last, a venture which he could hardly have risked a year ago."[96] Because of the Inspectorate's success, when Kurdish unrest flared up in Ağrı[97] in the late 1920s, this province was annexed into the Inspectorate with the hope that Diyarbakır would crush the insurgency there.[98] Ankara hoped that the Inspectorate would help defeat the Kurds' resistance to being incorporated into the Turkish nation.

Jews during the 1920s: the role of the Turkish language in assimilation

Like the Kurds, non-Muslims such as the Jews, Armenians, and Greeks, challenged the republic in the 1920s. Nonetheless, in the case of the non-Muslims, the dilemma was different: the non-Muslims were Turkish citizens; yet, the fact that they had not been part of the Turkish-Muslim *ethnie* of the Ottoman Empire hindered their full incorporation into the Turkish nation.[99]

However, the situation was not the same for the Jews and the Christians. The divergence in Ankara's approach to assimilate Jews and Christians makes clear this different standing. The Jews were in a unique historical position in relation to the Turkish nation. Unlike the Greeks and the Armenians, the Jews had not pursued separatist or nationalist ambitions during the last decades of the Ottomans. On the contrary, they had allied with the Turks during the dissolution of the Empire. For instance, in the aftermath of the 1908 revolution, when a conservative counter revolution had started in Istanbul, and the CUP had prepared an army in Salonika to crush this mutiny the Jews had joined this army with their own battalion.[100] Then, after Salonika had fallen to the Greeks in the First Balkan War, the Jewish population of the city had lobbied either to keep the city within the Empire, or make it into an international city.[101] Next, Jews had fought actively in the Ottoman army during the First World War.[102] Hence, whilst the Empire fell apart, with their support for the Porte,[103] the Jews had earned the title of "loyal millet."[104]

During the Turkish Independence campaign, the Jews, who suffered in the hands of the Greek armies as much as the Muslim Turks, again allied with the Turks. They aided the Kemalist forces and fought against the Greeks.[105] Accordingly, Turkish nationalism, which formed anti-Greek and anti-Armenian sentiments through its struggles with Greek and Armenian nationalisms, nurtured a neutral, if not positive, attitude toward the Jews. Then, unlike in other Balkan countries, such as Romania, where anti-Semitism became a vector of national identity to the extent that it created an ethnic divide against the Jews,[106] Turkish nationalism shied away from anti-Semitism. It exhibited a welcoming attitude toward the Jews. For instance, during the First World War, although the CUP banned the entry of Christian Ottoman refugees into the Empire,[107] it allowed Jewish ones.[108] Besides, upon arrival, these people were to enjoy the same privileges as the Muslims.

Given Turkish nationalism's benevolent attitude toward them, it could be expected that in the 1920s, the Jews would have a comfortable life under the republic. This, however, did not turn out to be the case. The end of the Turkish Independence War heralded an era of resentment toward the Jews.[109] In 1923, after the country's mercantile Greek and Armenian communities had been decimated, there was an expectation that Muslim Turks would fill the vacated business positions.[110] To facilitate this, the government initiated a campaign to make them dominant in the economy.[111] Although many Turks did emerge during this period as prominent businessmen, so did quite a few Jews.[112] That created a wave of hostility against them.[113] Accordingly, throughout the 1920s, there was growing anti-Jewish resentment among Turks and Muslims in the commercial centers of Western Turkey, such as Istanbul, Izmir, Edirne, Bursa, Tekirdağ, and Çanakkale, where a bulk of the Turkish Jewish community lived.[114]

In addition to economic competition, resentment toward the Jews was rooted in the fact that very few Jews were fluent in Turkish; and many spoke Judeo-Spanish. Turkish nationalists interpreted this as a sign that the Jews did not want to assimilate or that they did not care for Turkish.[115] There was further hostility toward the Jews since many of them spoke French. In fact, some Jews spoke only French, a language they had learnt in the French *Alliance Israélite* schools. These schools, which had been set up in the Near East since the mid-nineteenth century, had attracted the Ottoman Jews to a Western education along the Enlightenment lines. The *Alliance* system had been very successful. These schools not only enlisted thousands of Jewish pupils, but also assimilated many of them into French culture.[116] Most of their graduates spoke French as their daily tongue. When Jews had dropped Judeo-Spanish in favor of French, Turkish nationalists saw this as a proof of the Jews' condescension toward Turkish.[117]

Now the Jews were expected to prove their Turkishness by adopting Turkish. Subsequently, during the late 1920s, a public campaign arose to demand this. This campaign, titled "Vatandaş Türkçe Konuş" (Citizen Speak Turkish) started on April 26, 1927 when İnönü gave a fiery speech at the annual convention of the Turkish Hearths (Türk Ocakları), an organization of mostly intellectuals that served as a hotbed of Turkish nationalism. In his remarks, the Prime Minister emphasized the need for everybody in Turkey to speak Turkish. The government was going to transform all those who lived inside Turkey into Turks, at the cost of "no matter what happens."[118]

Next, the "Student Association of the School of Law of Istanbul University" (Darülfünun Hukuk Fakültesi Talebe Cemiyeti) started a campaign to invite everybody to speak Turkish.[119] The Association protested the use of minority and European languages in daily life. It wanted Turkish to be the only language spoken by the public. Although this campaign was unofficial, the fact that it was carried out by an officially recognized society gave it legitimacy. Jews, Greeks, Armenians, Circassians, Bosniaks, Arabs, and others were harassed in public for speaking their own languages. Signs were posted in theaters, restaurants, hotels, movie theaters, public ferries, and streetcars to recommend that everybody speak Turkish. The major target was the Jews.[120] Outside Istanbul, the brunt of the drive was felt in cities with large Jewish communities. In Bursa, for instance, the municipal government passed a decree banning the use of languages other than Turkish in public. Two Jews observed speaking Judeo-Spanish, were fined five liras.[121] In Izmir, a group of Turkish teachers prepared a letter demanding that the Jews "publish nothing in Jewish [*sic*]" and that all Turkish citizens speak Turkish only. The use of a language other than Turkish was an insult to Turkishness.[122]

In reaction to this, Avram Galanti (1873–1961), a Jewish scholar and a professor of ancient Near Eastern history at the Istanbul Darûlfûnun (University), wrote a book explaining why Jews did not speak Turkish.[123] So far, the Jews had shied away from Turkish not because of their lack of patriotism, but due to historic reasons. One of these was that in 1492, when the Sephardic Jews had come to the Ottoman Empire from Spain, they had brought printing presses with Hebrew/Judeo-Spanish (Ladino) typesetting. At that time, no printing press with Turkish typesetting had been available in the Empire. This had led the Jews to continue printing and speaking in Judeo-Spanish. By the time Turkish printing presses had been finally allowed in the Empire in 1712, it was already too late for the Jews to switch over to Turkish.[124] The spread of French among the Jews was an historical phenomenon, too. Since the Ottomans had ignored education, the Jews had not had a chance to receive Turkish instruction. Thus, many had attended the *Alliance* schools, which provided superior education, where they had learnt French.[125] Galanti argued that the fact that the Jews spoke Judeo-Spanish and French had nothing to do with their lack of patriotism. Professor Galanti concluded that this situation could be corrected by efforts from both sides. He urged the government to make education in Turkish available to the Jews and asked the Jews to start learning Turkish.

Another writer who argued for Turkification of the Jews was Munis Tekinalp (1883–1961), a Turkish nationalist of Jewish origin. Tekinalp had been one of the ideologues of Turkish nationalism since the 1908 revolution. He believed that the Jews could join the Turkish nation through assimilation.[126] To demonstrate this, Tekinalp had dropped his original name, Moiz Kohen, in favor of his Turkish name after the First World War.[127] Now, at the height of the language controversy in 1928, he wrote a book to advocate cultural Turkification. In this work titled, *Türkleştirme* (Turkification), he contended assimilation was possible if the Jews spoke Turkish. To outline some other means toward this, Tekinalp compiled a list of directives, the "Evâmiri Aşire" (Ten Commandments).[128] He demanded that the Jews:

- Adopt Turkish names
- Speak Turkish
- Make at least part of their prayers Turkish
- Teach only Turkish in schools

- Send their children only to Turkish schools
- Socialize with the Turks
- Join Turkish society
- Drop the mentality of being a minority
- Do their share in the economic sphere
- Know their citizenship rights.

Next, Tekinalp joined a group of Turkish and Jewish intellectuals in organizing the "National Cultural Union" (Milli Hars Birliği).[129] This promoted Turkification and the adoption of Turkish by the Jews.[130] However, such efforts did not bear many fruits.[131] There was neither mass adoption of Turkish nor other signs of swift assimilation among the Jews. On the contrary, the "Speak Turkish" campaign caused friction. This tension blew up on August 17, 1927, following the murder of a young Jewish woman named Eliza Niyego by a Turkish man. This murder was in fact the result of an amorous affair leading to a crime of passion. However, in its aftermath, thousands of outraged Jews marched through Istanbul's streets blaming the government for inactivity in the murder's investigation. The authorities retaliated by arresting a number of demonstrators.[132] Throughout the summer of 1927, pressure built up in the city. Nevertheless, the government's reaction, initially harsh then conciliatory,[133] led the Jewish anger to subside.

In the meantime, in Edirne, the campaign was turning violent. In April 1928, violent confrontations took place there between vigilante nationalist students and Jews. At this point, the government intervened in the campaign; Edirne's governor ordered that signs promoting the "Speak Turkish" campaign be torn down. Next, the Ministries of Education and Interior opened investigations against people involved in violence.[134] In a decree to the provinces, the Ministry of Interior asked that public order not be violated and asked the police to interfere in "case of a provocation or a threat in the name of 'Citizen Speak Turkish' campaign."[135]

In the interim, apparently "after the Jewish world outside Turkey had brought pressure to bear on Angora,"[136] the "Speak Turkish" campaign slowed down in April 1928, though it did not totally vanish. Newspaper articles in favor of the campaign continued appearing.[137] Nevertheless, the waning of this drive pointed at the failure of Turkish nationalism's expectations *vis-à-vis* the Jews. Although Ankara had aimed to incorporate the Jews into the body of the Turkish nation, its efforts had been hindered by linguistic and historic gaps between the Jews and the Turks.

Christians in the 1920s: an overview

Like the Jews, the Christians also challenged the notion that all of Turkey's inhabitants were the members of the Turkish nation. The Christians, too, had not been part of the Turkish-Muslim *ethnie* in the past and this stalled their incorporation into the Turkish nation.[138] Yet, even more instrumental in solidifying the walls between Christians and Turkish nation were events such the Armenian catastrophe, the Turco-Greek population exchange,[139] and the feeling that the Christians in Turkey had been "contaminated by a generation or more of foreign propaganda, culminating in open treason during the war [World War One] and armistice."[140] Accordingly, Turkish nationalism nurtured a robust antipathy toward Christians. Ankara did not attempt to assimilate them in the 1920s.

On the contrary, Turkey marginalized the Christian minorities. As early as 1920, the Kemalists took precautionary measures in this regard. On June 18, 1920, Ankara asked the local authorities to ban the free travel of Anatolian Armenians since they were "being armed by foreign powers."[141] On November 14, the government issued an order to deport the Greeks in certain villages of Suşehri, in the Black Sea hinterland, so that they "would not be proxy to political goals."[142] Greeks who lived along the Marmara Sea were also relocated to the interior.[143] Finally, on May 11, 1921, the government asked the authorities that Greeks near the western front, and Armenians along the southern front be deported to Sivas and Elazığ in the Anatolian interior.[144] These efforts could be linked to the wartime measures of limiting contact between local Greeks and Armenians and the invading Greek and Armenian forces. Yet even after peace, Ankara remained cautious toward the Christians. For instance, in September 1924, the Ministry of Reconstruction and Resettlement compiled lists of non-Muslim employees of the Water Utility of Istanbul.[145] On December 18, it wrote to Istanbul's Üsküdar-Kadıköy Water Utility Company (Üsküdar-Kadıköy Su Şirketi), asking it to fire non-Muslim employees, the bulk of whom were Greeks and Armenians.[146] These people were dismissed during 1925. On March 3, the Ministry thanked the company on this matter.[147]

Then, the government put pressure on the Greeks and Armenians (like the Jews) to relinquish various communal privileges, such as the right to run their own courts and schools that Turkey had granted them at the Lausanne Treaty of 1923. (First, the Jews renounced their privileges on May 23, 1925.) Armenians followed on October 17, and the Greeks on October 29.[148] Further action against the Christians' treaty rights followed. For instance, the government appointed "Turkish lady teachers to schools staffed by *frères* and Turkish men teachers to nuns' schools."[149] This led to the closure of a number of schools run by Christians.[150] Accordingly, benefits that had been guaranteed to the Christians by Lausanne were terminated.[151] Subsequently, the political situation of the Christian minorities deteriorated significantly in the 1920s. By the end of the decade, a diplomatic source noted that that Greeks and Armenians in Turkey

> receive discriminatory treatment throughout the whole country... They are forbidden to travel, they find in the larger commercial organizations that Government regulations tend to exclude them in favour of Moslems, in remoter districts their religious observances are barely tolerated and in some cases their churches desecrated, their tenure of property is made most precarious by unequal legislation, and in general they are discouraged from continuing their activities and very existence in Turkey.
>
> (FO, 371/14578/E729)

The situation was uncomfortable for the Greeks and other Christians in Istanbul, unpleasant for the Christians in the provinces, and worst for the Anatolian Armenians.

Greeks in the 1920s

In the 1920s, the shifting fortunes of the Greek community in Turkey were determined by the course of relations between Athens and Ankara. After 1923, protracted debates between Turkey and Greece on implementing the population exchange treaty, especially *vis-à-vis* the disposal of exchangee property, soured the relations between the two countries.[152] Athens and Ankara respectively used their control over Turkish-Muslim minority in Greece and the Greek-Orthodox minority in Turkey as leverage. These communities became hostages, their fate pegged to the dealings between Athens and Ankara. Hence, relations between Ankara and the Greek community in the country remained negative so long as Greece and Turkey maintained their differences. The first combustible issue in this regard involved the election of a new Patriarch of Constantinople. Until the Lausanne Treaty, Meletios IV had been the Patriarch of the Greek Church. However, Meletios' stand as a staunch supporter of the Greek invasion of Turkey rendered him *persona-non-grata* by Ankara. Greek Prime Minister Venizelos had concurred at Lausanne that if Ankara agreed that the Patriarchate remain in Istanbul, he would "recommend" that Meletios resign.[153] On June 27, 1923, the Patriarch appointed a *locum tenens* and left Istanbul due to "health reasons." After much deliberation, on December 6, the Church Synod elected Gregory VII as the new Patriarch. "Because he had refrained from displaying anti-Turkish sentiments during the armistice, Gregory was reckoned to be *persona grata*."[154]

Alas, Gregory's sudden death on November 16, 1924 necessitated new elections. The Holy Synod chose Constantine VI. This, however, created problems. The government contended that Constantine was among those Greeks considered exchangeable according to the Lausanne Treaty, which stipulated that all the Greek-Orthodox in Turkey, except for those people that had been living in Istanbul since 1918, had to leave for Greece. In January 1925, the Turkish authorities deported the Patriarch. A political crisis simmered. After much political wrangling, and the intervention of Athens to force the Patriarchate to accept the situation, the matter was settled on July 13, 1925. Basil III, a nominee name acceptable to the government, and a long-time resident of Istanbul, was elected by the Synod as the new Patriarch.[155] Even then, Ankara continued to press the Greek community in other matters, such as education and property ownership. During the 1920s, the government appointed Turkish teachers to Greek schools and imposed a new curriculum on them. It also shut down certain Greek schools for bureaucratic reasons.[156] Besides, on August 11, 1928, Ankara declared that the Greek community of Istanbul would not be allowed to own property outside the limits of the Greater City of Istanbul.[157]

There was pressure also on the insular Greek communities of Gökçeada and Bozcaada. These islands had been part of the Ottoman Empire until the

First Balkan War of 1912, when Greece had occupied them. At this time, the bulk of the islands' inhabitants were Greeks, with a large Turkish minority on Bozcaada. (In 1914–15, there were 3,538 Greek-Orthodox and 1,421 Muslims on Bozcaada, and 7,997 Greek-Orthodox and 92 Muslims on Gökçeada.)[158] De facto Greek rule over the islands had remained in effect until Lausanne. During the treaty negotiations, Gökçeada and Bozcaada were given back to Turkey due to their strategic proximity to the Dardanelles, on condition that they would be demilitarized.

The Lausanne Treaty had exempted the insular Greeks from the Turco-Greek exchange and added, "No inhabitant of the islands...shall be molested in Turkey." Additionally it stipulated that, "The islands of Imbros and Tenedos, remaining under Turkish sovereignty shall enjoy a special administrative organization composed of local elements...The maintenance of order will be assured therein by a police force recruited amongst the local population."[159] Despite these reassurances, however, many Greeks, including the elite of the community, fled before the islands were turned over to Turkey. (Accordingly, in 1927, the number of insular Greeks had dropped to 4,469 from 11,535 in 1914–15.[160]) To the dismay of the remaining Greeks, the "special administrative status" of the islands did not go into effect. Turkish officials were appointed to administrative positions on the islands. Ankara claimed, perhaps with justification given the nature of the recent emigration, that this was necessary since "there were no qualified islanders capable of fulfilling the functions of administration."[161]

The island Greeks suffered from this. For instance, their education was seriously undermined after 1923.[162] On December 15, 1926, representatives of Gökçeada and Bozcaada on Lemnos (Limni), a neighboring Greek island in the northern Aegean, wrote to the British Vice-Consul there to complain about Turkish rule. Although Turkey had been bound by Article Fourteen of Lausanne to "grant autonomy" to the islands, this had never taken place.[163] On the contrary, Ankara "was making every endeavor to Turkify the islands." For instance, "not a single Greek inhabitant is employed in the public services" and the "Greek schools are managed by Turkish schoolmasters whom the inhabitants are compelled to pay." Besides, while the authorities "enrolled conscripts and reservists whom they transport to Asia Minor," these men, "being afraid of oppression," deserted and escaped to Greece.[164] In 1927, students from Gökçeada in Athens forwarded another letter of grievance to the British Vice-Consul on Lemnos:

> The Turks, since they were first present on the Island, aiming for the humiliation and devastation of the residents, did not hesitate to engage in all vulgarities.... By coveting the seizure of the Schools by the Government and especially the acquisition of the Academic and of the Metropolitan Edifices, they used all means for the removal of all teachers.
>
> (FO, 286/11013/319)

This unfavorable situation for the Greeks lasted so long as Turkey and Greece were unable to come to terms over their differences.[165] Events took a dramatic turn in December 1928. Negotiations between Ankara and Athens on the Lausanne Treaty, which had been stalled earlier, started again following the election of a Venizelos government in Greece. Turkey and Greece moved to resolve their differences. This political rapprochement became palpable in 1929. Ankara now reevaluated its attitude toward the Greek minority. For instance, the proprietress of the Istanbul Greek daily *Ta Chronica*, who had been jailed in July 1929, in respect of a court decision that her paper's depiction of the Turkish army as "savage" had been "offensive to the dignity of the army,"[166] was released from prison in November following a decree that this publication had not been "offensive to Turkishness."[167]

Further rapprochement took place after Venizelos declared in February 1930 that, "Greece was attached to peace with the world and particularly with Turkey."[168] The grand finale of the honeymoon was during Venizelos' October 1930 visit to Ankara.[169] The premier officially dropped Greek irredentism toward Turkey by announcing that Greece had "definitely abandoned all designs on Constantinople."[170] Greece and Turkey entered an *entente cordiale*. That, in return, ameliorated the position of the minorities in both countries. Now, Turkey's treatment of the Greek minority changed significantly.[171] For instance, an American diplomatic source reported on August 20, 1931 that the "Turkish Minister of Interior is making a voyage to Imbros and Tenedos with the intention of installing autonomous administration, as provided by Article 14 of the Lausanne Treaty."[172] In another goodwill gesture, on February 19, 1935, Ankara passed a decree concerning "those exchangeable Greeks, who had somehow managed to remain in Turkey." The government stipulated that they "would be granted Turkish citizenship" and not forced to leave Turkey.[173] Thus, in 1930, the Greek minority seemed assured of relative stability and security.

Arab Christians, Jacobites, and other Eastern Christians during the 1920s

Compared to their brethren in Istanbul, the Christians in the provinces had a tougher time in the 1920s. In 1924, based on "reliable sources," the British Consul in Aleppo, Syria, reported the deportation of Christians from Anatolia and "Turkish Kurdistan." The Consul added with some disdain for the Turks that although "no general slaughter of the Christians is being carried out as far as can be seen," due to "the continued and growing xenophobia displayed by the Turks against all persons in Turkey not of Turkish race," the Christians were "being compelled to leave by force of circumstances, though not by definite orders, from the areas of Turkey" between Diyarbakır, Mardin, Urfa and Maraş.[174] At this time, Turkish government correspondence noted in 1924 that Armenians, who had returned to Urfa before the Turkish Independence War, were being gradually driven out.[175] Furthermore, British diplomats reported that, in addition to Armenians, Syrian Catholic and Orthodox Christians, "who have up to recently been left comparatively left in peace" were also leaving the country.[176] A Turkish government report by the Minister of Interior M. Cemil Ubaydın discussed these developments.[177] Among other things, this 1925 paper touched on the issue of Christians in the East. The government was to prevent the influx of "about two to three thousand Armenians in Diyarıbekir, as well as the Armenians, Jacobites, Chaldeans, Nestorians [Assyrians], and other Christians" in this area. Ankara was to facilitate the "expulsion of these mischievous elements that had been proxy to the British aims" in this area.[178] By 1930, the situation changed little: a British traveler to Mardin, in southeastern Turkey, noted that the Jacobites "were not happy," since they felt that "the circumstances were against them." They had their "ownership of land questioned and often denied." They were under "a steady if gentle, pressure" which resulted in a quiet exodus of Christians.[179]

Ankara was unfriendly also toward the Christian Arabs. Yet, suggesting that antagonism toward Arabs had not only religious but also ethnic roots, a British diplomat noted in 1924: "Muslims who are of Arab race are being slowly but surely compelled indirectly to leave Anatolia."[180] Even then, the situation was especially aggravated for the Christians. Orthodox and Catholic Arabs in Mersin and Tarsus, for instance, suffered from various restrictions.[181] During the negotiations of the Turco-Greek population exchange treaty, the government had insisted that Arabs who had "embraced the Orthodox faith are *ipso facto* Greeks and should consequently follow the latter into exile."[182] Ankara had wished to make the Arab Orthodox population of Mersin exchangeable.[183] However, these people had been allowed to stay due to the "decision of the Mixed Exchange Commission that they were not 'exchangeable' within the meaning of the Graeco-Turkish Exchange Convention of January 30, 1923."[184] This had angered Ankara to the extent that the Turkish press had accused the Mixed Exchange Commission of partiality.[185] Next, the government made life difficult for the Christian Arabs. For instance, the French Capuchin missions at Mersin and Tarsus, who tended to the Catholic Arabs, were not permitted to teach. British diplomats added, "They are even held up to all kinds of ridicule. At Tarsus, they are booed and even stoned in the streets by children and roughs, but at Mersina [*sic*] it is not quite so bad; they are even permitted to toll their church bell."[186]

Armenians during the 1920s: conflict and confrontation

Compared to other Christians, Armenians felt the brunt of Ankara's negative attitude during the 1920s, despite the fact that they were "better able to harmonize with the Turks than are the Greeks and the Jews; they have similar tastes and speak Turkish almost universally." Nevertheless, according to American diplomats, throughout the 1920s, Armenians suffered from "continual discriminations, particularly in matters of employment and travel."[187] By the mid-1920s, while it was complicated to be an Istanbul Armenian, it was even tougher to be an Anatolian Armenian. Then, small but concentrated Armenian communities remained in various provinces of north-central, central, east-central, and southeastern Turkey. It is difficult to estimate the exact number of these since the 1927 census had four categories: Armenian, Catholic, Protestant, and "Christian," in all of which they might have registered themselves. Diplomatic correspondence helps on this to an extent. The British reported in 1929

> It is true that there exists large numbers of Armenian women in Turkish houses, in the capacity of servants and concubines, but they and their Armenian children (who are brought up as Moslems) have become absorbed in the Turkish population, and their existence is not officially admitted. I doubt whether in the whole of Turkey outside of Constantinople there are even 10,000 Armenians living as such.
>
> (FO, 371/13827/E6397)

Calculations based on the 1927 Turkish census reveal higher numbers. In this year, it appears that there were 22,090 Armenians registered as such in the thirteen Anatolian provinces stretching from Siirt, Mardin, and Diyarbakır in the southeast, through Malatya, Elazığ and Sivas in east-central, and Kayseri, Yozgat and Ankara in the center, to Tokat, Amasya, Kastamonu, and Sinop in north-central. Additionally, 5,460 Catholics; 1,046 Protestants, and 6,151 "Christians" lived in this region.[188] Since at least some of these would have been Armenians, it can be estimated that 25,000–30,000 Armenians lived in these thirteen Anatolian provinces in 1927 (Map 5).

Provincial Armenians had problems especially in maintaining religious organizations. Then, they sought help from the Armenian Catholic Patriarchate, which relocated from Istanbul to Beirut in 1928.[189] After its move, the Patriarchate started lobbying internationally on behalf of the Turkish Armenians. On July 2, 1928, the Patriarch Pierre Terziyan petitioned the League of Nations in Geneva to complain about the maltreatment of the Armenians and the Armenian Catholic Church in Turkey. He asked the League to support the Turkish Armenians so that they could exercise "all that was assured to them by treaty."[190] However, the situation did not improve. On the contrary, it deteriorated significantly, especially in the Southeast: on the night of April 10, 1929, an Armenian priest, Yusuf Emirhanyan, was murdered in his house in Diyarbakır. When the British diplomats inquired about this homicide, they reported that "the Turkish reply is a particularly odious example of official hypocrisy whether the Diarbekir [*sic*] police took part in this murder (as it is not explicitly denied) or not." The event did not come as a surprise to the British diplomats, who noted that the "Christian community in Turkey can not hope for anything but persecution."[191]

Patriarch Terziyan protested the murder with a letter to the League of Nations. He claimed that "two police agents" had conducted this atrocity. Now, it would not be possible "to assure the safe administration of the Armenian Catholic Church in Diyarbakır." Terziyan asked the League to intervene in order "to achieve justice on behalf of the Christian victims" and "to ameliorate the condition of the survivors of our nation in Anatolia."[192]

It is not clear whether Father Emirhanyan's killing was politically motivated: British diplomats, who reported on this, first saw no reason why "the Turkish

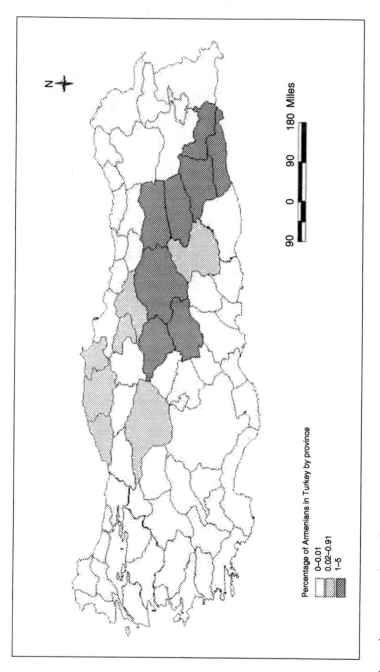

Percentage of Armenians in Turkey by province

◻ 0–0.01
▨ 0.02–0.91
▨ 1–5

90   0   90   180 Miles

Map 5 Armenian concentration in Central, East-Central, and Southeastern Turkey (1927).

Source: Büyük Atlas (1939).

police should not be guilty of such crimes against isolated Christians in the interior, provided the motive, usually robbery, be fairly strong."[193] Then, later on, they noted that Father Emirhanyan's murder was probably a private matter. Yet, regardless of its complicity in this matter, Ankara's indifference to the homicide exacerbated Armenians' fears about government hostility toward them. Following the murder, the police arrested Emirhanyan's wife, tortured her in prison, and vowed not to release her "until she told everything she knew."[194] This sent shock waves through the Anatolian Armenian community and ignited a scare among those around Diyarbakır.[195] Moreover, the slaying of an Orthodox priest in Mardin at this time only intensified the Armenians' feeling of insecurity. This time, the killing was apparently the work of the government:

> The local police called at the house of the orthodox priest and commenced to question him regarding a service he had held…During the cross-examination, the priest, who was a very old man, was accompanied by his servant, whom the police tried to order away, but he declined to leave his master. He was eventually obliged to leave to answer the door; upon his return he found only the mutilated body of his late master.
>
> (FO, 371/13818/E6101)

In the aftermath of this incident, the Catholic mission in Elazığ, whose flock was mostly Armenian was obliged to shut down. The priests here, including "two Armenians a Frenchman and a German," left "for Beirut on the 24–25th September."[196] The events triggered an exodus of Armenians from southeastern and east-central Turkey into Syria. Throughout the summer and fall of 1929, thousands of Armenians left for Syria. Most of them had to abandon their property since according to a decree dated January 1, 1929, Armenians in Turkey were not allowed, "to sell or bequeath their property," which, at death, "goes to the State."[197] In the interim, the Armenian Protestant Church in Harput was bombed and burnt. In addition, the Jacobite Bishop of Diyarbakır barely escaped an attempt on his life. Moreover, after further incidents, the Chaldean priest of the city "was escorted over the frontier."[198] These developments exacerbated the exodus and other Eastern Christians joined the exodus into Syria.

The number of refugees that fled to Syria at this time remains uncertain. American diplomats estimated that 10,000–20,000 Armenians moved.[199] The British initially noted that 30,000–40,000 were about to become refugees.[200] However, later on, they corrected their figure to 10,000–12,000.[201] On December 19, 1929, there was confirmation from Aleppo of 600 Armenian refugee families already there, "with 30–40 families arriving daily."[202] By February 1930, the British further re-estimated the total number of refugees to range between 2,000 and 2,500 or 3,000 and 4,000.[203] The Americans projected 5,373 refugees based on figures they had obtained from the Armenian Patriarchate.[204] On January 3, 1930, the British Consul in Tebriz, Iran wrote that Armenian refugees were also arriving into Iran from Van and Bitlis across the border. (The Consul added that Jews, however, "were not involved in an expulsion which apparently includes all Christian elements except the small and warlike Chaldean element."[205] In fact, the small community of Kurdish and Arabic-speaking Jews of eastern Turkey were treated well during these episodes.)[206]

At the apogee of the refugee crisis, on January 9, 1930, the Lord Mayor's Fund in London made a public appeal for money donations for refugee relief.[207] At this time, British records noted that so far, the French officials in Syria had "overlooked the absence of visas and have generously admitted a large number in view of the precarious situation." However, such behavior also indicated that this matter might be "under negotiation between the French government and Ankara."[208] Since the "French authorities have allowed this immigration on so large a scale," the British suggested that, "a tacit understanding exists with the Turkish government."[209] Hence, Ankara may not have been the sole factor behind the exodus. In fact, one diplomatic source wrote that despite its negative attitude toward the Christians, there appeared to be no

> deliberate pressure on the part of the Turkish Government to bring about this migration, though seeing that it is the natural result of its policy towards the minorities it may be supposed that the authorities view this departure with no regret. It is however, to their credit that very little actual brutality has been employed.
>
> (FO, 371/14587/E729)

Perhaps, hardships of all sorts may have played a role in causing the exodus. The British Ambassador noted that the provincial Armenians

> seem to have realized that life is impossible for them now in Turkey. They are not allowed to move about the country and trade as before. They are confined to the towns. They cannot have their own schools to bring their children up in. They often have no church, and more often, they have no priest. They cannot recover the property which they lost in the past.
>
> (FO, 371/14567/E1244)

American diplomats, who claimed "no evidence of the active maltreatment" of Armenians, also accepted economic hardship as a major cause of the exodus. They added, "There is evidence that pressure is being exerted in certain regions to force the Armenians from the country into the cities and towns and that the difficulty of obtaining their livelihood there is leading to their gradual emigration, particularly, to Syria." However, the Americans also reported that the "Agents of the Government are said to suggest to Armenian residents that it would be in their own interest to emigrate."[210]

Thus, it seems that coercion, government-instigated political and economic hardships, as well as public hostility all played a role in the exodus.[211] However, even so, fear may have been the most significant determinant of the exodus. In 1929, a refugee in Aleppo described the trauma of the Armenians in the

Turkish interior: "We have no means of existence; we are persecuted, suspected, robbed, ill-treated, thrown into prison, judged and if we are lucky, deported."[212]

There is also evidence that the exodus may have been possibly connected to agitation by Armenian nationalists, who wanted to get as many of their compatriots to Syria as possible in the hope of establishing a strong anti-Turkish presence there. A telegram on June 25, 1929 from the Turkish Consul General in Antwerp noted that Armenian nationalists led by Tashnak Party[213] member "Sotyon Harasanaryan," had held a meeting in Antwerp to discuss provoking a possible exodus of Armenians from Turkey to Syria.[214]

Whatever the reasons behind the exodus, the government did not attempt to stop it. In addition to its hostility toward the Armenians, a few other factors help explain this. First, Ankara was apprehensive of the anti-Turkish activity of Armenian nationalists. Turkey had a vivid memory of the assassination of various prominent Ottoman politicians by Armenians in the aftermath of the First World War in retaliation for the Armenian catastrophe of 1915. In reaction, on May 31, 1926, the TBMM passed Law Nr 882, which granted property to the families of Ottoman leaders assassinated by the Armenians. This law covered the relatives of prominent CUP members, including Mehmet Talât Paşa (1874–1921) Ahmet Cemal Paşa (1872–1922), Sait Halim Paşa (1863–1921), and Bahattin Şakir Bey (1877–1922), among others.[215] The legislation added that these families would be given property that belonged to fugitive Armenians. MP Recep Zühtü Bey (Soyak) (1893–1966) (Sinop), a close confidant and the private secretary of Atatürk, said this was a strong "warning message to assassins: you may execute a Turk through an assassination! But, we will raise his offspring with your money so that tomorrow, he will gouge out your eye and break your head."[216] In the interim, Ankara reacted against further Armenian attempts on republican cadres. Throughout the 1920s, the government thwarted many assassination schemes. During the fall of 1927, for instance, an assassin in the so-called Tokatlıyan affair, Mercan Altunyan, was caught in Istanbul, before he could make an attempt on Atatürk's life.[217]

Armenian conspiracies, French Syria, and Turkey in the 1920s

A second reason behind government hostility toward the Armenians was that in the 1920s, Armenian nationalists worked actively to build an anti-Turkish coalition around the country. This alliance included Turkish and Kurdish ex-army officers, Kurdish, Circassian, and Armenian nationalists, as well as representatives of Christian groups, such as the Assyrians (Nestorians), who had recently lost their homes in Turkey.[218] The nucleus of this grouping was Syria.[219] The French mandate government in Syria permitted activities against Ankara, such as anti-Turkish publications as well as assassins, who tried to cross to Turkey, to murder notable figures of the republic.[220] A 1929 letter from the Ministry of Interior noted a growing French-sponsored alliance of Kurds and Armenians in Syria. Another report, compiled by the General Staff of the Gendarmerie

(Jandarma Umum Komutanlığı—JUK), noted that the French were busy resettling Armenians in the Sancak of Alexandratta, south of the Turco-Syrian border and that the Kurds and the Armenians there were likely to cause trouble for Turkey.[221]

Ağrı uprising of 1930

In 1929, Turkey became aware of preparations for a Kurdish-Armenian uprising in the Ağrı region and along the Syrian border.[222] The nationalist Kurds and Armenians had seemingly decided to join forces against Kemalist Turkey. A report compiled by the JUK asserted that Armenians were arming and supporting the Kurds, across the Syrian and Persian borders, in preparation for a major offensive. In the Ağrı region alone, they had distributed 10,000 rifles to the Kurdish tribes. Hoybûn, a Kurdish-Armenian nationalist organization,[223] was preparing for an incursion into the Mardin province across the border in Syria.[224] This coalition of Armenians, Kurds (and Assyrians) took action in Ağrı in 1930, where a major uprising was launched. At the climax of the rebellion in July 1930, the American ambassador Joseph C. Grew (1880–1965) argued, "It would seem possible that minority organizations in the United States (Kurds, Assyrians, Armenians) may be drawn together in unity of action against the common foe, Turkey."[225]

Armenians, especially the nationalist Tashnak party, had a considerable role in the planning and financing of the Ağrı rebellion, which was conducted by Kurdish tribes.[226] Soon, clashes spread to Turkey's frontier with Iraq, where joint forces of Kurds, Assyrians, and Armenians crossed the border.[227] There were also simultaneous attacks from Syria. Feudal Kurdish chiefs in Turkey, whose influence had been lessened by the Inspectorate, as well as tribal Kurds, participated actively in the uprisings. Hoybûn played a prominent role in these efforts.[228] A letter to the US State Department by Vahan Cardashian, a Tashnakist in New York City, elaborated on this. Based upon a report from Hoybûn's Aleppo office, Cardashian noted that the chief of operations at Ağrı was an Armenian "who is assisted by several Armenian officers and technicians."[229] The Ağrı uprising was truly a multi-theatre campaign with many actors. American diplomats noted that,

> The Kurds of Persia, Iraq and Syria have already established armed contact with those of Turkey. They are now in possession of parcels of Turkish soil about Ararat, through Persia; in Hekkiari, through Iraq, and in El-Djezireh, south of Diarbekir, through Syria.
>
> (SD N 767.91/43)

The government's reaction was harsh: in 1930, the Minister of Foreign Affairs Dr Tevfik Rüştü Aras (1883–1972) told the British Ambassador Sir George R. Clerk (1874–1951) that the effective suppression of this rebellion "will extinguish all embers of discontent in other districts."[230] Ankara used airplanes in a counter-attack and mobilized 15,000 troops in Ağrı to suppress the uprising. It launched another 5,000 troops along the Iraqi and Syrian borders to fight the unrest.[231] Despite the tremendous challenge, the Turkish army was able to put down the unrests and the incursions, though with great difficulty,[232] and only after losing a few planes.[233]

It seems possible, at least without dwelling on the Armenian catastrophe of 1915, to link Turkey's antagonism toward the Armenians throughout the 1920s to such anti-Turkish efforts of Armenian nationalists. However, even then, it is striking that Ankara's seemingly innocent defensiveness was laced with ethnicism. Often being an Armenian in Turkey was reason enough to be suspected. In this regard, Ankara considered even those Armenians who had converted, dubious. For instance, on November 7, 1928, the General Directorate of Public Security (Emniyet-i Umumiye Umum Müdiriyeti—EUUM)[234] inquired from the governors of Istanbul and Edirne about a man "caught in İpsala,[235] who had given his name as Arif Hakkı [a Muslim name] and his domicile as Istanbul." Hakkı belonged to the Armenian millet. He was the son of Zenup from the Karakaşoğulları family, his real name was Kirkor, and "he had converted to Islam ten years ago." The letter demanded more information about Hakkı/Kirkor.[236] Determined to see Armenianness in a convert, the police was more than overly nationalist in its caution toward the Armenians.

Another aspect of vigilance was scrutiny of Armenians from other countries. A letter written from the Ministry of Interior on August 8, 1929 asked twenty-eight provinces to be watchful over the visit of three American-Armenian geologists, "Toros, Ermenak, and Hayık," to Turkey. The letter advised the authorities to "conduct serious investigation" about the aforementioned three, but "absolutely without their knowledge."[237] Ankara stretched its caution toward Armenians and Armenian-led activities as far as possible. On December 8, 1928, the Ministry of Interior wrote to the Inspector-General's office asking it to look for connections between a communist cell, recently uncovered in the Nizip district of Gaziayıntab [*sic*], and the Armenians (and the Circassians) there.[238]

Conclusion

During the 1920s, Islam's pivotal role in the formation of Turkish national identity and Turkey's demographic diversity clashed with Kemalism's understanding of the Turkish nation. While the Kemalists increasingly saw the nation as "an organic culture," defined through language and culture,[239] this meant, "the only way Kemalism could deal with those who were non-Turkish was through denial and assimilation." That led to conflicts between Ankara and the minorities. On the other hand, the legacy and trauma of the Armenian catastrophe and the Turco-Greek exchange burdened Turkey. These events, which Irving Horowitz describes as "ethnic homogenization, religious singularity, and nationalization,"[240] had created a deep rift between the Christians and Turkish nationalism. Coupled with the legacy of the millet system, which had separated the Muslims from the non-Muslims, this rift led the Kemalists to see the Christians as a separate ethno-religious community; citizens outside the body of the Turkish nation. Hence, primarily the heritage of the Ottoman Empire, and not language or political citizenship, shaped Ankara's attitude toward the non-Muslims.

Even then, now the Christians' weight in the Anatolian population was around 2 percent, down from 20 percent in 1912.[241] Anatolia had a large Muslim majority. However, in some places it was only a patchwork of partly assimilated groups, including the defiant Kurds, who challenged Kemalism's notion of the nation. In addition, the culturally isolated Jewish community seemed to have failed in assimilating into Turkishness. British diplomatic correspondence, which described 1928 as a "relatively happy one for the minorities for under this head there is little to record"[242] summarizes the problematic nature of the relations between the republic and the minorities as the country entered the 1930s.

3 Kemalism par excellence in the 1930s

The rise of Turkish nationalism

This new road we have blazed is an example to the nations
We are a fused mass, without classes or concessions
Knowledge is our vision and ideals our mode
If the world were doomed, we would not leave this road
We are the Turks; for the republic, our chest is a bronze shield
The Turk will not stop, the Turk to the front, the Turk forward.
(From a Turkish independence anniversary
marching song, 1933)

Menemen rebellion, Ağrı uprising, and SCF experience: the troublesome 1930

After the increasingly authoritarian 1920s, 1930 seemed to offer a respite: on August 12, 1930, the Free Republican Party (Serbest Cumhuriyet Fırkası—SCF) was established as Turkey's first opposition party since the TpCF in 1925. However, unlike the TpCF, the origin of the SCF was not grass roots. Rather, it was formed according to Atatürk's directives. The Turkish president thought of this as a means of funneling away the growing discontent in the country against the İnönü government.[1] Atatürk had his close friend and associate, Fethi Okyar, the Turkish ambassador in Paris, return from his post to take over the presidency of the SCF. Moreover, he made his childhood companion, Mehmet Nuri (Conker) (1881–1937), a compatriot Salonikan and an indispensable regular at his rakı parties, its Secretary General. The SCF was orchestrated to such an extent that, before its establishment, Atatürk, İnönü, and Okyar met to decide how many MPs it would have.[2]

Despite its controlled creation, the SCF soon evolved into an impromptu opposition party. For instance, on his trip to Izmir on September 4, 1930, Okyar was met by thousands of demonstrators, who greeted him with unprecedented euphoria and a spontaneous anti-government demonstration.[3] The masses stoned the CHP offices and clashed with the police. On September 7, a SCF rally drew more than 100,000 people in Izmir whose population was barely over 150,000.[4] The CHP followed the events with caution.[5] Soon, the developments caught Atatürk's attention, who started to question the idea of orchestrated opposition.

On October 5, the SCF fared better than anticipated in the municipal elections and captured a number of seats in various municipalities.[6] Increasingly, it started to look like a grassroots opposition party.

Moreover, it appeared that the Greeks, Armenians, and Jews were supporting the SCF, which was courting them.[7] In local elections, the SCF fielded 5 Greeks, 2 Armenians, and 2 Jews for the 42 councilmen positions of Istanbul.[8] In return, the minorities threw most of their support behind the SCF.[9] The CHP had a low opinion of this situation.[10] According to British diplomatic records, the party believed that "5 percent of the electors will vote for the Free Party [*sic*]," and that these people were "convicts enjoying temporary liberty, reactionaries... knaves who have sold their souls... fools who believe that their sugar and petro- leum taxes will cost less and that taxes and military service will be reduced; communists and finally Greeks, Jews and Armenians."[11] Then, there were rumors that the "Liberal Party [*sic*] urged the Kurds in Constantinople to support the liberals," and that it was courting the ex-Ottoman dynasty.[12] Atatürk decided to act. On November 17, on his recommendations, the SCF "abolished" itself, just three months after its formation.[13] This marked the advent of a new single-party era in Turkey.

By the end of 1930, the political mood in the country was acrimonious due to these events. The aforementioned Ağrı uprising of summer 1930 exacer- bated such bitterness. Although the rebellion was finally crushed, it caused great unrest.[14] Together with the failure of the SCF experience, it was one of the disheartening episodes of 1930 for Atatürk. Additionally, the Menemen incident, which took place before the year's end on December 23, aggra- vated Atatürk's frustration. This had started when a number of dervishes, led by Derviş Mehmet, a Cretan Muslim who belonged to the suppressed Nakşibendi Sufi order had taken arms and attacked government soldiers in Menemen, a small agricultural town north of Izmir.[15] The government had acted immediately: hundreds of people in various parts of Turkey were arrested on charges that they were part of the rebellion or that they were affiliated with the Nakşibendis. Many of them were tried in court martial, and twenty-eight were executed.[16]

Although, the regime swiftly crushed it, the Menemen incident heightened Atatürk's worries about popular unrest.[17] He decided to act on this by consoli- dating the CHP's hold on power. American Ambassador Grew contended that the Menemen incident alone triggered the advent of single-party rule in Turkey.[18] British Ambassador Clerk supported his American colleague:

> While religious opposition was being thus suppressed the President of the Republic made a tour of Turkey "with the exception of the eastern provinces" in order "to ascertain for himself the nature and extent of the anti-governmental feeling that had manifested itself at the municipal elec- tions in 1930 and during the life-time of the Liberal Party [*sic*], which had shortly been dissolved."

(FO, 371/16091/E222)

Atatürk returned from his three-month tour with observations about popular discontent:[19]

> He arrived at the conclusion that this feeling arose from the fact that the people in general were insufficiently instructed respecting the principles of the Republican Popular Party [*sic*] which alone guarded the revolutionary fervour, which alone could elevate the masses, and of which he himself was the head and from which the government was formed.
>
> (FO, 371/16091/E222)

The advent of High Kemalism

Now, Atatürk decided to launch a two-pronged policy: on March 3, 1931, he sent a letter to the CHP, asking for new elections.[20] A week later, he appointed Recep Peker (1888–1950), a staunch nationalist, as the CHP's new Secretary General. Atatürk was convinced that with these measures,

> the sound common sense of the Turkish people would return to power a Popular Party [*sic*] Government and would give that party a mandate to vote measures for the national good which experience gathered during his tour would enable him to suggest.[21]

Elections were held on April 24. The fourth term of the TBMM held its inaugural meeting on May 4. CHP was the only party participating in this. On May 5, the sixth İnönü cabinet took office as Turkey's new government.[22] The cabinet's program, which was presented to the TBMM by the Prime Minister on May 9, signaled the beginning of a fresh epoch. The program emphasized nationalism and the maintenance of order as its central concepts. It declared that "developing and securing a republicanist and populist national way of life and maintaining order, which is needed for political, national and economic progress" was a mission of this government.[23] In addition, the program cited republicanism, nationalism, and populism as the government's guiding doctrines.[24] This government's term, Turkey's tenth cabinet since May 3, 1920, when the first TBMM government had been formed in Ankara,[25] can be seen as the beginning of a new era, "Kemalism par excellence," under Atatürk. This period of High Kemalism, described by Ahmet Makal as "the hardening of the single-party regime,"[26] would last until Atatürk's death in 1938.

A number of factors differentiate this "Kemalism par excellence" from Kemalism in the 1920s. First, during the 1920s, Turkey had been trying to recover from the extensive warfare of the earlier decade. Between the Balkan Wars of 1912–13, the First World War, and the Greco-Turkish war of 1920–22, the country had suffered tremendous demographic and material devastation. For this reason, following the establishment of the republic on October 29, 1923, Turkey had gone through a period of physical and political re-structuring when Atatürk had focused his energy on establishing a secular republic. These tasks kept the regime busy during the 1920s.

By the beginning of the 1930s, when a secular republic had been firmly established and the country rebuilt, the regime was able to shift more of its attention to ideology. First, in a speech on September 24, 1931, Atatürk declared republicanism, nationalism, populism, étatism (statism), secularism, and reformism as the main principles of Kemalism.[27] A few weeks later, on October 16, 1931, Recep Peker voiced the CHP's commitment to these principles at a conference, which he gave to university students in Istanbul.[28] Then, throughout the course of 1930s, Ankara sanctioned these principles, especially nationalism and secularism, as it main tenets.[29] Consequently, nationalism's role in Turkish politics became more prominent in the 1930s than in the previous decade.

A third difference between the 1920s and the 1930s was that in the 1920s, Turkey had witnessed the two, however brief, periods of multi-party democracy. Although terminated abruptly, these epochs were signs of experimentation with democracy in the 1920s. As opposed to this, after the SCF experience, Turkey became an authoritarian, single-party state in the 1930s. Due to his worries about popular discontent, Atatürk moved to make the CHP into the country's sole political organization. He hoped that every citizen of Turkey "become a member of the party framework which was large enough to embrace every citizen."[30]

CHP's 1931 Congress

At this time, the Third General Congress of the CHP convened in Ankara, during May 9–16, 1931. At this venue, the party accepted a new program and by-laws. The CHP argued for the necessity of the new documents saying that they were "the organizational procedures of the party, which had been actualized, in accordance with lessons gathered from experience."[31] A close reading of these texts reveals the party's rising nationalist orientation in 1931.

The new program started by citing the CHP's founding principles. The earlier 1927 program had recognized republicanism, nationalism, and populism as the party's main tenets.[32] The 1931 program added étatism, secularism, and reformism to this list of guiding doctrines. Then, the program went into definitions. First, it described the "millet" (nation) as a "social and political community of citizens connected to one another through language, culture, and ideals."[33] This asserted that becoming Turkish was primarily cultural-linguistic, and then voluntaristic. In other words, one could subjectively see himself as a Turk only after learning Turkish and adopting the Turkish culture. The program emphasized the need for making Turkish into a national language and teaching "the ancient history of the Turks" to the nation.[34] Education was especially important since schools would raise citizens who would "respect and serve the Turkish nation, the Turkish Grand National Assembly, and the Turkish state."[35] After that, the program defined the *vatan* (fatherland) as the territory, "within our contemporary political boundaries, which nurtures the ancient and the exalted history of the Turkish nation and which hosts the nation and its relics, deep in its bosom."[36] Though this description repudiated irredentism, it also laid emphasis on Turkish history and the Turkish land. Such emphases prescribed a central role for Anatolia and Turkish history, not Islam or Ottomanism in the pantheon of Turkish nationalism.

The by-laws adopted at the 1931 Congress specified the CHP's growing ethnic-based nationalism. The seventh article of this, which clarified the conditions for membership in the party, stipulated that only "those Turkish citizens, who have not been in opposition to the national liberation movement, *who have been speaking Turkish* and who have accepted the Turkish culture and the Party's principles"[37] were eligible for membership to the CHP. This meant that the CHP was open to ethnic Turks, and closed to non-Turks, at least to those who had not *already* assimilated. By requiring ethnicity as a prerequisite, the by-laws called for an ethnic definition of nationality.

In practice, the party never fully closed its ranks to non-Muslims. This gap between practice and theory created confusion. A memorandum sent to the party branches from the Secretary General on May 5, 1933, addressed this. The CHP responded to queries from the branches on whether the "akalliyets"[38] (minorities) could be admitted into the party. The party did not object to that.[39] Yet, the fact that this correspondence had been necessary demonstrates that two years after the adoption of Article Seven of the by-laws, the CHP's local cadres were still not clear about how to see the non-Muslims. They were still trying to decide if they could consider the Greeks, the Armenians, and the Jews as Turks.[40]

Perhaps in an effort to answer this dilemma, Peker gave long lectures on the non-Muslims' position *vis-à-vis* Turkishness. (During the 1930s, Peker joined three other Kemalist ideologues, Yusuf Hikmet Bayur (1881–1980), Yusuf Kemal Tengirşenk (1873–1976), and Mahmut Esat Bozkurt, to deliver a series of conferences at the Istanbul Darûlfünun (University), where these four men became lecturers in 1934.)[41] In his lectures, Peker elaborated on Turkish nationalism and the non-Muslims' position in relation to the nation. In a 1931 speech at the Istanbul Darûlfünun, he said: "We need to voice our ideas on our Christian and Jewish citizens with equivocal clarity. Our party sees these citizens as full Turks, on the condition that they participate in ... the unity in language and in ideals."[42] Then, however, Peker inserted a caveat that even then, non-Muslims would not be considered as full Turks since, "according to daily-progressing historical evidence, the matter of blood ties and historical links between us and these masses is beyond our contemporary debate."[43] With these statements, Peker promoted a religio-ethnic definition of the nation. He excluded the non-Muslims from Turkishness and saw them fit only for Turkish citizenship. However, even this qualification came with a demand. Atatürk wrote that the need to be cautious toward the Jews and Christians would disappear only after they would "tie their futures and fortunes with ours."[44]

Peker also spoke on the non-Turkish Muslims' position *vis-à-vis* the nation, ignoring linguistic differences with them, and arguing instead that they could be considered Turks:

> We accept those citizens in the contemporary Turkish political and social community, as part of us, those citizens who accepted the ideas such as Kurdism, Circassianism, and even Lazeism and Pomakism. It is our duty to correct these false conceptions [among them].
>
> (Recep Peker, *CHF Programının İzahı*, 7)

The Secretary General saw all Muslims as citizens and as members of the nation. They were not to foster separate ethnic identities. Afet (İnan) (1908–85), another important ideologue of the republic, agreed with Peker. Calling names such as Kurd, Circassian, Laze, and Pomak as "mere labels," she said, "As the product of the authoritarian era of the past, these false labels have caused anguish and have had no effect on any member of the nation, aside from a few brainless reactionaries who are the tools of the enemy."[45] As in the 1920s, also in the 1930s, the Kemalists believed that all Muslims in Turkey were Turks regardless of their ethnicity. Turkish nationalism demanded complete assimilation from them.

CHP's 1935 Congress and the six principles of Kemalism

By the mid-1930s, thanks to the work of the CHP and its various subsidiaries such as the People's Houses,[46] the six principles of Kemalism had become into the established ideology of the country. At this time, on February 9, 1935, elections were held for the TBMM. Following this, on March 1, İnönü established his seventh cabinet. The new government's program, which was approved on March 7, repeated İnönü's commitment to nationalism.[47] In the meantime, the Fourth Congress of the CHP convened in Ankara, during May 9–16. This conference re-adopted the by-laws[48] as well as the program[49] of the 1931 congress. Peker said that the party's new program would guide the Turkish people so that they would not opt for the right or the left.[50] The new program repeated republicanism, nationalism, populism, étatism, secularism, and reformism as the party's principles.[51] In his speech during the congress, Peker argued for the necessity of these tenets for Turkey.[52] Populism was needed since with such a concept, the party would realize the goal of recognizing all citizens as equals. In the party's eyes, only those citizens who did not claim any privileges, constituted the people and only they were truly populist.

Étatism was the regime's ideal path for economic progress. In order to promote development, the state would protect all sectors of the economy, including capital, labor, peasantry, and commerce. However, the CHP would not be hostile toward private enterprise and capital. It would encourage private capital that functioned normally. The party opposed capital that exploited the people.[53] Next, came secularism. Peker's understanding of secularism was not anti-religious. Rather, it dictated the separation of religion from state matters since religion was a matter for the conscience.[54] Then, Peker spoke very briefly on reformism. He described this as the past efforts of the party to secularize Turkey. This implied that reformism had been achieved already, or was not to be pursued further.[55] Finally, Peker discussed nationalism and republicanism. Since Turkey was a republic, republicanism was one of the party's principles, and since new Turkey was nationalist, nationalism was a *sine qua non* for the CHP.[56]

The Inspectorates-General

Another process that characterized 1930s was the establishment of authoritarian rule in large areas of the country through Inspectorates-General (Umumi Müfettişlikler), regional governorships whose authority prevailed over all civilian, military, and judicial institutions under their domain. The First Inspectorate-General had been established earlier on January 1, 1928 in the southeast. During the 1930s, new ones followed. The idea behind this was to divide the country into large regions, six according to the initial plan, which would be ruled by appointed governors. This would optimize the country's administration by decreasing the number of provinces.[57] In practice, however, the Inspectorates were created only in regions that were considered strategic or turbulent areas by Ankara, or had witnessed Kurdish uprisings.

Three Inspectorates were established during the 1930s. The first of them, Trakya (Thrace) Inspectorate-General, was instituted on February 19, 1934.[58] The mandate of this covered the Edirne, Kırklareli, Tekirdağ, and Çanakkale provinces. With its seat at Edirne, the Thrace Inspectorate united the Dardanelles and the strategic Turkish provinces in Eastern Thrace under a common adminis-tration.[59] This fulfilled a major strategic goal: the Thrace Inspectorate provided a centralized military administration in an area of the country that flanked Bulgaria, the chief revisionist power in post-First World War Balkans. Thus, the creation of this Inspectorate was a security move by Ankara.[60]

In 1935, the government reorganized the Inspectorates and established new ones. (Laws Nr 2865, 2883, 2884, and 2885). Consequently, the Inspectorate-General in the southeast became the First Inspectorate and the Thrace Inspectorate-General, the Second. Then, two more were added.[61] Following İnönü's trip to the northeastern corner of the country, and upon his observa-tions,[62] a decree (Nr 2–3199) dated September 6, 1935, created the Third Inspectorate-General in this area. This covered the provinces of Erzurum, Kars, Ağrı (taken from the First Inspectorate General), Çoruh,[63] Gümüşhane, and Trabzon.[64]

With its seat at Trabzon, the Third Inspectorate had several aims: first, it coordinated the development efforts in the relatively poor northeastern section of the country. Second, it served to pacify Ağrı, a hotbed of Kurdish insurgency since the late 1920s. Third, this Inspectorate flanked the Soviet Union along the Caucasus border and acted as a security wall. That was important, since in 1934, the relations between Soviet Union and Turkey had taken a turn from the amicable state of affairs of the previous fifteen years. On June 25, 1934, Stalin had called the Soviet Ambassador in Ankara, Jacques Souritz, to Moscow. As the Soviet representative in Ankara since June 23, 1923, and as the doyen of the diplomatic corps in the Turkish capital, Souritz had been a friend of Atatürk, and his sudden departure had annoyed Atatürk. Then, on October 23, Stalin chose his new ambassador, Lev Mikhailovich Karakhan (Karakhanian) (1889–1937), an Armenian and the Soviet Deputy Commissar for Foreign Affairs since the 1920s. According to American diplomats, Karakhan "had trouble with Atatürk, shortly after arriving; he tore about Ankara in an expansive runabout."[65] Karakhan's ethnic origin as well as condescending behavior in Ankara "triggered distaste against him."[66] This created concerns about Stalin's motives toward Turkey,[67] and Turkey's relations with the USSR started to slip.[68] Accordingly, the Third Inspectorate might have been a sort of *cordon sanitaire* along the Soviet border.[69]

On January 1, 1936, government decree Nr 2–8823 set up the Fourth Inspectorate-General to incorporate a maverick region, Tunceli (former Dersim district, now made a province)[70] into the rest of the country. The Fourth Inspectorate also covered the provinces of Elazığ, Erzincan, as well as Bingöl (Genç or Çapakçur) district[71] all along the upper Euphrates basin.[72] The aim of this Inspectorate, established following İnönü's trip to the region,[73] was to tame Tunceli, the last area of the republic still under tribal control by the mid-1930s. With its rugged terrain, strong tradition of regionalism, and defiance toward central authority, Tunceli stood on the political margins of Turkish society. Kurdish ethnic particularism and the dominant Kızılbaş/Alevi faith in Tunceli furthered the region's alienation from the republic. For that reason, unlike the other Inspectorates, the appointee to this office was not a civilian, but an officer, General Hüseyin Abdullah Alpdoğan, who became the "Fourth Inspector General, the Governor and Commander of the Tunceli Province." While the Fourth Inspectorate-General centered on Tunceli, its seat was outside in Elazığ. This shows the extent to which the republic was unable to penetrate this province in 1936. Ankara felt uncomfortable sending the Tunceli commander there before its full subjugation.

During the 1930s, an overwhelming majority of Turkey's Kurds lived within the First, Third, and the Fourth Inspectorates. This provided the government with an instrument with which to rule the Kurds. Hüseyin Koca argues that the Inspectorates helped Ankara suppress "the nationalist, and mostly foreign inspired, Kurdish nationalist uprisings." He adds that they also promoted the development of Eastern Turkey and aided the government in fighting banditry, widespread in the East during the 1930s.[74] The Inspectorates enabled Ankara to create a special legal regime in large parts of Turkey (Map 6). Accountable only to the capital, the Inspectorates were administrative-military apparatuses with unprecedented powers. This phenomenon led to even more authoritarian rule in large parts of the country.[75]

First Turkish History Congress and the Turkish History Thesis

Together with the rise of authoritarianism, a key development of the 1930s was the crystallization of Kemalist nationalism. Interestingly, 1931, the year the CHP convened its Third Congress that heralded the rise of "Kemalism par excellence," was also the birth year of the *Turkish History Thesis*. The *Thesis* had initially been nurtured by Turkish Hearths' Committee for the Study of Turkish History (Türk Ocakları Türk Tarihi Tetkik Heyeti—TOTTTH). This committee had been established on April 28, 1930, when the Turkish Hearths had been independent. TOTTTH's members included prominent historians, intellectuals, and

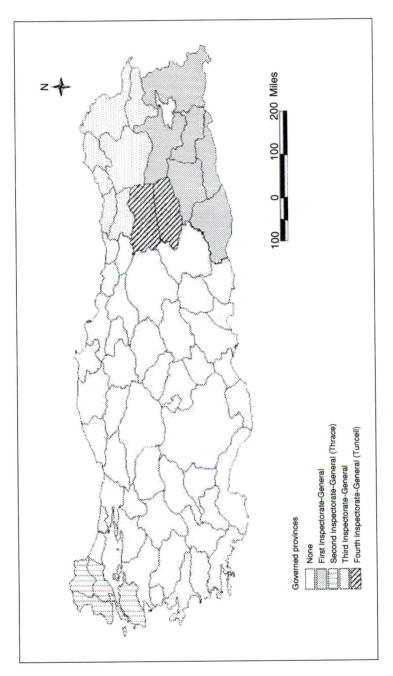

Map 6 Turkish provinces governed by the Inspectorates-General (1936).

Source: Büyük Atlas (1939).

ideologues of Kemalism, among them Akçuraoğlu Yusuf (Akçura) (1876–1935), the organization's President, Samih Rifat (Horozcu) (1874–1932), its Vice-President, and Dr Reşit Galip (1897–1934), its Secretary General, as well as Ağaoğlu Ahmet (Ağaoğlu) (1869–1939), Köprülüzade Fuat (Köprülü) (1890–1966), and Afet İnan. Atatürk instructed the TOTTTH to produce works on Turkish history. The first major study of the organization, a 606-page book titled, *Türk Tarihinin Ana Hatları* (Main Themes of Turkish History) was published in 1930.[76] This was a survey of Turkish history as reviewed by Turkish scholars.

When the Hearths were dissolved on April 10, 1931, the TOTTTH retained is membership but changed its name to Society for the Study of Turkish History (Türk Tarihini Tetkik Cemiyeti—TTTC). Atatürk dictated a program for this organization to İnan. The TTTC was responsible for disseminating Turkish national history, in Atatürk's words, "to its real owners, the Turkish people."[77] It would accomplish this "under the supervision and responsibility of the government authorities and the municipal governments, as well as with the help of the constant and unyielding propaganda activities of the CHP, via the People's Houses and the party's organs." The TTTC would also be helped by "the constant and effective publications in the daily papers and magazines, which would take place under the surveillance and supervision of the General Directorate of Press."[78]

Atatürk gave the society another mission with an eye for bolstering Turkish pride: the TTTC was to show that Turkish was the mother tongue of the great civilizations. To this end, the organization would establish a committee, the Society for the Study of the Turkish Language (Türk Dili Tetkik Cemiyeti—TDTC). Atatürk was convinced that Turkish and the Indo-European languages were related and that Turkish was the root of these languages.[79] The TDTC would launch a comparative survey on this to show that "Turkish is the mother tongue of the Sumerians, the Hittites, and the other ancient Anatolian civilizations, of the ancient Egyptians and the Cretans and of the Aegeans, who were the founders of the Greek civilization, and the Etruscans, the founders of the Roman culture." This would prove that "the Turkish language was the most influential factor in the development and progress of all the world languages."[80]

A second responsibility of the TTTC was to "synthesize and build" its aforementioned work, *The Main Themes of Turkish History*.[81] Soon, the organization produced a revised version of this book titled, *Türk Tarihinin Ana Hatlarına Methal* (Introduction to the Main Themes of Turkish History).[82] Then, it called for a conference of high school teachers in Ankara during July 2–11, 1932. Members of the TTTC, as well as university professors from various disciplines such as law, medicine, theology, fine arts, and literature, gathered in Ankara, ostensibly to discuss the works of the organization.[83] The main group of delegates at this conference, which was organized by the Ministry of Education, were teachers: 182 high school and secondary school teachers altogether. The venue, which was later titled the First Turkish History Congress, was in fact a workshop that aimed to instruct the teachers on the teaching of history.[84]

The Congress aimed to build a sense of nationalism in which teachers played a key role: during the congress, the delegates discussed "the history of Turkish civilization, anthropological characteristics of the Turkish race, and Turkish language and literature."[85] They also conferred on the *Turkish History Thesis*. A dictionary definition compiled during the 1930s that described the Turks as "a brave, heroic race of forty million that has inhabited Asia, and spread into Europe and Africa to conquer the world," summarized the essence of the *Thesis*.[86] The *Thesis* contended that the Turks were a great and ancient race.[87] İnan detailed this in a paper she presented at the Congress. She started that the Turks are a brachycephalic[88] people whose roots go back to Central Asia, where they lived thousands of years ago. In Central Asia, they had created a bright civilization around an inner sea. She asserted that when this inner sea dried up due to climatic changes, the Turks left their original home and moved in all directions to civilize the rest of the world. They went to China to the East; to India to the South; and to Egypt, Mesopotamia, Persia, Anatolia, Greece, and Italy to the West.[89]

This narrative had three implications: first, the Turks were the ancestors of all brachycephalic peoples, including the Indo-Europeans, whose origins went back to Central Asia.[90] Second, the Turkish race had created the civilizations in all the lands to which the Turks had migrated. Thus, the contemporary Turks were the inheritors of the glories of the ancient Sumerians, Egyptians, and Greeks, among others. Besides, they were the founders of the earliest civilization in Anatolia through the Hittites. A third implication was that since the Turks were its original autochthonous inhabitants, Anatolia was the Turkish homeland.[91]

The Congress's emphasis on race would help shape the thinking of Turkish nationalism. On the second day of the conference, Reşit Galip, a staunchly nationalist member of the TTTC, came to the floor. In his paper, "Türk Irkı ve Medeniyet Tarihine Umumi Bir Bakış" (An Overview of the Racial and Civilizational History of the Turks), Galip elaborated on this link between race and nationalism. While most studies on race claimed that the Turks belonged to the yellow race, a classification of races according to phrenelogical data would reveal different results. Galip contended that the Turk, "who is tall, has a long white face, a straight or arched thin nose, proportioned lips, often blue eyes, horizontal, and not slanted, eye lids" was "one of the most beautiful examples of the white race."[92] Contemporary Turks, as well as the original Turkish inhabitants of Central Asia, who had established civilizations in ancient Egypt, the Aegean, Mesopotamia, India, and Italy,[93] belonged to the Alpine branch of the brachycephalic white race.[94]

This accent on race needs to be accounted for. In this, the TTTC, as well as İnan and Atatürk, who did much of the actual work behind the *Thesis*,[95] seem to have been inspired by various West European scholars, especially anthropologists.[96] For instance, İnan had personal connections with the Swiss expert on races, Eugène Pittard (1867–1962). In the 1930s, she became his advisee in the Department of Anthropology at the University of Geneva, where she wrote a PhD dissertation on the Turkish race.[97] Atatürk is known to have read a number of seminal works on race,[98] including Pittard's *Les Races et l'Histoire Introduction Ethnologique a l'Histoire*,[99] as well as Joseph Arthur Comte de Gobineau's (1816–82)

Essai sur l'Inégalité des Races Humaines,[100] Alfred Cort Haddons's (1855–1940) *Les Races Humaines,*[101] Georges Montandon's *La Race. Les Races. Mise au Point d'Ethnologie Somatique,*[102] Jean-Marie Jacques de Morgon's *L'Humanité Préhistorique,*[103] and Joseph Deniker's *Essai d'une Classification des Races Humaines.*[104]

The rise of ethnic definition of the Turkish nation

The First History Congress ended with the affirmation of the *History Thesis* and the official view of what constituted Turkishness: race, ethnicity, and a long glorious history were the tripods of Turkishness; second, only people who spoke Turkish would be eligible for membership to the nation; and third, religion was deemed irrelevant in defining Turkishness. Although, since their emigration from Central Asia, the Turks had "crossed with other races," language had preserved their memories, cultural characteristics, and everything else that made them a nation, including their most cherished possession, the "Turkish intellect" (Türk aklı).[105] Since the Turkish language had conserved the characteristics of the nation, only Turkish speakers could claim to be Turkish. Atatürk had pointed at this even before the congress:

> One of the significant characteristics of the nation is language. One, who regards himself as a member of the Turkish nation, should before everything and in any case, speak Turkish. If someone who does not speak Turkish, claim membership to Turkish culture and community, it would not be right to believe in this.
>
> (İsmail Arar, *Medeni Bilgiler ve Atatürk'ün El Yazıları*, 371)

These emphases made ethnicity-through-language and race the main markers of Turkishness. According to İnan, "unity in political existence and homeland, as well as historical and ethical affinity" were also indicators of Turkishness.[106] During or after the congress, there was no mention of Islam in relation to Turkishness. In the 1920s, secularism had already pushed Islam to the margins of the society. Now, Ankara aimed to dethrone Islam in favor of a secular national identity. In this demarche against religion, secularism stripped the Turkish Muslims of their predominant collective identity. Ahmet Yıldız argues that the Muslims, who constituted nearly 98 percent of the Turkish population, now needed a new collective self. At this point, Kemalism offered them ethnic Turkishness as an alternative identity.[107]

However, this explanation does not fully account for the overwhelming ethnicism and racial orientation of the *Thesis*. In her book published in 1956, İnan elaborated on this. One of the driving forces behind the *History Thesis* was Atatürk, who saw this as a means of establishing the Turks as on par with the Western nations.[108] These questions had shaped the *Thesis*:

1. Who are the most ancient inhabitants of Anatolia?
2. How and by whom was the first civilization established in Turkey?
3. What is the Turks' place in global history and in world civilization?

4. If the establishment of a Turkish state in Anatolia by mere Turkic tribes is a myth, how can this be accounted for?
5. What is the real identity behind Islamic history? What role have the Turks played in Islamic history?

(Afet İnan, *Atatürk'ün Tarih Tezi*, 57–58)

In order to answer these questions, the *Thesis* pursued the following: first, it fought the idea that the Turks were incapable of establishing civilizations. According to the *Thesis*, since the early times, the Turks had always been civilized. The ancient Turks who had civilized Central Asia, had established the first civilizations of history in far away places such as China, India, Mesopotamia, the Nile Valley, Anatolia, and the Aegean,[109] to the extent that "the ancient Greeks used old Central Asian Turkish with minor differences in their dialect."[110] Accordingly, for instance, a fifth grade pupil would even learn in 1933 that it was thanks to "the efforts of the Berbers, who had been Turks, that the Arabs had crossed into Spain."[111]

Subsequently, the *Thesis* stressed the antiquity of the Turks to show that "Turkish history was not confined to Ottoman history."[112] Before the Ottomans, the Turks had established other bright states in Central Asia, including those of the Göktürks, Uygurs, and Karahanlıs. Next, the *Thesis* argued for direct lineage between the modern Turks and the ancient inhabitants of Central Asia.[113] While the Turks had civilized all the lands to which they had migrated, "today's Turks are the children of these Central Asian Turks."[114] Fourth, the *Thesis* claimed Turkish racial and historical continuity in Anatolia. Thanks to supposedly continuous Turkish civilizations in Anatolia from the Bronze Age and the Hittites to the Seljuks, Turkish racial stock had populated Anatolia for millennia. By asserting that the Turks were an ancient people in Anatolia, the *Thesis* deflated post-First World War claims by the Greeks, Italians, Armenians, and Kurds to Turkish territory.[115]

Then, the *Thesis* debunked the assertion that the Turks belonged to the "yellow" or the "Mongol" race. Although they originated from Central Asia, the Turks were in fact "a white and brachycephalic race."[116] The main reason behind this insistence that the Turks did not "belong to the yellow race," was Atatürk's personal interest in the issue, a fact apparent from İnan's accounts. İnan met Atatürk in 1928 in Bursa, when she showed him a French book which claimed that the Turks, who "belonged to the yellow race," were a "secondaire" people. When she asked him for his opinion on this, Atatürk reacted strongly and asked her to prove the contrary. Following this incident, İnan, then a high school teacher, was provided with government scholarships. After her education in Turkey, she went to Switzerland to write her doctoral dissertation on the Turkish race. A historian and anthropologist, she became Atatürk's intellectual friend and confidante. Thus, the *Thesis'* interest in proving that the Turks belonged to the white race[117] was deeply rooted in Atatürk's personal convictions, his offence at Western racism, as well as his intellectual relationship with İnan.[118]

The ramifications of the Turkish History Thesis

Cujus Regis illius motio

The ripple effects of the *Turkish History Thesis* were felt throughout the country. The People's Houses played a very active role in its dissemination.[119] The *Thesis* also surfaced repeatedly in newspapers and in publications of Turkish academics.[120] An example of scholarly works was one by famous historian İsmail Hakkı Danişmend (1889–1967). In his book, *Türklerle Hind-Avrupalıların Menşe Birliği*, (Common Origins of the Turks and the Indo-Europeans), Danişmend used the *Thesis* to argue that the Turks belonged to the White race and not the Mongol race. The language and racial origins of a people had to be the same. For that reason, it would not be possible to argue that the Turks, who belonged to the white race, spoke a language in the same family with the Mongols, who belonged to the yellow race.[121] Various linguistic similarities between Turkish and Mongolian could be attributed to the Turkish language's historical influence over the Mongolian language, and not to argue in favor of common racial origins of Turks and Mongols.[122] In support of this, Danişmend quoted from ancient texts, including the Avestan Zarathustra, to claim that the ancient Turks were Aryan and not Mongol.[123]

First Turkish Language Congress and the purification of the Turkish language

On September 26, 1932, High Kemalism took another important step with the convening of the First Turkish Language Congress in Istanbul. In many respects, this was an extension of the History Congress. First, it was organized by the TDTC, an association formed during the History Congress. Second, like the History Congress, the Language Congress had many school teachers in attendance.[124] A third and a more important link between the two venues was the ideological influence of the first over the second. Étienne Copeaux discusses this phenomenon,[125] which is also mentioned in a US diplomatic note:

> Namely, both the History and Language congresses tended to prove the potency and historical significance in ancient times, the decline under the influence of foreign influence of foreign factors and elements and, finally the renaissance under the Republican regime of the Turkish people and language respectively.

(SD, 867.402/48)

The statute of the TDTC confirmed these observations: the goal of the organization was "to bring out the genuine beauty and richness of the Turkish language and elevate it to the high rank it deserves among world languages."[126] In accordance with this, an emphasis on reviving Turkish and restoring it to its former glory resonated throughout the conference.[127] The delegates asserted that although it was a rich and ancient language, Turkish had been supposedly corrupted during the Ottoman era under the impact of Islam. Now, it needed to be reformed.[128]

MP Mehmet Şeref (Aykut) (1874–1939) (Edirne) advanced these arguments. He emphasized the need to revive Turkish to its old glory. While "throughout the recent centuries," Turkish had "died out in the written language;" it had "flourished" in the spoken, lay language.[129] Accordingly, now a gap existed between written and spoken Turkish, so much that the first, Ottoman Turkish, was very different from the second, people's Turkish. Galip added that due to this gap, "the language being taught at present could hardly be called Turkish "since it is intelligible only to one-tenth of the entire population of the country."[130] To alleviate this, Turkish had to be reformed based on the spoken language. Purifying the written language in order to bridge the chasm between spoken and written Turkish could achieve this.

The first signal of this effort came on July 12, 1932, when the TDTC changed its name. The words "tetkik" (study, investigation, research) and "cemiyet" (society), both of Arabic origin, were dropped from the name of the organization in favor of pure Turkish words, "araştırma" (research or investigation) and "kurum" (society). The Society for the Study of the Turkish Language (Türk Dili Tetkik Cemiyeti—TDTC) became the Society for Research on the Turkish Language (Türk Dili Araştırma Kurumu—TDAK).

This revealed the purification strategy: Arabic and Persian words would be replaced with pure Turkish ones. The latter would be gathered by collecting substitutes from the spoken language and second, by coining new words. Consequently, in November 1932, the parliament passed a decree asking the government organs all over the country to start collecting Turkish words "existing in the language, but not in the dictionaries."[131] Meanwhile the Ministry of Education declared a "linguistic mobilization."[132] In due course, lists of newly collected words, compiled mostly by schoolteachers started to flow to Ankara. By September 1933, about 125,000 word forms had been received by the TDAK. In a matter of a few weeks, a team of schoolteachers in Ankara screened them for mistakes and duplicates. This team published its list of collected words in 1934. In the meantime, the TDAK was also busy coining new words to replace foreign ones. During March 1933, the organization launched a public inquiry to seek the Turkish equivalents of such words.[133] It published ten to twenty newly coined proposals each day in the national papers asking for public feedback. Altogether, about 1,400 new words were publicized during this process. Then, the TDAK started publishing the *Tarama Dergisi* (Journal of Gathered Words), in which it periodically proposed replacements for words of Arabic and Persian origin.[134]

Accordingly, 1934 and 1935 were the zenith years of the language purification movement,[135] which Uriel Heyd describes as a state-orchestrated *tour de force*.[136] This explains the almost apocalyptic success of purification. The People's Houses were the most industrious participants in this movement. Members of the Houses worked hard to collect new Turkish words, which would replace the stock of Arabic and Persian words.[137] Purification efforts were not confined to the government sphere. On March 31, 1933, for instance, the Orthodox Christian Turks (Karamanlıs), led by Papa Eftim II, announced that they were adopting pure Turkish. Now, instead of Greek, they would use "that sacred tongue" in their services.[138] At the same time, the schoolteachers in Iğdır, a town in eastern Anatolia, announced their decision to "discard their Islamic names" to substitute them with "pure Turkish ones."[139] Name changes spread to all aspects of community life from theatres to banks. For example, the Istanbul movie theater "Cine Magic" became "Cine Turc" in 1933.[140] Even Atatürk changed his name. The president's middle name, Kemal, comes from Arabic. Atatürk and the republican elite, who had done so much to rid Turkish of Arabic's influence, showed their dislike for this Arabic name by modifying it. Accordingly, the Turkish leader adopted a new name, Kamâl, which supposedly meant "fortress" in old Turkish. This was official. Atatürk's identification card, on display at his mausoleum (Anıtkabir) in Ankara, bears the first name Kamâl.[141] (The republic's aversion toward Arab things was so strong that in October 1935, the Ministry of the Interior informed the provincial governors that a picture of Atatürk in Arab garb had been circulating around the country. Ankara asked all the provinces to confiscate such pictures.)[142] There were many other examples of name changes with ideological overtones. For instance, in 1934, the directors of the "Sanayi Kredi Bankası" (Industrial Credit Bank) changed its name to "Sümer Bankası" (Sumerian Bank).[143]

These name changes demonstrated the impact of the *History Thesis* beyond language purification. Since the *Thesis* had emphasized that the ancient inhabitants of Anatolia, Mesopotamia, and the Aegean were Turks, the purification campaign aimed to honor these bygone cultures through name givings. Many streets, schools, and neighborhoods followed suit. Another popular adoption was "Eti," the Turkish word for the Hittite Kingdom. On June 14, 1935, a new state bank for mining operations was named "Eti Bank."[144]

Atatürk's death and the end of a period of High Kemalism

Soon after the Second History Congress, Atatürk fell ill with cirrhosis of the liver. His health deteriorated, and he died on November 10, 1938.[145] This event marked the end of only one episode of High Kemalism. On November 11, the TBMM elected İnönü as Turkey's second president. Many aspects of High Kemalism survived Atatürk. (In fact, at this time, there was widespread concern among the non-Muslims that "given his hostile sentiments toward the minorities," life would be more difficult for them under İnönü.)[146] While Turkey remained staunchly nationalist after Atatürk, during İnönü's twelve-year term, Kemalism entered a new phase. In fall 1939, together with the rest of Europe, Ankara found itself engulfed in the Second World War. Whereas Turkey fell under a new set of domestic and international circumstances such as external threats, and a deep economic slump, 1939 can be seen as the beginning of a new era of "High Kemalism" under İnönü.

The ethno-racial definition of the Turkish nation vs Turkey's ethno-religious diversity

Between 1931 and 1938, the ideologues of High Kemalism established a specific ethno-racial definition of the Turkish nation. They claimed that all of Turkey's past and present inhabitants were ethnically and racially Turkish. In reality, inter-war Turkey was not an ethnically homogenous state. The 1935 census gives detailed data on the ethnic and linguistic diversity of the country. In that year, the Turkish population was 16,157,450, of whom 15,838,673 were Muslims. The rest included 125,046 Greek-Orthodox; 78,730 Jews; 44,526 Gregorian Armenians; 32,155 Catholics; 8,486 Protestants; 4,725 Christians; 559 without religion, and 12,965 others.[147] Although Turkish was the first language in the country, spoken by 13,899,073 people, 1,480,426 people spoke Kurdish. In addition, there were 153,687 speakers of Arabic; 108,725 Greek speakers; 91,972 Circassian speakers; 63,253 Laze speakers; 57,599 Armenian speakers; 57,325 Georgian speakers; 42,607 Judeo-Spanish speakers; 32,661 Pomak speakers; 29,065 Bosnian speakers; 22,754 Albanian speakers; 18,245 Bulgarian speakers; 15,615 (Crimean) Tatar speakers; 12,424 Spanish speakers; 10,099 Abkhaz speakers; 7,855 Romani speakers; 5,381 French speakers; 5,047 German speakers; 4,810 Russian speakers; 4,633 Italian speakers; and 4,369 Serbian speakers.[148] The question now was how Kemalist nationalism would deal with Turkey's diversity. Examples demonstrating this were the cases of the "Citizen Speak Turkish" campaign and the "Law on Last Names" of the 1930s.

Citizen, speak Turkish and adopt a Turkish last name!

> The Istanbul Chamber of Commerce announced that with the consent of the Ministry of Economy, it has given its approval to the use of Esperanto as an auxiliary commercial language.
>
> (From a US diplomatic memorandum dispatched from Istanbul to Washington, January 1932)

The "Citizen Speak Turkish" campaign of 1930s was spearheaded by the Turkish Jews. While the *History Thesis* had asserted that the Turkish language was key to both Turkish ethnicity and nationality, this meant that if the Jews started speaking Turkish, they could become Turkish. Hence, in 1931–32, concomitant with the emergence of the *History Thesis*, the Jews revived the "Speak Turkish" campaign that had gone into a hiatus since 1928.[149] The Jews of Izmir, a community in a unique position, were the initial flag bearers of this new drive. After the departure of the Greeks and the Armenians, they had become Izmir's only non-Muslim community, comprising more than 10 percent of its population. They were also the town's biggest non-Turkish speaking community, and had a large share in its economic life. Furthermore, during the 1930 elections, the Jews had thrown their support behind the SCF when it had emerged as a popular party in Izmir. All this had built a nationalist bitterness against them.[150] Perhaps the

re-initiation of the "Speak Turkish" campaign by the Jews here was their strategy
to alleviate antipathy against them. In December 1932, the American Consul in
Izmir, George W. Perry met with Emanuel Sidi, the head of the city's Jewish
community, to discuss the "Speak Turkish" movement. Mr Sidi said:

> The movement was quietly started more than a year ago by a group of young
> Jewish intellectuals, first in Milas and later in Izmir... it is now national in
> extent. The unique aim is to open up greater opportunities in public life for
> Jewish leaders: perhaps reminiscent of the time when, after the decay of the
> Byzantine Empire, Jewish business capacity obtained a recognition in the
> then new Turkey that proved markedly beneficial to the race. "Failing this"
> he declared, "we shall have to emigrate."[151]

(SD 867.4016 JEWS/3)

In 1933, Mehmet Asım, the chief editor of the Istanbul daily *Vakit*, repeated some
of Sidi's arguments. The Jews needed to assimilate the "Turkish language, culture,
and ideals." Unlike Greeks and Armenians, they had not been disloyal to the
Turkish regime. They had, however, remained a minority. Although the legacy of
the Ottoman regime seemed to set them apart from the Turks, there was no
ground for such a separation in the secular republic. There was no room for a
religious mentality. Asım concluded, "The Israelites will not be an ethnic minority
among the Turks."[152]

One of the staunchest proponents of the "Speak Turkish" campaign was
Atatürk's Executive Secretary and confidant, journalist Ruşen Eşref (Ünaydın)
(1892–1959). In a speech to the parliament on June 7, 1934, he spoke about the
Jews, "As if it was not enough that they did not speak Turkish, these had, also,
adopted a language [Spanish] that did not belong to them." Atatürk had shown
them that they are genuine Turks. Thus, the Jews "will one day learn that they are
Turks, and when they join to the Turkish nation, to us, they will understand that
they are happy and that they will not be able to find that pride in their previous
self." On the other hand, MP Şeref Aykut asserted that he would not propose the
expulsion or dispersal of the Jews. On the contrary, he asked that "these people,
who were highly talented in commerce... merge with the Turks, in accordance
with our Civil Law." The Jews could simply assimilate: "While the pride they
would get from Turkishness is infinite, the advantages they will derive from the
Turks are many. There is no other way for their representation."[153]

The Jews gradually reacted to these expectations that they speak Turkish. First,
the provincial elements gave in. In February 1933, Moise Efendi, the rabbi of
Kırklareli, a small town in Thrace, told his congregation at the end of services:
"I beg you from today to speak the beloved language of the noble Turkish race
and civilized proprietors of the great country in which we live."[154] The Bursa Jews
followed: "Fraternity" (Uhuvet), the organization of the city's Jews, decided to fine
those of its members who spoke "a language other than Turkish within the
precincts of the club."[155] The Ankara Jews came next, declaring that they had
adopted Turkish.[156] At the end of the year, İlyas Efendi, the rabbi of Diyarbakır,

made a tour of the provinces of the east and the southeast "calling upon the Jews to be baptized into the new Kemalist faith."[157] Finally, the Jews of Istanbul rallied. On November 23, 1933, they joined the Greeks and the Armenians in the city to further the dissemination of the Turkish language.[158]

Ironically, as the Jewish community leaders swiftly adopted Turkish, there was resentment among some Jews over this. For instance, a Jewish schoolteacher in Milas in Southwestern Turkey, who endorsed Turkification, was beaten up by some of his coreligionists.[159] At this time, Turkish Jewish intellectual Tekinalp appeared again to rally for Turkification. In 1934, together with Hanri Soriano and Marsel Franko, two prominent members of the Jewish community, he founded the Turkish Culture Association (Türk Kültür Cemiyeti) to promote the use of Turkish in public.[160]

The move by the Jews toward assimilation and the impact of the "Speak Turkish" campaign was felt also among Muslims who did not speak Turkish. British diplomats noted that Arabs, Circassians, Cretan Muslims, and Kurds were being targeted for not speaking Turkish.[161] In Mersin, for instance, "Kurds, Cretans, Arabs and Syrians" were being fined for speaking languages other than Turkish. Even speakers of West European languages were harassed. In April 1933, French-speaking British citizens in Mersin were reportedly attacked in public. In this town, where the Houses worked actively to promote the use of Turkish, many "hundreds of persons" were arrested "for speaking languages other than Turkish."[162] In a specific case in July 1934, a M. Chalfoun and a certain Jewish merchant were arrested in Mersin for speaking in French and Arabic with two Syrian merchants in town. These men, notables of Mersin, were released only after the Vali (mayor) of the town paid a visit to their lock-up.[163]

The "Speak Turkish" campaign was especially fierce in Mersin,[164] a town with a large Arabic-speaking community and many Greek-speaking Cretan Muslim immigrants. In January 1933, the American Embassy reported that "the inhabitants of a village near Mersina [*sic*] have decided to give up speaking Arabic and to speak Turkish—undoubtedly pure Turkish—instead."[165] In Mersin, the antipathy against those who did not speak Turkish was so strong that at a People's House meeting in July 1934, some young attendees demanded that non-Turkish speakers be "beaten up and forced to speak Turkish only."[166]

In 1935, the "Speak Turkish" campaign gained new momentum.[167] The drive was invigorated with a fiery speech given by İnönü at the CHP's Fourth Congress. In his address, the Prime Minister emphasized the need for everybody in Turkey to speak Turkish: "From now on we will not keep quiet. All citizens who live with us will speak Turkish."[168] Following this, the National Union of Turkish Students (Türk Milli Talebe Birliği—TMTB) initiated a drive to invite the public to speak Turkish only. This unofficial campaign aimed to make Turkish the sole language heard in public. Those people who did not speak Turkish were openly harassed. Signs were posted in public places asking everybody to speak Turkish. At this time, a series of nationalist articles appeared in various papers in support of the campaign.[169] For instance, the daily *La République* published an article in French on "Turks unable to speak Turkish." The paper noted that failure to learn Turkish "may trouble the harmony of social coexistence."[170]

Minorities responded to this new wave by further promoting Turkish speech and assimilation. For instance, Msgr Roncalli (1881–1963) (the papal nuncio in Istanbul and the future Pope Jean XXIII) gave a sermon in Turkish.[171] In 1935, a small number of Greeks and Armenians connected to the CHP organized the Turkish Association of Secular Christians (Türk Laik Hristiyanlar Birliği) in order to promote assimilation.[172] Yet, the real pressure of this new wave was on the Jews. In 1936, the municipal governments of Edirne and Tekirdağ, towns with large Jewish communities, passed decrees to fine those who spoke languages other than Turkish in public.[173] On February 26, 1936, Bursa and Lüleburgaz, two other towns with Jewish communities, banned the use of languages other than Turkish in public.[174] In reaction, during Yom Kippur services in September, Jewish community leaders in Istanbul recommended that community members speak Turkish.[175] Nationalist articles in favor of the campaign, which targeted the Jews for not speaking Turkish, appeared in the press in 1937.[176] Because of such vigilance, the number of Jews and others who spoke languages other than Turkish started to decrease.[177] This was apparent in the censuses. For instance, while 84 percent of the 81,872 Jews had declared Judeo-Spanish as their mother language in 1927, only 54 percent did so in 1935. This sharp decline was not due to assimilation, since the percentage of Judeo-Spanish-speaking Jews rose to more than 63 percent in 1945, and then to over 71 percent in 1965.[178] Hence, it seems that in 1935, while some Jews declared Turkish as their mother tongue because they might have actually dropped Judeo-Spanish, many others did so for the sake of convenience and since they felt intimidated. The following 1936 article by Mahmut Esat Bozkurt contextualizes the intricacies of this phenomenon:

"The Question of the Minorities"
Another day again, I was going from Istanbul to Ankara ... The former (Roman law) professor of our university, Mişon Vantura joined me ... Dear Professor Vantura voiced a few reproachful reminders. I reflected on them. I said to him:
—I am sorry to hear what you have told me. But, what upsets me is not this but the current situation. What I would like to know first is: Are you Turkish?!

He replied right away:
—No need for doubt. I am, and we are Turkish. I said:
—But, what is the proof of that? That your name is (Günisberg!) and your language is Spanish? And that you don't speak Turkish when you are with the others, unless you feel compelled to do so?!
It was as if he smiled. I said:
—These things that bother you will change one day, and when they do, there will be no problems. I mean, when the new Turkish becomes your mother tongue and your last name Cengiz,[179] there will be no more problems.
. . .

I ask myself: How many Jewish citizens speak Turkish at home? And how many of these have Turkish names? so I told *Mişon Vantura*:

—You have educated many a youth for this country. Often times, you did whatever you could to help your country. I like you, and you need to be appreciated for these points. But, let's be straightforward on this: you can claim two kinds of Turkishness: one of these is cultural Turkishness in your consciousness. The other one is Turkishness by laws and regulations.

(Hakkı Uyar, *Sol Milliyetçi Bir Türk Aydını*, 233–37)

Bozkurt was convinced that if the Jews wanted to assimilate, it was not enough for them to speak Turkish; they also had to adopt Turkish names. Law Nr 2741, the "Soy Adı Kanunu" (Law on Last Names) of June 21, 1934 proved that Ankara shared these expectations. The first article of this law stipulated, "Every Turk is obliged to bear a last name in addition to his first name." The third article added, "Names of foreign races and nations could not be adopted as last names."[180] During the parliamentary deliberations, MP Refet Bele (1881–1963) (Istanbul) objected to this article: "I am tired of those whose origins are not the same as mine, trying to join me. If this person has the name of a foreign race, and if his origin is not the same as mine...I would prefer to recognize him with the seal on his forehead and as he is."[181] The Minister of Interior, Kaya explained the need for the third article:

In regards to foreign names, the greatest responsibility of this country is to annex into its own community all those people, who live within its boundaries... Why should we keep using names such as Memet, the Kurd, Hasan the Circassian, or Ali the Laze...Doing this will show the weakness of the dominant element in this country...If the person has even the slightest feeling of being different, let's erase that in schools and in society. Then, that person would be as Turkish as I am, and he would serve the country. There are many examples of people from foreign races who have served the country in this manner. Why should we separate them from ourselves and stamp them with the seal of foreigner?

(TBMM Zabıt Ceridesi, term IV, vol. 23/1:249)

In these arguments, both the Minister and the MP referred explicitly to Turkey's non-Turkish Muslims. While Bele objected to these groups' assimilation through adoption of Turkish names, Kaya countered that this was the path to take:

The biggest responsibility of a government is to assimilate all who live within its boundaries into its own community...While many people did not assimilate [in the past], the Ottomans suffered from that. Otherwise, today, our boundaries would have started on the Danube.[182]

After long deliberations, the clause was passed into law to Kaya's satisfaction. Now, the government had created yet another tool for assimilation, especially of the non-Turkish Muslims. This ushered in an era of nationalist fervor *vis-à-vis* last names. The Houses joined this process actively and launched a campaign to promote Turkish names.[183] However, since most Turks already had last names,[184] the intent of this law was not to give new last names to the entire population. Rather, the act aimed to force the citizens to have their last names recorded, so that they could be screened for Turkishness.

As soon as this law went into effect, people started registering. While some citizens were allowed to keep their last names, registry was not permitted when these names were not Turkish, or if they did not sound Turkish. To regulate this, the government issued a regulation on December 20, 1934: names ending with "yan, of, ef, viç, is, dis, pulos, aki, zade, mahdumu, veled, and bin" could not be registered.[185] This made it impossible to register respectively Armenian, Bulgarian, Macedonian, Bosnian, Serbian, Croatian, and other Slavic last names, as well as Greek, Cretan, Persian, Georgian, or Arabic last names. The statute demanded that citizens of all religious and ethnic backgrounds have Turkish last names only. This had deep repercussions amongst both Muslim and non-Muslim minorities. Scores of Jews changed not only their last names, but also their first names. The list below gives a sampling of these names:[186]

Jewish name and last name	*Turkish name and last name*
İsrael Kohen	İsmail Kan
Dr Behar	Dr Bayar
Abraham Naon	İbrahim Naon
Nesim Guerera	Orhan Girner
Kemal Levi	Kemal Leventer
Albert Karaso	Alber Karasu

Another new last name involved Atatürk. Until 1934, the Turkish leader was officially referred to as Gazi (veteran) Mustafa Kemal. On November 24, 1934, the parliament passed Law Nr 2622 to give him an extra last name, Atatürk, which meant the "father of the Turks." The TBMM dictated that the name Atatürk was being reserved for him. It could not be adopted in any form by anybody else in the country.[187] This was doubtless a sign of a great reverence for his cult. A choral piece from a play written in 1932 had already signaled this:

> Just as the homeland is under the enemy's boots
> Again, a commander leads the Turks
> He is the first one to feel the might of the nation
> He is the one to challenge the world on his own
> When the world sees the Turks' might in his person
> All Its vengeance towards them turns into affection
> An unbreachable sea he is
> The miracle the Orient has been expecting for centuries.
> (Nabi Yaşar, *Mete*, 67–68)

Conclusion

Ayhan Aktar, Rıfat Bali, and Taha Parla argue that in its view of Turkishness, Kemalism broke away from Ziya Gökalp's thinking. While Gökalp had mostly emphasized religion, ethics, aesthetics, and socialization as the denominators of the nation, the Kemalists turned to ethnicity as the underlying factor of Turkishness.[188] Yet, as the "Speak Turkish" campaign demonstrated, although Kemalism increasingly favored ethnicity as a marker of Turkishness in the 1930s, it did not close down the gates to voluntary Turkification. This refutes Erik Zürcher's argument that Kemalism's idea of "organic culture" (language, and ideals by birth and not through voluntary selection or socialization) represented a break with Gökalp's idea of voluntary Turkification.[189] Although the Kemalist ideology focused on the Turkish race, as the "Speak Turkish" campaign and the Law on Last Names demonstrated, in practice, Ankara kept the avenues of assimilation open to those who were not ethnically Turkish, especially Jews and non-Turkish Muslims. Such assimilation was enforced; yet, it was inclusionary. In this regard, the desire to integrate the Jews was especially significant. This shows that not racism, but a form of intolerant nationalism shaped Turkey's attitude toward the Jews in the 1930s. Ankara regretted the fact that the Jews did not speak Turkish and had not assimilated. It expected that they integrate by adopting the Turkish language and Turkish names. Thus, unlike in many other interwar European countries, where racial walls divided the Jews and the Gentiles, Kemalist Turkey did not regard the Jews as racial outsiders.

At least in theory, Kemalism's vision of the Turkish nation in the 1930s included even the Christians. Proceedings of the Second History Congress demonstrated such a desire *vis-à-vis* the Armenians. In another example along this line, in 1938, Nadir Nadi (Abalıoğlu) (1908–91), a staunchly pro-Kemalist and nationalist journalist, argued it was scientifically proven that Armenians and Turks had the same racial origins.[190] Thus, it appears that under the rubric of Turkish race, Kemalism was willing to accept not only the Anatolian Muslims and Jews, but, wishfully, even Armenians, somewhere into the body of the Turkish nation.

Although the merits and methods of this policy may be questioned, the way Kemalism co-opted the notion of race suggests that in the 1930s, Ankara's practices appeared to favor the conventional, nineteenth-century usage of the term race, when this had been synonymous with nation. In the early twentieth century, Nazism and other racist ideologies transformed the word race with modifiers such as biology, genetics, bloodline, and physical attributes. This is also the view of race that one sees in the *Turkish History Thesis* and the *Sun Language Theory* (a theory coined in the 1930s which suggested that Turkish was the root of other languages), where Turkish "brachycephalic" race and Turkish nationality appear synonymous. Yet, although race had an important role in the ideology of Turkish nationalism in the 1930s, it does not seem to have been central to all of Ankara's practices. If acts such as the "Speak Turkish" campaign are taken into account, it would appear that what the Kemalist perception of race was, was closer to this word's nineteenth century connotations than to its twentieth century meaning.

Hence, in the practices of 1930s Kemalism, race usually referred not to a biological community, but to a national one. True, in the Kemalists's mind, this was an immutable category. Yet, it was defined through language and not by biological factors.

Consequently as the example of the "Speak Turkish" campaign reveals, ethnicity-through-language emerged as one of the primary bearers of Turkishness in the 1930s. This created dilemmas for the country's minorities. Turkey demanded that they assimilate by adopting the Turkish language and even change their names. As a result, Ankara's definition of the nation-through-language and the country's demographic diversity seemed bound to clash.

4 Who is a Turk?

Kemalist citizenship policies

Citizenship as a political tool in interwar Europe: an overview

High Kemalist Turkey of the 1930s is a demonstrative case of the authoritarian nation-state of interwar eastern Europe, in which a single nation dominated various minorities. Greece, Bulgaria, Romania, Yugoslavia, Hungary, and Poland are other examples of this kind of state that usually started as a multi-party democracy in the 1920s, and ended up an undemocratic regime or dictatorship in the 1930s.[1] (Iran was another case with some features of the prototype.)[2] Notwithstanding their differing levels of economic and social development, these states shared political affinities. Poland, Romania, and Yugoslavia were established on the premises of integrative nationalist ideologies.[3] Bulgaria and Greece failed in their efforts for territorial expansion at the expense of their neighbors. Hungary and Turkey were truncated former Empires with hurt national prides. In the 1930s, these states went through a radicalization of nationalism and a swing to the right.[4] Eventually, Turkey and Poland became quasi-corporatist states with authoritarian single-party regimes. Bulgaria, Yugoslavia, and Greece developed into repressive dictatorships while Romania and Hungary evolved into quasi-fascist regimes.[5] Then, in certain respects, these states resembled Italy and Germany to the west.[6]

It seems that the interwar east-European polity saw itself as an omnipotent nation-state. Here, the census served as a political tool for the state.[7] With this, the government could politically enumerate its citizens.[8] The state regarded its citizenship as a privilege and used the nationality benchmark to decide on this. It screened its citizens as well as citizens-to-be, denaturalizing those deemed unsuitable and naturalizing those considered desirable.

Turkey exhibited many characteristics of this interwar state. The Kemalist government passed numerous laws and executive acts and used various administrative measures to define the ranks of its citizenry. Ankara had a specific, ethno-religious perspective of the nation: it defined the Turks in relation to the Ottoman Muslim millet, and the non-Turks in relation to the Ottoman Christians. Using this as a litmus test, Ankara granted citizenship to many aspiring persons, while banishing some of its own from this privilege.

Turkish censuses under High Kemalism

Kemalist views of citizenship are reflected in the information sought in the 1935 census, the only general population survey carried out by High Kemalism under Atatürk. A comparison of the ethnic and religious classifications in this census with the census nomenclature from the 1920s and the late Ottoman era demonstrates the evolving nature of Turkish nationalism into the 1930s.

The last census of the Ottoman Empire, taken in 1914–15, had used only religious categories. It had not collected any data on languages spoken by the Ottoman population. With the exception of the Roma, who had been lumped into a separate class, this census had divided the Ottoman population into various confessional groups. These included the Druzes, Jews, Muslims, Yezidis, as well as Christians, who had been counted as Armenian Catholic, Armenian Gregorian, Bulgar, Chaldean, Coptic, Greek Catholic, Greek Orthodox, Jacobite, Maronite, Nestorian, Old Syriac, Protestant, Roman Catholic, Russian Cossack, Syriac, Serb, and Vlach.[9] The census had recognized a medley of religious and ethno-religious identities for the Christians.

On the other hand, the census had recognized all Muslims in the Empire as one community, overlooking their ethnic diversity. Such differing categorization of Muslims and Christians was rooted in the late millet system, which viewed the Muslims of the Empire as one group and the Christians as divided into various ethno-confessional units, organized in different churches. Yet, even then, in private, Istanbul gradually showed interest in the ethnic diversity of the Muslim population of the Empire. During 1914 and 1915, for instance, the CUP government collected confidential data on the ethnic heterogeneity of the Muslims in the Anatolian provinces.[10]

The first census of the republic in 1927 represented an evolution of this position. Now, Turkey was paying official attention to the diversity of the Muslim population. The government collected data on languages spoken by Muslims including Arabic, Albanian, Bulgarian, Circassian, Greek, Kurdish, Persian, Tatar, and Turkish.[11] On the other hand, unlike the CUP census, the republican survey did not seem alert toward the wider ethno-religious diversity of the Christians. Religious groups recognized in the 1927 survey included only Muslim, Jewish, Armenian, Catholic, Orthodox, Protestant, and "Christian" (all other Christian denominations).[12]

Again, the government's actual demographic interest was far more varied than these categories suggested. Throughout the 1920s, Ankara vigorously collected data on the country's ethnic diversity. For instance, in 1927, the Directorate General for Resettlement (İskân Umum Müdüriyeti—İUM) recorded detailed statistics on Turks, Tatars, Bosniaks, Kurds, Alevis, and Muslim Roma, who lived in the villages of the Polath district of Ankara.[13]

In other examples, the government gathered data on Turks, Muslim Roma, Bosniaks, Bulgars, and Romanian immigrants, who had been resettled in the Ayaş district of Ankara.[14] Then, in 1928, the İUM demanded from the local authorities in the Düzce district of Bolu to compile lists of villages with non-Turkish inhabitants. Since Düzce had large Circassian and Abkhaz populations, this must have aimed at gathering statistics on these communities.[15]

The 1935 census signaled further attentiveness toward the country's ethnic diversity. Now, High Kemalism collected more detailed data on the ethnic breakdown of the population, especially that of the Muslims. In 1935, the government acknowledged a long list of languages spoken in the country, including Abkhaz, Albanian, Arabic, Armenian, Bosnian, Bulgarian, Circassian, Croatian, "Czechoslovak," Dutch, English, French, German, Georgian, Greek, Hungarian, Italian, Jewish, Kurdish, Laze, Persian, Polish, Pomak, Romanian, Romany, Russian, Serbian, Spanish, Swedish, Tatar, and Turkish.[16]

On the other hand, however, like the 1927 census, the 1935 survey also used a limited number of religious categories. The government gathered data on eight confessional groups: Armenian, Catholic, Gregorian, Jewish, Muslim, Orthodox, "Christian," and Protestant.[17] The Gregorian grouping in this census, which did not exist in 1927, differentiated Apostolic Armenians from the non-Gregorian (Catholic and Protestant) ones.

The presence of fewer Christian categories in the republican censuses than in the Ottoman censuses can be explained. With the end of the Ottoman Empire, some Christian denominations such as the Copts and the Maronites, whose historical centers were outside the country, had become negligible in the country. However, Turkey still had many Eastern Christians, including Chaldeans, Jacobites, and Assyrians. The census counted none of them. Besides, unlike in the Ottoman era, the republican count identified all ethnic groups within the Protestant and the Catholic Churches as one community. In its official business, Ankara refused to acknowledge various smaller Christian groups. This lessened the chances of foreign intervention in their favor, an irritatingly frequent phenomenon during the late Ottoman era. Hence, the residual "Christian" category in the 1935 census lumped together many Christian groups and made it difficult for them to be enumerated as a separate minority.

On the other hand, although High Kemalism did not compile public statistics on the diversity of Christian communities, in private it gathered mass amounts of data on them. In 1930, the Directorate of Population Matters (Nüfus Umum Müdürlüğü—NUM) wrote to fifteen provincial governors in central, eastern, and northern Turkey inquiring about Armenian, Greek, Catholic, Jacobite, "Old Jacobite," Chaldean, and Protestant populations.[18] Then, on May 3, 1933, the EUUM asked the governor of Ağrı to compile a register showing the number of Armenians, Assyrians, Jacobites, and Chaldeans in this province.[19] Ankara's attention to this matter was obsessive. On June 22, the EUUM wrote to Ağrı again. It asked why the governor had not provided information on the number of Armenians, Assyrians, Jacobites, and Chaldeans within the province, as per its earlier request.[20]

Another communication shows that although the government classified all Catholics and Protestants as one community in the censuses, it was aware of ethnic heterogeneity within these groups. On May 20, 1933, the EUUM wrote to the Mardin province concerning an earlier statistical table sent from there. This had listed 1,990 Protestants living in 374 households in Mardin. "Since Protestantism is only a sect," the letter said, a breakdown of this number "according to nationality" was needed.[21] Like its Ottoman predecessor, Turkey was interested in the ethno-confessional diversity of the Christians.

Thus, it appears that Ankara's lack of attention toward the ethnic variety of the Christians was limited to the official censuses only. Throughout the 1930s, the government enthusiastically collected confidential data on the Christians, especially the Armenians. For instance, a 1931 correspondence asked all authorities to "inform the Ministry of Interior of the increases and decreases in the number of Armenians."[22] Ankara's concern on this was extensive. In 1933, for instance, the Ministry of Interior wrote to the governor of Tekirdağ, in response to an earlier correspondence from him, asking if it was certain that there were no Armenians in the province. If there were any, Ankara wanted to know their exact number.[23]

The government was especially concerned about the number of rural Armenians left behind after 1915. For instance, on May 7, 1933, the EUUM sent a communiqué to the governor of Gümüşhane inquiring about Armenians in the villages there.[24] If there were Armenians in a province, then Ankara queried their exact location. In a similar instance, in a letter on May 13, 1933, the EUUM asked if Armenians lived exclusively in Yozgat city. The dispatch questioned the number of Armenians in each district, sub-district, and village in Yozgat.[25]

The authorities collected confidential data on the Muslim minorities, too. For example, in December 1930, Ankara wrote to fifteen provinces in central, eastern, and southern Turkey inquiring about the number of Kurds, Arabs, Circassians, Chechens, and Lezgis.[26] A 1933 letter by the NUM further demonstrated its awareness toward the ethnic heterogeneity of the Muslim population. The Directorate demanded from the Antalya province a village-by-village and quarter-by-quarter breakdown of Turks, Kurds, Arabs, Circassians, Georgians, and others.[27]

The government was especially concerned about the Kurds. It wanted to know how many of them lived in which province, even in those with few Kurds. An example of that was a letter sent by the NUM in December 1930. This asked twenty-nine provinces, including heavily Kurdish ones in the East, but also typically non-Kurdish provinces as far west as Kocaeli on the Marmara Sea, to inform Ankara about the number of Turks and Kurds in each.[28]

The comparison of the late Ottoman and Kemalist statistical categories reveals that between the 1910s and the 1930s, the governments developed an interest in the ethnic diversity of the Muslims. The Kemalists wanted to know how many Muslims in Turkey did not speak Turkish. Additionally, the republic recorded the confessional diversity of the Christian communities in the detailed ways of the Ottomans. These sensitivities demonstrated the evolving nature of Turkish nationalism from a basic disregard for the ethnic diversity of the Muslims in the 1910s into the assimilationist tactics toward the Muslims in the 1930s.

The privileged position of the Turks among the Turkish citizens

In the interwar era, Kemalism saw both Turkishness and Turkish citizenship as privileges. Ankara passed many laws to favor the Turks over the non-Turks. For example, as early as February 1924, the TBMM adopted a law exempting companies that belonged to Turkish citizens from paying customs duties for ships and boats that they purchased as imports. During the deliberations on this law, it became clear that the parliament had in mind Turks and not Turkish citizens for the exemption. In the discussions, MP Zülfü (Tiğrel) (1876–1940) (Diyarbakır) asked how to interpret Turkishness in the case of companies that had foreign capital. Saraçoğlu Şükrü (Saraçoğlu) (Izmir) (1887–1953), who had prepared the draft law, replied: "We mean whatever the laws understand from the words, Turk and Turkish companies." MP İsmail Kemal (Alpsar) (Çorum) inquired: "Are we calling the Armenians and the Greeks, Turkish?" MP Zeki (Kadirbeyoğlu) (Gümüşhane) responded, "They have never been Turkish."[29]

With the meaning of the clause "Turkish citizens" clarified, on May 12, 1928, the TBMM passed Law Nr 1246, stipulating that "the right to establish boy scouts units or other scouting groups under any other name or title, in or outside schools, belongs exclusively to Turkish citizens."[30] The government was cognizant of the rise of nationalist athletic militias elsewhere in Europe, and was making sure that non-Turkish minorities would not be able to establish such groups in Turkey.

The apportionment of privileges to Turks continued throughout the 1920s, with the laws gradually substituting the term "Turk" for "Turkish citizen." On March 15, 1926, for example, the TBMM passed "Memurin Kanunu" (Law on Government Employees).[31] The fourth article of this manifested that "one had to be a Turk to be a government employee."[32] During the deliberations on this law in the parliament, MP Mustafa Faik (Öztrak) (1882–1951) (Tekirdağ), who spoke on behalf of the committee that had drafted the law, said,

> "We have made being a Turk a condition for becoming a government employee. A prospective government employee naturally needs to be a Turk . . . those other than the Turks cannot be government employees under any conditions."[33] Then, this law demanded that the government maintain records for all its employees. These files would contain information on the employee's "name, alias, religious denomination, and nationality."[34]

This would help Ankara track the ethnicity of all its employees to make sure that it could favor Turks.

Another piece of legislation that prescribed privileges for Turks came on April 11, 1928, when the parliament adopted Law Nr 1219.[35] This stipulated that doctors had to have a degree from the Medical School of the Istanbul Darülfünun and that they had to "be Turks."[36] Dentists, midwives and nurses, too, had to be Turks.[37] A following article of the law furthered the Turks' privileges: it was possible for "doctors who are Turks," who had diplomas from foreign schools, to have their degrees recognized by the Ministry of Health so that they could practice medicine.[38] This option was not enacted for doctors who were not Turks.

The preferential treatment of the Turks increased during the 1930s under High Kemalism. For example, "Cemiyetler Kanunu" (Law on Associations), passed in June 1936 prohibited the establishment of organizations and associations representing ethnic and religious minorities.[39] Then, caution against non-Turks became more blatant. For instance, on July 25, 1931, the TBMM approved "Matbuat Kanunu" (Press Law), which imposed strict measures on press freedom in Turkey, and, at the same time, favored the Turks: only they could own magazines or journals. The legislation added that all publishers had to have a diploma from higher institutions of education. If a publisher held a diploma from a foreign country, then he needed to be fluent in Turkish. Moreover, people "who had served the enemies' goals during the Turkish Independence War" would not be allowed to publish newspapers or journals.[40]

On June 11, 1932, the TBMM passed Law Nr 2007. This allocated a number of occupations in the country exclusively to Turkish citizens. This exclusivity affected both professionals such as veterinarians, chemists, stockbrokers, as well as people whose jobs required little or no formal training such as maids, janitors, chauffeurs, and night watchmen.[41] The law gave non-Turkish citizens a 1933 deadline, and with an amendment later on a 1935 deadline,[42] to stop practicing these jobs. It obliged employers to fire the non-citizens after the deadline. This banned non-citizens, especially some Istanbul Greeks, who were Hellenic citizens, from a variety of jobs.[43] Many of them were unemployed. According to American diplomatic records, more than 15,000 left the country as a result.[44]

With the rise of High Kemalism, in the late 1930s, legislation started to be partial to the Turkish race, too. A law adopted in 1938, which regulated the travel of foreigners within the country, granted certain exemptions to foreigners who were of the Turkish race.[45] This was perhaps a reaction to pan-European developments. A parliamentary memorandum written on this law argued that the preference given to the Turkish race was not necessarily due to a national feeling, but rather because of "the methods that were in effect in many Balkan and European countries."[46]

By the late 1930s, various laws had established many privileges for the Turks in the country.[47] In some of them, the government had tacitly favored ethnic Turks, under the clause "Turkish citizens." In others, it had openly sided with ethnic Turks. Ankara sanctioned this position in its administrative acts as well: in 1933, for example, the General Directorate of Public Security (Emniyet İşleri Umum Müdiriyeti—EİUM) wrote to the governor of Ağrı. It asked why the governor had hired Kurds, who had recently been allowed to return to Ağrı, after their earlier forced resettlement in Western Turkey. Were there "no Turks or Turkish immigrants, who could have been employed instead of such rebels and their families?"[48] In the eyes of the High Kemalist government, ethnic Turks were the preferred citizens.

While Turkish citizens became privileged, the government devoted utmost attention to defining them. This involved the processing of citizenship in order to disbar the undesirables and invite the sought-after elements. International law recognizes *jus soli* and *jus sanguinis* as the two means of achieving citizenship. *Jus soli* defines citizenship based on one's birthplace or domicile, while *jus sanguinis* prescribes citizenship through bloodline. Legislation passed in Turkey during the interwar era demonstrated a blend of these two approaches. On the other hand, in its administrative acts, Ankara showed partiality toward *jus sanguinis*.

Denaturalization cases

Denaturalizations in accordance with Law Nr 1041

On May 23, 1927, the TBMM passed Law Nr 1041. "Those Ottoman subjects who had stayed outside Turkey during the Independence War," and had not returned since then would lose their citizenship.[49] Accordingly, many former Ottoman subjects had their citizenship terminated in accordance with Law Nr 1041. For instance, in 1932, the government rescinded the citizenship of six people, since "they have not returned to our country till now and because they have not participated in the national struggle."[50] In another case, in 1937, 164 people were denaturalized since they had not participated in the Turkish Independence War.[51] Various similar acts denied citizenship to many people, a majority of whom were non-Muslims. Most of them had left the country during and after the First World War. Some others were Armenian survivors of the deportations of 1915 who were now outside Turkey.

Law Nr 1041 affected all the minorities. For instance, on July 4, 1931, following a request from the Ministry of Interior, the Prime Minister's office signed a decree "to denaturalize twenty-seven people in accordance with Law Nr 1041."[52] The people on this list were Greek-Orthodox (Melchite), Catholic, and Alawite (Nusayri) Arabs.

Non-participation in the Turkish liberation campaign was the crux of Law Nr 1041's application. In 1931, two Armenians, "Mircan and Aram of Erbaa, sons of Mihran," had their citizenship rescinded since they had "fled the country with Armenian passports during the national struggle," and "have not served in the army."[53] Then, a certain Arab, "Mehmet Nâsır, of Mersin, the son of deceased Nâsır, of the sons of Ahmet Ağa" lost his citizenship in accordance with Law Nr 1041 since he had "collaborated with the French and the Armenians during the occupation."[54] In another case, an "Arab Nusayri Salih, of Tarsus," the "son of deceased Halil, of the sons of Kâhil," had his citizenship terminated as he had allegedly helped the French and the Armenians during the war.[55]

Furthermore, in 1930, a Nusayri, "Halil Fatum of Mersin, son of Mehmet" was denaturalized for not "having participated in the Independence War."[56] In other examples, "Norisan of the Armenian Protestant community, the daughter of Partamyan," "Aram Kazaryan of Van, son of Agop," and "Circassian İzzettin of Düzce, son of Hapaç," lost their citizenship.[57] Occasionally, other criteria seemed to suffice for the termination of one's citizenship. For instance, "İsmail Tevfik (Tevfik Süleymanoviç), a man of the Bosniak race, born in Izmir" was denaturalized in 1937.[58] Although "he knew Turkish, İsmail, who had left for Yugoslavia thirty years ago, insisted on speaking Serbian." Moreover, since İsmail, who worked as the director of a nursery in Brčko, had moved "away from Turkish culture," the government decided in favor of terminating his citizenship.[59] At times, people lost their citizenship without a specific reason. For instance, a certain Jew, "İlya Ferman, son of Nesim and born in Istanbul," who had left the country in 1917, and had later returned to Turkey, lost his citizenship since "he did not possess the necessary qualifications."[60]

Denaturalizations in accordance with Law Nr 1312

Soon after Law Nr 1041, on May 23, 1928, the government passed Law Nr 1312, "Türk Vatandaşlığı Kanunu" (Law of Turkish Citizenship).[61] Law Nr 1312, too, prescribed the conditions for losing citizenship. Its ninth article asserted that the Cabinet of Ministers could denaturalize people who took "the citizenship of other countries without special permission from the government" or joined the armies of other countries. The tenth article of the law further demanded: those who had "served a foreign state in any capacity" would lose their citizenship if they did not abandon their positions within the deadline granted to them by the authorities.[62]

In practice, these articles made it possible for the government to terminate the citizenship of ex-Ottoman citizens, especially Armenians, who had left the country during the 1910s, and had become the citizens of other states. In a 1930 interview with the British representative to the League of Nations in Geneva, the Minister of Foreign Affairs, Aras confirmed this: "*Le Gouvernement turc maintient toujours son point de vue que les Arméniens, habitant à l'étranger, ayant perdu la nationalité turque...*"[63]

Accordingly, Ankara terminated the citizenship of many Armenians and other non-Muslims in accordance with Law Nr 1312. For instance, a decree published on April 2, 1936 listed thirteen Armenians, nine Jews, three Greek-Orthodox, one Latin Catholic, one Christian Arab, and one Bulgarian, who lost their citizenship subsequent to the tenth article of Law Nr 1312.[64] In other demonstrative cases, in 1930, a Jewish woman, "Viktorya, daughter of İzak Arditi" was denaturalized since she had adopted US citizenship without permission from the government;[65] and in 1932, the government removed "Protestant Toma, son of Yakop Usugarip"[66] from citizenship.

There were many other examples of denaturalizations of non-Muslims during the 1930s consequent to Law Nr 1312. Among these were, a "Maronite Catholic, Maron Eyub, son of İlyas, from Mersin,"[67] a "Syriac Catholic, Yusuf Efendi, son of Cercis, of the sons of Istanbullu, resident at number 99 in the Şeyhullah quarter of Mardin,"[68] "Masis, son of Anderyos, of the Armenian millet, resident on the Kapulu Bağ Street, in the Feriköy quarter of Istanbul,"[69] "Maryos Dallalyan, an Armenian Catholic, resident at number 14 in the Nüzhetiye quarter in Mersin."[70] These people lost their citizenship in accordance with Articles Nine and Ten of the Citizenship Law.[71]

Law Nr 1312 affected the Muslim minorities, too: in 1933, for instance, "Halil, son of Haydar, from the Suruç district of Urfa and of the sons of Kurd Ahmet Ali," was denaturalized.[72] In other cases, "Süleyman, of the Arab race,"[73] and "Circassian Mehmet Arif (Arif Hikmet), resident at number 26 in the Türebey quarter in Bergama,"[74] lost their citizenship, as did a certain "Circassian İsmail, son of Mehmet, from Yozgat," who had fled to Syria, joined the Circassian units, and collaborated with the Armenians.[75]

Articles Nine and Ten affected scores of Muslims of undeclared ethnicity. Most frequently, these people were denaturalized for allegedly having served in the intelligence units or armies of foreign countries. An analysis of available cases reveals that such people were from areas of the country that had Muslim minority populations. Hence, they were possibly not ethnic Turks. For instance, a certain "Hamit efendi, son of Hacı Hasan, resident of the İstil village of the Midyat district," possibly an Arab or a Kurd, was denaturalized in 1931.[76]

In other cases, taking Soviet citizenship or employment by its intelligence units were the major causes of denaturalization. For example, in 1935, the government issued a decree that a certain "Zekiye, originally from Batum," likely a Muslim Georgian, "but now resident in Posof, Kars," lost her citizenship for "becoming a Soviet citizen and working for the Cheka."[77] Then, "Abdülkadir, son of Mehmet of the Orta quarter of Hopa," likely a Laze, was denaturalized in accordance with Article Nine of the Citizenship Law, too. Abdülkadir had become a citizen of the USRR without permission from the Turkish government.[78]

Denaturalizations in accordance with the Statute on Traveling

In 1933, Turkey issued 'Seyrisefer Tâlimatnamesi' (Statute on Traveling). Alongside Law Nr 1041 and the Citizenship Law of 1928, this act regulated the return of Armenians and other Anatolian Christians to the country. At a first glance, the statute appeared to be benevolent toward people who had left the country in the past; in reality, the statute prevented the former Anatolian Armenians from returning to Turkey. The third article of the statute stated: "Persons who have gone to foreign countries with passports issued by the government of the TBMM or the Turkish republic could return to Turkey."[79] This clause seemed to promise the right to return to many Christians who had left the country. However, "thousands of persons who [had] left Turkey during the Allied occupation of the Straits Zone bearing passports issued by the Allied authorities" were excluded from this. That was the case especially for the Armenians. An American diplomat noted: many Armenians "living in the United States fall, of course, under this category and there is apparently no provision for their return."[80]

Another article of the statute did seem to make it easier for the Armenians and the others to return. Turkish subjects who,

a. went to a foreign country without providing themselves with any passport whatever,
b. went to a foreign country bearing an Ottoman passport,
c. having resided heretofore for as long as five years in a foreign country, have failed to apply to a Turkish consulate for registration and for obtaining of a Turkish certificate of nationality or for passport,

(SD, 867.0128/5)

could apply to a Turkish consulate for permission to return to Turkey. However, the procedure was that the consulates would send these people's applications to the EUUM. Only after investigation by the police, and approval for citizenship in accordance with the laws, the applicants would be able to return. US diplomats noted that since it "would be rare to discover an Armenian or other non-Moslem of Turkish origin who has resided abroad for any considerable time whose conduct has been uninterruptedly correct with regard to his Turkish allegiance," this article did not promise the right to return for many non-Muslims. While most of these "persons have evaded military service," and since "many have actually enlisted for service against Turkey and many have obtained naturalization abroad," the authorities would not have a difficult time finding "materials to be embodied in unfavorable recommendations" against their applications. Although many Armenians and others petitioned to return to Turkey in accordance with the Statute on Traveling, the government was not reported to be issuing documents to these people to facilitate their repatriation.[81]

Among all the groups that had left the country in the past, the Armenians were the most disadvantaged *vis-à-vis* the execution of the Statute on Traveling. In 1933, the EUUM warned the local authorities that "Armenians, who have escaped from our country at various times because of an assortment of reasons, are apparently coming to our country with other countries' passports or Nansen Passports," which are internationally recognized refugee identity cards issued by the League of Nations. Ankara wanted the authorities to prevent this.[82] A 1931 petition to the League of Nations by Mr Pashalian, Secretary General of the "Comité Central des Refugiés Arméniens," discussed this further. While Turks and Jews who had left the country without Ottoman passports were allowed to return if they applied to Turkish consular offices with their current passports,[83] this was not the case for the Armenians, who had to prove that they were former Ottoman nationals. Since the return of the Ottoman Greeks to Turkey had been regulated by the recent Ankara Convention of June 10, 1930, the Armenians were alone in facing discrimination *vis-à-vis* the application of the Statute on Traveling.[84]

During the late 1920s and the 1930s, Ankara denaturalized many ex-Ottoman citizens using Laws Nr 1041, 1312, and the Statute on Traveling. A large majority of these people were Christians, and a few were Jews and Muslims. Ethnic Turks were a slim minority among these people. True, very few Turks that had left the country during the Independence War became the citizens of other countries or worked for their armies and intelligence units. Hence, the low number of Turks denaturalized should not be surprising. Besides, in its denaturalization decrees, Ankara did demonstrate that the people who lost their citizenship had retroactively violated the laws by taking the citizenship of another country, or serving its army and intelligence units. Hence, these terminations were technically legal.

Nevertheless, it is striking that the denaturalization orders universally mentioned the ethnicity of the people who lost their citizenship. This suggested a link between the government's acts and Turkishness, while implying the purported culpability of the minorities. According to the Kemalists, the minorities had proven disloyal to the republic. With Laws Nr 1051 and 1312 and the Statute on Traveling, Ankara deprived them from Turkish citizenship, favoring *jus sanguinis*. This was especially the case in deportee Armenians vs the Statute on Traveling. This 1933 act had the effect of preventing the repatriation of these Armenians. Law Nr 3519, "Pasaport Kanunu" (Passport Law) passed on June 28, 1938 completed this process. People who came to Turkey without papers documenting their citizenship would not be admitted into the country.[85]

Naturalization cases

Law Nr 1312: East-Central Europeans, Hellenic Greeks, and White Russians

The naturalization policies of interwar Kemalist republic worked to grant citizenship to many former Ottoman Muslims, yet in some narrow instances, Turkey made exceptions toward European Jews and Christians in accordance with the principle of *jus soli*. The fifth article of Law Nr 1312 asserted that aliens, who had resided in Turkey for five years or more, could petition for citizenship.[86] The sixth added that people who did not fulfill the conditions articulated in Article Five could be granted citizenship in accordance with the decision of the Cabinet. These clauses favored *jus soli* and made it possible for non-Turks to gain citizenship after fulfilling a minimum residency requirement. Accordingly, scores of non-Muslims became citizens subsequent to Article Five. However, a study of these cases reveals that they were conditional. In other words, exceptions were made to specific groups so that they could be naturalized in accordance with Law Nr 1312.

The first group was the Istanbul Greeks, the so-called *établis*. These were Hellenic Greeks. Although not Turkish or Ottoman citizens, these people had been permitted by Lausanne to remain in Istanbul because they had been established in the city before the fall of the Ottoman Empire, hence, their name, *établis*. In the 1930s, some Hellenic Greeks who were willing to convert to Islam, or at least adopt Turkish-Muslim names, were given citizenship. For example, in 1934, a Greek woman, "Marika, born in Salonika to Argiro" became a citizen with her new name, "Meral,"[87] and in 1937, "Vasiliki, the daughter of İstavri Dimitri" was granted citizenship on the same principle with her new name, "Fatma Türkân."[88]

Other Hellenes achieved citizenship in accordance with Article Five. "Marika, a Greek citizen, who was born on Andros in 1895," and had converted to Islam, became a citizen in 1935,[89] while "converted Fotini Yanapulo (now Fethiye), whose domicile is Istanbul," became a citizen in 1938.[90] In a rare incident that did not involve conversion, a Greek, "Dimitri Bakalopulos, son of Yorgi Bakalopulos, whose business interests grossed 10,000 liras, and his wife Zafira," became citizens in 1932.[91]

A second group of non-Muslims toward whom exceptions were made in accordance with Article Five, were Christians and Jews from Central Europe.[92] The government extended special leniency toward them, especially if they converted, or adopted Turkish names. For instance, in 1934, the government granted citizenship to "Polish subjects, Karl Polzav (Cevat Alp), son of Güstav, and his wife, Roza (Radiye)."[93] Similarly, Hungarian "Jozef and his wife Elizabet" were made Turkish citizens in 1935 with their new Turkish names, "Turan," and "Fethiye."[94] Other examples of naturalizations of converted Central Europeans included a Czechoslovak,[95] a Hungarian,[96] an Italian,[97] a Soviet family,[98] an Austrian,[99] and a Romanian.[100] These people became citizens in accordance with Article Five of Law Nr 1312. There was leniency even toward the Balkan Christians, if they converted. For instance, a certain "Elisoveta (Saadet)," from the "Slavic race, born in Titel,"[101] the wife of "Mehmet, from the Bosnian race and born in Hasel," and "Manol Kostof (Mehmed)," born in Constanza, became citizens in 1934.[102]

In addition to conversion, other factors supplemented one's chances for citizenship. "Service for Turkey and the Ottoman Empire" helped especially: in 1933, for example, the government admitted "Robert Özer (Zeki) and his wife Alfrida (Aliye)" from Lithuania to citizenship after they adopted Islam.[103] Özer, who had arrived in Turkey in 1892, had served as a civil engineer at the Fevzi Paşa–Diyarbakır rail line, and this helped the couple's naturalization.

Germans, too, could become citizens, if they met such conditions. A "German subject, Robert (Rıfat), who had "fought along the Black Sea Coast during the war, served the Turks," and worked as a valuable "train driver in the Çerkeş district of Çankırı," became a citizen on November 3, 1934, after he converted to Islam.[104] Valuable skills strengthened one's case for citizenship: for instance, "Karl Mazarik," an Austrian subject and the "orchestra director at the Ankara Palas [Palace]," state guesthouse in Ankara, became Turkish under his new name "Hasan Basri" in 1935.[105] In addition, a "Czechoslovak subject, Arthur Koronfelt (Ahsen Kemal), son of Maks, who had worked as an engineer in tunnel, viaduct and bridge construction on the Fevzi Paşa–Diyarbakır rail line," and had converted to Islam, became a citizen on November 7, 1934.[106]

Marriage to a Turkish Muslim also improved one's prospects: a "Russian political refugee, Pavli Aleksandroviç Bojeno, who had come to Turkey in 1920," married a Turkish woman, became "Celâl Kâzım," and was granted citizenship in 1934.[107] In another case, a "subject of the Russian Tsars, Aleksi Vilademir" was made a citizen after he had converted to Islam, "entered our community through marriage with a Turkish girl," and adopted a new name, "Servet Efendi."[108]

Throughout the High Kemalist era, a significant number of people, from Hungary, as well as Austria, Czechoslovakia, Germany, Italy, Lithuania, Poland, Romania, and Russia, many of whom were Jewish, became citizens in accordance with Law Nr 1312, mostly thanks to conversion.[109] Adoption of Islam may have been only ostensible in some of these cases. For instance, on March 18, 1934, a "Pole, Firiç Rafael Lihtendal, son of Maks," a Polish Jew, was granted citizenship. Lihtendal, who did not change his first name, and who we may assume did not convert to Islam, simply adopted a new Turkish last name in order to become a citizen. Interestingly, his new last name, Songurtekin (auspicious white falcon), had a Central Asian resonance.[110] In some other cases, not even superficial conversion was mentioned: in 1935, for instance, "Herman Guincke, who is a doctor at the German Hospital and his wife, Marn," became citizens in accordance with Article Six of Law Nr 1312.[111]

White Russians did not require conversion either; a unique incident involving a mass number of Christians, the only such case under High Kemalism. White Russians had fled to Turkey in the aftermath of the 1917 Revolution. While many of them had later gone to third countries, some had stayed in Istanbul. By the 1930s, only a few had become citizens in accordance with Article Five of Law Nr 1312. For instance, in 1934, a Russian refugee, "Leon Vasileviç Civanof" had become a citizen with his Turkish-Muslim name, Abdullah Arslan.[112] By the mid-1930s, a majority of the White Russians still lacked citizenship. Meanwhile, the passing of certain laws favoring Turkish citizens had made life difficult for them.[113] For example, Law Nr 2007 of June 11, 1932, which had reserved many jobs for citizens, had inconvenienced the White Russians greatly. Most of them who were affected by this law worked in fields and could lose their jobs. In reaction to this humanitarian crisis, the government issued a decree on May 29, 1934, granting citizenship to 986 White Russian families.[114]

The case of the White Russians and the naturalization of East-Central Europeans demonstrated that Kemalism did not view citizenship as a racial category. Non-Turks, too, could become citizens, if they fulfilled specific criterion such as de facto conversion, possession of valuable technical skills, marriage to a Turk, or a record of service for Turkey. Yet, with the notable exception of the White Russians, nominal adoption of Islamic identity through the embracing of a Muslim name was the common dividend of most of these cases. Then, it can be assumed that nominal Islam was a *sine qua non* for access to Turkish citizenship in the minds of the Kemalists. For this reason, the republic was lenient in granting citizenship to scores of Christian or Jewish East-Central Europeans, Hellenic Greeks, and Balkan Slavs, if they were willing to adopt Muslim-Turkish names or convert. However, even then, Ankara did not extend its leniency to the Armenians.

There were only a few cases of naturalization of Armenians in the 1930s. One of them involved a certain "Kigork Karpiç and his wife." These two were Persian nationals who owned "Karpiç," Ankara's most popular, and according to some, "only" restaurant in the interwar era. The couple was granted citizenship on February 28, 1935 so that they would not lose their jobs in accordance with Law Nr 2007 and be forced to shut down Karpiç.[115] An other case of naturalization of an Armenian involved a certain Persian national, "Filori (Fikriye Emel), born in Izmir, and the daughter of Karabet." This woman had a Muslim name, hence, was possibly a convert.[116] Yet, since these examples involved Armenians who were citizens of another country, it appears that under High Kemalism, the gates of Turkish citizenship were shut tight to the Ottoman Armenians. They could not hope to be naturalized.

Naturalizations in accordance with Law Nr 1312: immigrant Muslims

While it blocked the ex-Ottoman Christians from citizenship, Ankara permitted large-scale immigration of ex-Ottoman Muslims, especially from the Balkans. These people were granted citizenship consequent to Article Six of Law Nr 1312. For instance, on October 17, 1929, an act made "437 Yugoslav, Bulgarian, Romanian, and Italian (Dodecanese) Muslims," citizens.[117] Then, on October 23, 1929, "438 Muslims from Russia, Syria, and Iraq" were similarly granted citizenship.[118] Next, on November 20, 1929, "483 Muslims from Yugoslavia, Bulgaria, Romania, Greece, Iran, and Syria" became citizens.[119] In other examples, on July 12, 1931, "184 Muslims from Yugoslavia, Bulgaria and Russia,"[120] and on September 21, 1932, "384 Muslims from Yugoslavia, Bulgaria, Romania, and Albania" all became citizens in accordance with Article Six of Law Nr 1312.[121]

The rise of Turkish nationalism in the 1930s impacted the Kemalist policies toward the Balkan immigrants. Throughout the 1920s and the 1930s, hundreds of thousands of Turkish and non-Turkish Muslims, who came to Turkey, earned citizenship through Article Six of Law Nr 1312. In these cases, the government did not require Turkishness as a prerequisite for citizenship. Rather, it was enough for one to be an Ottoman Muslim, especially from the Balkans, in order to become a citizen. However, even then, starting with the rise of High Kemalism, an emphasis on Turkish ethnicity worked its way, at least, into the text of the naturalization policies. While the government continued to admit Turkish and Muslim immigrants, it changed the way it described them. Until 1931, the naturalization decrees referred to the immigrants not as Turks, but as Muslims.[122] However, in 1931, the word Turk appeared to describe them. In a first example along this line, the Cabinet of Ministers signed a decree on August 17 that, "A northern Turk, İbrahim Akçura, son of Musa Akçura, will be admitted to Turkish citizenship."[123]

Throughout the 1930s, the word Turk gradually replaced the term Muslim in reference to the immigrants. For instance, a document dated March 4, 1933, stated, "Twenty-three Turks will be admitted to Turkish citizenship."[124] By late 1933, "Turk" had become the common way of describing immigrants who until a few months before, would have been registered as Muslims. For instance, a decree on April 14, 1933 wrote that, "277 Turks from Yugoslavia, Bulgaria, and Romania would be naturalized."[125] Another order stipulated on August 5, 1933, "165 Turks from Yugoslavia, Bulgaria, and Romania will be given Turkish citizenship."[126] As "Turk" became the dominant way of identifying immigrants in 1933,[127] the term Muslim disappeared from the immigration documents.[128]

All these immigrants were accepted since they were Muslims, hence potential Turks. Yet, while Turkey allowed non-Turkish Muslim immigrants, it also wanted to conceal this fact: then, during 1934–35, "person," a more neutral term, replaced the word Turk.[129] For instance, a decree dated August 5, 1934, noted, "60 persons," who had come to the country as immigrants, were to be naturalized.[130] On September 4, 1934, another document said, "330 persons will be granted Turkish citizenship."[131] In other examples, "745 persons, who had arrived in the country as migrants of refugees," were given citizenship on October 17, 1935,[132] and another "272 persons" on November 11, 1935.[133] By the end of 1935, the word person had become the most common way of identifying the naturalized immigrants.[134]

In the 1920s and the 1930s, Muslim and Turkish immigrants came to Turkey from three main countries: Bulgaria, Romania, and Yugoslavia,[135] as well as a variety of other places in the Balkans, the Near East, and the Caucasus. Until the rise of High Kemalism, as we have seen, the government called them "Muslims." From then on, until 1935, it referred to them as "Turks." After that, Ankara switched to "persons." The immigrants originated from the same countries, but the government's name for them changed over time, reflecting the rise of Turkish nationalism, and a consequent desire to cover up the fact that the immigrants were exclusively Muslims and not exclusively Turks. While Turkey left its doors open to non-Turkish Muslim immigrants, under the category "persons," the ethnicism of Kemalist nationalism was being practically compromised.

Race and ethnicity in Turkish citizenship policies in the 1930s

Even then, Turkish ethnicity continued to affect Kemalism's notion of citizenship. This was the case especially in the administrative practices of the government *vis-à-vis* the citizens. In the early 1930s, Ankara started using ethnicity as a criterion with which to evaluate them. For instance, with the advent of High Kemalism, the words, "race, and nationality" appeared often in the police records. On April 6, 1932, the EUUM wrote to the governor of Ağrı province. Ankara asked for an investigation on the "race and nationality" (ırk ve milliyet) of a certain Hacı Sadık of Nahcivan (Azerbaijan).[136] The term nationality "milliyet" here stood not for citizenship but ethnicity. A clear example demonstrating this was the case of Peter Gaytena, a teacher and an Italian citizen, who lived "at Nr 16, Cami Street, in Büyükada, Istanbul." On September 20, 1935, the EİUM wrote to Istanbul inquiring about his nationality."[137] Since the government was questioning the nationality of an Italian citizen, this meant that in Ankara's eyes the term nationality "milliyet" stood for ethnicity or religion, but not citizenship.[138] Meanwhile, on July 6, 1932, Ankara wrote again to Ağrı concerning Hacı Sadık. Sadık was of "the Kurdish race," he ought to be expelled to Iran immediately.[139]

Ethnicity was an important criterion, with which the government watched and judged its citizens. In March 1935, for example, the Police Headquarters in Ankara inquired from the governors of Balıkesir, Çanakkale, and Istanbul about the race of a certain suspect named Galip.[140] The sensitivity of the police on race and ethnicity extended even to its own staff: on March 8, 1935, the EİUM wrote to the governor of Izmir about a police officer in Kuşadası, who had been sheltering "an Armenian woman, named Bedia, also known as Tırvanda." Ankara wanted to know the "nationality" of this officer.[141] In another example of sensitivity on this, in 1931, the EUUM informed the First Inspectorate-General and the provinces that Kâzım Aslan, a former police officer in Ankara, was "of the Arab race."[142]

Not being ethnically Turkish could be a reason for becoming a suspect, too. A remarkable example along this line was recorded in a 1935 letter from the EİUM to the governor of Aydın. In this dispatch, Ankara requested information about the Tepe village in the province. Too many police-related occurrences had been reported there lately, "Are the inhabitants of this village Kurdish?" asked the letter. Then, it added: "How many Turks are there in Tepe?[143] In a similar case, Ankara sent a dispatch to the Muş province asking about the inhabitants of another restless village. "Are the inhabitants of this rebel village Kurds?" inquired the communiqué. "Are there many incidents in this village? How many Turks are there?" it asked further.[144]

At the apogee of High Kemalism in 1935, the notion of "Turkish blood" became an interchangeable term for Turkish ethnicity in the government documents. On October 9, for example, the EİUM wrote to the Thrace Inspectorate-General about a certain refugee named Ali: "Since Ali is of Turkish blood," if the investigations did not reveal anything negative against him, "he may be accepted into our country," said the dispatch.[145] In another letter on October 14, the EİUM wrote that if a certain Bayram, an escapee from Iran, "is of our blood and if there is nothing negative about him," he may be accepted into the country.[146] An additional example came in a communiqué from the Executive Private Secretary (Hususi Kâlem Müdürlüğü—HKM) of the Ministry of Interior. In this letter dated September 1, 1936, the HKM wrote to the sub-district governor of Yalova, Istanbul. The Secretary emphasized the importance of Turkish ethnicity and perhaps the need to favor it:

> It is reported by a trustworthy source that a certain Musa Erkan, a Bulgarian immigrant, who resides in Çiftlik village of your district, is being abused and beaten by the gendarme from the local station. Since plans are being made to densely populate your district with immigrants from Bulgaria, who have clean Turkish blood, your highness would, of course, not accede to agree to the flight of such Turkish immigrants, who have settled there.
>
> (Ministry of Interior—Turkey [hereafter DV], HKM 2.1090)

Conclusion

In its naturalization policies in the interwar era, Ankara blended *jus soli* and *jus sanguinis*. Turkey granted citizenship not only to ethnic Turks, but also to Ottoman Muslims who immigrated to the country. Ankara even naturalized converted East-Central European Christians and Jews, Hellenic Greeks, and both Christian and Jewish White Russians. In these cases, race and ethnicity seemed unimportant. Nationality-through-religion emerged as the most common way of gaining citizenship. The government processed citizenship as a category exclusive to the former Muslim millet. When non-Ottoman Christians converted, they could "join the Muslim millet" and become eligible to obtain Turkish citizenship. Since they had not belonged to the Muslim millet, Christian ex-Ottomans, most notably the Armenians, were unlikely to obtain Turkish citizenship, even when they converted. Due to the legacy of the millet system, Ankara saw former Ottoman Christians as a separate ethno-religious community, outside the body of the Turkish nation. Hence, religious heritage of the Ottoman Empire, and not race, determined the means of achieving Turkish citizenship.

In the interim, in policies *vis-à-vis* its own citizens, Ankara favored *jus sanguinis*. Interwar Turkey considered ethnic Turks as first-class citizens. It collected information about the nationality of citizens in order to favor ethnic Turks and screen the minorities. While the security apparatus treated all ethnic and religious groups with suspicion, the government tilted to ethnicism.

The rise of ethnicist nationalism in Turkey was not a novelty. In the 1930s, other countries in East-Central Europe, as well as Turkey's neighbors in the Middle East, experienced similar political developments. The interwar Greek state, for instance, adopted an ethnicist attitude toward its citizens.[147] Similarly, Egypt witnessed the rise of "integral Egyptian nationalism" during the 1930s.[148] Ethnic nationalism was a pan-European and Near Eastern phenomenon in the 1930s, and Turkey was one of the finer examples of this.

5 Defining the boundaries of Turkishness

Kemalist immigration and resettlement policies

The Kurds of the Eastern provinces, the Arabs of South-Eastern Anatolia, the Moslems from Russia, from the territories detached under the Treaty of Lausanne, the Greek islands, Greece, the Balkans and Roumania will be scattered among pure Turkish populations, so that they may lose the characteristics of the countries and districts of their birth, and, in a generation, be Turkish in speech.

(From a British Embassy memo sent to London, October 1934)

The nature of immigration to Turkey in the 1920s and the 1930s

Throughout the 1920s and the 1930s, Muslim immigrants, mainly from the Balkans, but, also the Black Sea, Aegean islands, Cyprus, Sancak of Alexandratta (Hatay), Middle East, and the Soviet Union poured into Turkey. Turks and Muslims of the former Ottoman Empire came to the country that they considered home.[1] The pull factor was so strong that Turkish immigrants arrived from as far as Yemen,[2] Trans-Jordan,[3] and Finland.[4] According to one estimate, between 1921 and 1939, 719,808 people entered the country as immigrants.[5] Another calculation puts the number of immigrants from 1923 through 1938 at 801,818.[6] In any case, this was a sizable influx given that in 1927, the country's population was 13,542,795. The bulk of the immigrants were Balkan Turks and Muslims who faced harassment and discrimination in their homelands.

In accepting these immigrants, Ankara recognized Islam as the key for access to Turkey. Turkey signed treaties with Greece and Romania to facilitate emigration from these countries, and entered accords with Albania, Armenia, and Bulgaria to regulate citizenship-related matters with these countries. Interestingly, these treaties mentioned not the Turks, but Muslims as the primary object of Turkey's interest. On December 2, 1920, for instance, Ankara signed the Gümrü (Alexandropol) Treaty with Armenia. Yerevan would protect the rights of its Muslim population and Turkey would observe this process.[7] Then, on May 31, 1925, Ankara entered a treaty of friendship with Albania. Since many Muslim Albanians had immigrated to Turkey during the Ottoman era, this treaty was vital in determining these peoples' status. It stipulated that people "who are originally from the territory of Albania and who are now in Turkey, will be Turkish citizens."[8] This recognized the Albanians in Turkey as citizens.[9]

On October 18, 1925, Ankara signed a treaty of friendship with Sofia.[10] Whatever language they spoke, Muslims born in Bulgaria who had immigrated to Turkey in the past were Turkish citizens. On the other hand, "Turkish citizens who spoke Bulgarian and were Christians would be accepted as a Bulgar minority by Turkey."[11]

Immigration treaties with Greece and Romania also mentioned the Muslims, and not exclusively Turks.[12] The 1923 population exchange agreement with Greece asserted "Greek subjects, who belonged to the Muslim faith" would be exchanged with "Turkish subjects of the Greek-Orthodox faith."[13] With this, Ankara acknowledged religion as the base of immigration to Turkey. Consequently, Turkish-speaking Greek-Orthodox Karamanlıs were sent over to Greece, while the Greek-speaking Muslim populations of Crete and Yannina came to Turkey. Ankara wanted all the Greek-Orthodox Christians to leave the country so that the exchange would be as complete as possible. Accordingly, on July 22, 1923, the Ministry of Justice declared that until "life goes back to normal," applications "by the non-Muslims to convert will not be accepted."[14] This shut the doors for the Greek-Orthodox who hoped to exempt themselves from the exchange by converting to Islam. In another measure, on January 20, 1924, the government declared that marriages between exchangeable non-Muslim women and Muslim men, which would exclude these women from the exchange, would not be allowed.[15]

Twelve years after the completion of the Turco-Greek exchange, in 1936, Turkey signed an immigration treaty with Romania. This determined that "the Muslim Turkish population, which lived in the Dobrudja," would be allowed to immigrate to Turkey.[16] The specific mention of "Muslim Turks" in this text excluded the Greek-Orthodox Gagavuz Turks from the scope of this emigration. Once again, the government recognized Islam as a prerequisite for immigration to Turkey.[17]

There were, however, objectors to the use of a religious criterion in immigration. One of these was the poet Yaşar Nabi Nayır (1908–81). After his trip through the Balkans, in 1936, Nayır wrote a book entitled, *Balkanlar ve Türklük* (The Balkans and Turkishness). He argued in length about the Turkishness of the Gagavuzes. Ethnically and linguistically, there was no doubt that they were Turks.[18] Hence, Nayır asserted that the Gagavuzes should be allowed to come to Turkey.[19] Another objector to the use of a religious criterion in immigration was Hamdullah Suphi Tanrıöver, the chairman of the Turkish Hearths between 1912 and 1931, and Turkey's Ambassador to Bucharest during the 1930s. Tanrıöver also protested the exclusion of the Gagavuzes from the body of Turkish emigration from Romania. In addition, he argued that the Karamanlıs, "the Turcophone Greek-Orthodox Christians of Central Anatolia" who belonged to the "original stock" of Turks, should not have been sent to Greece in accordance with the population exchange. These people had been the "purest-blooded Turks in Turkey." Their forced emigration to Greece had been a mistake. As a result of the exchange, "Turkey had lost many thousands of her best Turkish-speaking elements, and in return had received a smaller number of Cretan and other immigrants who were Greek in everything but religion."[20]

Despite such protests and notwithstanding their belief in the ethnic definition of the nation, the Kemalists were aware of Islam's role in nation building, especially, *vis-à-vis* the (non-Turkish) Balkan Muslims. Like the Turks, the Balkan Muslims descended from the Muslim millet of the Ottoman Empire. Moreover, compared to the Anatolian Muslims, they were mostly better educated and more prosperous. Since Turkey was underpopulated and devastated in the 1920s, Ankara needed the human capital of these people. Thus, not only due to ideology, but also for demographic and economic reasons, the Kemalists left the country's doors open to the Muslim immigrants from the Balkans. In fact, Ankara actually promoted immigration from the peninsula.[21] (On the other hand, it discouraged migration from the Dodecanese,[22] Sancak of Alexandratta,[23] Cyprus,[24] and Western Thrace. Ankara wanted to preserve the Turkish communities in these regions, where Turks enjoyed special legal regimes, possibly so that the Turkish character of these neighboring territories could be maintained.)

A major reason behind the flow of migrants from the Balkans was the push factor. During the interwar era, Muslims on the peninsula continued to face antagonism. Many saw Turkey as a place where they could escape harassment. For instance, the Pomaks in Bulgaria, who were "baptized by force by order of Holy Synod backed up by policemen" and had been given Bulgarian names after 1913, emigrated to Turkey *en masse* during the 1920s and the 1930s. Bulgaria wanted to retain the Pomaks, whom it considered original Bulgars, and convert them to Christianity.[25] Hence, it denied them passports. However, as religious persecution made life too difficult to bear, the Pomaks fled to Turkey.

Consequently, immigrants arrived from a variety of Balkan countries. In addition, some others came to the country from Cyprus, Sancak of Alexandratta, Iraq, Iran, and the Soviet Union, opting to live in a Turkish state. The Caucasus Turks also immigrated to escape Soviet communism. A British report from 1928 recorded this diversity of immigrants:

> They [the Kemalists] advertise the desire of the Cypriots, Syrians and other Muslim inhabitants from the Dodecanese Caucasus and elsewhere to settle in Turkey. The press states that land and houses made vacant by the departure of the Greek elements are being apportioned to Cypriots in the Smyrna neighborhood; that land in North-Eastern Turkey is being prepared for a large influx of Moslems from the Caucasus, that Eastern Turkey is being populated by emigrants from Yugoslavia, Bulgaria and Greece in considerable numbers.

(FO, 424/268/E129)

The Resettlement Law of 1926

As the Ottoman-Turkish Muslims poured in, Ankara needed legislation to cope with the influx. The first resettlement law, "İskân Kanunu" (Nr 885) was adopted on May 31, 1926. This law started by defining who could qualify as an immigrant. During the deliberations of this law, the TBMM agreed that Turkish culture "hars" would be the basis of future immigration to Turkey.[26] Hence, the second article of the law stated: "Those who don't share the Turkish 'hars'...will not be admitted as immigrants."[27] After Gökalp, the word culture in the Kemalist understanding, referred to Islam and the Turkish language, as well as the common past and values of the Ottoman-Turkish Muslims. This facilitated the immigration of Turkish and Muslim ex-Ottomans into Turkey. Simultaneously, it blocked out formerly Ottoman non-Muslims. In a demonstration of this, on January 19, 1929, the İUM asked that Greeks coming from various places should not be admitted as refugees since their "resettlement and maintenance is not possible" because of "economic hardships."[28]

While Ankara admitted non-Turkish Muslims, it launched a coordinated resettlement policy during the 1920s to prevent the country's de-Turkification. This policy also aimed at enhancing the Turkish character of the population. For instance, on October 15, 1925, the İUM decided that the Maraş province, "whose inhabitants are of various elements, needed Turkish immigrants."[29] In another example, in 1926, the İUM asked that Turkish immigrants coming from Russia be "resettled in Van and the nearby villages on the Van plain,"[30] a heavily Kurdish area.

With the same aim in mind, the government also made sure that non-Turkish Muslim immigrants would not establish a demographic base in any part of the country. For example, in 1929, the Ministry of Interior asked the Izmir province to be careful about the increased "population density" of Albanians and Circassians in the Bergama district. This could not be allowed. The governor needed to disperse these groups around.[31] In another example, in 1935, the NUM wrote to the Thrace Inspectorate-General, "Due to weather conditions, it is not possible to send the Pomaks who have arrived from Yugoslavia away for resettlement. It is acceptable to resettle them away from the border and in areas not inhabited by other Pomaks."[32]

Additionally, Ankara tried to block off non-Turkish immigrants from the Balkans if it deemed them non-assimilable. In the government's eyes, when Muslim immigrants originated from culturally non-Turkish parts of the Balkans, such as the Epirus, being Muslim was not a reason enough for their entry into Turkey. During the Turco-Greek population exchange, for instance, it seemed likely that the multinational commission in charge of population transfers would send Muslim Chamuria (Akarnania) Albanians, who lived in the Epirus, to Turkey. Some of these people declared to the mixed-exchange commission in Parga, Epirus, that they were Turks. Hence, the commission allowed them to be included into the exchange.[33] Ankara was apparently anxious about this situation,[34] worrying that these people were not ethnic Turks.[35] Thus, it resisted the immigration of Chamuria Albanians. Originating from a culturally non-Turkish, if Muslim, part of the Balkans, and possessing a relatively strong sense of Albanian nationality, these people could be difficult to assimilate. In the end, when some Chamuria Albanians immigrated to Turkey, Ankara quickly made it possible for them to leave for third countries: a decree of May 6, 1925 said: "240 people of the Albanian race, who had come from Greece with the population exchange could leave for abroad."[36]

In another case that demonstrated Ankara's wish to differentiate between Turkish and non-Turkish immigrants from the Balkans, on October 8, 1928, the İUM wrote to the governor of Edirne, concerning immigrants from Greece. Those, who were "of the Turkish race," would be resettled in Edirne (along the border with Greece), while others "of the Greek race" would be relocated away from the border, to the Çanakkale province, across the Dardanelles in Asia Minor.[37]

The resettlement policies toward the Kurds in the 1920s

As it aimed to facilitate the country's repopulation and Turkification, the Resettlement Law also focused on domestic population issues. It authorized the Ministry of Interior "to relocate the nomadic tribes and others around suitable centers."[38] (The word nomad in the republican jargon was a euphemism for the Kurds, and the occasional Roma, the only unsettled groups in Turkey by the late 1920s.) Consequently, this clause allowed the government to uproot the Kurds from their homelands and resettle them elsewhere, among the Turks. That opened the way for their gradual assimilation. In noting this, Minister Aras told British Ambassador Clerk in 1926, perhaps somewhat exaggerating, that "the Turkish Government were determined to clear out the Kurds out of their valleys, the richest part of Turkey to-day, and to settle Turkish peasants there." These Kurds would be resettled among the Turks. Clerk reported alarmingly, "His Excellency said that they would be treated as were the Armenians."[39]

In fact, resettling the Kurds among the Turks was not a novelty. This had been a popular measure throughout the Ottoman era. Especially during the later phases of the Empire, the Porte had resorted to relocation of the Kurds in order to assimilate and pacify them, while promoting economic growth and increasing the Muslim ratio in different parts of Anatolia.[40] However, despite the legal framework provided by the 1926 Resettlement Law, the relocation of the Kurds did not become a widespread policy in the 1920s. One reason behind this may be that Turkey's view of the Kurdish question gave priority to security over resettlement. In 1930, Aras told the British representative to the League of Nations in Geneva

> *Par la suite que la politique du Gouvernement turc au sujet des Kurdes consiste pour le moment à une occupation militaire d'un pays, de nature à garantir l'ordre, et au désarmement complet et absolu de la population. A l'avenir il envisage la possibilité d'une intense colonisation turque, de façon à noyer les Kurdes dans une masse considérable de population turque.*

(FO, 371/14578/E)

Accordingly, the number of Kurds moved to Western Turkey between 1920 and 1932, totaled a mere 2,774, out of the 742,720 people, who were resettled in the country during that period.[41] (Of this sum, 499,239 were exchangees "mübadil," covered by the Turco-Greek population exchange treaty, and 172,029 were non-exchangees "gayr-i-mübadil" [immigrants from Greece and the other neighboring countries, not covered by the population exchange treaty, hence their name, non-exchangees]. In addition, 14,312 people resettled in this period were "harikzedes," those people who had lost their homes due to wartime destruction, especially the burning of towns by Russian, Greek, and Armenian forces between the First World War and the Turkish Independence War. An additional 35,936 people in the resettled population were refugees, while 18,430 people were classified as the "native populace."[42])

Turkey resorted to forced relocation of the Kurds mostly to pacify the insurgent elements. For instance, following the 1927 uprising in Ağrı, the government passed Law Nr 1097. This stipulated the relocation of "about fourteen hundred individuals from Ağrı vilayet and the Eastern martial law area to the Western provinces."[43] These people were free "to travel around the Western provinces." However, they were not to return to the East. In another case of limited resettlement, on November 20, 1927, Ankara moved forty-one people, in ten households in Bitlis province, to Western Turkey.[44] There was compulsory relocation of the Kurds also in the aftermath of the abortive Ağrı uprising of 1930. At this time, the government was reportedly planning to replace the Kurds in this area with Turks. In July 1930, Aras told Clerk that after the rebellion "it would be necessary to re-people the whole district with Turkish refugees from elsewhere."[45] Kurdish nationalist leadership, such as members of leading Kurdish families, was also subjected to relocation, especially if implicated in anti-government uprisings. A British traveler to Eastern Turkey noted in 1929 that because of such policies, "there is not, I was told, a single wealthy or powerful Kurd in Turkish Kurdistan to-day."[46]

In addition to forced relocation, other measures, too, affected the Kurdish population. In 1927, for instance, Turkey closed its border with Iraq. This blocked the trans-national migrations of Kurdish tribes, such as the Koçars along the Iraqi frontier. Ankara prevented them from returning to Turkey in its efforts to seal its international boundaries.[47] Meanwhile, a case of resettlement of Kurds constituted a benevolent act on behalf of Ankara.[48] This involved the Halikanlı tribe that lived near the Persian border. The Halikanlıs had sided with the Turks during the 1930 Ağrı rebellion. After a 1931 Turco-Persian border rectification, they had been left on the Iranian side of the boundary.[49] The Halikanlıs applied for permission to enter Turkey to escape punishment from Teheran for collaborating with Turkey.[50] During November 1931, 300 Halikanlı families were moved away from the Persian frontier and resettled in Tekirdağ, in Thrace. In the same month, "112 persons belonging to the tribe arrived in Izmir via Trabzon and Istanbul. These people as well as the 726 head of cattle that belonged to them were sent to the Aydın district by rail."[51] The Halikanlı tribe was unique also since the government issued a decree on April 20, 1932, making 300 of them citizens.[52]

In addition to the Kurds, other groups such as the Armenians were also subjected to limited resettlement in the 1920s. For instance, a 1928 letter from the governor of Aksaray asked the Ministry of Interior for permission to relocate three

Armenians from Mardin who had been resettled in the Arapsun district of Aksaray. These Armenians, "Atabel, son of Şahin, Kirkor, son of Yorki, and Ohannis, son of Kevork," had been unable to make a living in Arapsun and were in financial despair. The governor asked if the men could be relocated to Aksaray, where they could engage in trade and make a living.[53]

Given the limited nature of the Kurds' relocation during the 1920s, much of the ambition *vis-à-vis* their forced resettlement remained on paper or in rumors. For instance, an alleged 1928 scheme by the government to import 60,000 Muslims from the Caucasus for settlement among the Kurds, did not take place.[54] Then, in 1930, American diplomatic sources reported that a rumor had come their way that "the Turkish authorities plan to exterminate the Kurds and repopulate Turkish Kurdistan with Turks now resident in Soviet Russia, notably Azerbaijan, where they are numerous."[55] Such a scheme, too, did not actualize.

Another piece of news concerning enforced relocation came from Mersin, a province with large Arabic and Greek speaking elements. British diplomats reported in 1934: "There is a rumor in circulation at Mersin that the non-Turkish elements of this region will soon be ordered by the Government to migrate to districts allotted to them in the interior" of Turkey. Although, this incident did not take place, that and similar rumors were significant. They had the "effect of causing a great deal of disquietude amongst the thousands of the inhabitants to whom such a law would be applicable."[56]

The Resettlement Law of 1934

While Turkishness was defined through ethnicity under High Kemalism, population engineering in the service of Turkish nationalism emerged as a valuable concept. Then, despite its low-level application in the 1920s, the idea of assimilating the Kurds through relocation survived into the 1930s. A new Resettlement Law (Nr 2510) passed on June 13, 1934 demonstrated this.[57] During the discussions of this law in the TBMM, MP Mustafa Naşit Hakkı (Uluğ) (1902–77) (Kütahya) said: "The Resettlement Law is distinguished as one of the foremost laws of the revolution since it will soak all, who live in this land, with the honor and the appreciation of being Turkish."[58]

The Kurds in High Kemalist resettlement policies

The first article of the new Resettlement Law stated: "the Ministry of Interior is assigned the powers to correct... the distribution and locale of the population in Turkey in accordance with membership to Turkish culture."[59] The law designated three areas in Turkey with which to actualize this policy: Zone 1, set aside for "populations who share the Turkish culture"; Zone 2, for the "... relocation and resettlement of populations which are to adopt the Turkish culture;" and Zone 3, closed to resettlement and habitation due to "sanitary, economic, cultural, political, military, and security" reasons.[60]

People who lived in Zone 1 areas and were of Turkish origin, but had forgotten Turkish, were to be resettled in Zone 1, "in villages, towns, and cities, whose population shared the Turkish culture."[61] Tribal or nomadic people, as well as individuals "who did not share the Turkish culture"[62] would not be allowed to settle in, or enter Zone 1, even if they were its native inhabitants. Tribal populations in Zone 1 areas who did not speak Turkish would be resettled in Zone 2, except in the following (Zone 1) districts:

a. "Areas in which resettlement is forbidden or limited in accordance with the decision of the Cabinet of Ministers."
b. "Those parts of the First, Third and Fourth Inspectorates that are set aside for the resettlement of Turkish immigrants from foreign countries."
c. Certain areas in Diyarbakır, Siirt, Van, Bitlis, Sivas, Erzincan, Erzurum, Malatya, Mardin, Urfa, Bingöl, Ağrı, Iğdır, Tunceli, Gümüşhane, Maraş, and Gaziantep, such as a "twenty kilometer belt on both sides of railway lines, radial sectors centered around urban zones, planes, mining zones and regions, lake Van basin," border zones, river valleys, as well as Iğdır, Erzincan, Elbistan, and Malatya planes.

(Naci Kökdemir, *Eski ve Yeni Toprak*, 166–70)

The focus of these articles was the Kurds, whom the laws described in varying ways such as "tribal populations that do not speak Turkish,"[63] "people who do not share the Turkish culture,"[64] or "people who are not of Turkish origin and do not share the Turkish culture."[65] Accordingly, the clauses above banned the Kurds from relocating to Zone 1 areas. In accordance with this, on July 12, 1932, the Ministry of Interior wrote to the First Inspector General's office in Diyarbakır. Ankara had screened a group of people from Erzurum and Kars who wanted to resettle in Muş. The Kurds in this group were not to be allowed, while it was all right for the others to move to Muş.[66] In another case, on September 30, 1935, Ankara told the Kars province that those refugees from Yerevan, "who were reported to be from the Kurdish race," could not be resettled in Ağrı province. These people needed to be sent to "a district in Zone 2."[67]

The government planned to resettle Turks in Zone 1 areas, from which the Kurds were banned. This would enable Ankara to carve an axis of Turkishness into the Kurdish heartland in the East. In an example of attempted colonization, an executive act of 1939 dictated the resettlement of immigrant Turks in specific strategic areas in the east, from which the Kurds would be excluded.[68] With this policy in mind, the government gave the right of way to Turks from the eastern Black Sea littoral, the most densely populated area of the country, for resettlement in the East.[69] This policy had been predicted as early as 1925 in the aforementioned "Report on Reform in the East."[70] This document had called for priority to be given to the inhabitants of Trabzon and Rize provinces for resettlement in the Murat river valley and the Lake Van basin.[71] Now, on November 5, 1933, Ankara decided to resettle "9,836 landless peasants from Trabzon and Çoruh [Artvin] vilayets around lake Van."[72]

The next step was that the Kurds would be resettled in Zone 2 areas, where they would mix with the Turks. Article 9 of the Resettlement Law stated: "the Ministry of Interior is entitled to... resettle migrant Roma and nomads, who don't share the Turkish culture, by spreading them around to Turkish towns and villages" in Zone 2.[73] Since the Turks and the Kurds shared a common religious identity, it was expected that the Kurds could assimilate if they were integrated with the Turks. Hence, the Resettlement Law stipulated that Kurds who were resettled had to stay a minimum of ten years in their new homes.[74] If, however, these policies failed, the Ministry of Interior was empowered to

> Take the necessary cultural, military, political, social, and security measures against those, who share the Turkish culture but speak a language other than Turkish, or against those who don't share the Turkish culture. These measures, not to be applied collectively, are resettlement and denaturalization.
>
> (İskân Kanunu, Nr 2510, 1158)

High Kemalist governments resorted to increased resettlement of the Kurds during the 1930s. In 1932, for instance, security forces stormed various areas of unrest and deported the Kurdish inhabitants of these regions to the provinces in the West.[75] Even then, however, the relocation of the Kurds did not turn into a mass program. The total number of Kurds moved to the West in the 1930s was 25,381 people, in 5,074 households.[76] Still, the government closely monitored any resettlement of the Kurds. In 1933, the NUM asked the Kırşehir province about the "race of the inhabitants of Kazaklı village who had applied for resettlement in the Çat village." Were these Turks or Kurds? Ankara would not make a decision on this unless sufficient information was provided.[77] In another case, the Ministry of Interior wrote to Tokat about the resettlement of Turks and Kurds. "It is permitted that the Turkish Doygel tribe be resettled in the Çerdiken and Sarı Tarla villages of the Pazar sub-district." However, it is not desired that "the Kurds congregate in these two villages or elsewhere and establish independent Kurdish villages. The Kurds who want to assemble therein should be resettled in Turkish villages, one household in each."[78] In another case, in 1932, Ankara adopted a decree to move "440 people of the Kurdish race who lived on the remote and unreachable Aygar Mountain, on the border between Çorum and Yozgat provinces," to more "suitable locations."[79] This aimed for the subjugation of these tribal Central Anatolian Kurds by putting them under closer government scrutiny.

Race and ethnicity in Turkish resettlement policies in the 1930s

Concomitant with the *Turkish History Thesis*, race and ethnicity became important concepts in the resettlement policies, especially in the 1934 Resettlement Law. Article 7 of this legislation stipulated that "immigrants who belong to the Turkish race 'soy' might settle wherever they wish, so long as they have not applied for material help from the government." However, those "immigrants who don't belong to the Turkish race" had to "settle where the government had asked them to, whether or not they had requested aid from the government."[80]

During the discussion of this law in the parliament, Minister Kaya said that the term "soy" in this legislation meant race.[81] The word race, used often in the Kemalist laws and acts, referred to a national community, defined through ethnicity, language, or religion. Ethnicity was an important concept in the High Kemalist acts on immigration. For instance, in 1932, the NUM asked the Ağrı province about a number of refugees who had recently crossed the border with the Soviet Union. Ankara wanted to know the "race of 220 people, who had been sent there form Kars; 180 people, who were reportedly refugees; ten men and eight women, who had sought asylum in Tuzluca; 260 people, who had come to the Iğdır district with the hope of finding asylum; and the 5,000 people, who had been resettled in Iğdır."[82]

In another letter to Ağrı in 1932, Ankara inquired about a certain refugee named Mirza Ali. It was unlikely that this man, who had come from Iran, had been pressed to flee from there. Another reason ought to be behind his attempt to seek refuge in Turkey. Ankara inquired about this as well as Mirza Ali's race.[83] Investigations about refugees' and immigrants' race multiplied during 1932. On July 18, for example, the EUUM asked the Kars province about the race of a refugee, a certain Molla Veli.[84]

In its immigration and resettlement policies, Ankara gave special preference to the idea of Turkish race. For instance, during the 1930s, the government permitted into Turkey only immigrants of the Turkish race from the USSR and the Middle East. In October 1933, the NUM wrote to the governor of Kars, a province on the Soviet border, "Non-Turks will never be admitted into the country." If they had entered "our national boundaries earlier, they will be returned to their origin, Russia." If Russia refused to accept them, then they would be dropped at the Iranian frontier.[85] In a similar communiqué, in 1933, Ankara asked Urfa, on the Syrian border, to deny entry to a number of people, who "are not of Turkish race."[86]

In a similar case of preferential treatment toward people of the Turkish race, on July 25, 1933, the NUM wrote to the governor of Kars, asking him not to return refugees from Adzaria (Georgia), who were of the Turkish race, to Russia.[87] Then, on October 9, 1935, Ankara sent a dispatch to the Thrace Inspectorate about a certain Ali. If this man "is of our blood" and if "investigations on him do not yield any negative evidence about him," then, he was to be admitted into Turkey.[88] In another document, on October 5, 1937, the government wrote to Ağrı about a refugee of Turkish race. "This man is not to be treated as a foreigner since he is of the Turkish race," the letter said.[89] The notion of ethnicity also guided the High Kemalist resettlement policies. On July 2, 1933, the NUM wrote to the First Inspectorate-General regarding people from Giresun, who had asked to be resettled within the Inspectorate-General: "If it could be proven that these people from Giresun are Turkish in regards to their blood and language," then they could be given free land to resettle around Van.[90]

Armenians in the High Kemalist resettlement acts

While it favored Turkish ethnicity in resettlement matters, Ankara showed caution *vis-à-vis* the Christian minorities, especially the Armenians. On September 6, 1938, for example, it asked, "Armenians, who lived in the Efkere village of Kayseri be resettled away from military installations and bases."[91] Similarly, in November, Ankara inquired from the Yozgat province about the emigration of Armenians to Kayseri, writing, "Since there is no reason, it is striking that these families are moving in groups to other places." The communiqué asked the governor of Yozgat to conduct an investigation.[92] Then, on December 14, Ankara ordered the governor of Kayseri to observe whether Armenians "who have emigrated to Kayseri from the Fahralı village of Boğazlıyan, were resettling in the vicinity of military installations and bases."[93]

On the other hand, in 1936, the government issued a decree that an Armenian, "Ohannes (Ahmet Hidayet), son of Vian," should be transferred to and resettled in Kastamonu.[94] While this act used Ohannes' former non-Muslim name, this proved that Ankara still saw him as an Armenian despite the fact that he had converted to Islam. Ohannes was dealt with punitively and sent for resettlement. In a similar example, in 1937, a decree asked that "Eyub (Agop) of Erzurum, and Sadık, the gavur [infidel, Christian] of Hasice, who had settled in the Nizip" district of Gaziantep, and had engaged in smuggling and spying, were to be sent, together with their families, to Niğde in Central Anatolia for resettlement.[95] Although the two suspects had Turkish-Muslim names, the decree mentioned an Armenian name for Eyub, and spoke of Sadık as an infidel. This implied that, in Ankara's eyes, Armenian ethnicity was embedded in an immutable religious marker. This idea of an unassailable ethno-religious identity was central to High Kemalists' perception of Armenians, whether converts or Christians. It determined the nature of action against them. In these cases, Ohannes, Eyub, and Sadık were resettled in Central Turkey.

Central Turkey was pivotal in both Kemalist and Ottoman resettlement schemes.[96] The governments considered it demographically sound to settle non-Turkish groups there, while middle Anatolia is a high plateau surrounded by steep mountains, and populated by Turkish peasant stock. If minorities lived in the midst of Turkish peasants, this would facilitate their assimilation. Moreover, since Central Turkey is cut off from the country's coastlines by mountain chains, the minorities' relocation here would not pose a security problem. This explains the resettlement of many "undesirable elements" in the middle of the country throughout the interwar years. A demonstrative example along this line came on the eve of the Second World War. On February 13, 1939, the government issued a decree that refugees fleeing to Turkey from Greece and Bulgaria over the Thracian border "should be resettled in Central Anatolia."[97]

The immigration matrix

Despite its tilt toward ethnicity in resettlement and immigration matters, the High Kemalist state still allowed certain non-Turks as immigrants.

	Settled	Nomadic
Of Turkish culture and origin	✓	✓
Of Turkish culture but not of Turkish origin	✓	✗
Not of Turkish culture or origin	✗	✗

Figure 1 Matrix of Turkishness.

The Resettlement Law highlighted this: "following approval by the Ministry of Interior, settled or nomadic individuals of Turkish origin and settled persons who share the Turkish culture" would qualify as immigrants.[98] A deductive reading of this clause reveals that it banned the immigration of:

- "settled persons who don't share the Turkish culture" and
- "nomadic individuals of non-Turkish origin."

Meanwhile (Figure 1), the clause permitted the immigration of:

- "settled or nomadic individuals of Turkish origin" and
- "settled persons who share the Turkish culture."

According to Gökalp's definition, the term "Turkish culture" in this law referred to the common heritage, history, traditions, belief system, values, and mores of the Ottoman-Turkish Muslims. For that reason, the clause, "people who did not share the Turkish culture" in this law referred to non-Muslims. (British diplomats agreed with this interpretation: "It could be established that persons in Turkey of non-Turkish culture are the same as the non-Moslem minorities."[99]) Then, it can be argued that the phrase "settled persons who don't share the Turkish culture" in the Resettlement Law applied to urban non-Muslims in Turkey's vicinity, including Greeks, Bulgarians and other Balkan Christians, as well as the Russians, Armenians, Georgians, and Jews.

On the other hand, the term "nomadic individual" was a Kemalist euphemism for the Kurds and Roma in Turkey. When applied to potential immigrants, this would also cover other nomadic groups in Turkey's neighborhood in the 1930s, including the Arabs, Assyrians, some Circassians, and similar Caucasus Muslims. Hence, the Resettlement Law, which prevented "nomadic individuals of non-Turkish origin" from immigrating, blocked off the Kurds, Roma, Arabs, Assyrians, Circassians, and other Caucasian Muslims.

The meaning of the clause "settled or nomadic individuals of Turkish origin" is clear. This referred to ethnic Turks from the Balkans, Cyprus and the Dodecanese, as well as Azeris, Balkars, Karaçays, Karapapaks, Tatars, Terekemes, Turkmens, and other Turkic groups in the country's vicinity. Finally, the phrase "settled persons who share the Turkish culture" needs elaboration. While the term "Turkish culture" referred to Ottoman-Turkish Muslims, this clause covered the urban Ottoman-Turkish Muslims around Turkey. As a High Kemalist euphemism, the phrase "settled persons who share the Turkish culture" applied mostly to the non-Turkish Balkan Muslims and allowed them to come to Turkey.

Balkan and Caucasus Muslims in the High Kemalist resettlement policies

Consequently, under High Kemalism, as discussed before, Turks from the Balkans, Aegean, Middle East, Black Sea, and the Caucasus, as well as non-Turkish Balkan Muslims were let in to the country. Altogether, 229,870 immigrants and refugees came to Turkey from 1934 until 1945.[100] For instance, between June 1, 1933 and November 1, 1934, 9,806 people arrived from Bulgaria; 4,471 from Russia; 4,337 from Romania; 3,342 from Yugoslavia; 1,161 from Iran; 420 from Syria and the Sancak of Alexandratta; 413 from the Dodecanese Islands; 63 from Greece (Western Thrace); and 23 from Cyprus.[101]

Non-Turkish Muslim immigrants were part of the Ottoman legacy. High Kemalist intellectuals and politicians understood this. MP Dr Refik İbrahim Saydam (1881–1942) (Istanbul), who wrote "Esbabı Mucibe Lâyihası" (Memorandum of Statement of Reasons) in support of Law Nr 2510, elaborated on this. During its earlier phases, the Ottoman Empire had implemented a successful Turkification strategy. Resettlement policies had been an important part of the Empire's assimilationist vision. Nevertheless, later on, when non-Turkish Muslims had been given privileges, their assimilation had been curtailed. As the Ottoman Empire collapsed in Europe during the nineteenth century, with "reverse migration," many Ottoman Muslims from the Balkans had fled into Anatolia. Then, the "artificial Ottomanization" process of the Tanzimat era, which had promoted civic Ottoman citizenship, had hindered the Turkification of these elements. "A conscious assimilation policy toward the resettlement of these masses" had not been followed. Serious attempts had not been made to integrate the non-Turkish Muslims into the Turkish culture and nation. Now, this issue needed to be addressed. Saydam concluded: "It is time to enhance the Turkish population through state-led measures."[102]

During the deliberations of the Resettlement Law, MP Hasan Ruşeni (Barkın) (1884–1953) (Samsun) drew further on Ottoman mistakes with regard to non-Turkish Muslims' assimilation. Since the beginning of the Empire, "millions of devşirme [recruited] aliens had fallen in love with the Turkish advance, joined the

Turkish ideal, merged into the Turkish culture, unified into the Turkish blood, and proved of great use to us." However, in its later years, the Empire had recognized only religion and left all the minorities by themselves. Therefore, "various Muslim and Turkish groups who spoke foreign languages had lived as separate millets and clusters within the Empire, differing from one another with respect to their dissimilar traditions and even their diverse clothing." The groups that had seen "the Turks as siblings for ages due to their inspiration from religion" had not merged with them because of the Empire's mistakes. The 840,000 Circassians, who had arrived in 1864, as well as the Georgians, Abkhazes, and Lazes were examples to these people. The failure to integrate the non-Turks had come to the point that now there were even Turks who had lost their identity and assimilated into other Muslim communities. The Turks who lived among the Arabs and had integrated into their culture exemplified this problem.[103]

Another view on the assimilation of Muslim minorities came from "İskân Kanunu Muvakkat Encümen Mazbatası" (Official Report by the Temporary Committee for the Resettlement Law). This report, dated May 27, 1934, cited Albanians, Circassians, and the Abkhazes as examples of Muslim groups that had failed to integrate into the Turkish nation. Although these immigrants "belonged to the Muslim community and were adjacent to the Turkish race in their belief," they had not integrated. Now, Ankara had to melt them. Taking "unity in ideals, unity in mind and first and foremost, unity in language, as the basis of the nation," Ankara was to "amalgamate and alleviate the domestic and transboundary forces of Turkishness." It was the "Turkish republic's goal and ideal to link everything to the great Turk."[104]

Subsequently, the policy during the 1930s *vis-à-vis* the non-Turkish Muslim immigrants was to assimilate them. An indicator of this was Ankara's awareness on non-Turkish Muslims, who had been resettled in a compact way in the past and had escaped assimilation.[105] Now, the government wanted to determine the names of these villages, where "alien dialects" were spoken. It asked the authorities to distribute populations that spoke "alien dialects" to nearby Turkish villages.[106] The policy toward non-Turkish Muslim immigrants was to resettle them among the Turks and dilute their concentration. The following article of the Resettlement Law pointed in this direction. Those "whose mother tongue is not Turkish might not establish towns, villages, and worker or artisan units."[107] This strategy was applied vigorously, even to the smallest groups. For instance, on June 28, 1933, the NUM wrote to the First Inspectorate-General that "eight Albanians in six households, who had recently come from Yugoslavia, be resettled in Elâziz province in a dispersed fashion."[108] There was no need to resettle immigrants of the Turkish race in this manner.[109]

Hierarchy in immigration to Turkey

High Kemalist immigration policies emphasized primarily Turkish ethnicity and secondly, nationality-through-religion. "İskân Muafiyetleri Nizamnamesi" (Statute on Exemptions from Settlement), an executive act that went into effect on

December 27, 1934,[110] asserted that those who "belonged to the Turkish race and culture" and "maintained their Turkish citizenship but lived in other countries," were to be accepted as immigrants to Turkey.[111]

Furthermore, Article 3 of this statute, which instructed the Turkish consular offices on issuing immigrant visas to aspiring immigrants, stipulated that "people who belong to the Turkish race" might be given immigration visas without approval from the Ministry of Interior, so long as they were not in need of material help upon their arrival in Turkey. However, "those who share the Turkish culture but don't belong to the Turkish race" might not be issued immigration visas without approval from the Ministry of Interior, even if they declared that they would not need material help upon arrival in Turkey.[112]

Another executive act from the 1930s, "İskân ve Nüfus İşlerinin Süratle İkmali Hakkında Tamim" (Circular on the Speedy Disposal of Resettlement and Population Matters) also used ethnicity as a tool with which to view the candidates to Turkish citizenship.[113] This circular commanded the local authorities to swiftly grant citizenship certificates to those immigrants who had not yet been naturalized. "Those who belong to the Turkish race, or those who share the Turkish culture, speak Turkish, and know no other languages" were to receive their naturalization papers without inspection.[114] Pomaks, Bosnian Muslims, Crimean Tatars, and Karapapaks were to be treated likewise. As for Muslim Georgians, Lezgis, Chechens, Circassians and Abkhazes, they were to be given nationality certificates only after being investigated by the Interior Ministry. On the other hand, Kurds, Arabs, Albanians, and other non-Turkish speaking Muslims, as well as Christians and Jews, were not entitled to receive naturalization papers.

This executive act established five hierarchical categories among the aspiring immigrants (Figure 2). The first was ethnic Turks, who were to receive their documents immediately. The second group included the Crimean Tatars and

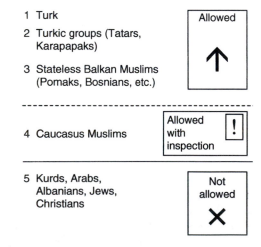

Figure 2 Priority in immigration.

Karapapaks, who were welcome since they were ethnically related to the Turks. The third category comprised the Balkan Muslims: Pomaks and Bosnians. Though not ethnically Turkish, these people were seen as easy to assimilate, as they lacked strong national movements or independent states with which they could identify. Consequently, they were to receive their papers on the spot.

Vigilance toward the Caucasus Muslims

Then came the non-Turkish Caucasus Muslims, such as Georgians, Lezgis, Chechens, Circassians, and Abkhazes, in a category below the non-Turkish Balkan Muslims. This implied caution toward the Caucasus Muslims. Why was this the case? Like the Balkan Muslims, the Caucasus Muslims were numerically small communities without independent homelands. However, the Circassians, the largest group of Caucasus Muslims in Turkey, had a relatively powerful national movement. In addition, there were still vestiges of nomadism among them in the Caucasus, and Ankara disfavored the nomads. Also, Soviet rule over the Caucasus led Ankara to view immigrants from this region as likely communist agents. Finally, there was the simple reason that Ankara favored the Balkan Muslims. The republican elite, itself drawing heavily from the Balkans, cherished the Ottoman-Muslim-Turkish heritage of the peninsula. It saw the Balkans as a gateway to Europe, to which it aspired to stay connected. American Ambassador Grew wrote on this and the Turks' emotional view of the Balkans: for Turkey, "the death of a peasant in the Balkans is more important than the death of a king in Afghanistan."[115]

Accordingly, due to a complex set of reasons, Ankara preferred the non-Turkish Muslims from the Balkans to those from Caucasus. Thus, the "Circular on the Speedy Disposal of Resettlement and Population Matters" asserted that Caucasus Muslims could receive their papers only after having been investigated. High Kemalist Turkey found vigilance necessary toward them. In an example of this, in 1932, the EUUM had asked the governors of Turkish provinces along the Black Sea coast to "deny entry to a group of Laze refugees of 300 families from the Soviet Union who had arrived in Batum with the intent of migrating to Turkey."[116] The provinces were to take all necessary precautions to prevent this group from coming to the country. In another example, in 1934, Ankara advised prudence about a certain "Halil İbrahim Horan of Çoruh," who lived in Gaziantep, near the Syrian border. Horan, with a Laze-sounding last name was from Çoruh, a province with a large Laze population. Hence, he was likely a Laze. Ankara asked that he be resettled in the "interior of the country."[117]

Watchfulness over communism also played into Turkey's aversion towards the Caucasus Muslims. During the 1930s, Ankara was wary about this and possible espionage activities by the Caucasus Muslims coming from the USSR. For instance, on November 2,1937, the government ordered that refugees from the Soviet Union were not to be admitted into Turkey. In case of a *fait accompli*, those who managed to enter the country were to be "resettled at least fifty kilometers away from the Soviet border."[118] In another example of vigilance toward the

Caucasus Muslims in relation to the Soviet Union, on October 18, 1933, the EUUM wrote to the governors of Çoruh, Kars, and Ağrı, the Turkish provinces along the Soviet border. People who were not of Turkish race, who had crossed the "Russian border as refugees in groups or individually," ought to be denied asylum and returned to their places of origin.[119] Then, on July 16, 1938, Ankara wrote to the Inspectorates-General, and the northeastern and Black Sea provinces about a group of Lazes, who were expected to arrive from the USSR. They were reported to be employed by the Russian intelligence and were working at the "Lazistan kolkhoz." The authorities were to be alert toward them and others entering Turkey from the USSR. They were to gather information on these people, their "nationality, real identity, previous trips to Russia, the dates and reasons of such trips, their jobs and reputation in Russia, and the number of languages they spoke."[120]

To the extent that Ankara was cautious toward the Caucasus Muslims, as these documents show, it also distinguished among them. For example, Ankara especially disfavored the religiously conservative Lazes, whom it saw as likely threats to secularism, and the mostly nomadic Circassians, whom it incriminated in Circassian nationalism. On the other hand, Ankara seems to have favored the Georgian Muslims. These were a settled community, not involved in Georgian nationalism, and liberal in their interpretation of Islam. Accordingly, the government accepted many of these people as immigrants. For example, in 1939, Ankara wrote to the Kars province regarding twelve Georgian Muslim immigrants that these could be accepted as refugees.[121]

After the Caucasus Muslims, the fifth and the last category in the immigration hierarchy included the Christians, Jews, Kurds, and various other Muslims. The people in this grouping were not to receive naturalization papers under any circumstances. The Christians were in this list for a simple reason. Turkey wanted to see their population diminish. For example, in December 1930, the EUUM warned the Kars province not to accept any Armenian refugees.[122] Then, in May 1933, it wrote to the Ağrı province concerning Armenian and Georgian refugees who had apparently arrived there from the Soviet Union. They were to be deported immediately.[123] The flow of refugees from Russia must have continued throughout the summer of 1933, since Ankara wrote to Ağrı again in July 1933, asking the governor "to return Armenian refugees back to Russia."[124]

In a similar case, on April 14, 1932, the EUUM sent a communiqué to the country's border and coastal provinces about a group of refugees, who had recently left Greece to go to the Soviet Union and had been denied entry by Moscow. After providing the authorities with a list of names of 14 Armenians, 2 Greeks, and 1 Russian, the Directorate asked the authorities to deny access to these people at entry points. If seen within the country, these were to be arrested immediately.[125] In other cases, on May 24, 1933, the EUUM asked the Ağrı province that Armenian and Georgian refugees be sent to the First Inspectorate-General, which would expel them through the country's southern border.[126] The fear that refugees from the Caucasus might be communists might have added to the aversion toward them. On July 31, Ankara demanded that "Armenian refugees from Russia, Miran, son of Mişon, and Dinov, son of Agop, be returned to their origin" immediately.[127]

In another example of refusal of Christian immigration, in June 1933, the Ministry of Interior responded to the inquiry of the Secretary General of the President's Office about a certain "Mr. G. K. Hungari, who had asked for permission to colonize the Istranca region," a mountainous zone in Eastern Thrace, along the Bulgarian border. It was not possible for those "who do not share the Turkish culture to be accepted to our country like that," said the communiqué. Thus, Mr Hungari's request had been turned down.[128]

The group of undesirables for immigration also included Muslims, such as Albanians, Arabs, Roma, and the Kurds. The republic considered them difficult to assimilate, therefore a potential threat. The Albanians and the Arabs among them had independent states and strong nationalist movements, thus their assimilation would not proceed smoothly. In fact, as early as 1922, Ankara had been apprehensive about Albanian and Arab immigration.[129] It believed that the Albanians had not assimilated well enough into the Turkish society.[130] Consequently, Turkey prevented them and the Arabs from immigrating. In 1933, for instance, Ankara wrote to the governor of Gaziantep asking that a certain refugee, "Ahmet, son of Ali, of the Arab race" be returned to his country of origin.[131]

The Roma, too, were unwanted. Law Nr 2510 which regulated the entry of refugees into Turkey, established that people, "Who did not belong to the Turkish culture, anarchists, spies, migrant Gypsies," could not, under any conditions, come to the country as refugees.[132] During the interwar era, the government maintained a watchful attitude toward the Roma, a group whom the Turks, like their neighbors, considered unwelcome.[133] Ankara scrutinized them and kept detailed tabs on their number.[134] If the government discovered Roma, who were not citizens, it deported them immediately.[135] In addition, Ankara followed a strict policy of enforced resettlement of Roma.[136] On January 22, 1933, for example, the governor of Mersin complained to the Ministry of Interior about 146 Roma refugees, originally from Kolos in Old Greece. While they had not been settled yet and since they could "violate order and security within the province," the governor asked for recommendations on what do with them. Ankara replied on March 7 that they should be resettled in the Turkish villages of Mersin, one household in each. Although they had asked permission to do so, the Roma were not to move to other provinces. They were to be strictly subjected to the "forced resettlement law."[137]

The republic was especially careful toward the Kurds. Turkey banned the Kurds from immigrating to arrest the growth of its own Kurdish community; the largest and least assimilated non-Turkish Muslim community in Turkey. For instance, on July 26, 1933, the NUM asked the governor of Van and the First Inspectorate-General not to accept "five hundred households of refugees of Kurdish race."[138] In another example, on December 2, 1931, the Ministry of Interior wrote to the Artvin province, "The movement of Kurdish refugees of the Hemşin tribe ought not be delayed until the spring." Rather, they were to be deported immediately.[139] In other cases, on February 25, 1932, the EUUM asked the governor of Artvin to deport a "Caucasian Kurd, a certain Ali, son of Hamit, and of the Hemşin tribe," to Iran.[140] Then, on June 22, 1938, Ankara wrote to the First Inspectorate-General and the governor of Hakkâri about a certain "Murat, of the Kurdish race," who had arrived as a refugee. "Murat and his family are to leave Turkey or are be handed over to the Iraqi government," the communiqué said.[141]

Given the chance, Ankara even got rid off its own Kurdish population. Following a border rectification with Iran in July 1933, the Ministry of Interior wrote to Ağrı concerning the inhabitants of the "Çavmao/Cavzer," a village that had been given to Iran in accordance with recent borders realignment. The Ministry wanted to know "in twenty-four hours, the nationality of this village's inhabitants as well as their language."[142] The following week, apparently after Ağrı's response, Ankara asked "the inhabitants of this village be left in Iran, since they are Kurdish."[143]

The spirit of High Kemalist immigration and resettlement policies

The resettlement and immigration policies of interwar Turkey were instituted with a nationalist vision. The government was acutely aware of the presence of non-Turks in different parts of the country. For instance, Prime Minister İnönü pointed at this in notes he took during his trips throughout the country in the 1930s. On July 6, 1935, in Siirt in the Southeast, he noted that this province was "entirely Arab and Kurdish."[144] Two days later, in Bitlis, he remarked that this was "a sole most powerful center of Turkishness, a Turkish city."[145] Then, İnönü elaborated on dealing with this issue. On July 12, he wrote in Muş, depopulated since the First World War: "If the Muş plain is left unoccupied, that would be very dangerous. If it were resettled, it would become a bastion of Turkishness. If this were to be left empty, in addition to the external threats, the Kurds would fill it up eventually. Then, a monolithic Kurdistan shall be formed."[146] Accordingly, Kemalist policies aimed to mold the ethnic map of Anatolia and Thrace. A British diplomat wrote

> In short, Turkey's only policy to-day is to rid itself of every extraneous population, without real regard to the eventual results on her population and in the hopes of building up in course of time from the remnants a homogenous Turanian people. Her Arabs, Armenians, Greeks, Jews and, indeed, any people that can, possibly, by tradition, sentiments or blood be linked however remotely to other countries she eyes with the same suspicion as in the past and is determined to supplant and even to root out.
>
> (FO, 424/268/E129)

The 1934 Resettlement Law was an important component in such vision. Even with a cautious interpretation, this and the accompanying legislation provided the government with the necessary tools to knead "all Moslem elements into one whole, entirely Turkish in character, speech, manner of life and outlook."[147] One British diplomat noted this:

> The Kurds of the Eastern provinces, the Arabs of South-Eastern Anatolia, the Moslems from Russia, the territories detached under the Treaty of Lausanne, the Greek islands, Greece, the Balkans and Roumania will be scattered among pure Turkish populations, so that they may lose the characteristics of the countries and districts of their birth, and, in a generation, be Turkish in speech, dress, habits and outlook, undistinguishable from their old-established neighbors.
>
> (FO, 371/17970/E6434)

Turkishness and the Turkish race were central in this design. British diplomats saw the Resettlement Law as "an important stage in the creation of the completely Turkish state." Ambassador Sir Percy Loraine (1880–1961) suggested that this legislation would usher in "a union of the Turkish races, i.e. Pan-Turanianism in a new form, since it seems to me that instead of Turkey's sovereignty being extended over areas inhabited by Turks, these Turks shall be attracted and encouraged to settle in Turkey itself.[148] In confirmation of this, on November 18, 1935, Minister Kaya told the TBMM, that, thanks to concerted policies, Thrace had been settled with "tens of thousands of people of our race."[149] He added: "One of the principles of our general population policy is that the Turks abroad come here. The arrival of the Turks from abroad is not only related to the population business. We see this, also, as a matter of feelings, compassion, humanity, and justice."[150]

6 Secularized Islam defines Turkishness

Kurds and other Muslims as Turks

The history of Van and Diyarbekir eyalets under the Ottoman Empire is the story of the oppression, assimilation and alienation of the Turkish population, Turkish language, and Turkish culture in these places.[1]

(From an article by Şevket Süreyya (Aydemir)
(1897–1976), June 1932)

Why were the Kurds the biggest challenge to Kemalism?

Given the rising ethnic-based definition of the nation under High Kemalism, which dictated that all of Anatolia's inhabitants were Turkish, and while the legacy of the Millet system led the Kemalists to view all Anatolian Muslims as Turks, the regime in Ankara expected that all Anatolian Muslims would merge into the Turkish nation. This process worked fairly smoothly for most non-Turkish Muslims, except for the Kurds. The Kurds were a formidable challenge to Ankara's desire to craft a new Turkish nation. This was on account of the fact that they were different in many ways than the other non-Turkish Muslim groups in the country. First, the Kurds were the only sizable non-Turkish group in Turkey, comprising more than 10 percent of the population. Second, they were the majority of the population in many provinces in Eastern and Southeastern Turkey where they formed a large and contiguous non-Turkish zone. Third, the Kurds were isolated from the rest of the country by the harsh geographical features of Eastern Turkey, as well as by lack of proper transportation and communication means between the East and the rest of the country. Finally, the Kurds were much poorer than the rest of the country's population.

The Kadro movement and the Kurds: "Are the Kurds a nation?"

The Kadro circle of 1930s, one of the prominent intellectual movements of High Kemalism, devoted much energy to analyzing the Kurdish question. The Kadro movement was set up in 1932 by a group of young intellectuals who gathered around the journal, *Kadro* (Cadre), to speak for a radical form of Kemalism.[2]

The most notable writers of *Kadro*, which appeared in January, were: Şevket Süreyya (Aydemir), İsmail Hüsrev (Tökin) (1902–94), Vedat Nedim (Tör) (1897–1985), Burhan Asaf (Belge) (1899–1967), and Karaosmanoğlu Yakup Kadri (Karaosmanoğlu) (1899–1974). These men shared a leftist past and an affiliation with the Turkish Communist Party (Türkiye Komünist Partisi—TKP) in the 1920s.[3] (Aydemir had earned a degree at the University of the Workers of the East in Moscow). Moreover, the five were united by a nationalist passion for the republic.

Kadro saw Kemalism as a "fourth way," that was neither fascist, communist, nor capitalist.[4] Since Turkey was at a pre-capitalist stage of development, it could not adopt capitalism, socialism, or fascism, which the movement regarded as "the advanced stage of capitalism."[5] According to the Kadroists, the Kemalist revolution and the Turkish "national liberation movement" had created a *sui generis* political structure in the country. "Türk Nasyonalizmi" (Turkish Nationalism) dominated this system,[6] which was a reaction against colonialism and imperialism.[7] The Kadroists contended that non-stop Kemalist revolution would save Turkey from the vices of the other systems, such as class struggle, domination of the capitalist class, or colonialism.[8] The ideal path for Turkey was a state-run, national, and capitalist economy.[9] Kemalism would create a society without classes, a homogenous mass without privileges.[10]

Although the Kadroists extolled Kemalism and statism, and while Kemalism promoted étatism at this time, since it did not like independent movements, High Kemalism never adopted *Kadro* as its brainchild. Mustafa Türkeş argues that the Kadroists were aware of this limitation. Accordingly, they used self-censorship.[11] In return, Kemalism tolerated *Kadro*. In due course, *Kadro* evolved into the voice of an officially marginal, yet radical, and colorful intellectual movement. The class analysis of the journal crossed with its solidarist views, while the movement's espousal of authoritarianism contrasted with its refusal of fascism, Nazism, or communism. The Kadroists rejected liberalism and warned about the ills of capitalism. Instead, they promoted a solidarist and étatist path.[12] With this puzzling synthesis, they elaborated on Turkey's problems. Occasionally, they did not agree with Ankara. However, while staunch nationalism and secularism deeply colored *Kadro*'s contents, this made the movement's theses easier to digest for the regime. Nevertheless, Ankara's patience with the Kadroists gradually wore out. In October 1934, the government appointed *Kadro*'s concessionaire, Yakup Kadri Karaosmanoğlu as ambassador to Albania. Turkish press laws stipulated that government employees could not own journals, or other periodicals. Except for Karaosmanoğlu, all the Kadroists were government employees. Now, he had become one, too. Thus, the journal stopped publishing; Karaosmanoğlu went to Tirana, and the other Kadroists to their government jobs.[13]

Although it was tolerated only briefly, and while the regime never fully endorsed it, *Kadro* was an important publication of Turkey in the 1930s.[14] The journal embodied a radical interpretation of Kemalism, laden with economic reductionism. However, if this were shaved off, the Kadroist writings could be regarded as representative examples of Kemalism's approach to Turkey's problems in the 1930s. Two of *Kadro*'s main interests were Eastern Turkey and the Kurds. The journal identified feudalism as the biggest problem in the East.[15] The tribulations there were rooted in the fact that feudal Kurdish landlords, who had controlled this region for centuries, had oppressed its free Turkish peasantry. This had been the case especially during the Ottoman era, when "twelve Kurdish principalities" and "nine individually divided governments" had existed in the region.[16] Consequently, the Ottoman government had never established itself in the East, where Kurdish feudalism had liquidated small landholding, and enslaved the free Turkish farmers.[17] This had resulted in the Kurdification of the region's Turkish population.[18] Religion had played a role in feudalism's domination over Turkish peasants, too. In fact, in the struggle "between Turkish social and economic order on the one hand, and Kurdish feudalism on the other, *tekke* [religious shrine] had been a brutal institution of Kurdish feudalism."[19] Meanwhile, due to feudalism, while market forces had developed elsewhere in Turkey, they had not laid roots in the East.

Because of Kurdification, there were villages in the East whose inhabitants did not speak Kurdish, but who claimed to be Kurds. Consequently, Turkishness was a latent phenomenon there. How else, for instance, could one explain the fact that "seventy percent" of the names of villages and road passages in Dersim (Tunceli) were "genuine Turkish." According to the Kadroists, Dersim was a special area *vis-à-vis* Turkishness. There were villages here that had dropped Turkish as recently as five to ten years ago. Besides, especially in Dersim, "the places vacated after the reversal of the Armenian element had not been populated by Turkish immigrants." This had allowed "the feudal lord, an element of the mountains and high planes, into the valleys and the low plains."[20] However, the "order and discipline" of new Turkey had prevented the "onslaught of a terrible feudalism to the gates of our cities in the East."[21] Now, the "liquidation of the feudal order was a natural matter for the Turkish revolution."[22] Aydemir wrote

> The remaking of the nomads into the peasants, the re-tilling of deserted hamlets, and the opening of roads and passages to a happy and crowded Turkish population that feels secure about its life and property *is not the most arduous of the tasks that revolutionary Turkey has undertaken.*
>
> (Aydemir, "Derebeyi ve Dersim," *Kadro*, 6, 45)

The subjugation of the Kurds was not a nationalist issue. "Is there a Kurdish nation when there is not a Kurdish national movement? We will reply no to this," said Tökin.[23] Not a Kurdish nation, but a conglomerate of Kurdish-speaking tribes as well as Turkish elements, which had been forced to speak Kurdish, lived in the East. "We cannot find the qualities that a nation bears in these Kurdish speaking tribes," asserted Tökin. In keeping with Durkheim, the Kadroists contended that as a "high social category," the emergence of the nation required "a solid division of labor, as well as shared economical, political, cultural, and historical interests" among its members.[24] The Kurdish tribes did not possess these qualities. Thus, the Kurds were not a nation. The movement also asserted that as a result of Kurdification, many Turkish villages had succumbed and assimilated into the Kurdish speaking tribes. This had created social and economic as well as security problems.[25] In Aydemir's words,

> What the new Turkey inherits from the old Ottoman Empire in these places is a primitive society that lives on an un-enchanted piece of land and that has not found its homogeneity. The methods and forms that dominated the internal and external economic relations of this society were the brutal methods and principles of a backward and loathsome feudalism.
>
> (Aydemir, "Derebeyi ve Dersim," *Kadro*, 6, 45)

Consequently, Turkey's Kurdish question was not an ethnic issue but a problem with economic and security dimensions. Because it endangered the maintenance of order in the country, this problem needed to be resolved as soon as possible.

Kemalism and the Kurds: 1920s into the 1930s

The High Kemalists agreed with the Kadroists on the Kurdish issue, especially regarding the security and reverse Turkification dimensions of this question. Throughout the 1930s, Ankara's approach to the Kurds emphasized maintaining order and discipline. The Kemalists believed that the establishment of a strict regime in the East would prevent future problems there. The mistakes of the Ottomans *vis-à-vis* the region could be undone if the Kurds and feudalism were subjugated to the republic. In this regard, Ankara's efforts to modernize the East were buttressed by Kemalism's global project of Turkey's Westernization. These attitudes, however, were not novel. In fact, one of the elements of continuity between the 1920s and the 1930s was Ankara's treatment of the Kurds. Secularist modernization, maintenance of order, "reverse assimilation," and liquidation of feudalism were the pillars of Turkish policy toward the Kurds both in the 1920s and the 1930s.[26]

The Kemalists had acknowledged the Kurds as a possibly separate ethnicity only for a brief period during the Independence War of the early 1920s.[27] At this time, Turkish nationalism had allied with the Muslim minorities in the country against the Greek, Armenian, and Allied forces.[28] In recognition of this, Atatürk had noted in 1920:

> The various Muslim elements who live within the limits of the circle that we have drawn as our national boundaries are our genuine brothers, who have mutual respect for each other vis-à-vis race, region, and morals. Consequently, we would not desire to do anything contrary to their wishes. It is certainly clear to us that the Kurds, Turks, Lazes, Circassians, etc., all the Islamic elements within our national boundaries share joint interests and that they have decided to work together.
>
> (Borak, *Gizli Oturumlarda Atatürk'un Konuşmaları*, 109)

Following the establishment of the republic in 1923, and with the beginning of secularization in 1924, Kemalism had reneged on its alliance with the Kurds and other Anatolian Muslims. Ankara had proceeded to make Turkey into a nation-state for the Turks. This was revealed, for example, in the republican rhetoric. According to Ergun Özbudun, whereas until 1924, the Kemalists used the word "Muslims" in addressing the public, this disappeared from the republican texts soon after.[29] Accordingly, for instance, in 1926, the Ministry of Education issued an order that "names such as Kurd, Laze, Circassian should not be used, as they harmed Turkish unity."[30] The Kurds and the others were now regarded as Turks.

The Kurds resisted this. Martin van Bruinessen argues that until the 1920s, Kurdish nationalism had been a weak political force, limited to the educated urban elites and the tribal leaders.[31] However, Kemalism's approach to the Kurds after 1923–24 fanned Kurdish nationalism into a mass movement.[32] In this process, centralization of power in Ankara caused the mostly tribal Kurds to resent Ankara's interference in their life, while secularization propelled the Kurds, most of whom were conservative Muslims, to develop an aversion toward Kemalism. The Kurds also refused to abide with the government's emphasis on Turkishness instead of Islam as the cohesive link between the country's inhabitants. These factors explain the many Kurdish insurgencies during the 1920s, including the Şemdinli, Raçkotan, Raman, Eruh, Pervari, Çölemerik (Hakkâri), Beytüşşebap, Koçgiri, Mutki, Biçar, Asi Resul, and Savur incidents.[33] These mutinies, though they were crushed immediately, kept patches of Eastern Turkey in constant turmoil. More regional rebellions, including the First and Second Ağrı rebellions,[34] Tendürek and Zeylan insurgencies,[35] the 1930 Ağrı upheaval, and the Şeyh Said uprisings, challenged the authority of the republic in controlling the East. (In addition to fuelling Kurdish unrest, the tension between Kemalist nationalism and the Kurds also led to a hardening of Turkey's regime. The 1930 Ağrı rebellion played a cataclysmic role in the fermentation of High Kemalism. In the aftermath of this event, as well as the aforementioned religious mutiny in Menemen and the TpCF incident, Ankara toughened in 1931. Thereafter, the Kurds and the Turkish state were at odds more than before.)

Ankara's task in the East was further complicated by the sheer poverty of this area. During the 1910s, demographic losses as well as destruction of infrastructure had impoverished much of Turkey. However, unlike Western Anatolia, where mass resettlement of immigrants had restored the region's agriculture and infrastructure, Eastern Turkey, whose population had remained sparse, had not been able to recover from the devastating warfare of the 1910s, as well as the deportation and annihilation of the region's Armenians during 1915.[36] An example was the plain south of Mardin. Whereas until the end of the Ottoman Empire, this had been an important cotton- and grain-producing area," now production there barely satisfied the local needs. Another case demonstrating the legacy of material devastation of the 1910s was Harput. A British traveler wrote in 1929:

> In other days, Harput was a prosperous town, whose population was largely Armenian. It also had a large American college and was surrounded by orchards. To-day the Armenians and the orchards are no more, troops are

quartered in the American college buildings, which are dilapidated in appearance, and the town has shared the fate of nearly all Armenian villages in Turkey. Hardly one stone remains upon another.

(FO, 371/13828/E3538)

Even villages had not been able to recover from the 1910s. The same British diplomat traveling to Ulaş, near Sivas, wrote, "The once large village of Ulash was in such a state that, like my chauffeur and servant (both Turks), I thought there must have been an earthquake. They asked a passer-by. The answer was a laconic, 'This was an Armenian village.' "[37]

Additionally, enforcement of new boundaries between Turkey and her Arab neighbors, which cut through the East, exacerbated the region's economic woes. These boundaries hurt the area's established trade connections, while lack of communication between the East and the rest of Turkey rendered new commercial links difficult. In consequence, by the early 1930s, economic depression was perhaps a bigger "menace to the continuance of the Angora [Ankara] régime" in the East than was Kurdish nationalism.[38]

The Dersim uprising

His Excellency Pasha, it is not as difficult as you presume to leave the Kurds, whose assimilation to Turkishness has been proven de facto impossible, alone on their own in Kurdistan.... You should be certain that imprisoning the Kurds is more difficult than killing them...If, in spite of everything, you do not have mercy on the poor Anatolian boys, who spill Muslim blood while dying with a Muslim bullet, you should know that, the Kurd has always excess blood in his veins, which he will spill while dying and while killing.

(Open letter from Celadet Ali Bedirhan to Atatürk (1893–1951) (January 1931))

As Bedirhan, a leader of the nationalist and tribal Kurdish opposition to Ankara in the 1930s, pointed out, the Kurds would be obstinate in their resistance to the Kemalist efforts to assimilate and pacify them. Despite this, Ankara's Turkification policies continued into the 1930s.[39] The government monitored nationalist activities among the Kurds,[40] whom Ankara distrusted. For instance, in December 1930, the Authority for the Provinces (Vilayetler İdaresi—Vİ) in the capital wrote to the governor of Erzincan concerning his recent firing of a certain "İbrahim Efendi, the ex-director of Danzik, a sub-district of Pülümür district." Because "the director of Danzik is Kurdish and since he is not trustworthy," his termination on grounds of "his Kurdishness, poor penmanship, and many dialectical mistakes" was justified, said the communiqué.[41]

Moreover, High Kemalist officials influenced by the *History Thesis* were convinced that the Kurds were not a separate nation. For instance, a certain "Colonel Nuri Bey from the Turkish General Staff" told a British major in 1931, "The Kurds are of very mixed and doubtful national origin and have no national unity." The "racial differences between the Kurds, and the Turkomens, Circassians and Armenians" were "very doubtful." The Colonel added, since Kurdish "bears a strong resemblance to the Turkish dialects spoken in parts of Anatolia, such as the lower slopes of Ercis Dag," the Kurds "derive largely from the Seljuk Turks, who preceded the Ottoman invasion."[42] While Ankara doubted that the Kurds were a separate ethnic group, it barred Kurdish nationalist publications from entering into the country. For instance, a decree on August 1, 1934 banned four books issued by Hoybûn.[43] Publications with the word "Kurdistan" were outlawed, too. These included *Der Grosse Weltatlas*,[44] a German atlas, which showed a map of Kurdistan, and *Der Adler von Kurdistan*[45] (The Eagle of Kurdistan), a German novel.

In the interim, by the early 1930s, Eastern Turkey had become relatively quiet.[46] A British diplomat noted that

> Travellers go unescorted. The roads are freely patrolled by couples of gendarmes, but not, so far as I saw, by troops. Cars and motor-buses seem to go freely in all directions, . . . I had no escort given to me. The only places where I met a military patrol (of some twenty men in each case) were at either end of the gorge in which Bitlis lies.
>
> (FO, 371/19828/E3538)

Yet, although, "there is no doubt that tranquility reigns east of the Euphrates," it was "also clear that that tranquility is dependent on force."[47] This improved security situation was accredited to the Inspector-General, Dr Öngören. Although the Inspector had been criticized for acting as a "super-vali" (super governor), the British diplomats noted that he deserved some recognition. His policies, which included more than repression and violence, deal with the East in the right way. Edmonds, a British traveler to Eastern Turkey, wrote

> When the soldiers had done the dirty work of repression, the civilian Inspector-General arrived with a policy of conciliation and with the army subordinate to him, but adequate to ensure absolute respect for his rule. He has the confidence and backing of Angora. He is able to give to the officials under him confidence and backing such as they would never have if directly dependent on the distant capital. On the other hand, he is able to represent to Angora local needs and aspirations, and by his prestige to obtain for them intelligent and sympathetic treatment.
>
> (FO, 371/14579/E2678)

Perhaps Edmond's adulation for Öngören should be taken with a grain of salt. It appears that the British man had been very impressed by his Turkish counterpart: "He is a worker, but he goes to see things himself. He is genial, tactful and broad-minded." The Inspector's exposure to the British Empire made him even more appealing: "He has been to Bombay, studies Anglo-Indian administration and makes his officials start work at 7:30 and stop at 1." Edmonds went as far as to propose that Dr Öngören, a "cultured" man, would "make a good Ambassador in London whenever a change is wanted."[48]

Even if Edmond's positive remarks about the Inspector were to be treated with caution, by the early 1930s, Turkey east of the Euphrates was calmer than before. In this regard, Ankara saw this river as a barrier between the two halves of the country. In June 1933, for instance, the EUUM asked the governor of Urfa to continue requiring special permission from travelers, who wanted to cross to the east of the Euphrates.[49] An executive order, issued in September 1935, emphasized this ban, especially *vis-à-vis* foreigners.[50] By the mid-1930s, thanks to Dr Öngören's regime, only two areas east of the Euphrates were not under Ankara's absolute rule. These were Dersim, a rugged landmass along the upper Euphrates tributaries, and Sason, a small, narrow gorge on the anti-Taurus chain.[51] In order to address this, first, Ankara declared the Sason valley a "forbidden zone," to which entry was banned.[52]

With a rocky, mountainous area larger than 6,000 km², Dersim was a much bigger area than Sason. By the mid-1930s, Dersim had a population of as many as 65,000 to 70,000 people.[53] A majority of this was Zaza-speaking Alevi Kurds, who were a minority among the more numerous Kurmançi-speaking Sunni Kurds. In the government's eyes, this set Dersim's population (Dersimlis) apart from the rest of the Kurds. As Alevis, the Dersimlis indeed differed from the majority Sunni Kurds. Since Sunni Islam had traditionally regarded Alevism as a heresy, and while a majority of the conservative Sunni Kurds looked down on the Alevis, the Dersimlis did not associate with the larger Sunni Kurdish community. Their reaction to the Şeyh Said uprising had demonstrated this. At this time, although most Sunni Kurds in Muş, Diyarbakır, and Elazığ had sided with the rebellion, the Alevi Kurds in Dersim and elsewhere had either remained neutral or joined the Turkish army against Şeyh Said.[54] Kemalism's abandonment of Sunni Islam as Turkey's state religion had not only granted the Dersimlis (and other Alevis) equality but also emancipated them. Secularization had freed them from centuries of persecution, rooted in the Ottoman Empire. Hence, it could be expected that Dersimlis and all other Alevis, who had much to gain from Kemalist secularization, would embrace the republic.

According to Ankara, if faith separated the Dersimlis from the rest of the Kurds, so did language. The Dersimlis spoke Zaza, a minority Kurdish language unintelligible to the majority Kurmançi speakers.[55] Consequently, the Kemalists believed that the Dersimlis were ethnically different from the rest of the Kurds. In fact, they contended that the people in Dersim were not genuine Kurds, but Turks, who had assimilated to Kurdishness. A 1936 report, written by General Alpdoğan, the Inspector-General of Tunceli (Dersim) province, and the Commander of Tunceli, supported this.[56] Based "on scientific research and his trips to the area," the General-Commander asserted that the inhabitants of Dersim were ethnic Turks.[57] Such views on Dersim region had also been popular during the 1920s. A report[58] written by the Speaker of the TBMM, Abdülhâlik Renda had argued that the Dersimlis were Turks, who thought of themselves as Kurds due to their Alevi faith.[59] Kâzım Karabekir, one of the commanders of the Turkish Independence campaign, had also argued that the Dersimlis were of Turkish origin.[60] Hence, according to Ankara, the Zaza Alevis of Dersim had a weaker claim than the Sunni Kurmançis to Kurdishness.

Nonetheless, by the 1930s, Dersim was neither a devotedly Turkish area of the country nor an exemplary province. In addition to its unique ethno-religious identity, the region's traditionally autonomous and tribal culture contributed to its rogue character. An American diplomat noted in 1931 that "the mountaineers in this region, organized as bandits," were "terrorizing the surrounding country." These people were "within the fatherland but outside the law."[61] A 1934 report[62] by Hilmi Ergeneli, who succeeded Dr Öngören as the Inspector-General between 1933 and 1935, elaborated further

> The vagabond units of the Dersim tribes roam the districts of Sivas, Erzincan, and Elazığ for plunder. However, it cannot be said that the government has actual control over them. Although, certain government organs state that there has been no progress in the political goals and activities of these people, it has been reported that pro-Kurdish propaganda is being carried out among the Dersimlis and that various foreign spies have been in touch with this region.
>
> (Prime Minister's Republican Archives—Turkey
> [hereafter BCA], KL 69 D 457 EN, 25)

Ankara believed that Dersim was an area of lawlessness that needed to be tamed. A report that Prime Minister İnönü wrote after his trip to Eastern Turkey in 1935,[63] argued

> We will establish the Dersim province according to a new method. An active duty lieutenant general will be its governor, and uniformed active duty officers will be its district governors. Whenever possible, retired officers will be given the position of government employees. The governorship will be organized as an army corps headquarters, suitable for this goal, and it will have branches for security, roads, finance, economics, justice, culture, and health. The matter of justice will be simple, private, and absolute.... Excluding the fixed gendarme units, there will be at least seven mobile gendarme battalions under the governorship.... Roads and army stations will be built in 1935 and 1936. If ready by the spring of 1937, two organized army divisions will be put under the authority of the governorship. All Dersim will be swiftly cleansed of arms.... Then, shall begin the ensuing process of shaping up Dersim.
>
> (Öztürk, "21 Ağustos 1935, İsmet
> Paşa'nın Kürt Raporu," 437)

In view of that, on December 25, 1935, the TBMM passed "Tunceli Kanunu" (Tunceli Law).[64] A decree (2–3823) of January 1936 set up the Fourth Inspectorate-General. Tunceli (the former Dersim district, now made a province with a new name), Elazığ, Bingöl (the former Genç province now renamed Çapakçur), and Erzincan provinces were included in this Inspectorate.[65]

The relative success of the First Inspectorate had prompted the government to propose the Inspectorate for Tunceli. However, a major difference between these two was that while the First Inspectorate had been a civilian organization, the Tunceli Inspectorate was a military affair. The appointee to this post was an army corps commander who would "retain his contact with the army and the benefits of the authority of his military rank." He would be "entrusted with the execution of death sentences, except those subject to appeal." Şükrü Kaya argued that the "reorganization of the Vilayet of Tunceli" was necessary since Tunceli was a tribal and backward region, similar to "areas in France, Italy and in Greece." Backwardness here explained "the failure of the previous attempts to cope with the people of Dersim." Now, the "republic had decided to establish within this zone the civilized organization enjoyed by the country as a whole."[66] Thus, Ankara's approach toward Tunceli was as much about modernization, centralization, and de-feudalization as it was about nationalism.

The Tunceli Inspectorate's mandate covered Dersim's neighboring provinces. This was an attempt to encircle the area. In accordance with this, in March 1936, the General Directorate for Citizenship Matters (Vatandaşlık İşleri Umum Müdürlüğü—VİUM) wrote to the Third Inspectorate-General in Trabzon. Turks from the Kelkit district of Gümüşhane, and the Tercan district of Erzincan were to be resettled in "Erzincan, to enhance an important urban Turkish center like Erzincan, which lay to the north of an area inhabited by the Kurds."[67]

Once in place, the Fourth Inspectorate focused on building roads, bridges, and *gendarme* stations throughout the region. Now, Ankara's power was felt more strongly here.[68] It appeared that the government would finally crush Dersim's feudal chiefs and independent tribes. Soon enough, Dersim rebelled in the spring of 1937. A band of Kurdish rebels destroyed a bridge and then killed a party of officers. Next, a federation of tribes issued an ultimatum to the government that "no posts of troops or gendarmerie should be established in the Dersim, that no bridges should be built, that no administrative units should be organized." They also requested that they be permitted to continue carrying their guns and added, "They should continue to meet their taxes, as in the past, through bargaining on the part of their chiefs."[69]

Ankara acted with full force to crush the uprising. Around 25,000 soldiers in four army divisions, a cavalry regiment, and *gendarmerie* units were deployed.[70] These units were accompanied by twenty warplanes, one of which was flown by Sabiha Gökçen (1913–2001), Atatürk's adopted daughter, and the world's first female fighter pilot. Nevertheless, the government was faced with a challenge. The mountainous terrain of the region made it difficult for the troops to gain bridgeheads. Moreover, poor transportation and communication links disabled the logistics of the Turkish operation. These factors gave the tribesmen, who fought a guerilla war, the upper hand during the summer of 1937.

At this time, Seyid Rıza, the leader of the uprising and a tribal chieftain, appealed for international help. On June 30, he wrote a letter to the British Foreign Secretary, which he signed "Le Généralissimeau Dersim." With a nationalist rhetoric, Rıza argued that his people had risen against Ankara's assimilation efforts:

> *Depuis des années le gouvernement Turc tente d'assimiler le peuple Kurde et dans ce but opprime ce peuple, interdisant les journaux et les publications de langue Kurde, persécutant les gens qui parlent leur langue d'origine, organisant des émigrations forcées et systématiques des territoires fertiles du Kurdistan aux territoires incultes de l'Anatolie où ces émigrés périrent en grand nombre.*

(FO, 371/20864/E5529)

Rıza emphasized the ferocity of the Turkish forces and mentioned the use of chemical gas and weapons as well as the bombing of civilians and villages. Even then, his efforts did not bring any help. Still, the Kurds were able to hold on to their bases and inflict damage on the Turkish forces. Even General Alpdoğan admitted, "The casualties on the Turkish side had been heavier than amongst the Kurds."[71]

The government was alarmed by the situation. Besides, the Fourth Inspectorate had evidence that "suspicious characters from the south, among whom was an Armenian" had recently entered Tunceli. Ankara worried that the uprising could be linked to groups in Syria, such as the Armenians.[72] Additionally, the government had determined earlier that "a few Armenians" lived in Tunceli "here and there."[73] This added to fears about Armenian complicity in the event, exacerbated when Turkish forces captured some Armenians among the rebels in September 1937.[74]

By late 1937, Ankara changed its strategy. As winter approached, the government decided not to penetrate any further into the region. Now, the goal was a slow but full-scale mop-up operation. Accordingly, "no attempt would be made to occupy the whole disaffected area in 1937." Instead, the Turkish forces would "advance to a given line…and stop there, while measures to pacify the land win over the Kurds would be initiated." The army encircled the area to logistically suffocate the tribal resistance.[75] The siege of winter 1937 cut the rebels' supply lines and seriously decreased their capabilities. In the summer of 1938, the army advanced into Tunceli. British diplomats noted that, it attacked indiscriminately and caused many civilians casualties.[76] After much bloodshed on both sides, the Turkish forces finally crushed the uprising in October 1938, a month before Atatürk's death.[77]

As High Kemalism under Atatürk ended, so did the last of the Kurdish uprisings in Turkey for many decades to come. After the subjugation of Tunceli in October 1938, Eastern Turkey entered a long period of calm. Professor Hans Henning von der Osten, a German archaeologist who traveled though this area in 1938, somewhat naively described the background of the long peace that would prevail until the 1980s:

> The Kurds…are generally abandoning their nomadic mode of life and settling in villages, have come to take pride in considering themselves citizens of Turkey, frequently intermarry with the Turkish population, send their

children to the Government schools, and have come to constitute a loyal and law-abiding element in the population.

(SD, 867.00/3060)

However, to the extent that they seemed to be docile, the Kurds were also aloof toward the republic. A sign of this was their lack of participation in the CHP's organizational structure. By 1938, the CHP had branches in all Turkish provinces except for all those east of the Euphrates, including Ağrı, Bingöl, Bitlis, Diyarbakır, Elazığ, Hakkâri, Mardin, Muş Siirt, Van, Tunceli, and Urfa.[78] That Turkey's ruling party was established in none of the predominantly Kurdish provinces is striking. High Kemalism had made the Kurds into obedient yet inactive members of the republic.

High Kemalist policy toward the Circassians and other Caucasus Muslims

While Kemalism acted harshly to assimilate the Kurds, it resorted to more benign means toward the lesser Muslim minorities. Ankara watched the minor Muslim groups with caution and monitored any nationalist activities. This called for a cultural policy. For instance, the government banned publications in Muslim minority languages. Accordingly, on June 9, 1932, it outlawed the entry of a Circassian primer in Latin characters into Turkey.[79] Circassian nationalist publications were also targeted. For example, a government order of December 27, 1937 forbade "The Caucasus Quarterly," a Circassian journal published in Paris.[80]

Meanwhile, Ankara observed anti-government activities among the Circassians at home and abroad. It especially followed Çerkes (Circassian) Ethem, an early hero of the Independence War. Ethem had joined the Turkish campaign against the Greeks in 1919–20, together with his brothers and a powerful band of Circassian irregulars. Later, he had connected his forces to the Green Army, a coalition of nationalist, "Islamic, anti-Imperialist, corporatist and socialist" forces. This political body had been established with Atatürk's approval to boost the morale in the nationalist camp.[81] Soon, however, Ethem had become a powerful figure in it. In reaction, Atatürk had disbanded the Green Army. Then, Ethem had broken from the nationalist forces. In January 1921, when Ankara had ordered him to disband his forces, Ethem had refused and mutinied. After an unsuccessful campaign against the Kemalists, he had fled and taken refuge with the Greeks. Following this, a Circassian Congress was held in Greek-held Izmir, attended by Ethem and other Circassians. Those at the meeting claimed that the Circassians, who were Aryans, were members of the White race, which had created civilizations. As such, they were grateful for the protection extended to them by the Greek authorities in Anatolia.[82] Despite this and various other Greek efforts to court them,[83] however, most Circassians remained loyal to the Kemalists. Yet, the republic explained Ethem's treason through his national origin. In addition to the Ethem incident, a 1920 Düzce uprising by the Abkhazes, the Circassians' ethnic kin, sharpened the government's fears about the loyalty of these people to the republic.[84] In the 1930s, Ankara had worries that Ethem, who had settled in Trans-Jordan, would lead the Circassians to ally with the Armenians and the Kurds to assassinate Atatürk or other leaders of the republic. Consequently, Ankara observed the nationalist activities of diaspora Circassians as well as those at home.[85]

One such case of Circassian conspiracy started in 1935. On August 14, the British Foreign Office in London informed Ambassador Loraine that, "a report has reached H.M.G. from a source whose reliability cannot be guaranteed, but which may be well-informed, that a group of Turkish and Kurdish terrorists sailed from Beirut on July 1930 with the intention of making an attempt on the life of the President of Turkey."[86] On August 16, the Turkish government issued an alert on this issue to its local authorities. Ankara also noted that a band of Circassian assassins from Trans-Jordan and an Armenian from Athens would enter Turkey to join these efforts.[87]

Consequently, the republic became extremely wary toward the Circassian diaspora. Many intelligence reports tracking the activities of Circassians abroad appeared in the summer and fall of 1935.[88] For example, on September 15, Ankara informed the Aegean and Western provinces that Ethem, his brother Emin, and "twenty people, of whom about 9–10 are Circassians and the rest, Armenians" were on Eşek Adası (Aghatonissi), in the Dodecanese islands, right across the Turkish coast in the Aegean.[89] In another case, on August 20, the EİUM notified Istanbul and Bolu provinces that a certain "Circassian Cemil," who had recently entered the country from Greece, needed to be screened since he had been "mischievous" in Western Thrace, where he lived.[90]

Ankara was also cautious toward Circassians from Syria, given the fact that the French authorities there were known to be harboring Circassian nationalists. For instance, on March 29, 1932, the EUUM replied to an earlier letter from the governor of Maraş regarding his request for permission to deport "Circassian Sadettin," a man of Syrian citizenship to Syria. If Sadettin were a suspicious and harmful person, then his domicile in "our country is undesired," said the dispatch.[91] Similarly, on November 12, 1938, Ankara wrote to the governor of Izmir about a certain "Circassian Kemal Rıza" of Syrian nationality. The authorities were to follow this person's movement within Turkey and observe his contacts.[92]

Native Circassians were followed, too. Especially after the discovery of the 1935 assassination conspiracy, the government scrutinized the activities of Turkish Circassians, whom it found suspicious.[93] An example was a certain "Circassian Osman, son of İlyas." On September 13, the EİUM warned the governor of Çanakkale to keep him under watch.[94] In another communiqué, on October 2, Ankara asked the "Southern provinces with Circassian populations" to be careful about the activities of those Circassians implicated in nationalism.[95] The dispatch also pointed at the possibility of collaboration between Circassian nationalists, Kurds and Hoybûn.[96] Then, on October 12, Ankara wrote to the governors of Afyon and Antalya about Circassians there. A report from the governor of Kütahya had noted that, "Many Circassians have left Kütahya for Afyon and Antalya to work in railway building." Ankara asked Afyon and Antalya to "keep these Circassians under close surveillance, especially their links with mischievous people abroad." Since it was likely that "mischievous people who had entered our country would be among these workers," the EİUM wanted caution on this.[97] In another example of alertness, on October 15, the government asked a vast number of provinces to be diligent in following and apprehending possible assassins. Bolu province, which had a large Circassian population, was especially responsible to "heavily investigate Circassians, who would travel to Ankara."[98]

Such qualms about the Circassians fed doubts toward other Caucasus groups, too. Among them were the Lazes. Even before 1935, they had been on the government's radar screen. For example, on July 17, 1933, EİUM wrote to the governor of Çoruh, concerning a certain "Ahmed of Erbaa." Since it had been determined that Ahmed had engaged in "Lazeism activities," he needed to be sent to Ankara for interrogation.[99] Besides, the government believed that Athens had established an anti-Turkish alliance of Lazes, Circassians, and Pontic Greeks to restore the Caliphate. Such a front would have been appealing for the Lazes, generally conservative Muslims, who had been obstinate in their refusal to hail secularism. In view of this, Ankara monitored the Lazes, since it considered them suspicious due to their links with the pro-Caliphate movement, Pontic Greeks, Circassians, Athens, or all of them.[100]

In view of this perceived conspiracy, even Muslim Georgians, the Lazes' neighbors, were considered dubious.[101] For example, on September 15, 1935, the EİUM asked the Governor of Çoruh, a province with a large Laze and Muslim Georgian community, whether there were "any previous inhabitants of Hopa or the Gümüş village of Rize," who lived on the Greek island of Lesbos (Midilli). "If there are any former residents of your province living in foreign countries now, information is needed on how and when these people have left the country" said the letter. The dispatch asked the governor to track "the situation of Lazes, Georgians and other suspicious elements, who live within your province and who have the potential to cause harm."[102] Next, on August 14, Ankara inquired from the Governor of Istanbul about the suspicious activities of a Georgian named Hasan in İzmit.[103] Since this man had been contacting the Armenians in İzmit and while he was connected to the assassination attempts, his case needed to be investigated.

Ankara's attentiveness toward the Circassians, Lazes, and Muslim Georgians widened to include almost all Caucasus Muslims, including the Chechens.[104] In an example along this line, on September 5, 1935, for example, the EİUM asked the governors of Kocaeli, Balıkesir, Aydın, and Çanakkale, provinces with sizable large Caucasus communities, to report their estimate of "firearms in the hands of civilians, especially in those areas, populated by the Lazes, Georgians, Abkhazes, Lezgis, and Circassians."[105] In this regard, even the non-Caucasus groups came under scrutiny for their links with the Circassians. For instance, Ankara deemed a certain Jew, "David, who lived in Haifa" and worked in a construction business, doubtful. David, who had entered Turkey and had been arrested, had "confessed to giving money to Circassian Ethem."[106] Additionally, a Cretan Muslim, "Mehmet, son of Mahmud," who had close links with the Circassians, was also implicated in the Circassian assassination conspiracy.[107]

High Kemalist policy toward the Nusayris, and the Hatay Conundrum

The Nusayris, also called Alawites, are Arabic-speaking heterodox Muslims whose faith shows similarities to that of Alevis. A significant number of them live today in Southern Turkey, around the Mersin and Iskenderun Bays. The story of the Nusayris in the 1930s is a unique and entertaining juxtaposition of the *Turkish History Thesis* with Turkey's geopolitical ambitions. In the late 1930s, the government claimed that the Nusayris were ethnic Turks who descended from the Hittites.[108] This was closely linked to the events in the Sancak of Alexandratta, (henceforth Sancak), an autonomous part of interwar French Syria, which had a population of mostly Turks, Nusayris, and other Arabs, as well as Christian groups. Although the Turks were the largest community in the Sancak, and the Nusayris the second, neither group comprised a clear majority in the Sancak's population. Ankara hoped that depicting the Nusayris as Turks, and winning them over to the Turkish side would help secure a "Turkish majority" for controlling the Sancak, before the province fell under Syrian rule as per Franco-Syrian agreements in the late 1930s.

The Sancak was a wealthy Mediterranean enclave. Until the end of the First World War, it had been an Ottoman administrative unit (sancak) within the vilayet of Aleppo. At the end of the First World War, the Franco-Turkish armistice line of October 21, 1918 had cut through it.[109] However, in 1920 the French had violated the armistice line. They had gathered a Syrian legion among the Armenian deportees from Cilicia and Asia Minor, and launched an invasion of the Sancak and Cilicia. When a 1921 counter-attack by Turkish forces had pushed them out of Cilicia, the French had remained in control of the Sancak.[110]

During the ensuing peace negotiations between Paris and Ankara, the Kemalist government had objected to French control of the region and had brought up the issue of the large Turkish community here. The wealth of the enclave made it attractive too. İskenderun (Alexandratta), the Sancak's largest city, was a bustling, cosmopolitan Levantine port. Antakya (Antioch), its second largest town, was on fertile farmland, along the Asi (Orontes) River. The Ankara (Franklin–Bouillon) Treaty of October 20, 1921 had taken a middle position on the Sancak's ownership. While the accord left the Sancak in French-mandated Syria, it satisfied some Turkish concerns.[111] It called "for the establishment of a special administrative regime for the district of Alexandratta"[112] and gave the Turkish language official recognition there. It also obliged the French to "appoint Turkish officials in those regions with a Turkish majority" and "set up schools for the promotion of Turkish culture."[113] Additionally, in a symbolic recognition of the Sancak's separate sovereignty from Syria, the treaty allowed the district to have a special flag. In return, Turkey gave up its rights on the region. In 1920, the League of Nations granted France the mandate for Syria and Lebanon.[114] Then, at Lausanne, Ankara renounced "all rights and title whatsoever over or respecting the territories to the south of this [Turco-Syrian] frontier."[115]

Relations between Turkey and French Syria in the 1930s

Nevertheless, the relations between France and Turkey remained cool. Throughout the 1920s and the 1930s, Ankara had reason to believe that Quai d'Orsay was using Syria as a logistics base for various anti-Turkish groups. American diplomats reported in 1931 that as part of their designs *vis-à-vis* Turkey, the French mandate authorities were resettling Armenian refugees along Syria's border with Turkey to create an Armenian government there.[116] A Turkish report added that the French were

> Courting the Hoybûnist Armenians, Jacobites, and Kurds and planning to create a Christian majority in Elcezire [El Jeziraah, Mesopotamia] with the intent of establishing a buffer state there, taking Elcezire under control, and using this buffer state against Turkey and Syria, and that the French allowed the elements in Elcezire to cross the border into Turkey for thievery and vagabondism.
>
> (DV, EUM 1.G.3/31268)

The Sancak controversy of the late 1930s

The already sour relations between Ankara and Paris deteriorated further in the mid-1930s, once the Sancak issue came under the spotlight. At that time, nationalists in Syria were agitating against French colonial rule. In 1936, Paris agreed to grant Damascus independence. The draft of the Franco-Syrian treaty drawn in 1936 stipulated that, "Sancak would remain autonomous under Syrian sovereignty."[117] This angered Turkey and started the Sancak debate. On October 9, 1936, in a diplomatic note, Ankara asked if France would consider having negotiations with the Turkish inhabitants of the Sancak, separate from those with Syria.[118] Paris replied the next day that it was prepared to grant the Sancak autonomy within a future Syria.[119] When on October 23, France and Syria signed a friendship and alliance treaty,[120] asserting that the Sancak would become a part of Syria, though with a special status,[121] the Turks protested. In his speech to the parliament on November 1, Atatürk announced

> A prominent and important matter that keeps our nation occupied every day and every night, nowadays is the fate of 'İskenderun–Antakya' and its vicinity, whose genuine owners are pure Turks (*bravos, applauses*). We need to approach this issue seriously and with gravity (*prolonged standing ovation, bravos, hoorays*).
>
> (*Atatürk'ün Söylev Demeçleri*, vol. 1, 410)

Ankara wanted the district to become an autonomous, if not independent, pro-Turkish buffer zone between Turkey and Syria.[122] However, according to the figures provided by the French mandate officers in 1936, the Turks were only 39 percent of the Sancak's population of 219,000. The rest of the population was

28 percent Nusayri Arab, 11 percent Armenian, 10 percent Sunni Arab, and 8 percent other Christians. (The remaining 4 percent comprised of Kurds, Circassians, Jews, and others.)[123] Although the Sancak was 80 percent Muslim, it was not majority Turkish. Moreover, it had a nearly equal number of Arabic and Turkish speakers. It seemed that for a valid argument in favor of the Sancak's independence from Syria, a majority of the district needed to be Turkish. To achieve this, Ankara adopted a policy of recognizing the Nusayris as Turks. High Kemalist ideologues started writing about them and the Sancak with a nationalist twist. The *History Thesis* emerged on the scene. First, the name of the Sancak became Hatay, after the ancient Hittites. Then, its inhabitants became "Eti Türkleri" (Hittite Turks) in the official parlance of the republic.[124]

Agop Dilaçar produced a book to substantiate these claims: *Alpin Irk, Türk Etnisi, ve Hatay Halkı* (The Alpine Race, Turkish Ethnie and the People of Hatay).[125] According to him, Sancak's name had been Hatay in the Neo-Hittite period. Now, the district could revert to its original name. Dilaçar added that anthropologically, there was no difference between the people of Anatolia and those of Hatay.[126] Both belonged to the Inner-Asian (*innerasiatisch*) type of the Alpine race, a category also called the Near Asian (*vorderasiatcish*) race or *Homo Tauricus*. Hatay was full of archaeological and anthropological traces of this race. The inhabitants of Hatay, even those who spoke Arabic, were not Semitic; rather, they were the descendants of the ancient Hittites.[127] Since, according to the *History Thesis*, the ancient Hittites were Turks, these Arabic-speaking inhabitants of Hatay were Turks, too.

Prof. Hasan Reşit Tankut (1891–1980) a Turkologist, continued further. In his work, titled, *Nusayriler ve Nusayrilik Hakkında* (About the Nusayris and Nusayrism),[128] Tankut argued that anthropologically, historically, and ethnographically, there was no doubt that the Nusayris were the descendants of the Alpine Hittites of Asia Minor.[129] They had spoken Turkish until the persecution of their cult belief by Sultan Selim II during the Ottoman era.[130] Only then, had they switched to Arabic in reaction to Ottoman policies.[131] This was music to the regime's ears: in April 1938, the CHP sent a copy of Tankut's book to all the People's Houses branches in the country.[132]

In the meantime, the Franco-Turkish dispute continued to evolve. On January 11, 1937, Ankara presented to Paris a memorandum, outlining its thesis, that Hatay, Syria, and Lebanon were confederate states and, as such, Hatay had the right to determine its future.[133] Surprisingly, the French replied with a conciliatory letter.[134] Upon Paris' proposal, Turkey and France submitted their differences to the League of Nations. On January 27, 1937, the League adopted a resolution[135] that Hatay be made into a "separate entity." Although "the State of Syria" would "be responsible for the conduct of its foreign affairs," Hatay would have "full independence in its internal affairs."[136] The League asked Ankara and Paris to agree on a treaty to facilitate this.[137] A Franco-Turkish commission was formed to discuss Hatay's future. This culminated in a long negotiation process through the winter of 1937. At this time, nationalist Turks and the Arabs were at odds: most Turks wished to see total independence, and most Arabs wanted incorporation into Syria.[138] Meanwhile, sentiments rose in Turkey over the Hatay issue.[139] The daily *Cumhuriyet* initiated a nationalist campaign in favor of Hatay's annexation to Turkey.[140] Atatürk commented that the Hatay issue had become an indispensable cause for him.[141] During the summer of 1937, Ankara amassed 30,000 troops on its border with Hatay.[142] Finally, Turkey and France reached an agreement. On May 29, they signed a treaty for an independent Hatay state, whose territorial integrity they guaranteed.[143] The accord gave Hatay a constitution and an army,[144] with 1,000 local soldiers and 2,500 more from the Turkish and the French forces, each. The Turkish troops entered Hatay on July 5.[145]

France was lenient toward Turkey on this issue since, together with the United Kingdom, it desired to keep Ankara content and away from a possible alliance with the Axis. Hence, subsequent to their agreement on Hatay, Ankara and Paris signed a friendship treaty on June 23, 1937.[146] The two countries were joined by the United Kingdom and became allies in the Mediterranean against fourth parties.[147] In support of the Franco-Turkish friendship, in May 1937, Minister Kaya wrote to the governors of Istanbul, Izmir, and Adana (Seyhan) asking them to convey the importance of this alliance to the chief editors of Turkish newspapers in their provinces.[148]

In the interim, the independent Hatay state was established on November 29, 1937. The Franco-Turkish agreement mandated by the League of Nations, stipulated that the future state of Hatay would have a parliament whose members would be determined in a two-stage election. Article 17 of The League of Nations regulations on this matter said that in the first stage, electors "shall register...as members of one of the following communities: 'Turkish community', 'Alawite community', 'Arab community', Armenian community', Greek-Orthodox community', Kurdish community', 'other communities'."[149] Article 32 added, "For each community, there shall be one elector at the second stage for 100 duly registered electors at the first stage."[150]

Following this, the new Hatay government started a population registry, which quickly turned into a politicized census. That prompted nationalist mobilization and agitations, which led to communal violence in 1938. Arab nationalists organized in the League of National Action rallied to keep Hatay part of Syria and make sure that the Arabs would have a majority in the registry process. In this, Christian Arabs and Armenians joined the Muslim Arabs.[151] There were reports that some Kurds and Circassians too, connected to this front.[152] Still, the Armenians were especially strong in this camp. On February 5, 1938, for instance, Ankara wrote to Tayfur Sökmen (1892–1980), a Hatay Turk, an MP in TBMM between 1935 and 1938, and the first president of Hatay republic: twenty Armenian Tashnaks had left Beirut for Hatay to agitate for the Arab cause there.[153]

On the other hand, although France had taken a conciliatory attitude toward Turkey, now it seemed to complicate the matters. A letter by the EİUM on February 13, 1938 noted that the French were arming the members of the Kurdish Hoybûn, Armenian Tashnak organizations, as well as the Assyrians to "provoke various elements against Turkishness."[154] The French seemed to have approached the Nusayris, too.[155] They were also trying to recruit the Circassians.

On January 7, 1938, the Emniyet Umum Müdiriyeti—EUM wrote that the French were interested in bringing Çerkes Ethem, the hero of Circassian nationalists and a staunch opponent of Kemalist Turkey, to Hatay to win over the Circassians there.[156]

Turkey helped the Hatay Turks. Ankara had envisaged that Hatay would become an independent Turkish state, and worked actively toward this goal. On August 13, 1937, Ankara wrote: "In reference to Hatay's fate, it is a given and compulsory fact that we need to take advantage of those Hatay Turks in Turkey so that the Turks in Hatay may gain the majority in the elections."[157] The government asked the local authorities to make lists of all employees who were originally from Hatay. These would be sent over to Hatay for population registry. In a similar memo on January 4, 1938, Ankara threatened action against Turks of Hatay origin who were unwilling to go to Hatay to register and vote.[158] In another communiqué, it pointed at İskenderun as "the weakest point in the Turkish community of Hatay." Sökmen was to work on this.[159]

Turkey and the Hatay Turks were joined in these efforts by some of the Circassians and the Nusayris.[160] In accordance with the *History Thesis*, Ankara had been considering the Nusayris to be ethnic Turks. As Hatay's second largest ethnic group, they were vital for the Turkish plans. Their cooperation would give the Turks a numerical majority in Hatay. Consequently, Ankara launched a campaign to win the Nusayris. The government favored the Turkish Nusayris to show to those in Hatay that life would be good for them under its rule. On May 29, 1937, the EİUM recommended the governor of Adana to treat well "our Turkish brothers, the so called Alevis, who we know are united with us in race."[161] The union of Turks and Alevis in Syria would "give the Turks a numerical majority in Hatay against the alliance of the Christians and the Armenians." Then, Ankara courted the Nusayris in Turkey with the hope of getting their brothers in Hatay to support the Turkish cause.[162]

Ankara took further steps toward this end. On January 10, 1937, it informed the governor of Adana that, "It has been decided to elect a Nusayri to the parliament." The governor was asked, "to suggest the name of a person in Adana or Mersin, who has contributed to the national movement, whose connection to Turkishness and our national revolution is undoubted, and who is influential among the Nusayris."[163] He replied on January 14: even in the worst days of the French occupation, when "Turkishness seemed to have collapsed beyond recovery," the Nusayris had allied with the Turks. While others had taken advantage of the situation and "betrayed the motherland and Turkishness," the Nusayris "had strictly refused the most appealing and glimmering proposals by the French."[164] The letter ended with a list of four Nusayri candidates for the TBMM. In the interim, Turkey courted the Nusayri notables in Hatay for influence over the masses.[165] For instance, on May 24, 1938, Ankara wrote that Sökmen "would present as gifts seven pistols to the Alevi notables of the Harbiye, Süveydiye, and Karamut sub-districts of Antakya."[166]

Ankara's attitude led some of the Nusayris in Hatay to register as Turks for the elections. Still, the competition between the Arabs and the Turks was tough.

Especially following Ankara's activities to promote Hatay-born Turks to return to the region, skirmishes broke out between Arab and Turkish militia. The People's Houses established in Hatay played an active role in this process.[167] Then, during the summer of 1938, the French interfered with a helping hand for the Turks and cracked down on the Arab League of National Action. Finally, the registry ended and the results were declared. In the Hatay parliament, which had 40 representatives, the Turks would have 22, Nusayris 9, Armenians 5, Sunni Arabs 2, and the Melchites 2 seats.[168] Since the Turks had the majority in the parliament, they would dominate the political life of the short-lived Hatay republic.[169]

Subsequently, Hatay was gradually incorporated into Turkey. First, its legal code was synchronized with Turkey's. For example, on October 15, 1938, Ankara sent a draft citizenship law to Sökmen, then Hatay's president. This code, based on the Turkish Citizenship Law of 1928, was to be adopted immediately.[170] Second, on December 31, Turkey's new Minister of Interior Affairs, Refik Saydam, asked Sökmen to make sure that Turkish would be the official language of the State of Hatay.[171] Third, Hatay adopted the Turkish Lira as its currency and started using stamps issued by the Turkish Postal Authority.[172] At last, following a Franco-Turkish agreement, on June 23, 1939,[173] the Hatay parliament voted to join Turkey.[174]

An exodus of anti-Turkish groups accompanied this event.[175] An estimated 22,000 Armenians; 10,000 Nusayris; 10,000 Sunni Arabs; and 5,000 Christian Arabs left Hatay for Syria during 1938–39.[176] Now that the Turks were a demographic majority in Turkey's newest province, the government reversed its policy of courting the Nusayris. In a letter to Sökmen on December 31, 1938, Ankara wrote that since there were also "Arabs, Armenians, Orthodox, Kurds, Circassians in Hatay, who were Sunnis or belonged to various Christian denominations," the sympathy thus far shown to Alevis needed to be terminated in order to not offend these others.[177] Another change *vis-à-vis* the Nusayris was in Turkification policies. All this time, the Kemalists had been arguing that the Nusayris were Turkish. Now, after the termination of its strategic alliance with the Nusayris, Ankara could insist that they be taught Turkish. This would help them merge into Turkishness. On July 26, 1938, the government initiated this policy and made funds available for it.[178] In a specific case, on August 8, Ankara allocated 10,000 TL for the Adana and İçel provinces so that Nusayris there could be taught Turkish.[179]

High Kemalist policies toward the Arabs and the Albanians

Although Ankara favored the Nusayris between 1936 and 1938, this did not mean that it would take a pusillanimous attitude toward the other Arabs in the country. On the contrary, while the challenge of Arab nationalism in Hatay exacerbated Ankara's vigilance, the government constantly monitored the Arabs and their nationalist activities. Ankara collected information about Arabs, whom it considered a security threat. For example, in October 1935, the EİUM informed the governor of Adana about "Şükrü, the Arab," who had been traveling with Saadettin Haydar, and who was a suspected spy. Ankara wanted him to be followed closely.[180] In other cases of surveillance on Arabs, in 1936, Şükrü Kaya sent a report to Recep Peker about a certain "Dr. Nuri Fehmi Ayberik, from Gaziantep," the president of the City Club of Gaziantep. This man had appropriated the People's House garden in Gaziantep for the exclusive use of the City Club, causing grievance in town. Action was necessary on Ayberik also since he was an Arab from Basra who had a bad character, and was known to be carrying "Arab feelings and spirit."[181] In another example of vigilance on Arab nationalism, in October 1937, the EİUM alerted the First Inspectorate-General, and the governors of Urfa and Mardin, about a certain "Hüseyin, son of Mehmed, who lived in the Mucipli village of the Nusretiye sub-district of Harran." This man had been agitating among the Arabs against the Turks. Additionally, he had traveled to Mardin and Viranşehir to meet with Arabs. Ankara asked the authorities for an exhaustive investigation on Hüseyin's "nationality, citizenship, actual domicile, past history, and contacts at home and abroad."[182]

In addition to Arabs, other Muslim minorities were also monitored for possible anti-government and nationalist activities. A notable group was the Albanians. For example, in May 1936, the EİUM wrote to the Inspectorates-General and the provinces. After pointing at the latest political troubles in Albania, the dispatch said there was a possibility that a member of the Ottoman dynasty might become the King of Albania. This necessitated extra caution toward Albanians coming to Turkey. Besides, there was evidence that an Albanian assassin would soon enter the country to kill Atatürk. Moreover, Bektashi babas (religious community leaders) would allegedly be sent from Albania to get in touch with their Turkish counterparts. In view of this, Ankara warned the authorities to be extremely vigilant toward Albanians visiting Turkey and the possible links that they might have in the country.[183]

In a specific correspondence about Albanian nationalism, on November 6, 1936, the Minister of Interior replied to an inquiry by the CHP's Secretary General about possible nationalist activities by Albanians. Following a review of high-ranking Albanian government employees, an investigation on Albanians in Ankara and the potential links of these people to nationalist organizations, the Ministry had determined that none of these men had the potential to "possess a political idea." There was no risk that Albanian nationalist circles existed in Ankara.[184]

Conclusion

Throughout the 1930s, Turkey used a variety of precautionary means toward her Muslim minorities. In this regard, the Kurds, the largest and the least-assimilated Muslim minority, were singled out. The government targeted Kurdish tribalism in order to incorporate vestiges of Kurdish autonomy, such as Dersim, into the republic. In addition, Turkey closely monitored the lesser Muslim groups. Ankara was careful about the anti-government and nationalist activities among them. It appears that in the 1930s, the government followed a double-pronged policy *vis-à-vis* the Muslim minorities. It persistently pursued the assimilation of these groups, while observing nationalist activities among them with caution. In this regard, Turkey saw nominal Islam (the Muslim identity and culture shared by these groups) as the glue that bonded them to the Turkish nation. Even under staunch secularism, Islam carved the way to Turkishness for these groups. The cultural, military, and administrative means that were available to Ankara under High Kemalism helped catalyze this process. Thus, it appears that in the 1930s, Kemalism had most of the ingredients as well as the ideal circumstances to ferment the Anatolian Muslims into a national community. In other words, the 1930s presented Ankara with a golden chance to amalgamate the rump Muslim millet into the Turkish national community. The PKK insurgency in the 1980s, and the full-scale Turkish nationalist reaction to it in the 1990s would reveal that, with the exception of parts of the Kurdish community, Turkey would indeed succeed in bringing all Anatolian Muslims into the fold of Turkishness. Herein lie Kemalism's success and its predicament.

7 Ethno-religious limits of Turkishness

Christians excluded from the nation

> This program of Minorities is essentially the latest phase of a conflict between the radically opposed political ideals; Ottomanism or federation of the heterogeneous, and Turkish or homogenous nationalism.
>
> (Dispatch from the American Embassy in Turkey, December 1938)

A general overview

Relations between Ankara and the Christian minorities improved in the 1930s. The government felt more secure about the Christians. The first sign of this came as early as 1929, when Ankara lifted a ban prohibiting non-Muslims in Istanbul and Izmir from traveling beyond these cities' municipal limits. A government decree of May 8 stipulated, "Non-Muslim Turks are free to travel to spas such as Bursa, Tuzla, Yaluva [sic], Çeşme within the months of May, June, July, August, and September, for health needs and necessities."[1] These restrictions were further relaxed in 1931.[2] Finally, in 1932, Ankara allowed near-complete freedom of movement to non-Muslims. While previously, they had needed "special authorization to travel" and had been "forbidden to exercise property rights outside their place of residence,"[3] now they were allowed to go anywhere in the country, provided they did not stay for more than three months. A symbolic sign of Ankara's ease toward the non-Muslims came in 1933. The daily *Akşam* reported that non-Muslims would

> Henceforth be admitted to the Turkish Sports Federation and may represent Turkey in international competitions. At the same time, it came out that the Red Crescent Society had for some time been extending to non-Moslem schools its distribution of clothing to poor school-children, a practice not heretofore allowed.
>
> (SD, 867.9111/389)

A second aspect of the relations between the government and the Christian minorities in the 1930s was that Ankara got along better with some Christians than the others. For instance, the affairs between Ankara and the Greek community moved in a positive direction in the aftermath of the 1930 Turco-Greek rapprochement. On the other hand, although after the exodus from Southern Turkey, the Armenians had entered a relative period of calm, the relations between them and the government were still marked by tensions. As in the 1920s, Ankara viewed them with caution. Similarly, the Jacobites, Chaldeans, and the Assyrians faced their share of difficulties. Such developments had a direct impact on each Christian community. Accordingly, while the number of Greek-Orthodox individuals increased in this decade, the number of Armenians and other Eastern Christians plummeted. Census data bears testimony to this. Republican surveys do not provide a precise picture on these communities, since the religious categories in the censuses varied from one tally to the next. Nevertheless, the evidence shows an increase in Greek population and a decline in Armenian and other Eastern Christian populations in the 1930s. For instance, while there were 109,905 Greek-Orthodox in 1927, there were 125,046 in 1935,[4] a rise of 13.8 percent.[5] During the same period, the overall Turkish population increased by 22.2 percent, from 13,542,795 to 16,157,450. On the other hand, the number of Armenians and other Eastern Christians, which, excluding the Catholics and Protestants, was 101,740 in 1927,[6] dropped to 60,480 in 1935.[7] That meant a decline of 41.1 percent.

In the interim, Ankara's staunch secularism shaped the affairs between the Catholics and the government. In the 1930s, Ankara disfavored the religious establishments, Islamic and otherwise. Such "anti-clericalism" extended into the realm of affairs with the Vatican. Turkey refused to recognize the Catholic Church. For instance, in 1934, the TBMM issued a law that religious garb could not be worn in public,[8] except by the heads of the recognized religious communities, which excluded Roman Catholics. According to British diplomatic records, the list included

> Rifat, president of Religious Affairs, Angora.
> Photios, Patriarch of the Orthodox Greeks, Constantinople.
> Papa Eftim, head of the Orthodox Turks.
> Mesrop Naroyan, Patriarch of the Gregorian Armenians, Constantinople.
> Vahan Koçaryan, head of the Catholic Armenians, Muş.
> Isak Şaki, *locum tenens* of the Grand Rabbinate, Constantinople.
> Oton Cilaciyan, head of the Armenian Protestant Community, Constantinople.
> Dionysios Varuhas, head of the Catholic Greeks.

(FO, 371/19040/E4264)

Msgr Roncalli, the Apostolic Delegate to Turkey, was not among the privileged ecclesiastics. This was since, in Ankara's eyes, he "is not only a foreign ecclesiastic himself but represents a foreign hierarch of whom this lay State has no official cognizance."[9] Subsequently, Ankara tried to block communication between the Turkish Catholics and the international Catholic community. For example, in October 1937, the government banned a pamphlet titled "Lettre Collective des

Evêques Espagnoles," sent "from Paris to the Jacobite and Chaldean priests in Cizre, and signed by the Spanish cardinals."[10] In the interim, the number of Catholics went from 39,511 in 1927 to 32,155 in 1935, a decrease of 18.6 percent mostly due to emigration.[11] The smaller Protestant community seemed to fare better. Its number, 6,658 in 1927, climbed to 8,486 in 1935, with an increase of 36.4 percent. This rise may have been due to people who had registered themselves as "Christians" earlier now chosing for the "Protestant" option.

Greeks under High Kemalism

Of all the Christian groups in the country, the Greeks were the most comfortable in the 1930s. In the earlier decade, they had been hostage to the bitter relations between Ankara and Athens. Like the Turks in western Thrace, the Greek community in Turkey had not felt welcome. However, this situation changed in the 1930s subsequent to the détente of 1929–30, and the improved relations between Athens and Ankara. Venizelos' aforementioned renunciation of Greek territorial claims *vis-à-vis* Turkey diminished Ankara's perception of a Greek threat. The warm reception of İnönü and Aras in Athens in 1931 further alleviated Ankara's fears.

Another event that shifted Turkey's security perception was that Athens took action against the *Yüzellilikler* (The Group of One-Hundred-Fifty), a group of anti-secularist Muslims and Turks who had been exiled from Turkey in the 1920s. Most of them had lived in Western Thrace, where they led activities against Turkey.[12] Ankara considered the presence of these people along the border a security threat. In 1931, Athens expelled many of the *Yüzellilikler* to Alexandria, Egypt. This was welcome in Ankara as a goodwill gesture and contributed further to the rapprochement.[13] (In fact, Ankara was so relieved by this move, there were even rumors that it would expel the leaders of the breakaway Turkish-Orthodox Church in return.)[14]

Now, Turkey and Greece viewed each other differently. Accordingly, bilateral cultural exchange flourished. For example, on April 11, 1932, a group of 150 Greeks, including the players and fans of the *Apollon* soccer team were allowed to come to Izmir to play against Turkish *Altay* and *Karşıyaka*.[15] Turkish and Greek "university students, journalists, football teams, theatrical companies and political and military leaders exchanged frequent visits."[16] In the meantime, Ankara was careful about the exchangees. When some exchangees who had come to Turkey from Greece, petitioned to travel to Greece, Ankara wrote: "It is likely that this will set up a precedent for the subsequent travel of exchangees from Greece to Turkey," and "open the country's doors wide" for them, who "could come back." Accordingly, the excursion was banned on July 22, 1933.[17] When Greek exchangees did come to Turkey, the government put them under special restrictions. For instance, unlike other Hellenic citizens, exchangee Greeks were allowed to stay in Turkey for up to three months only upon their visit.[18]

In the interim, the *Entente Cordiale* of 1930, "one of the most durable diplomatic engagements concluded during the interwar period,"[19] proved to be a blessing for both the Greek minority in Turkey and the Turks in Greece. Ankara and Athens changed their views of these communities. A symbolic sign came on August 26, 1932, when the Istanbul Greek community organized a fund-raiser dance for its schools. İnönü and Aras attended this event, "fraternizing for several hours with the Greeks."[20] In another example of government ease, the "Greeks were allowed to move freely in the interior of Turkey, a privilege hitherto enjoyed only by the Muslim and Jewish Turkish citizens."[21] In demonstration of this, in May 1933, Ankara wrote to the governors of Trabzon and Erzurum, regarding the journey of Greek (and Armenian) builders, who were Turkish citizens, to Erzurum for the construction of a teacher's school. "Since these men are of Turkish citizenship, they are not subject to obtaining special permission for travel within Turkey" said the communiqué.[22]

Further ameliorating the Greek minority's condition, the government "raised the sequestration on property and bank accounts" owned by them.[23] Besides, the wives, minor children, and unmarried daughters of Istanbul Greeks were allowed to return to the city. Although the *établis* Greeks suffered setbacks after the promulgation of the aforementioned Law Nr 2007, things were relatively better for them too. Many were granted citizenship in the 1930s, in accordance with the lenient attitude of the government (see Chapter 4).

The situation of Bozcaada and Gökçeada Greeks also improved following a 1931 visit by Minister Kaya to the islands. Since Ankara's fears of a Greek attack on Turkish territory were now eliminated, the government abandoned its policy of making life difficult for the insular Greeks, so that they would leave these strategic outposts guarding the Dardanelles.[24] Ankara even allowed some island Greeks who had gone to the United States to return. Meanwhile, on July 29, 1936, Turkey signed the Montreux Treaty with the United Kingdom, France, the Soviet Union, and a number of other powers and Balkan states. This accord abrogated the clauses of the Lausanne Treaty, which had created a special, non-militarized regime for the Turkish Straits, including Bozcaada and Gökçeada. The Western powers acceded to Turkish control of the Straits in return for Ankara's neutrality *vis-à-vis* Nazi Germany. Accordingly, on July 29, 1936, Turkish forces entered the islands. Now that it had absolute control, Ankara permitted the election of Greeks to local administrative posts on the islands.[25]

The crowning act of Turkey's moderation toward the Greek minority came in 1935, when Nikola Taptas, a renowned doctor, and a prominent member of the Greek community, was elected to the TBMM, upon recommendation from the government. Interestingly, however, Taptas did not become a deputy from Istanbul, where 97 percent of the Greeks lived, but from Ankara, where none did. To complicate matters, İstamat Zihni Özdamar, a lawyer and a leader of the Turkish-Orthodox Church,[26] was elected to the TBMM as another representative of the Orthodox community. Although the Turkish-Orthodox Church was a tiny one, the government treated it on par with the Greek-Orthodox Church. Özdamar was a noteworthy choice also since he had set up the aforementioned "Turkish Association of Lay Christians" (Türk Laik Hristiyanlar Birliği), which claimed that the Christians in Turkey were Turks in need of secularization.

After he became a deputy, Özdamar wrote a report promoting the Turkification of non-Muslims. Refusing to call these people "minorities," he contended, "Turkish citizens whose religion is not Islam are Turks." Like Tekin Alp, Özdamar asserted, "All Turkish citizens who take refuge in the Turkish flag and understand the Turkish culture, whose hearts and souls are inspired by the Turkish homeland, are Turks regardless of their denomination, and are an inseparable Turkish whole within the state." He added, since language had a huge impact on feelings, "we Turks would want our children to study altogether in Turkish schools and speak in the Turkish language." Then, "Regardless of their religions, Memet, Dimitri, Kaspar, and Mişon will coalesce in these official schools under the Turkish flag, the Turkish teacher, inspiration, and education, and will be raised as one Turkish element, devoted to his country." Özdamar closed by saying, "I am so happy that I am a Turk."[27] An important part of Özdamar's vision had already been enforced: in 1931, when the government had passed Law Nr 1774 stipulating that, "Children of Turkish nationality who enter school in order to receive primary instruction may attend Turkish schools only."[28] Now, all pupils would learn Turkish at the earliest stage of education. Although, non-Muslim high schools continued to function, in the end, compulsory primary education in Turkish paved the way for linguistic assimilation.

Özdamar's position on Turkification, his election to the TBMM, and Ankara's preferential treatment of the Turkish-Orthodox Church hinted at the government's qualms about the Greek community: Ankara hoped to maintain its leverage over the Greek-Orthodox Church. Hence, the Turkish-Orthodox Church surfaced occasionally during the 1930s. For example, in 1930, Özdamar "managed to appoint himself the chief trustee" of Balıklı, Istanbul's major Greek hospital.[29] Then, in the 1930s, the Turkish-Orthodox community started having problems in burying its dead. The Fener Patriarchate refused to allow them to be interned in Greek cemeteries of Istanbul, which were under its administration. The government acted to alleviate the situation. In January 1932, Ankara asked Istanbul to set aside a cemetery for the Turkish-Orthodox.[30] Although that did not materialize, the incident showed the government's commitment to the Turkish-Orthodox community. In return, these people demonstrated their loyalty to Turkishness. For example, in 1930, Eftim and the others appealed to the authorities to have the information on their identity cards changed to "Turkish-Orthodox" from "Greek."[31] During the language purification movement, the Turkish-Orthodox took "pure Turkish" last names. Patriarch Papa Eftim became Papa Zeki Eren Erol on October 27, 1935, and Pulluoğlu İstimatis made his name İstamat Zihni Özdamar.[32]

Ankara's favorable treatment of the Turkish-Orthodox Church was linked to its caution toward Fener. While the Lausanne Treaty had recognized the Patriarchate only as the spiritual leader of the Greek-Orthodox in Turkey, Ankara wanted to make sure that Fener would not revert to its previous international status under the Ottoman Empire as the leader of the global Orthodox community. In view of that, in October 1935, the EİUM wrote to the governor of Istanbul. Patriarch Fotyos had reportedly visited the Greek consulate. He needed to be reminded, "The Patriarchate is a Turkish institution, he is a Turkish citizen, and that it is in his interests to obey and respect the Turkish laws in all his business."[33]

In other instances, too, Ankara exhibited caution toward the Greek community as well as its heritage. For example, on March 29, 1932, the General Directorate for Cemeteries (Mezarlıklar İşleri Umum Müdürlüğü—MİUM) wrote to Izmir province regarding the Greek cemetery in town. On December 15, 1931, Izmir had requested permission from Ankara to build a stadium on this cemetery, which had recently become its property. Now, Ankara wrote that this would be allowed if Izmir "sold the tombstones or used them in the construction of the stadium."[34] On April 6, 1932, the MİUM demanded further action on this. If Izmir were slow, "Greece's demands would increase, and the danger of giving this graveyard to the Hellenes would rise."[35] Apparently, the matter was urgent: on April 12, the Directorate told Izmir again to start construction immediately.[36]

In other examples of trepidation toward the Greek heritage, on November 2, 1938, the EİUM wrote to the governor of Çoruh about Greeks, who had converted to Islam. Since these people "were reportedly holding services," Ankara asked the governor "to explain why deserted and run-down churches have not been destroyed until now."[37] Though there is no evidence that these Greek churches were destroyed later, watchfulness over Greeks extended even to the MPs. A report by the Private Secretary of the Interior Minister noted that the Greek-Orthodox MP Taptas was "having a five-story apartment built for himself at number 14, on Yuvakin Patrikaya Street, in Kolonaki, Athens."[38]

Eastern Christians under High Kemalism

In addition to the Greeks, Turkey was also prudent toward the Eastern Christians, including the Assyrians, Chaldeans, and the Jacobites. Ankara watched the movement of these groups in the country. In October 1935, for example, the EİUM wrote to a number of Turkish provinces, to which a number of Chaldeans and Jacobites had recently traveled, inquiring the whereabouts of these people.[39] Then, in March 1939, the governor of Mardin wrote to Ankara that he was having a Jacobite suspect, "Yusuf Devli, who is son of Baho, a merchant in Mardin," kept under surveillance.[40] In this regard, Turkey was wary especially toward the Assyrians. These people had allied with the Russians and the British in the First World War. Many of them had been killed in the following conflicts. Most others had left their traditional homeland in Hakkâri for Northern Iraq during these catastrophes.[41] Afterwards, the Assyrians had proven hostile towards the Kemalist republic, participating in a number of anti-Turkish campaigns, including border incursions of 1923–25 and 1930.[42]

By the early 1930s, Assyrians in Northern Iraq were demanding recognition from London for their efforts on behalf of England. Consequently, Britain hoped either to settle these unruly tribesmen in Northern Iraq[43] or to return them to their former homes in Hakkâri. In 1932, through the Iraqi Prime Minister, the British asked Ankara if it would agree to the Assyrians' return to Hakkâri. If not, the British were ready to exchange a portion of Northern Iraq, inhabited by the

Barzani tribe, for parts of Hakkâri, where the Assyrians could settle. Aras refused the offer. However, he added that Turkey might consider the proposal if she were released "from her minority obligations under the Treaty of Lausanne [the various cultural and religious community rights that Ankara granted the Greeks and the Armenians]." Alternatively, Turkey could agree to the Assyrians' repatriation to Hakkâri in return for obtaining "Duck's Beak," the easternmost part of Syrian El Cezire, an area sandwiched between Turkey and Iraq, where the French had been resettling Armenians and other Christians with the hope of creating an anti-Turkish zone. The Foreign Office refused the Turkish proposals.[44] For the British, Ankara's demands, which they described with disdain as "grotesque, even for one of Tevfik Rüştü's brainwaves"[45] seemed determined to prevent the Assyrians from returning. In support of this assumption, in November 1931, the General Command for Gendarme (Jandarma Umum Komutanlığı—JUK) wrote to the First Inspectorate-General in regard to a group of Assyrians who had arrived as refugees from Iraq. "These are to be expelled as soon as possible," said the dispatch.[46]

In addition to the Assyrians, their Uniate kin, the Chaldeans were also unwanted by Ankara. For example, in July 1938, the EUM wrote to the First Inspectorate-General and the governor of Hakkâri regarding Chaldean refugees from Iraq. "Since there are strict orders about not allowing any Chaldeans into our country," these refugees, "whom we consider undesirable, are to be deported to Iraq immediately," said the order.[47] Such attitudes toward the Eastern Christians were anchored in the fact that these people did not enjoy official recognition on par with the Armenians or the Greeks.[48] For example, on March 6, 1932, Ankara wrote to the First Inspectorate-General about the recent election of Ignatius Afram I Barsoum as the "Kadim Süryani" (Old Syrian/Jacobite) Patriarch. Since the "government does not recognize an entity under the name of the Patriarchate of the Old Syrians," it was not interested in this election.[49] In another case of non-recognition, on April 28, 1937, Ankara banned literature sent to Jacobite priests from Haifa.[50] A declaration from Patriarch Afram met the same fate on June 7, 1937.[51]

Armenians under High Kemalism

Similar to the Eastern Christians, the Armenians were also in distress in the 1930s, with the government remaining hostile to them. One reason behind this was the memory of the war between Turkey and Armenia between 1917 and 1920. This created an image of Armenians as anti-Turkish. Turkey's reading of the Armenians' collaboration with the Russians during the First World War and Armenian nationalism in the Ottoman Empire exacerbated this perception. Hence, Ankara was cautious and even antagonistic towards the Armenians. A second reason behind Ankara's rancor was the constant anti-Turkish lobby efforts of the diaspora Armenians. While at least a part of such international efforts aimed to raise relief funds for the survivors of 1915, the government saw various Armenian nationalist conspiracies in them. Accordingly, Ankara viewed

Armenian lobbying with resolute suspicion. American diplomats elaborated on this

> The *Vakit* says that the Armenians are intensifying their anti-Turkish propaganda, having extended their activities even to Finland, where a violent brochure in several languages is responsible for the collection of considerable contributions for Armenian relief. It is too bad that several decades ago some foresighted Turk did not rise up and warn his people of the eventual pecuniary usefulness to the Armenians of persecution, deportations and massacres.
>
> (SD 867.9111/335)

Turkey was also bothered that the Armenian campaigns aimed to convince the international powers to pressure Ankara so it would extend leniency to the Armenians. On April 21, 1931, the Secretary General of the "Comité Central des Réfugiés Arméniens," Mr Pashalian complained to the League of Nations about the poor treatment of Armenians in Turkey.[52] Another case of such lobbying came in 1932, when the Armenian Gregorian Church council met in Echmiazin, Soviet Armenia, to elect a new Catholicos (Patriarch). Ankara refused to allow the Turkish Armenians to travel to Echmiazin to participate in this.[53] On October 7, Ohannes Essayan, who represented the Armenian refugee organizations in Greece, sent a petition to the League of Nations to protest this.[54] On December 11, Aras wrote to Geneva to expand on the Turkish position. According to Article Thirty-Eight of Lausanne, the government was ready to protect the religious freedoms of all citizens. However, while Ankara did not recognize the international religious authority of the Armenian Catholicos, and since the election of a Catholicos did not constitute a religious matter under Article Thirty-Eight, the participation of Turkish Armenians in this election was not stipulated by Lausanne.[55]

Nevertheless, Essayan continued with his lobbying. In 1936, he wrote a letter to the British Secretary of State. Then, London was about to sign the Montreux Convention with Turkey. Essayan reminded the Foreign Office of Turkey's treatment of minorities and added, "I therefore consider the Montreux Conference as a heavensent opportunity for us to obtain the redress of our legitimate grievances."[56] Such lobbying did not sit well with Ankara. In fact, these efforts exacerbated Turkey's fears that the Armenians were conspiring against it. Accordingly, during the 1930s, Ankara remained guarded toward Armenians abroad. For instance, on May 29, 1936, the EİUM wrote to the governor of Istanbul about "Jorj Greguvar Hisarof," a French citizen. It was possible that this man was Armenian. Hence, he needed to be followed upon entering Turkey.[57] Then, on May 18, 1936, the EİUM inquired about an Armenian who had jumped off a ship and managed to enter Istanbul. The Directorate wanted information on this person.[58]

Turkey was careful about foreign Armenians, especially when it feared they could be Tashnakists. For example, in November 1931, the EİUM issued a warning about a number of foreign Armenians including "Anliyan, a tobacco tradesman in Jerusalem, Topalyan, a carpet merchant from America, and Hacı İstefan, originally from Bursa, but now a tobacco salesman in Beirut." These men, known to have links to the Tashnak, were traveling through the country and had made acquaintances with Turkish Armenians. Accordingly, Ankara was collecting information about them.[59] In this regard, foreigners who established contacts with Turkish Armenians were also suspects: in October 1931, the EİUM warned Istanbul about a Romanian, "Tranko Yaşi, who was in Istanbul as a member of the Romanian delegation for the Balkan Conference, and had contacted various Armenians during his sojourn." This man was reportedly "a known Armenophile." Thus, he needed to be scrutinized.[60]

Armenian assassination attempts against the leaders of the Republic

The final and perhaps most decisive cause of government caution toward foreign (and by extension native) Armenians was their involvement in assassination attempts, both alleged and actual. In the 1930s, Armenian nationalist organizations such as the Tashnak continued with their attempts to assassinate the Turkish leaders. This aggravated Ankara's concerns. In April 1930, the EİUM informed a number of provinces about eight Armenian assassins, who would be arriving from Aleppo.[61] Then, in the fall of 1931, a Tashnak plot to kill İnönü unraveled. An Armenian, Agop Apikian, whom the government believed was connected to the "Armenian revolutionary Hrant Janikian," was discovered aboard a Romanian steamer in Istanbul.[62] Though Apikian committed suicide before his arrest,[63] and while British diplomats viewed the Turkish evidence regarding his attempt on İnönü's life to be "fantastic,"[64] for Ankara, this was a real threat. In view of this, the government was alarmed. On November 8, the EİUM warned the authorities about four Armenian assassins, who would be coming from Beirut via Aleppo. The letter also mentioned other potential assassins arriving from the Dodecanese islands, Bulgaria and Cyprus.[65] On November 16, another communiqué referred to fifteen would-be assassins, who would be leaving Beirut "under the leadership of Küçük Antranik."[66]

Throughout the early 1930s, Turkey tracked many would-be assassins from Syria and Lebanon, as well as Egypt, Greece, Romania, and France.[67] While most of these people were Tashnakists, there were even Hoybûnists among them.[68] In Ankara's eyes, collaboration between the Armenians and the Kurds played a big role in the assassination plots.[69] According to the government, there were other parties involved in these schemes, too: in July 1932, for instance, the EUUM notified the First Inspectorate that the Tashnak party was trying to convince Armenians in France and Syria to go to Germany to obtain citizenship documents. "The German Consulate in Paris has told the Tashnak Central Committee that it is prepared to give any help to Armenians who will go to Germany," said the dispatch. On the other hand, Armenians in Syria were reportedly crossing to Iran, where they bought Persian citizenship. Then, these people traveled to Germany with the hope of coming to Turkey from there. Since "the activities of the Armenian *komitecis* [*komitadji*] and the Armenians in general, who are the enemies of our nation, have increased lately," said the letter, "caution is necessary towards them."[70]

In the meantime, new assassination schemes were discovered. In March 1935, Ankara warned the provinces that twelve Tashnakists in Aleppo had sworn to enter the country in order to kill the Turkish leaders.[71] Then, a major plot against Atatürk unraveled on September 19. The EİUM alerted the authorities that a group of Turks and Kurds from Syria, and Armenians from the Greek island of Lesbos, would come to Turkey to make an attempt on the president's life.[72] Then, in October, Ankara discovered two other plots by Armenian and Circassian assassins from Syria.[73]

The events stemming from French Syria soured Ankara's perception of its neighbor. Throughout the 1930s, the government had evidence that Tashnakists, Circassians, and Kurds in Syria were working for, and even spying for, the French.[74] Additionally, the Turkish press, especially the daily *La République*, highlighted the resettlement of Armenians along the Syro-Turkish border, Hoybûn's tolerated activities and the creation of Circassian militia units in Syria. These events, which were seen as signs of Damascus' and Paris' open hostility to Ankara,[75] caused uproar.[76] They led to a deterioration of Ankara's already poor opinion of French Syria. In the interim, although the assassination attempts subsided in the late 1930s, Ankara's wariness toward the Armenians did not decrease. On April 6, 1937, for instance, the EİUM wrote to the governor of Kocaeli about an Armenian contractor, a Turkish citizen, who had been permitted to construct a quarantine station in Tuzla. This man needed to be scrutinized during his work.[77]

Caution and ethnic bias toward the Armenians

This case of prudence toward the Armenian contractor was not unique. In fact, Ankara focused extensively on local Armenians. In addition to the government's fears that these people could be involved in assassination attempts, a variety of other factors help explain such caution. First, Ankara followed local Armenians for their suspected links to communism.[78] Second, it investigated their sympathy for Armenian nationalism. For example, in 1931, the First Inspectorate-General reported about "Hüsrev, a known Armenian *komiteci* [*komitadji*]." There was evidence that this man was collaborating with other Armenians in nationalist activities.[79]

Accordingly, Ankara followed the local Armenians if they moved suspiciously or too frequently within the country. For instance, in November 1931, the government alerted the governor of Erzincan about a certain "Agop of Arapkir, son of Serkis, an Armenian subject, who lived in the Ortaköy quarter of Istanbul." This man, who repaired sewing machines, had been traveling to Erzincan and Erzurum for his job. He needed to be investigated.[80] Two days later, Ankara informed the First Inspectorate that Armenians traveling through the country were being scrutinized for their links with Armenians abroad.[81] Then, on November 25, the EİUM sent a letter to Istanbul about a certain Armenian "İstepan Zaker Papasyan, or İstefan Çalıkyan who has been arrested recently after his trip to Çanakkale." Ankara wanted to know this man's "record in the post-1918 armistice period, his family's reputation, the date, and reasons for his trip from Istanbul, as well as his possible links with Armenian *komitecis*."[82]

The government also scrutinized local Armenians if they traveled abroad too often. For example, in October 1931, the EİUM alerted Istanbul about "Kalost Canyan Ohanis, who had spent seven years in Europe." The Directorate wanted to know if this man was connected to the *komitecis*.[83] Then, in 1935, the EİUM advised all the provinces and Inspectorates that since "there is a persuasion that the Armenian element will be a proxy to all sorts of evil," Armenians who traveled abroad often were to be investigated regarding "their links, connections, and correspondence with the foreign countries." When Armenians came from abroad, they and their belongings were to be searched thoroughly. On the other hand, suspicious Armenians were to be followed if they were in Istanbul or in Ankara at the same time with the republican leadership.[84]

Finally, throughout the 1930s, Ankara prudently followed people with possible Armenian heritage. According to the government, such people were Armenians even after they converted to Islam. Perhaps more than anything else, this demonstrated that in Ankara's eyes, being an Armenian was not a religious matter. Rather, Armenianness was an immutable identity inherent in all those who were or had been Armenian.[85] Vigilance was necessary toward them since all Armenians were implicated in anti-republic activities. This led the government to be wary even toward Armenians who had converted to Islam. In an example demonstrating this, on April 28, 1932, the EUUM warned the governor of Istanbul about "Mazhar, reportedly an Armenian who had converted, who worked as a janitor at the [official] Anatolian News Agency, and engaged in negative propaganda there." The dispatch asked Istanbul to find out more about this man's identity and connections.[86] In other examples along this line, on September 30, the EİUM alerted the First Inspectorate about "Sıtkı [a Muslim name], high school senior student of Armenian blood." Ankara wanted to know the real name of this student.[87] Next, on November 6, 1936, the Ministry of Interior informed the CHP about "Hamparsom Onnik, an Armenian born of Eblanka, a Serb mother." This man had converted to Islam and become Enis Baba Özkan. Now, he was a businessman, interested in becoming an MP. Caution was necessary on him.[88]

The government's attention to this matter was overly cautious. Even the possibility that one's parents may have been converted Armenians made one the object of attention. For example, in March 1937, the EİUM warned the governor of Balıkesir about a certain "Mahmut Nedim, whose father's name is Abdullah." Because Abdullah was a name typically given to converts, this had "caused a suspicion that Nedim may be Armenian." Hence, investigation was needed on Nedim's parents' birthplaces and their "genuine origin."[89] Then, in September 1938, the EUM sent a dispatch to the governor of Kırşehir about "Edip Kamil, a tenth-year student at the military lycée." Earlier, Kırşehir had told Ankara that this man's family "is of Turkish race." However, later, it had written that Kamil's mother "is an Armenian convert." Now, Ankara wanted precise information on this person and "his blood."[90] In this regard, the government was careful toward its employees, too. For instance, in January 1933, the governor of Yozgat, Sami wrote in self-defense to the Ministry of Interior, to refute claims by Yozgat's local notables that he was Armenian (or Russian):

> His Excellency, the Minister, my parents are Turkish, so is my (120) years old grandfather, who lives in Istanbul. I was born in Pasinler.... My personal records are present in file at the Ministry...I have many relatives, who were martyred by the Armenians.
> (DV Yozgat Vilayeti Mektup Kalemi 17, November 1933)

Ankara's wariness *vis-à-vis* the Armenians also shaped its cultural policy toward them. For example, in September 1938, the Ministry of Interior wrote to the First Inspectorate-General about an Armenian guerilla bandit who had been caught in Nusaybin. This man had confessed that the priest of the Armenian Derikira church in the Beşiri district had collaborated with him. Because the priest had supported banditry, he was to be sent to Beşiri, and his church was to be vacated.[91]

Accordingly, vigilance toward Armenians extended to their cultural institutions. For example, during 1932, a controversy brewed in Istanbul over the possession of the Pangaltı Armenian cemetery, "a very large and very valuable piece of property in the heart of Pera, between the Harbie military school and the Taxim municipal park." The Istanbul Municipality claimed possession of this cemetery on grounds that the Patriarchate did not own a title deed to it. The City intended to divide the cemetery into lots and sell these parcels. The money accumulated from this would be spent for "providing the city with modern cemeteries and purchasing equipment to the end of its taking over the exclusive business of burying the dead." The Armenian Patriarchate brought the matter to court. It argued that although it did not have a title deed, it still had a right to own the cemetery. Turkish laws permitted the acquisition of a title deed for a property after "fifteen years of uncontested occupancy." The Patriarchate, which had held usufruct of the cemetery for a longer time, requested its ownership.[92] However, upon the findings of a commission of academics in land cadastres, on July 19, the courts passed a decision unfavorable to the Patriarchate.[93] The Armenians lost the cemetery. In due course, the cemetery was razed and its land was used to build a number or parks, public and commercial buildings.

Another issue that demonstrated unfriendliness toward the Armenians emerged in June 1935. News arrived that the Metro Goldwyn Mayer Company would produce a film based on Franz Werfel's 1933 work on the Armenian catastrophe, titled, "Forty Days on Musa Dagh." The government reacted harshly: if the film were made, then Turkey would not only ban it, but all Metro Goldwyn

Mayer productions.[94] Ankara also approached the American diplomats with the hope of facilitating Washington's intervention in this matter.[95] The Turkish reaction heightened further. The Kadroists, for instance, objected vigorously to the movie.[96] Nadir Nadi Abalıoğlu pointed in his daily *Cumhuriyet* that Werfel, the author of the book, was Jewish. Likewise, Henry Morgenthau (1856–1946), the American Ambassador to Turkey between 1913 and 1916, "who drew attention to the alleged bad treatment of Armenians during the war was also of that faith." Nadi concluded with an anti-semitic remark that, the evidence of these Jews "is biased and can be disregarded."[97] These people were trying to make money by distorting the circumstances.

The Turkish Armenians joined in and "condemned the action of the Jews in exploiting regrettable incidents of the past to the prejudice of the brotherly feelings between the Armenians and the Turks." Then, "Turkish Armenian intellectuals" held a meeting in the courtyard of the Pangaltı Armenian Church. At this gathering, "an effigy of the offending author was solemnly burned, together with a copy of his book." The nationalist euphoria over the movie seemed to be all-encompassing: "the local Jews, likewise, though expressing doubts that Werfel was one of their race, duly expressed their scorn of his work."[98] Meanwhile, the Turkish efforts produced results: upon a request by the US government, Metro Goldwyn Mayer shelved its plans of making this movie.[99]

A related aspect of Ankara's cultural policy toward the Armenians was the banning of nationalist literature or works, including those on the Armenian deportations of 1915. For example, in 1933, the government barred the entry of "*Hayrenik* (Fatherland), a Tashnak journal issued in Boston," USA, into Turkey.[100] Other titles such as *Lesser Armenia and its Capital Sivas* (Küçük Ermenistan ve Onun Payitahtı Sivas), *What I Saw During the Deportations From Sivas to Aleppo* (Tehcirde Sivas'tan Halep'e kadar Gördüklerim), and *In Memoriam of the Armenian Children* (Ermeni Çocuklarına Hatıra) were banned in July 1934.[101] The next month, "*Baykar* (Struggle), an Armenian newspaper distributed in the USA" was forbidden entry into Turkey.[102] This was followed by others, including "the daily *Aramazt* (Ahuramazda), printed in Athens,"[103] "a book titled, *My Beloved Armenia* (Sevgili Ermenistan), issued in Chicago,"[104] "*La Passion de Cilicie*, published in Paris,"[105] "the daily *Zartonk* (Awakening), circulated in Beirut,"[106] "Maşek Seroyan's *The Armenian Question* (Ermeni Meselesi), printed in Beirut,"[107] and "the daily *Azad Hosk*, distributed in Sofia by the Tashnak."[108]

Turkish Armenians at the end of the High Kemalist era

As the closing stages of High Kemalism under Atatürk, the Armenians seemed to become more pliant. A 1936 speech given to the parliament by Armenian MP Berç Türker (Keresteciyan) (Afyonkarahisar) characterized this best. (Türker, a banker, had been credited with saving Atatürk's life in 1919, when Atatürk had been trying to leave Istanbul for Anatolia to organize the Turkish liberation campaign. Türker had reportedly informed Atatürk that his ship would be attacked, earning credit for preventing Atatürk's death or capture by the British. Now, in 1935, he was elected to the TBMM representing the Armenian community. Interestingly, at this time, he changed his Armenian last name, Keresteciyan [the son of lumberjack] to Türker, meaning "the Turkish soldier/man.")

On June 28, 1938, Türker gave a speech to the parliament in favor of the aforementioned Law on Associations. This law banned the establishment of associations on the basis of family, minority community, race, ethnic origin, class, religion, sect, or denomination. It also outlawed associations that "disturbed political and national unity."[109] The law, which prevented the Armenians (and other non-Muslims) from establishing ethnic-religious associations, also voided their privileges: "All imperial edicts, decrees, statutes, decisions, and regulations, which cover the law and privileges of the minority communities in Turkey are annulled."[110] Of all the MPs, Türker came to the floor to defend this law. However, it seems that he had not volunteered for this: "Dear Friends, as you know my oratory powers are very weak. I usually write my speeches. Nevertheless, they have given this law to me with an extraordinary urgency. I have not been able to analyze it and write my speech."[111] The duty to support the Law on Associations had been given to Türker in a *fait accompli*.[112] However, even then, the MP did a good job. He noted that while this legislation mentioned minorities, "This word chimes unpleasant for our ears." It "recalls any group that had been proxy to the foreign powers in the era of the capitulations." Now, the minorities "have joined the god in the other world" said Türker, amidst the laughs of his colleagues.[113] As the law was being voted in the TBMM, the Armenian MP showed his full support by cheering, "Long Live the Turkish Republic."[114]

Conclusion: a legacy of uneasiness toward Christianity and the Christians

It appears that, in the 1930s, Ankara had a mostly negative stance toward the Christians. In addition to the reasons outlined above, this phenomenon appears to have been rooted in anti-Christian instincts of Turkish nationalism. This, in return, was due to two historical developments. First, the ethnic cleansing of the Ottoman Muslims by the Christian powers and the recent conflicts with the Christian nations led the Turks to identify Christians as adversaries. Second, Turkish nationalism possessed a dislike toward Western Churches, which had proselytized for Catholicism or Protestantism in the Ottoman Empire.[115] For a long time, these Churches had sided with the local Christians against the Porte. Now, the republic opposed them and hoped to thwart their activities. In view of this, Turkish nationalism had a negative attitude not only toward the missionaries but also toward Christians as a group.

The antipathy *vis-à-vis* Christianity was also linked to contemporary developments, more specifically to Kemalist secularism. In 1932, American diplomats described the government's policy toward religion as one of "contemptuous tolerance."[116] Ankara especially wanted to wipe out religion's influence in education and diminish all religious influence.[117] In accordance with this, the government targeted the Islamic religious establishment, organized in various sects and orders. For example, in January 1938, the EUM demanded that Alevi babas, who collected donations in the Muş province, be censured.[118] Then, a report from the Ministry of Interior in April 1936 noted that twenty-three women and seventeen men, who lived in the Haçka village of the Akçaabat district and had been caught in a Nakşibendi *zikir* ceremony, were sent to the court. Nineteen of them were arrested.[119] In another example, in September 1935, the EİUM asked the authorities to investigate the Sufi Kadiri order. Ankara wanted to identify its members and leaders, and asked that they be kept under close surveillance.[120]

In this regard, the government also targeted the Christians. With their missionary traditions, the Catholics and the Protestants were particularly beleaguered. For example, in 1932, Ankara discovered that some "servants in the German mission had become Christians" in Maraş.[121] Some of them

> went to Ankara and in an interview with the Minister of the Interior demanded their rights as Turkish citizens and contended, that since the Constitution provided for liberty of conscience, the local administrative and police authorities were acting illegally in their attempts to interfere with the religious convictions of adult Turkish citizens.

> (SD, 867.404/208)

In reaction, in July 1933, the EUUM wrote to Maraş: foreign Protestants, who, "had been using religion for the benefit of their interests, and had engaged in mischievous conduct in this regard," were to be deported immediately.[122] When the US Embassy intervened on behalf of them, Ankara agreed to let the two Americans among them stay, but the German sisters, who belonged to the "Deutsche Hilfsbund für Liebeswerk," were obliged to leave for Syria. Ambassador Clerk explained Ankara's leniency toward the American women also through the government's anti-clericalism: "The greater severity shown toward the German ladies is doubtless due to the fact that they are members of a religious sisterhood, which is not the case with their American friends, who are simply Congregationalists."[123]

In other cases of vigilance toward missionaries, in February 1933, British diplomats noted that the government was expelling Mr Alford Carleton, an American missionary who lived among the Assyrian Christians in Mardin. This expulsion, which targeted missionary work, also showed that "the Turkish government did not care for the presence in the Eastern provinces of foreign representatives."[124] Then, in March 1935, the EİUM asked that an Albanian, "Atandali," who had been "conducting missionary propaganda," be expelled.[125]

Ankara was also careful on conversions. For instance, on July 15, 1935, the EİUM warned the governor of Istanbul about "Nusret Emil, who had converted to Catholicism." This man was not to "be allowed to conduct religious propaganda."[126] The government was wary about Christian publications, too. It banned them, including a pamphlet called *The Humanity of Jesus* (İsa'nın İnsanlığı),[127] a book titled, "*Deo Gratios*, published in Nancy, France,"[128] and another book printed in Istanbul, *Imitation or Following the Messiah* (Imitation yahut Mesihe Uymak).[129] Attentiveness toward religious publications extended also to the local Christians: in 1936, the Directorate-General for Press (Basım Genel Direktörlüğü—BGD) asked that the "regular pro-religious publications of the Istanbul Armenian daily, *Jamanak*" be terminated.[130]

Accordingly, it seems that, in the 1930s, the government was wary not only toward Christians and their missions, but also toward the idea of Christianity. US Ambassador Grew elaborated on this: "In the eyes of the government and indeed the Turkish people, even the application of so-called 'unnamed Christianity' let alone attempted conversion, is the wavering away of impressionable youth from spiritual allegiance to the Turkish state."[131] Perhaps, this explains the current resentment held by some Turks toward Christian proselytizing in the country. As in the High Kemalist position toward Christianity and Christian minorities, the contemporary antagonism *vis-à-vis* Christianity in the country seems to be rooted more in nationalist feelings than in religious intolerance. In other words, in the same way High Kemalism saw Christianity as an anational affront to Turkishness, today most Turks view Christianity as a challenge to their national identity. Rather than confronting the Turks' Muslim faith, Christianity stands as a challenge to their nominal Islamic identity.

8 Jews in the 1930s
Turks or not?

Thrace, the focal point of Jewish concentration in Turkey

At a first glance, the Jewish experience in the 1930s seems similar to that of other non-Muslims. Like the Armenians and other Eastern Christians, the number of Jews also declined in the 1930s: while there had been 81,872 Jews in Turkey in 1927,[1] there were 78,730 in 1935.[2] Whereas the country's overall population increased by 22.2 percent during this period, the Jewish population decreased by 2.6 percent. Many Jews left the country each year for the Americas, Palestine, or France.

The biggest annoyance for the Jews throughout the 1930s was the "Citizen Speak Turkish" campaign. In Istanbul and Izmir, this drive affected all non-Turkish speakers. However, outside these cities, the initiative was especially fierce in Thrace and the Dardanelles, areas with relatively large Jewish communities. (In 1927, while Jews were 0.60 percent of the country's overall population, they were 5.07 percent of the Thracian population, including the Dardanelles and Istanbul.[3] In Edirne and Çanakkale they comprised more than 15 percent of the population, and in Tekirdağ they were around 5 percent.[4] There were also smaller Jewish communities in Gelibolu, Lapseki, Kırklareli, Uzunköprü, Babaeski, Lüleburgaz, Çorlu, and Silivri.)

Ankara's attitude toward the Thracian Jews and Bulgarian revisionism concerning Thrace

The presence of so many Jews in Thrace would have perhaps gone unnoticed, had it not been for the fact that Turkish nationalism had a particularly sentimental view of Thrace. The daily *Zaman* (Time) noted this in 1935:

> If Ankara is the heart of Turkey, Thrace is her head. If Turkey is a European country, it is entirely thanks to Thrace ... Certainly, the area of Thrace is not considerable. Compared to that of Anatolia it is not even one-thirtieth. But the value of this parcel of ground which connects us with the European Continent is immense ... Turkey would not exist without the

Marmara and the Straits. Without them she would become a state of third class in international politics.

(SD, 867.014/68)

Besides, Ankara viewed Thrace as a strategically pivotal area, flanking Bulgaria, the revisionist power of interwar Balkans. In the 1930s, Sofia was in a growing alliance with Italy, the major revisionist power in the Mediterranean. At this time "Italy was popularly credited with having a hand in the refusal of Bulgaria to yield to the persuasions" of the other Balkan countries to join the Balkan Pact, which Turkey and Greece were trying to foster.[5] Ankara believed that Rome was arming Bulgaria, which might attack Turkish Thrace.[6] This caused great discomfort to Turkey,[7] and exacerbated Ankara's fears about Bulgarian designs toward Turkish Thrace. In 1932, in an interview with the Yugoslav daily *Politika* Aras noted this:

> If the Bulgarians wish it, let them take not only Thrace but the whole of Turkey!...But I must tell you that we've had too many lessons in the past to be ready to embark on new adventures now! We will never adopt an aggressive front, and are friends with all who desire to be friends.

(SD, 767.00/40)

In view of the situation, first, Turkey tried to reach a mutual understanding with Bulgaria.[8] A team of Turkish diplomats visited Sofia in fall 1932, to secure Sofia's accession to the Turco-Greek Pact of Friendship. This failed.[9] In 1933, while passing through Sofia, Aras invited Bulgaria to join the ongoing treaty negotiations between Turkey, Greece, Romania, and Yugoslavia for a Balkan Pact. Once again, the Turkish call went unanswered.[10] At this time, public attitude toward Bulgaria soured. In view of this, a 1933 decision to raze a Turkish cemetery in the Razgrad district of northeastern Bulgaria to make way for a new park created uproar in Turkey. When news reached Istanbul, a mob attacked the Bulgarian consulate.[11] By 1934, Bulgaria was Turkey's only neighbor, dissatisfied by her borders, with whom Turkey had less than normal relations.[12] On February 9, 1934, Turkey, Greece, Romania, and Yugoslavia signed the Balkan Pact. Except for Albania, which was an effective Italian colony, Bulgaria was the only Balkan country that did not participate in this collective security treaty. Subsequently, Ankara was guarded toward Sofia. For example, during the winter 1935 government crisis in Greece, when Bulgaria amassed troops on the Greek border, Turkey responded by moving troops into Thrace, along the Bulgarian frontier.[13] Sofia protested this strongly.[14]

In view of the perceived Bulgarian threat, Turkey saw Thrace, with its relatively high number of Jews (13,000 Jews, 8,000 of them in Edirne[15]) as the underbelly of the republic. A majority of the Thracian Jews did not speak Turkish and had not received the "Speak Turkish" campaign warmly. To complicate the matter further, at this time, Ankara did not enjoy military control over the Straits. The Lausanne Treaty had created an international regime and a non-militarized status for the Dardanelles, the Bosphorous, and the adjoining areas in Thrace, including towns such as Tekirdağ, Silivri, Lapseki, Çanakkale, and Gelibolu, all of which had Jewish populations. Turkey did not fully trust the Jews. In Ankara's eyes, the presence of so many Jews in this sensitive area would create a security concern if the Jews were disloyal. It would be difficult to defend Thrace and Istanbul in the case of a Bulgarian attack, for example.

The government decided to act on this matter. First, it tried to improve the security situation in Thrace. Law Nr 2393, passed on February 19, 1934, instituted the aforementioned Thrace Inspectorate-General. This put the Dardanelles and Thrace under an Inspector-General. Second, it amassed troops on the Bulgarian frontier.[16] Third, Ankara passed the aforementioned Resettlement Law, which went into effect on June 21, 1934. One of the aims of this was the Turkification of Thrace. In a speech to the parliament on November 18, 1935, Kaya noted: "one of the fundamentals of our resettlement policy is bringing the Turks here from abroad." Then, he added, "The number of people, who have been resettled in Thrace until now is 65,000, including those from Romania, Bulgaria, Yugoslavia. In the course of specific times ahead, we would like to see one million people in Thrace, excluding Istanbul."[17]

Jewish exodus from Thrace, the 1934 Thracian incidents

Last but not least, while aspiring to make Thrace more defendable, when anti-semitic publications appeared and as the aforementioned "Speak Turkish" campaign took a radical turn in Thrace, the government turned its head the other way, hoping that such efforts aimed at intimidating the Thracian Jews would perhaps convince them to be more loyal citizens. One of these anti-semitic publications was *Orhun*, issued out in Edirne by Hüseyin Nihal (Atsız) (1905–75), a young schoolteacher and one of the ideologues of Turkish racism. The first issue of *Orhun* appeared in November 1933. The journal included many anti-semitic treatises, attacking the Jews. For instance, on March 21, 1934, Atsız labeled the Jews and communists as the Turks' two enemies.[18] On May 25, he issued a warning to the Jews: "Germany has become the first country to solve the Jewish question," said Atsız. If the Jews do not behave, "And then if we get mad, we will not just destroy the Jews like the Germans, but we will scare them," he added. Then, he concluded, "As the saying goes, it is better to scare the Jew than to kill him."[19]

In the interim, a second anti-semitic journal, *İnkılâp* (Revolution), emerged in April 1933. This was published by another young racist and anti-semite, Cevat Rıfat (Atilhan) (1892–1967), who would later become Atsız' nemesis.[20] *İnkılâp* appeared in Izmir. Interestingly, Izmir and Edirne, the home of *İnkılâp* and *Orhun*, both had large Jewish communities that had rivaled the Turks economically since the departure of Christians. In addition, public resentment in both cities was widespread against the fact that the Jews did not speak Turkish.

Like *Orhun*, *İnkılâp* also published many anti-semitic articles and found inspiration in Nazism. According to Shaw, Atilhan's ascent was thanks to German help. For example, he was invited to Germany after Hitler's rise to power, where he met Julius Streicher, the publisher of Nazi propaganda journal *Der Stürmer*. Upon his return to Turkey, Atilhan started *İnkılâp*.[21] In May 1933, he wrote that Jews had betrayed the Turks during the Balkan Wars and the First World War. He asked the Turkish youth "to not trust the sons of this race that has betrayed your race, fatherland and history."[22] Atilhan also charged that the Jews did not speak Turkish, did not shop at Turkish stores, did not employ any Turks, and were "hostile to Turkish culture, Turkish civilization, and Turkish nobility."[23] In May 1934, Atilhan moved his journal to Istanbul and renamed it *Milli İnkılâp* (National Revolution). He augmented his praise for Nazi Germany and increased the tone of his virulent anti-semitism.[24] *Milli İnkılâp* wrote: "When a Jew changes his name and says that he is a Muslim, that does not make him a Turk. Turkishness is a matter of blood and character." Then, the journal went further and called for an economic boycott of Jewish businesses: "The future of the nations, which are not sovereign, is weak. We have to defeat the Jew in the economic sphere."[25]

It is difficult to estimate the impact of these anti-semitic journals on the Turkish population, especially in cities where many Jews lived. Aktar argues that due to sparse communication networks, lack of a nationwide radio broadcast, and the low level of literacy, these publications and the anti-semitic hysteria created by the Nazis' resonated little in Turkey at this time, especially in small towns, such as those in Thrace.[26] Thus, not anti-semitism but Turkification policies led to animosity against the Jews. Aktar's argument is undercut at least in part by the fact that an economic boycott started in Çanakkale against the city's successful Jewish community exactly at the time when *Milli İnkılâp* called for one in May 1934. At this time, the Jews of Istanbul petitioned Ankara, complaining about *Milli İnkılâp*. The Interior Ministry replied that it did not approve anti-semitism and that it would act accordingly toward *Milli İnkılâp*. However, "since the necessary administrative and legal steps would take time, the Jews need not worry further about this," said Ankara.[27]

By June, Jews in Çanakkale were getting threatening mail, telling them to leave town or risk death. On June 21, some of the Jews were attacked and beaten. Jewish homes were looted. Three days later, new hostile letters were delivered to leaders of the community, while the boycott was hardened. Anti-semitic pamphlets, signed by "The League of Turkish Youth," were passed around. These said: "Son of Turkey, do you not feel bitter at heart when you give money to our economic enemies?"[28] Such events triggered an exodus from the town. About 1,500 of Çanakkale's Jews took refuge in Istanbul. On June 30, the boycott spread to other Thracian towns. American Ambassador Peet Skinner (1866–1960) noted that "word was passed around, in some mysterious manner, that they [the Jews] would have to go, and being by nature a timorous people, their disposition is to take no chances but to get out as quietly and rapidly as possible." Many Jews received "offers for the purchase of their property on absurdly low terms, and my informant suggested to me that this perhaps furnished the key to an understanding of the situation," that "there might be a concerted plan to spread alarm among the Jews."[29]

In the interim, on July 3, two prominent members of the Istanbul Jewish community, Gad Franko (1881–1954) and Mişon Ventura had a meeting with Atatürk, in which they requested his intervention in the matter.[30] The president replied positively. That night, however, the situation got out of hand. Jewish homes and businesses were attacked and looted in Kırklareli; many people were beaten and harassed.[31] The next morning, most Jews there escaped to Istanbul, while others took refuge in Edirne, home to more than half of the Thracian Jews. In Edirne, food dealers reportedly received "orders from the nationalist pogrom bands not to sell food to the Jews under pain of severe reprisals."[32] As the incidents continued, the events led to a spiraling of fear. The Jews in Edirne and other towns joined the exodus. A large number of the 13,000 Thracian Jews—3,000 according to the government[33] or 7,000–8,000 according to British Ambassador Loraine[34]—fled to Istanbul in a matter of a few days.

Who was responsible? A government account

On June 5, Ankara had the situation under control and quiet prevailed in Thrace. In his speech to the TBMM, İnönü said that the government would punish those responsible for the exodus. Kaya arrived in Edirne with a team of investigators. Upon the conclusion of this on July 11, the government issued a declaration. Ankara linked the exodus to the following "historically-rooted developments":

> It appears that Anti-Semitism began in Thrace during World War I and it continued during the Armistice and the fight for Independence. After having been suspended during the early years of the Republic, it has penetrated the country once more during the last few years with more vigor and following new formulas obtained from different parts of the world, Anti-Semitic articles published recently in certain journals have troubled the relations of Turks and Jews.
>
> (Shaw, Turkey and the Holocaust, 17)

However, the Jews were not blameless in this wave of anti-semitism: "There are reciprocal complaints," said the report. "The social peculiarity in Turkey that Jews persist in preserving a foreign language and culture, causing a presumption against some of them that they are spies, and dangerous to the security of the country in demilitarized zones." The report added that this perception had been abused in the aftermath of the Resettlement Law of June 13, 1934, which had stipulated that the government is "entitled to take the necessary cultural, military, political, social, and security measures against those, who share the Turkish culture but speak a language other than Turkish, or against those who don't share the Turkish culture."[35] In view of this,

> [r]umors were also put into circulation throughout the Republic, beginning about the middle of June, to the effect that the Government desired to dislodge the Jews of Thrace but preferred that the movement should not be accomplished in broad light of day, but by means of...pressures.
>
> (Shaw, Turkey and the Holocaust, 17)

According to Ankara, local hooligans had perpetrated the exodus. In the aftermath of the Thracian Incidents, pointing at the government's benevolence toward the Jews, MP Necip Ali Küçükzade (Küçüka) (1892–1941) (Denizli) argued that the exodus could not have been inspired by Ankara: "the fact that numerous German Jews have recently been engaged as professors as the Istanbul University," said Küçüka, "the recent regrettable incidents in Thrace had their source in purely local commercial competition."[36]

Who was responsible? A diplomatic account

American diplomats saw things differently. They alleged that government officials, including the governor of Kırklareli, had taken part in the hostilities, which had aimed "to intimidate and boycott the Jews."[37] The Thracian events would have been inconceivable without Ankara's consent. Consul Charles E. Allen noted:

> It is all but impossible to believe that any official in Thrace,—and some officials, notably the Vali of Kirklareli seem to be involved—or any considerable number of individuals would have set out to intimidate and boycott the Jews without the assurance that this had the approval of Ankara.
>
> (SD, 867.4016.JEWS/12)

Allen linked the exodus to government policies, including the Thrace Inspectorate and the Resettlement Law.

> It was generally assumed that making them [the Jews] flee was part of the program which includes the recently-inaugurated special régime for European Turkey and the refortification of the Straits, in other words, a deportation for political and military reasons.
>
> (SD, 867.9111/419)

The idea was "to get rid of the Jews but at the same time to make it appear that they had left on their own."[38] American diplomats added that in this, anti-semitism did not motivate the authorities. American *Charges D'Affaires ad Interim* in Istanbul, G. Howland Shaw added that he did not believe "for a moment the responsible leaders in Turkey entertain any Anti-Semitic sentiments."[39] The exodus had been facilitated by "a desire to have an exclusively Turkish population in the region in question."[40] Ambassador Skinner, too, connected the exodus to the recent Resettlement Law as well as a well-camouflaged government campaign.[41] British diplomats supported this: while the Resettlement Law had stipulated that people who did not share the Turkish culture could not form more than 10 percent of a town's population when being resettled, this could be interpreted that in Thrace, where the Jews comprised a significant portion of the urban minorities, the government would not permit this situation any more.[42] Allegedly, this motive had been the catalyst for the exodus. "Witness the expulsion of the

Jews," wrote British Ambassador Skinner. "Already, the minority populations of Thrace have been moved out, and now it is the turn of the Jews.[43]

American diplomats also linked the exodus to the "recent decisions of a military character affecting Thrace."[44] British Ambassador Loraine added, "The whole district is to become, at any rate virtually, a military zone."[45] American representatives in Bulgaria supported these predictions: Turkey would militarize its Thracian frontier "to establish a precedent for the eventual fortification of the Dardanelles." In this regard, not only Jews but all non-Turks were unwanted in this region: four Bulgarian families had been expelled from near Edirne, and it was expected that "several hundred Bulgarians now residing in the Adrianople [Edirne] district would be obliged to leave."[46]

Loraine's above analysis proved correct: the government used the exodus to Turkify Thrace and render its demilitarized areas less vulnerable. The establishment of the Thrace Inspectorate-General, and the appointment of İbrahim Tali Öngören, whom Skinner described as someone "familiar with rough and ready processes for getting things done," to this post evidenced Ankara's military concerns.[47] In this regard, government encouragement of the exodus seemed plausible, a suggestion which British Ambassador Loraine supported:

> The Commercial Secretary has learnt, from what he considers a reliable source, that notwithstanding the decelerations of Ismet Pasha and the Minister of the Interior, the Turkish Government decided some time ago to clear Thrace of the Jewish element. This was to be effected by a very slow process, such as the institution of a gradual boycott, the working of minor incidents, and so on.
>
> (FO, 1011/174)

Despite Ankara's wishes to conduct the exodus in an orderly fashion, however, the plans had gotten out of hand:

> Unfortunately for the Turkish Government, the oral instructions to this effect which were given to the local authorities, were according to my informant, passed on by them to the unofficial Turkish institutions and were carried out, no doubt as a patriotic gesture, by an organized and sudden move instigated by the Turkish Sporting Club.
>
> (FO, 371/17969/E4905)

In proving the organized nature of the exodus, Loraine also noted that the director of the Ottoman Bank in Kırklareli, who was a Jew, had been warned by a friend, a member of the Sporting Union, that "there was going to be trouble shortly and that he better leave the town."[48]

Who was responsible? An academic account

The many historians evaluating the Thracian Incidents have not reached a consensus on who or what caused the exodus. Avner Levi blames it on anti-semitic publications and agitation by Nazi Germany.[49] He highlights that the "Night of the Long Knives" of June 30 in Germany took place only a few days before the Thracian incidents. Atilhan and his men saw this as a sign to take action.[50] Since Thrace is part of Europe, Nazi Germany, which wanted to cleanse the entire continent of Jews, would have encouraged the Jews' expulsion from here.[51] Finally, Levi argues that the coincidence between the exodus and the Resettlement Law was "either fate or accident."[52] Thus, he does not see any clear government responsibility in the incidents.[53]

Stanford J. Shaw concurs with Levi in blaming the exodus on "Nazi-inspired propaganda," and refutes Ankara's responsibility.[54] Haluk Karabatak, who agrees with Shaw's thesis on Nazi inspiration, nonetheless, puts the blame on "Kemalist racism." He sees the incidents also as a product of Ankara's Turkification policies as well as the 1934 Resettlement Law.[55] On the other hand, Bali, like Loraine, sees the exodus as the result of a well-planned, long-term strategic government plan.[56] Yet, like Levi and Shaw, Bali also ties the incidents to the anti-semitic publications.[57] In addition, he argues that the exodus was linked to the "anti-Jewish Speak Turkish" campaign.[58]

Zafer Toprak asserts that the current research does not lead him to blame Ankara for the exodus. He sees culpability for this in the local cadres of the CHP.[59] Aktar goes a step further, and views local government and CHP cadres as the main perpetrators of the exodus.[60] However, unlike Karabatak, Shaw, and Levi, Aktar refuses to see racism or Nazi inspiration as a cause. He adds that Turkey in the 1930s did not have the necessary ideological or sociological capital, which presaged the birth of modern racism.[61] Action against the Thracian Jews was not rooted in racism. Rather, it was tied to the government's fears *vis-à-vis* Sofia and Rome. In Ankara's eyes, the Jews, who lived in this sensitive area, constituted a security threat.[62]

Who was responsible? A conclusion

A classified communiqué from CHP provides evidence that Toprak and Aktar may be correct in their interpretation of the exodus: in this letter sent to the CHP's local branches right after the exodus, Recep Peker shed light on Ankara's and the party's responsibility in this. Peker wanted to know why the local authorities had not informed Ankara of the events until the beginning of the expulsions. He asked when the local cadres had become aware of the movement against the Jews. Peker also wanted information on the complaints the CHP had received on this matter prior to the events, as well as copies of all relevant correspondence. Then, the Secretary General queried the names of people in the party, who might have taken part in the incidents. Peker also questioned whether anyone in the CHP had taken advantage of the incidents for personal gain.[63] Since Peker was searching for possible accomplices in this classified report, it would appear that the CHP's presidency was unaware of the exodus until it started. Besides, the government seemed truly aggravated by the event. The aforementioned decree of July 12 said that Ankara would "prevent pressure for emigration and boycotts."[64] It would make sure that "all offenses brought to the attention of the judiciary will be judged speedily." Moreover, it would not allow "opposition to the return of the Jews." The communiqué added, "The government will not permit in Turkey any provocations or suggestions of enmity against citizens. It expects the press to show prudence with regard to sowing of contagious and susceptible discord amongst citizens."[65]

The aftermath of the 1934 incidents

Regardless of the CHP's supposed culpability or Ankara's hypothetical responsibility, the government's aloofness toward the plight of the Thracian Jews after the exodus meant they had few means to go back. American diplomats noted, "Nothing appears to have been done in a material way toward returning the expelled Jews for their firesides or indemnifying them for the losses incidental to their flight." If one watched the government's reaction to the events, it seemed that "in a few years, at most, the Jews will have effectively disappeared from this region."[66]

Indeed, the majority of the Jews who left their homes did not return: the community of Uzunköprü was never repatriated. Most Jews who had fled Çanakkale and Kırklareli stayed in Edirne,[67] while others remained in Istanbul. The number of Thracian Jews declined. While there had been 10,402 Jews in the four Thracian provinces in 1927, there were 7,555 in 1935.[68] It appears that official assurance given to the Thracian Jews had not sufficed. In the meantime, on July 14, the press stopped reporting about the event. Then, the mayor of Kırklareli, the president and vice-president of its Chamber of Commerce, "who were arrested in conjunction with this incident" were acquitted in August 1934. The courts condemned only "six persons of unimportance" to "terms of not less than six months' imprisonment" in relation to the incidents.[69] Measures that fell short of restoring all property, the punishment of only minor figures implicated in the exodus, as well as the "hands off-policy of the authorities" seemed aimed to discourage the Jews from returning permanently.[70]

As a result, Jewish emigration from Thrace continued after 1935, while overall Jewish emigration from Turkey increased.[71] Accordingly, whereas between 1927 and 1935, the Jewish population in the country had decreased by 2.6 percent, by 1938, this rate of attrition had peaked to as high as 9 percent.[72] Yet, even then, the government aimed to appease the Jews. The first indicator of this was the election of a Jewish MP, Dr Samuel Abravaya (Marmaralı) (1875–1954), to the TBMM in 1935 as a goodwill gesture.[73] On the other hand, although it did not bring full justice to the victims of the exodus, Ankara veered away from anti-semitism. A clear sign of this was the banning of anti-semitic publications after the Thracian Incidents.

Anti-semitism in Turkey in the 1930s

The case of the anti-semitic publications and press

Right after the exodus, on July 16, 1934, Atsız wrote an article in *Milli İnkılâp*, in which he defended actions against the Jews. According to this, blood, and not language, was the main marker of Turkishness.[74] "To be a Turk, first you need Turkish blood," said the author. This implied the Jews could never be Turkish, even if they spoke Turkish. In response, Ankara initiated a crackdown on *Milli İnkılâp* and other anti-semitic publications. İnönü noted, "anti-semitism is neither a Turkish product nor part of the Turkish mind."[75] Accordingly, *Milli İnkılâp* was banned on July 16, 1934, less than a fortnight after the Thracian Incidents. Atilhan had various other anti-semitic publications. These included conspiratorial novels such as "*Yahudi Dünyayı Nasıl İstila Ediyor*" (How the Jew Invades the World),[76] and "*Sina Cephesinde Yahudi Casuslar*" (Jewish Spies on the Sinai Front).[77] Atilhan also wrote "*İğneli Fıçı*" (The Needled Barrel),[78] a book on how Jews abducted and killed Muslim children in needled barrels to use their blood for Passover matzoh. Another of his works, "*Suzi Liberman 'ın Hatıra Defteri*" (The Diary of Suzi Liberman)[79] was the story of a Jewish spy in Palestine who worked for the British during the First World War. Ankara scrutinized these works,[80] most of which were banned. For example, a decree of September 17, 1936 outlawed the "Diary of Suzi Liberman."[81]

There were also other anti-semitic publications elsewhere in the country. A popular one among them was *Karikatür* (Caricature), a comic magazine that had a large number of anti-semitic illustrations.[82] Another one was Rıza Çavdarlı's "*Tarihte Yahudiler ve Düşmanlık Sebepleri*" (Jews in History and the Reasons behind Animosity Toward Them).[83] In the late 1930s, Ankara banned many of these publications,[84] as well as many others, including Cevat Özelli's work, "*Asrın Gailesi Yahudiler*" (Jews, the Trouble of the Century).[85]

Furthermore, the government scrutinized the press for anti-semitism: for instance, on September 30, 1936, the Ministry of Interior wrote to the CHP's Secretary General about an article in the Istanbul magazine, *Türkiye'nin Sesi* (The Voice of Turkey), which contended that the Turkish press was under Jewish control. This piece also linked communism and Freemasonry to the Jews. Since "this publication would create discord among the citizens, "the Ministry asked that the issues of this magazine be confiscated.[86] In another example along this line, in 1939, the BGD of the Ministry of Interior sent an order to the governors of Istanbul, Izmir, and Adana. Lately, there had been anti-Jewish articles in the press. "These publications, which took place under the influence of foreign countries," could lead to anti-Jewish episodes. For this reason, the Directorate asked the governors to convey the "necessary messages" to the newspaper concessionaires in their provinces.[87] With this, Ankara was making sure that spontaneous anti-Jewish drives would not flare up in the country.

Next to Atilhan and Atsız, perhaps the single most important anti-semitic publisher in the 1930s was Yunus Nadi Abalıoğlu, a nationalist journalist, who issued the pro-Kemalist dailies *Cumhuriyet* and *La République*. The emergence of anti-semitism in Nadi's papers coincided with the Nazi's rise to power. Germany did invest in propaganda efforts in Turkey in the late 1930s. In 1937, Berlin opened up a German Information Office in Istanbul that issued *Die Türkische Post*, a Nazi publication. In addition, Germany courted various Turkish journalists, among them, Nadi,[88] whose anti-semitic attacks heightened in the late 1930s. For example, in 1938, he wrote a number of articles about the alleged Jewish boycott of the Tokatlıyan Hotel in Istanbul. The manager of this hotel was an Austrian who sympathized with the Nazis. After the *Anschluss*, he had started flying the Nazi flag next to the Turkish flag in front of the hotel. Nadi argued that, in reaction to this, the Jews had started boycotting Tokatlıyan.

American diplomats argued to the contrary: "There is no evidence that there has been an organized effort to boycott the hotel." The Americans explained Nadi's attitude on this through his "strong pro-German bias."[89] This was understandable since a reliable member of the Embassy staff reported that Nadi had been "receiving remuneration in the form of certain customs quota facilities for the exportation to Germany of Oriental carpets." (Nadi allegedly offered his services to all sorts of business interests: American diplomats wrote that "numerous private commercial interests *of all nationalities* [*sic*] doing business in Turkey declare that Yunus Nadi has on many occasions offered them his journalistic support 'for a fair price'."[90]) Nevertheless, because of his anti-semitism, Yunus Nadi earned the nickname "Yunus Nazi" among his colleagues.[91] Liberal journalists among them, Ahmet Emin Yalman (1888–1952) and Zekeriya Sertel (1890–1980), the editor of the liberal daily *Tan*, vigorously criticized him for his anti-semitism.[92]

Was Turkey anti-semitic in the 1930s?

In the late 1930s, in addition to scrutinizing anti-semitic publications, Ankara also became careful about the "Speak Turkish" campaign. For instance, on December 19, 1938, the BGD wrote to the governors of Istanbul, Izmir, and Adana:

> We have come across various publications in the December issues of the newspapers, such as Kurun and Son Posta about the minorities not speaking Turkish. Since such publication is not to the benefit of the country, I request that you yourself convey it personally to the responsible people of all newspapers and journals these [publications] be stopped immediately.
>
> (DV BGD 5 825/32)

Edirne was especially under inspection. For instance, in September 1938, Ankara asked the governor there to investigate a banner, "which has recently been hung up on a tree across from the building of the Thrace Student Hostel." This poster demanded that everybody in Edirne speak Turkish. The people responsible for this had to be apprehended immediately. Similar acts were not to be tolerated.[93] With this, Ankara aimed to make sure that new "Speak Turkish" drives would not begin in Thrace.

In view of this, the government monitored the emigration of Jews from Thrace. On December 1, 1938, the EUM informed the Bursa province about reports that Edirne Jews had held a meeting, in which they had decided to move to other provinces that had low Jewish densities. Members of Edirne's

Jewish community would be traveling to Bursa to investigate this town for a possible relocation scheme. Ankara wanted such activities to be monitored.[94] Then, on December 5, the EUM wrote to the governor of Istanbul regarding "Mordeşe Abuaf, known as Mordehay, a Jew from Thrace." Ankara wanted to know more about the activities of this man, who was in Bursa. In addition, it demanded information on whether Mordeşe Abuaf was among the people, who were reportedly searching for possible resettlement locations for the Edirne Jews.[95]

The government hoped to prevent potential anti-Jewish hysteria. A sign of that came in a communiqué, issued on January 28, 1939. This letter written to all the provinces and Inspectorates said, "Our country does not have a Jewish problem, the way some other countries do. We have no restrictive precautions on Jews, who are born on Turkish soil, raised as Turkish citizens, and recognized as Turkish citizens by our laws."[96]

Jewish immigration to Turkey in the 1930s

The case of German and Austrian professors in 1933

More proof of Ankara's distance from anti-semitism was the case of Jewish immigration to Turkey in the 1930s. Ironically, while some Jews were leaving the country, others were arriving. There were two waves of Jewish immigration to Turkey in the 1930s. The first of them involved a small but important group of professors in 1933–34. In the aftermath of the aforementioned university reform of 1933, and starting with Hitler's rise to power, many professors escaping from Nazi Germany arrived in Turkey. There were also musicians, politicians, artists, and architects among these people, who came for a variety of reasons. With the exception of two, all of them were German Jews[97] who fled the Reich to escape anti-semitic laws. Not only Jews, but also social democrats, liberals, or socialists left Germany to avoid persecution for their convictions.[98]

Professor Albert Malche (1876–1956) from the University of Geneva, who conducted the university reform, facilitated these refugees' access to Turkey. In this endeavor, his Swiss colleague Professor Schwärtz, a consultant to "German intellectuals who were obliged to leave that country for political or racial reasons," helped Professor Malche.[99] Turkey willingly admitted these refugees. The fact that Istanbul University had just been reformed and purged of some of its staff, and whilst the government was trying to establish schools of higher learning in Ankara, meant that many positions were offered to them. Turkey's benevolence in accepting these scholars including Ernst Reuter, Wilhelm Röpcke, Rudolf Nielsen, Philip Schwärtz, and Fritz Arndt, among others, greatly benefited Turkish universities. Many disciplines, previously weak in the country, were enhanced by these refugees, who contributed to the establishment of new schools in Ankara that would be consolidated into the Ankara University in 1946. Most of these scholars stayed in Turkey until the end of Second World War, when they left for West Germany or America.[100]

Jewish immigration to Turkey in the late 1930s

A second wave of Jewish immigrants came to Turkey in the late 1930s. These were mostly German and Austrian Jews, escaping Hitler. As Nazi persecution became more severe, Ankara allowed the relatives of Jews residing in Turkey to enter the country.[101] In reaction to this, MP Mehmet Sabri Toprak (Manisa) (1877–1938), the Minister of Agriculture between 1925 and 1927, who had been born in Bosnia, and who himself was of immigrant origin, wanted Jewish immigration to be strictly banned and submitted a draft law to the TBMM. He argued that Turkey should accept only Jews who were artists or were experts in the sciences. Alluding to the fact that the Jews in Turkey did not speak Turkish, Toprak added that all immigrants were to become fluent in Turkish a year after their naturalization. In case of a failure to do so, these people were to be deported.[102]

The government killed Toprak's drafts on the TBMM's floor. The Interior and Foreign Affairs Committee of the parliament unanimously rejected these proposals.[103] In regards to Toprak's request to ban Jewish immigration, the Committee of Foreign Affairs asserted, "the Government already had the power to take any measures desired in regard to immigration and that such a law was unnecessary." With regard to Toprak's second proposal, the Committee argued, "There was no reason for enacting such a law since there already existed legal provisions relative to the use of the Turkish language in public."[104]

According to British diplomats, the unanimous rejection of Toprak's bill in the TBMM meant, "The considerable and prosperous community of Istanbul need have no qualms for their security."[105] The British added that Turkish Jews appeared to be reasonably secure and that "antisemitic legislation had no basis of reality in Turkey."[106] Writing on Toprak's proposals, the CHP's official daily *Ulus*, supported this assertion: "Our measures for defending the right, honor, dignity and the interests of Turkish citizens living in the country are satisfactory and sufficient to render absolutely useless extreme proposals such as those which have been rejected."[107]

An interesting development at this time *vis-à-vis* Jewish immigration was a proposal by Dr Chaim Weizman, the president of the World Zionist Organization, "for the immigration of 100,000 German Jews into Turkey, in return for a large loan to be made to Turkey," which the British diplomats estimated to be as much as £50,000,000, or even higher.[108] Weizman told Ambassador Loraine that regarding this matter he had been in touch with Sami Günsberg, an Ashkenazi Turkish Jew, who was Atatürk's dentist. Günsberg had come back to Weizman and asked him to arrange for a loan from private Jewish funds for Turkey. Weizman added that this loan "might influence Turkey in favor of the Jews, more particularly in favor of a Jewish National Home in Palestine." That could make Turkey into a counterweight against "less friendly Arab countries, such as Iraq."[109] Ankara replied that although "the Jews are our genuine fellow-citizens," and while "their legal rights are guaranteed," it is not possible to "permit the immigration of Jews who are being driven out of other countries in Europe." This reaction to the possibility of mass Jewish immigration was similar to those in other countries of Europe and elsewhere. However, even then, the Turkish Prime Minister added that "Jewish refugees employed in Turkey as specialists (doctors and professors) would be permitted to remain with their families until their contracts have expired." (As discussed in Chapter 4, these people were granted citizenship so that they could stay in the country.) American diplomats noted, once again these statements "indicate that there is little Anti-Semitism in Turkey, at least for the present."[110]

Anti-semitism was indeed not the motive behind Ankara's rejection of Weizman's proposal. Rather it was Turkish nationalism, which dictated the refusal of mass immigration of all non-Turks. This was shown also in Turkey's reaction to another case of proposed immigration. In 1938, London inquired if Turkey would be willing "to absorb all or some of the 800,000 Arab Fellahin who would presumably be leaving the territory of the Jewish state and would require resettlement elsewhere," in case a Jewish state was created in Palestine. Ankara reacted negatively to this proposal since, according to Aras, "the Turkish republic was determined to be an as near as possible racially homogenous Turkish state." Turkey, which "wished to assimilate her minorities," could not be expected to receive more non-Turks. Besides, Ankara "wished to live in amity and bon voisinage with the Arab states that had already got or shortly would get their independence."[111]

The death of Atatürk and the arrest of Italian Jews

The complex nature of Jewish immigration to Turkey in the 1930s demonstrated that Ankara resisted Nazism and European-wide anti-semitism. In this regard, Atatürk, whom the Turkish Jews believed treated them favorably, had a special role. Accordingly, the Jews were upset by news in 1938 that Atatürk was fatally sick.[112] In view of this, Atatürk's successor Celal Bayar's (1883–1987) speech on January 11, 1938 aimed to reassure them: "There is no Jewish problem in the country. There is no minority problem at all. We do not intend to artificially create a Jewish problem because of external influence. We will not allow external currents to influence us."[113]

Still, Atatürk's death on November 10, 1938 upset the Jews. There was a perception among them and other non-Muslims that various anti-minority measures of the government were inspired by İnönü and his associates. The fact that İnönü had now become the president worried them.[114] Besides, at this time, the government's arrest of Italian and German Jews and rumors that these people were going to be deported caused distress. These arrests were made in accordance with the aforementioned Passport Law and the Law on Residence of Foreigners (Yabancıların İkâmeti Hakkında Kanun). These laws stipulated that foreigners who were in Turkey without valid passports would be deported, and that "Stateless persons could not reside in Turkey." These clauses had the potential of targeting the stateless Jewish refugees in Turkey.[115] That provoked fears that they could be sent to fascist Europe, where they would face persecution. This was troublesome especially for the German Jews, since, as a British diplomat noted, "all German and ex-Austrian subjects are required to produce a certificate of 'Aryan' descent" at their Embassy "before their residence permits are renewed."[116]

The problem was even worse for the Italian Jews, who constituted a majority among those that these laws would affect. Most of these people were in fact Turkish Jews, who, for various reasons in the past, had obtained Italian citizenship to take advantage of capitulations and other privileges granted to foreigners. The fact that these Turkish Jews would be deported to fascist Europe caused alarm within the community. This led to fears about possible anti-semitism by İnönü. Then, the government instantly addressed the situation. Hüseyin Cahit Yalçın (1874–1957), a prominent Istanbul journalist, wrote an editorial in his dailies, *Sabah* and *Journal d'Orient*. In a piece "directly inspired by the new President,"[117] Yalçın first addressed the Jewish concerns *vis-à-vis* the İnönü regime:

> To begin with, we can say at once that there is no problem at all regarding Jews, who are Turkish citizens. The Constitution gives full political rights for Jews, who have been living and working in Turkey for centuries... The Constitution of the Republic makes no distinction among its citizens in regard to religion or race... In sum, they [the Jews] can live in all parts of the country, without being considered separately from the mass of citizens who are Muslims. These words are not a problem nor a wish, nor do they have any particular objective. They express the simple reality of today. This is so much the case that it would have been useless to even raise the question if there were not a Jewish question causing anxiety in the world.
>
> (Shaw, *Turkey and the Holocaust*, 26–27)

This was a relief for the Jews.[118] Yalçın also wrote on the issue of the arrests: because of "a small mistake by our police" subsequent to the Passport and Residence Laws, there had been an order to expel "Italian and German Jews resident in Turkey who had been deprived of their citizenship because of anti-semitic legislation. The order was subsequently revoked," wrote Yalçın.[119] He added, "pressure was brought on the Italian Government, which had finally agreed to extend their passports,"[120] and that subsequently local authorities had become more lenient toward Jews with Italian and German passports.

Nevertheless, Yalçın added that this compassion did not mean that Ankara would allow mass immigration of European Jews into Turkey: "We shall not permit the immigration into our country of Jews who, in certain parts of the world, suffer a lack of tranquility." But Turkey would still permit a few foreign Jews: "There are, however, foreign Jews in Turkey who are working as specialists. During the period of their contracts we will receive their immediate families as our guests on the condition that they remain as guests and are not admitted to Turkish citizenship."[121] British diplomats confirmed this: "While the general policy of the Turkish Government is to prevent foreign Jews from entering Turkey no discrimination appears to be exercised against them when foreign specialists are engaged for work which cannot be undertaken by Turkish subjects."[122]

Conclusion: Jews in the 1930s, Turkish nationalism vs anti-semitism

This selective immigration policy of Turkey, as well as the emigration of Turkish Jews in the 1930s should not be interpreted as an argument for anti-semitism. Turkey's vision of the Jews in the 1930s lacked such a component. The anti-anti-semitic policies of the government, as well as Jewish immigration in the 1930s support this point. In this regard, the government did not view the Jews as a racially alien category. Ankara treated local and foreign Jews favorably compared to other European countries. Hence, even after the controversial arrest of Italian Jews, it continued admitting Jewish refugees from Italy.[123] German Jews were also allowed to come to the country. For instance, on January 6, 1939, Ankara accepted Emma Peters, "of the Jewish race from Vienna, the mother of Prof. W Peters, Professor Emeritus of child psychology at the University of Istanbul." Peters was allowed to remain in the country for the duration of her son's residence.[124] On this day, the government also let "Jetti Thaler, a nanny of Jewish race, who worked for MP Şükrü Koçak from Erzurum," to stay in Turkey.[125] Then, on March 6, another decree permitted "Manelok Olga, a German Jew, and resident in Slovakia," and "the mother of Dr. Verner Laquesir, a laboratory assistant at the obstetrics and gynecology clinic of Istanbul University," to come to Turkey. The doctor's mother could stay in the country until the end of her son's tenure.[126] In another case on the same day, the government let "Martha Engelman, resident in Berlin, the mother of a German Jew, Konrad Engelman, who worked as an expert in the accounting division of *Denizbank*," to come to Turkey. "Mr. Engelman's sister, Suzan" was also granted this privilege until the expiration of Mr. Engelman's contract.[127]

Accordingly, in many instances in 1939, Ankara permitted Jews from Europe to come to Turkey. This tolerance, at a time when almost no country in Europe offered Jews safe haven, points at the absence of anti-semitism in government policies. True, the 1934 Incidents had scared the Jewish community. However, not anti-semitism or racism, but nationalism and security perceptions seem to have played a role in these incidents. Thus, it was Turkish nationalism that shaped Turkey's attitude toward the Jews in the 1930s. Ankara hoped that the Jews would assimilate by adopting the Turkish language and taking over Turkish names. This points at two significant conclusions: first, unlike in many other inter-war European countries, in the 1930s, race did not separate the Jews from the majority in Turkey; second, and more importantly, anti-semitism was impotent in the country at the brink of the Second World War.

Conclusion

Understanding Turkish nationalism in modern Turkey—the Kemalist legacy

The characteristics of Turkish nationalism in the interwar period

The 1930s witnessed the advent of an étatist, authoritarian, and nationalist state in Turkey. The swing to the political right was rooted in both domestic and international factors. Kemalism opted for authoritarianism, first, in the face of mounting domestic opposition to secularization and nation-state building. Besides, while Turkey had come to regard the West as a model, and since Atatürk's idea of modernization followed Europe, the bankruptcy of democratic regimes in the continent had repercussions in Turkey.[1] Ankara turned away from democracy and adopted an authoritarian line. Yet, even then, Turkish nationalism did not break away from its earlier roots, including the 1920s, when secularized Turkey had moved to discard religion. Then, Ankara had officially focused on a voluntaristic, territorial, and political understanding of the nation. The republic had voiced this in its 1924 constitution, the CHP documents, as well as a number of speeches by its leaders.

However, even so, religion played a major role under this rubric. After Kemalist secularization, nominal Islamic identity as well as the cultural heritage of the former Muslim millet became important in defining Turkishness. This was evident in Ankara's day-to-day practices, which demonstrated that it viewed the country's Muslims as Turks and Christians as outsiders. The government's reaction to the Armenian exodus of 1929–30, or its treatment of Greeks and Eastern Christians exemplified this desire to isolate the Christians from the body of the Turkish nation. Then, as in the case of the Kurds in the 1920s, Kemalism regarded all Muslims as members of the Turkish nation. Accordingly, Islam was a subtle but definitive marker of Turkishness in the 1920s.

On the other hand, as the "Speak Turkish" campaign demonstrated, language increasingly became a component of nationality too. This was part of an assimilationist vision, which aimed to integrate the Muslims and Jews into the body of the nation through their adoption of Turkish.

In the 1930s, under the *Turkish History Thesis*, ethnicity and race joined religion and language as markers of Turkishness. (Race became central especially in High Kemalist highbrow works and school textbooks.) As proven by many administrative documents, race was indeed an important component of the relations between Ankara and the citizens in the 1930s. For instance, in 1939, the Ministry of Interior wrote to the First Inspector-General about immigrants fleeing Kürtdağı, a mountainous region in Syria, which had just experienced an anti-French rebellion: "It has been observed that refugees coming from Kürtdağı comprise a significant number ... the racial situation of these refugees be investigated" said the communiqué.[2]

Still, this emphasis on race was nuanced: it did not necessarily denote immutable biological characteristics, passed down genetically. Rather, as elaborated in the *History Thesis*, in the High Kemalist understanding, "race" often meant ethnicity-through-language. This opened up Turkishness to Jews, if they learned Turkish. On the other hand, Islam's pivotal role in shaping the Turkish nation compromised the notion of race further, leading to the ethno-religious definition of Turkishness. These factors made it possible for the non-Turkish Muslims to become Turkish.

The Anatolian, Balkan, and Black Sea Muslims vis-à-vis Turkishness

This explains why, even when ethnicity and race were central in the High Kemalist thinking, non-Turkish Anatolian, Balkan, and Black Sea Muslims, including the Kurds, were seen as assimilable, if they learned Turkish. A 1939 statement from Ankara to the governor of Hakkâri, Turkey's most heavily Kurdish province, pointed at this: "I report that in this district, men and women have been registered at nations' classrooms [of the literacy campaigns] and that they are being taught our language and letters."[3] The mass immigration and naturalization of Balkan Muslims also demonstrated High Kemalism's desire to assimilate the rump Muslim millet. Not only Turks, but also non-Turkish Ottoman Muslims, who had immigrated to the country in the past, or wanted to come to Turkey now, were seen as assimilable. Ankara was so firmly committed to this mission that it was ready to ignore the fact that such groups existed at all. In December 1938, the Minister of Interior, Refik Saydam wrote: "Unconstitutional phrases such as '... is being investigated as a member of the Circassian race ...' have been attracting our attention. The Circassians are Turkish citizens and are Turks by race."[4]

However, while High Kemalism was committed to the full assimilation of non-Turkish Muslims, it also nurtured caution toward them. As shown in many administrative acts, Ankara remained wary of these communities, especially the more sizable ones, such as the Circassians and the Arabs. In this regard, the government was particularly cautious toward the Kurds. Yet, as the Kadroists aptly elaborated, High Kemalism saw the Kurdish question not just as an ethnic issue, but as a dilemma with nationality, security, centralization, and modernization components. Accordingly, for example, when Ankara unleashed full forces to crush the Dersim uprising, it aimed to both modernize and assimilate the region's Kurds. Resettlement policies, too, facilitated the Kurds' Turkification. The governor of Malatya, a province with a mixed Turkish-Kurdish province, wrote in March 1939:

> Since there is not a single Turk in the Kahta district, and while there are people engaged in Kurdishness, who have established ties to the south [Syria], and who own a significant portion of the land there; for the good of the state these people need to be relocated away from this area [Kahta].
>
> (DV HKM 1793, Telegram Nr 313)

The Jews vis-à-vis *Turkishness*

Thanks to the ethno-linguistic definition of Turkishness, High Kemalism kept the avenues of Turkishness open to the Jews, too. In this undertaking, Ankara's efforts were challenged by the legacy of the Ottoman past, namely, the Jews' separation from the Ottoman Muslims under the millet system, a condition that now put them on the periphery of Turkishness. Even so, the naturalization of many east-central European Jews and the mostly Jewish White Russians, the "Speak Turkish" campaign, as well as Jewish immigration to Turkey in the 1930s proved that Ankara did not see the Jews as outsiders. High Kemalism distanced itself from anti-semitism. True, as in the case of the Thracian Exodus, there were anti-Jewish incidents in the 1930s. Yet, such occurrences were due more to Ankara's security perception than to anti-semitism. British diplomats, otherwise critical observers of interwar Turkey, gave Ankara credit on this matter: "antisemitic legislation has no basis of reality in Turkey."[5]

The Ottoman Christians vis-à-vis *Turkishness*

While Kemalism attempted to assimilate the Jews, it saw the Ottoman Christians as inassimilable into Turkishness. Since Turkish ethnicity was conterminous with Balkan-Anatolian Islam, as revealed by the denaturalization of former Ottoman Christians, these people were seen outside the Turkish nation. Given the legacy of the millet system, which had separated the Ottoman Muslims from the Christians, and also due to the recent conflicts with the Christian nations of the Empire, Kemalism conceived the Ottoman Christians outside Turkishness, and the Ottoman Muslims inside Turkishness. (This separation of Ottoman Christians from Turkishness did not necessarily create a prejudice against non-Ottoman Christians. As the naturalization of the east-central European Christians in the 1930s evidenced, High Kemalism saw them as assimilable, though in limited numbers.)

While High Kemalism viewed the Ottoman Christians as non-Turkish, the position of the Armenians in this equation was especially sensitive. The continuing anti-Turkish activities by Armenian nationalists inside and outside Turkey, especially various attempts by them to assassinate the leaders of the republic, induced contemporary government antagonism toward the Armenians. Events surrounding the sudden collapse of the Anatolian Armenian community during the First World War led Turkish nationalism to label Armenians as alien. The 1917–20 wars between Turkey and Armenia added to the image of Armenians as a hostile people.

The denaturalization of former Ottoman Armenians, as well as Ankara's wariness toward Armenians in the 1930s illustrated such feelings. What is more, High Kemalism showed caution even toward Armenians who had embraced Islam, including those whose parents had converted. In this regard, religion marked Armenian ethnicity, thus almost turning into a racial indicator. The legacy of the millet system, the catastrophes of 1915–20, as well as the ethnicism of the 1930s made it possible for Turkey to imagine the Armenians as non-Turkish.

Subsequently, Turkish nationalism remained hostile to the Armenians and other Ottoman Christians. Religion created an ethno-national boundary between them and the Ottoman Muslims. With its immigration policies, Ankara blocked the former Ottoman Armenians from coming to Turkey. Furthermore, the government marginalized the Ottoman Christians, especially the Armenians, but also the Jacobites, Chaldeans, and Assyrians, even those living in Turkey. For instance, the official historiography produced during the 1930s omitted the Armenians, an autochthonous people in Anatolia, as well as Armenian history from its account of Turkish history.[6] Consequently, there are no direct references to them in the resettlement laws of the 1930s.

Kemalism's three zones of Turkishness

In conclusion, it appears that High Kemalism had three overlapping, but inexact categories of Turkishness. The first was territorial. This definition, the most inclusive of the three, was embodied in the 1924 constitution. It registered all inhabitants of Turkey as Turks. The second definition, less inclusive than the first, was religious. This was embedded in the millet system, and articulated in the 1930s highbrow works, textbooks, and CHP documents. Due to the legacy of the millet system, the Kemalists saw nominal Islam as an avenue toward Turkishness: all Muslims in Turkey were potential Turks. This religious definition led to a number of conflicts. First, by barring the non-Muslims from the nation, it contradicted the territorial definition of Turkishness. Second, it was not always consistent: although all Turks were Muslims, not all Muslims were ethnic Turks. The third and the least inclusive definition of Turkishness under High Kemalism was ethno-religious. This definition was best observed in the day-to-day acts of the state.

First, Ankara saw only those people who were ethnically Turkish as Turks. Second, it used religion to classify non-Turks into two hierarchical categories, Muslim, and non-Muslim. It favored the former over the latter. The millet system helped the Kemalists view the Balkan, Anatolian, and Black Sea Muslims as one community with the Turks. Ethnic Turks were not a solid majority in Turkey. If the non-Turkish Muslims assimilated, they could enhance the Turkish population. Hence, the Kemalists were willing to accept them as Turks, provided that they adopted Turkish. Still, Ankara would not forget that these people were not ethnic Turks. Accordingly, the government remained cautious toward the non-Turkish Muslims, especially the Kurds, the largest, and the least-assimilated group among them. It denied the Kurds (and other Muslim groups) a separate national identity and screened them to prevent their number from increasing. In its efforts to assimilate these communities, Ankara strived to reshape the ethnic map of the country

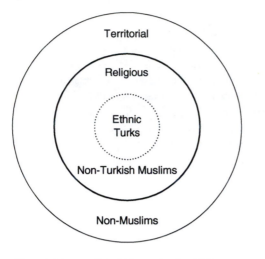

Figure 3 Zones of Turkishness in the 1930s.

through a planned relocation policy. When presented a chance, it resettled the Muslim minorities among the Turks in order to facilitate their integration into the Turkish population.

Thus, in its interaction with the country's ethnic and religious minorities, High Kemalism produced three concentric zones of Turkishness: an outer territorial one, reserved for the non-Muslims (with the Jews closer to the center than the Christians); a middle religious one, reserved for the non-Turkish Muslims; and an inner ethnic one, reserved for the Turks (Figure 3). A 1933 directive to Kars and Artvin provinces, along the country's border with the Soviet Caucasus, demonstrated the existence of these circles in the minds of the republican administrators. This dispatch discussed the conditions under which refugees from the Soviet Union would be admitted to Turkey. People who "are Turkish or share the Turkish culture," were to be accepted as refugees and sent into the First Inspectorate-General (an area with a heavy Kurdish population) for resettlement. Others, "who are not Turkish, but speak Turkish or are married to a Turkish girl, are to be arranged for resettlement in Central Turkey" (the solidly Turkish heartland). The rest of the people, "who do not belong to the Turkish race or share the Turkish culture" could not be admitted as refugees under any conditions, said the dispatch.[7]

Of the three zones of Turkishness, the outermost "territorial conceptualization of Turkish national identity or citizenship became eroded" quickly.[8] Accordingly, today, in this scheme of concentric circles of Turkishness, the further away a group is from the center, the more unaccommodating is the state toward it. Only when a group is located in the innermost, ethnic zone, does it enjoy close proximity to the state. Moreover, while groups from the religious layer are expected eventually to move into the inner ethnic core, groups from the territorial zone are strictly confined to the hostile margins of the society.

The saliency of ethno-religious nationalism in the former Ottoman sphere

Despite its idiosyncrasies, the situation in Turkey in the 1930s was not unique. Other interwar Balkan countries, too, resorted to demographic measures as a means of ethnic engineering. Then, these states followed ethno-religious nationalisms. For instance, Sofia relocated Bulgarian immigrants from Greece along the country's Black Sea coast, an area that was not solidly ethnic Bulgarian. Likewise, Bucharest resettled Vlach immigrants from the southern Balkans into the Dobrudja, one of Romania's ethnically most diverse regions.[9] In this regard, the situation in Greece was especially poignant. The interwar Greek state marginalized the non-Orthodox minorities in the country, including the Muslim Turks, Pomaks, Albanians, and Roma,[10] as well as the Sephardic Jews and the Greek Catholics.[11] Athens aimed to get rid of these communities. On the other hand, Greek nationalism saw Orthodox Albanians, Bulgarians, Macedonians, and Vlachs as potential Greeks to be absorbed into the nation.[12] Greece refused to recognize these communities as separate ethnic groups.[13] In the official Greek parlance, for instance, Orthodox Macedonians and Bulgarians were "Slavo-phone Greeks."[14] Besides, Athens forbade the public and private use of the Macedonian and Bulgarian languages.[15] To add insult to injury, when the Macedonians who had immigrated to the US came back to Greece, Athens expelled them upon their return to the country.[16]

Although non-Orthodox and non-Greco-phone people were only 6.20 percent of Greece's population in 1928,[17] since they were concentrated in certain cities and provinces, this gave them significance in the government's eyes.[18] Consequently, Athens used its resettlement policies to address this situation. After the Turco-Greek population exchange, for instance, it resettled Anatolian Greeks in Macedonia, Thrace, and Salonika in Northern Greece, which had a heavy minority presence.[19] Then, throughout the interwar period, Greece remained alert toward the non-Orthodox and non-Greco-phone minorities. In fact, even today, Greece seems to discriminate against these groups.[20]

Understanding Turkey's nationality-related dilemmas: the Kemalist legacy

The nationalization-through-religion that dominates nationalisms in Turkey (and Greece) points at the saliency of the millet system and ethno-religious identities in the former Ottoman lands. Accordingly, even today these factors define contemporary Turkishness (and Greekness).[21] This explains the following religion-and-nationality-related dilemmas within modern Turkey:

1   Turkey is unsympathetic to the idea of Muslims, such as the Kurds, being distinct ethnic groups.[22] This is because Turkish nationalism is assimilatory and open toward all the Muslims in the country. While many of these people have already willingly and successfully assimilated, Turkey cannot comprehend why it is difficult for the others to merge into the nation. In addition,

when groups such as the Kurds resist incorporation, Turkish nationalism reacts, demanding the assimilation of the Kurds, whom it sees in the ethno-religious zone of Turkishness. The ideological roots of the Kurds' Turkification lies in the juxtaposition of ethnic and religious definitions of the nation under High Kemalism.

2   There is a tension in Turkey between Islam as a religion and Islam as an iden-tity. This is a product of the overlapping processes of secularism and nation-alization of the recent past. At present, while nominal Islam is a marker of Turkishness, Islam as a faith is outside the public sphere. Accordingly, when parties resort to introduce Islam into the political sphere, they encounter resistance from Turkish secularism, as in the case of the Welfare Party (Refah Partisi—RP) in the early 1990s, or the Virtue Party (Fazilet Partisi—FP) in the late 1990s.

3   As established by the High Kemalist attitude toward the missionaries, Turkey sees Christianity as non-Turkish, and Christians as outsiders. Hence, Ankara treats its Christians, however numerically insignificant they may have become since the 1930s, with suspicion. This explains why, for instance, even when Turkey acted relatively favorably toward its Greek minority in the 1930s, it still nurtured trepidations toward Greek heritage in the country. Kemalism saw the Ottoman Christians as unsuited for being Turkish and unfit for assimilation since they lacked the *sine qua non* of Turkishness: Islam. The origins of this antagonism lie in the incongruity between the idea of Turkey as a nation-state of the Ottoman-Turkish Muslims and the presence of Christians on Turkish territory.

4   Turkish nationalism is ambivalent toward the Jews. On the one hand, they are a non-Muslim minority, like the Christians. Yet, on the other, compared to the Christians, they are in a better position *vis-à-vis* Ankara.[23] Historically agreeable relations between the Turks and the Jews, and the absence of potent anti-semitism in Turkey rendered Kemalism tolerant toward the Jews. Consequently, unlike in many other interwar European countries, where racial walls separated the Jews from the Gentiles, High Kemalist Turkey did not set up such a divide. However, since language and the legacy of the millet system were important components of the notion of Turkishness, the Jews, who did not speak Turkish and who had not been part of the Muslim millet, remained on the margins of the Turkish nation.

5   Given her sensitivities *vis-à-vis* her Christian and non-Turkish Muslim com-munities, Turkey remains cautious today toward her neighbors that harbor nationalist causes among these groups. Ankara's wariness against interwar French Syria, which provided safe haven to nationalist Armenians, Kurds, and Circassians, illustrated this phenomenon. In the 1990s, this situation repeated itself, when Damascus provided refuge to the PKK. Turkey views its neighbors as a security threat when they shelter its non-Muslim and Muslim groups. Hence, today, these communities continue to burden Turkey in more than one way.

Notes

Introduction: Turkish nationalism today

1 Lately, though, reforms Turkey has carried out toward European Union (EU) accession, have led to an improvement in the non-Muslims' status. Since December 1999, when the EU recognized Turkey as a candidate country for membership, Ankara has moved fast to satisfy the EU's accession rules, Copenhagen Criteria, which stipulate among other things, "respect for and protection of minorities." This process has started a discussion on granting wider rights to the non-Muslims (as well as facilitating broadcasting and education in Kurdish and other languages spoken by various Muslim communities). For more on Turkey's EU reforms, see Soner Cagaptay, "European Union Reforms Diminish the Role of the Turkish Military: Ankara Knocking on Brussels' Door," *Policywatch*, no. 781, The Washington Institute for Near East Policy, August 12, 2003.

2 For more on this controversy, see *Radikal*, October 13, 1999, October 17, 1999, October 31, 1999, and *Hürriyet*, March 24, 2002.

3 For the background of Syrian support for the PKK, see Robert Olson, "The Kurdish Question and Turkey's Foreign Policy toward Syria, Iran, Russia, and Iraq since the Gulf War," in *The Kurdish Nationalist Movement in the 1990s*, ed. Robert Olson (Lexington, KY: University Press of Kentucky, 1996), 84–92.

1 From the Muslim millet to the Turkish nation: the Ottoman legacy

1 Anthony Smith, *Nations and Nationalism in the Global Era* (Cambridge: Polity Press, 1995), 57.

2 Smith, *Nations and Nationalism in the Global Era*, 57.

3 Anthony Smith, *Ethnic Origins of Nations* (Oxford: Basil Blackwell, 1986), 55.

4 Smith, *Ethnic Origins of Nations*, 15.

5 Smith, *Ethnic Origins of Nations*, 51–54.

6 Smith, *Nations and Nationalism in the Global Era*, 159.

7 For a first person account on this, see the Hebrew chronicle of Isaac Schulhof, a Jewish resident of Ottoman Buda. In his memoirs, translated into Italian, Schulhof details the fall of Buda to the Habsburgs in 1686. He elaborates on the traumatic nature of this event for the Ottoman Muslims and Jews, who were purged from the city following the Habsburg takeover through mass killings, forced conversions, slavery, and expulsions. "Megilat Oven" (La meghilla di Buda (1686)) trans. with a preface by Paolo Agostini, *Testimonianze sull'ebraismo*, 13 (Rome: Carucci, 1982).

8 Alexandre Popović, *L'Islam Balkanique* (Berlin: In Komission bei Otto Harassowitz-Wiesbaden, 1986), 183–87, 257–60; Mustafa Imamović, *Historija Bošnjaka* (History of the Bosniaks) (Sarajevo: Bošnjaka Zajednica Kulture Sarajevo, 1997), 280–99; and

Radovan Samardžić, "Srbi u Turksom Čarstvu" (Serbs in the Turkish Empire) in *Istorija Srpskog Naroda* (History of the Serb Nation) vol. 4, part 1 (Beograd: Srpska Književna Zadruga, 1981–93), 19–30. For more on the extermination of the Ottoman Muslims in these lands, see *Istorija Naroda Jugoslavije: početka XVI do kraja XVIII veka* (History of the Yugoslav Peoples: From the Beginning of Sixteenth Century to the End of Eighteenth Century) eds, Bogo Grafenauer, Jorjo Tadić, and Branislav Čurčić, vol. 2 (Belgrade: Prosveta, 1960), 496, 519–30, 587, 599–60.

9 In most cases, the destruction of Balkan Muslim communities was accompanied by the annihilation of the local Jewish communities. For example, when the Greek principality attained independence in 1821, not only Muslims, but also Jews in the Peloponnesus (Morea) and Attica were slaughtered by Greek forces. Yitzchak Kerem, "Jewish-Turkish Relations in the Greek Peninsula during the Nineteenth and Early Twentieth Centuries," in *Turkish-Jewish Encounters: Studies on Turkish-Jewish Relations through the Ages*, ed. Mehmet Tütüncü (Haarlem, the Netherlands: SOTA, 2001), 170.

10 Ernest Gellner, *Nations and Nationalism* (Ithaca, NY: Cornell University Press, 1983), 45.

11 Robert Shannan Peckham, "Frontier Fictions," in *National Histories, Natural States Nationalism and the Politics of Place in Greece* (London: I. B. Tauris, 2001), 40.

12 Kemal H. Karpat, "Millets and Nationality: The Roots of Incongruity of Nation and State in the Post-Ottoman Era," in *Christians and Jews in the Ottoman Empire*, ed. Benjamin Braude and Bernard Lewis (New York: Holmes and Meier, 1982). For case studies of nationalization-through-religion among the Balkan Christians, see Hugh Poulton, *Who are the Macedonians?* (London: Hurst and Company, 1995), 26–47; and Paschalis M. Kitromilides, "'Imagined Communities' and the National Origins of the National Question in the Balkans," *European History Quarterly* 19(2) (1989): 149–92. For a work that analyzes the impact of nationalization-through-religion in the Balkans, see Leon Volovici, *Nationalist Ideology and Antisemitism: The Case of Romanian Intellectuals in the 1930s* (Oxford: Pergamon Press, 1991). In this work, the author argues that one of the reasons for widespread anti-Semitism in Romania in the interwar era was the identification of Romanian nationhood with Orthodoxy. This led to the branding of the Jews as non-nationals and created a wall between them and Orthodox Romanians, 3, 30–35, 80–85, 95–113.

13 Maria Todorova, "The Ottoman Legacy in the Balkans," in *Imperial Legacy*, ed. Carl Brown (New York, Columbia University Press, 1996), *passim.*

14 Todorova, "The Ottoman Legacy in the Balkans," in *Imperial Legacy*, 66. For more on the persecution of the Balkan Muslims during and after the establishment of Greek, Serbian, Montenegrin, and Bulgarian states, see Popović, *L'Islam Balkanique*, 108–12, 113–34; 260–64, 265–67; 207–08, 294–96; and 66–73, 73–78; and Nedim İpek, *Rumeli'den Anadolu'ya Türk Göçleri 1871–1890* (Turkish Migrations from Rumelia to Anatolia 1871–1890) (Ankara: Türk Tarih Kurumu, 1994).

15 Justin McCarthy, *Death and Exile: The Ethnic Cleansing of the Ottoman Muslims, 1821–1922.* (Princeton, NJ: Darwin Press, 1995), 1. On the other hand, Cem Behar notes that between 1876 and 1895, 1,150,015 immigrants arrived in the Ottoman Empire. *The Population of the Ottoman Empire and Turkey*, comp. Cem Behar, Historical Statistics Series, vol. 2 (Ankara: State Institute of Statistics, 1996), 51. For two articles on the number of Muslim refugees fleeing into Anatolia before, during and after the Balkan Wars, see Justin McCarthy, "Muslim Refugees in Turkey: The Balkan Wars, World War I and the Turkish War of Independence," in *Humanist and Scholar: Essays in Honor of Andreas Tietze*, ed. Heath Lowry and Donald Quataert (Istanbul: Isis Press, 1993), 87–111; and İlhan Tekeli, "Osmanlı İmparatorluğu'ndan Günümüze Nüfusun Zorunlu Yer Değiştirmesi ve İskan Sorunu," *Toplum ve Bilim*, 50 (1990): 49–72. For detailed accounts of the persecution of the Ottoman Muslims and their ensuing flight to Anatolia, consult *Death and Exile*, 1–22, 59–108, 135–78; and Alexandre Toumarkine, *Les Migrations des Musulmans Balkaniques en Anatolie (1876–1913)*, (Istanbul: Isis, 1995), 27–78. For a case study, which examines the migrations of the

Crimean Tatars and the Caucasus Muslims, see Johannes Kläy, "Endstation 'Islambol'. Die Türkei als Assyland für muslimische Glaubensflüchtlinge und Rückwanderer *(muhacir)* im 19. und 20. Jahrhundert," in *Migrations en Asie: Migrants, Personnes Déplacées et Réfugiés*, ed. Micheline Cetlivres-Demont (Berne: Société Suisse d'Ethnologie, 1983), 9–82.

16 Kemal H. Karpat, "Historical Continuity and Identity Change," in *Ottoman Past and Today's Turkey*, ed. Kemal H. Karpat (Leiden: Brill, 2000), 22.

17 Kemal H. Karpat, "The Hijra from Russia and the Balkans: The Process of Self-Determination in the Late Ottoman State," in *Muslim Travelers: Pilgrimage, Migration, and the Religious Imagination*, ed. Dale F. Eickelman and James Piscatore (London: Routledge, 1990), 131–52.

18 Kemal H. Karpat, "Ottomanism, Fatherland and the 'Turkishness' of the State," in *The Politicization of Islam: Reconstructing Identity, State, Faith, and Community in the Late Ottoman State* (Oxford: Oxford University Press, 2001), 341–45.

19 Hakan M. Yavuz, "Islam and Nationalism: Yusuf Akçura, Üç Tarz-i Siyaset," *Oxford Journal of Islamic Studies* 4(2) (1993): 190–92, 207.

20 Hakan M. Yavuz, "The Patterns of Islamic Identity: Dynamics of National and Transnational Loyalties and Identities," *Central Asian Survey* 14(3) (1995): 360.

21 Kemal H. Karpat, "Transformation of the Ottoman State: 1789–1908," *International Journal of Middle East Studies* 3 (1972): 266.

22 For the emergence of the vatan concept among Turkish writers and intellectuals at this time, see Kemal H. Karpat, "Ottomanism, Fatherland and the 'Turkishness' of the State" in *The Politicization of Islam*, 329–35. Also, consult Şerif Mardin, *The Genesis of Young Ottoman Thought: A Study in the Modernization of Turkish Political Ideas* (Princeton, NJ: Princeton University Press, 1962), *passim*.

23 Selim Deringil argues that Namık Kemal popularized the "vatan" concept in his work, "The Ottoman Origins of Kemalist Nationalism: Namık Kemal's and Mustafa Kemal," *European History Quarterly* 23(2) (1993): 165–91.

24 In this play, Namık Kemal poetically eulogized the courageous defense of Silistre, a mostly Muslim-Turkish town along the Danube. The Ottoman army and the town's inhabitants rallied to defend Silistre against a numerically superior Russian army during the Crimean War. Consequently, Silistre became an icon of Turkish-Muslim love for "vatan." For this play in Turkish, see *Vatan yahut Silistre* (The Homeland or Silistre), ed. Kenan Akyüz (Ankara: Kültür ve Turizm Bakanlığı, 1988).

25 Feroz Ahmad, *The Young Turks: The CUP in Turkish Politics, 1908–1914* (Oxford: Oxford University Press, 1969), 152–53; and McCarthy, *Death and Exile*, 336.

26 Justin McCarthy, *The Arab World, Turkey and the Balkans (1878–1914): A Handbook of Historical Statistics* (Boston, MA: G. K. Hall, 1982), 60, 64–68. Contemporary scholarship disagrees on the number of Greeks, and Armenians in Turkey before the First World War since there are three censuses recording the population of the Ottoman Empire at that time. The first of these is the official Ottoman census of 1911–12, and the other two censuses carried out by the Greek Patriarchate in 1910–12, and the Armenian Patriarchate in 1912. My calculations, based on Justin McCarthy's work, *The Arab World, Turkey and the Balkans*: 69–83, reveal that the Ottoman census recorded 1,562,678 Greeks and 1,265,960 Armenians in today's Turkey (Istanbul, Anatolia, and Thrace) in 1912. On the other hand, the Greek Patriarchate's census puts the number of Greeks in Turkey in 1912 at 2,068,402. Alexis Alexandris, "The Greek Census of Anatolia and Thrace (1910–1912): A Contribution to Ottoman Historical Demography," *Ottoman Greeks in the Age of Nationalism*, ed. Dimitri Goncidas and Charles Issawi (Princeton, NJ: Darwin Press, 1999), 54; and Paschalis M. Kitromilides and Alexis Alexandris, "Ethnic Survival and Forced Migration," *Deltio Kentrou Mikrasiatikuon Spoduon* 5 (1977): 9–44, while the Armenian Patriarchate recorded 1,914,620 Armenians in Turkey in 1912. Raymond H. Kevorkian and Paul B. Paboudjian, eds, *Les Arméniens* (Paris: Editions d'art et l'Histoire, 1992), 53–60.

27 For a work that studies the spread of Turkish nationalism among the non-elites of the Empire, see Ercümend Kuran, "The Impact of Nationalism on the Turkish Elite in the Nineteenth Century," in *Beginnings of Modernization in the Middle East*, ed. William, R. Polk and Richard L. Chambers (Chicago, IL: University of Chicago, 1968). Kuran applies Miroslav Hroch's "three-stage theory" to Turkish nationalism to argue that in Turkey, nationalism started as a scientific movement among the elites. Then, it evolved into a literary movement. Only in the third phase, Turkish nationalism turned political to become popular with the masses. For Hroch's work explaining his "three-stage theory," see *Social Preconditions of National Revival in Europe* (New York: Columbia University Press, 2000).

28 Şerif Mardin, "The Ottoman Empire," in *After Empire*, ed. Mark von Hagen and Karen Barkey (Boulder, CO: University of Colorado, 1997), 115.

29 Alec L. Macfie, *The End of the Ottoman Empire 1908–1923* (London: Longmont, 1998), 76.

30 For the persecution of the Balkan Muslims during and after the Balkan Wars, by Serbia, Montenegro, Greece, and Bulgaria, see Popović, *L'Islam Balkanique*, respectively, 302–11, 135–47, and 74–77. Also consult the recently reprinted report of the inquiry by the international commission of the Carnegie Endowment, *The Other Balkan Wars: A 1913 Carnegie Endowment inquiry in retrospect*, with a new introduction and reflections by George F. Kennan (Washington, DC: Carnegie Endowment for International Peace, Brookings Institute Publications, 1993), *passim*. For more on the persecution of the Ottoman Muslims in the Balkan Wars and their flight to the Empire, see H. Yıldırım Ağanoğlu, *Göç: Osmanlı'dan Cumhuriyet'e Balkanlar'ın Makûs Talihi* (Migration, the Unhappy History of the Balkans from the Ottomans through the Republic) (Istanbul: Kum Saati, 2001), 44–98.

31 *Cumhuriyet*, October 17, 1931.

32 Mardin, "The Ottoman Empire," in *After Empire*, 117; Ahmad, *The Young Turks*, 154–55.

33 Ayhan Aktar, "Economic Nationalism in Turkey. The Formative Years, 1912–1925," *Boğaziçi Journal of Economic and Administrative Sciences* 10(1–2) (1996): 263–90.

34 Şükrü Hanioğlu argues that even before the Balkan wars, men of Balkan origins had dominated the nationalist movement, *The Young Turks in Opposition* (Oxford: Oxford University Press, 1994), 169–70.

35 This was accompanied by a proliferation of nationalist publications. Among these, the first general of the Turks by Necib Asım, *Türk Tarihi* (Turkish History) (Istanbul: Dar al-Matba'ah al-'Amirah, 1316 [1898 or 1899]) is especially striking. There were also various journals and newspapers published during this period. These included the journals, *Genç Kalemler* (Young Pens) and *Yeni Lisan* (New Language) in Salonika, and *Türk Yurdu* (Turkish Homeland) in Istanbul, as well as newspapers, such as *Hakikat* (Truth), *İkdam* (Progress), and *Sabah* (Morning). For more on this, see Hanioğlu, *The Young Turks in Opposition*: 169–70; David Kushner, *The Rise of Turkish Nationalism* (London: Frank Cass, 1977), 7–22, 30, 41–57; and Macfie, *The End of the Ottoman Empire*, 85–88.

36 Bernard Lewis, "History Writing and National Revival in Turkey," *Middle Eastern Affairs* 4(6–7) (1953): 218–29; and Mardin, "The Ottoman Empire," in *After Empire*, 115.

37 Karpat, "From Religion to Ethnic National Identity," in *The Politicization of Islam*, 357–73.

38 Hanioğlu, *The Young Turks in Opposition*, 170.

39 Before 1913, in addition to nationalism, the Young Turk regime showed interest also in other ideas including Ottomanism, Islamism, and Turkism. The CUP's commitment to these ideologies was linked more to a pragmatic desire to find a method with which to save the declining Empire than to its steadfast commitment to them. Consequently, even after 1913, when the CUP turned to nationalism, it continued to toy with other ideas. There are a number of works that discuss the CUP's shifting

ideological orientation in the period between 1908 and 1918. Of them, Feroz Ahmad's study, *The Young Turks* argues that depending on political developments, the CUP promoted various ideologies ranging from Ottomanism to Islamism and Turkism, 134–62. On the other hand, Masami Arai contends that although initially, it favored Ottomanism, the CUP switched to nationalism later in this period. The Committee saw Turkism as a tool with which to save the decaying Empire, *Turkish Nationalism in the Young Turk Era* (Leiden: Brill, 1992), 1–65. Hasan Kayalı points at Islamism in the Young Turk policies between 1908 and 1918. He sees this policy not as a product of the party's dedication to Islam, but rather due to the CUP's desire to transform the Empire into a viable state that would appeal to its mostly Muslim Arab citizens. As for the alleged Turkist policies of the CUP, these were in fact centralizing measures that aimed at reforming the Empire. Save such pragmatic utilizations of ideology, the state was essentially Ottomanist throughout the decade between 1908 and 1918. *Arabs and the Young Turks: Ottomanism, Arabs, and Islamism in the Ottoman Empire, 1908–1918* (Berkeley, CA: University of California Press, 1997). Finally, Jacob M. Landau draws attention to Pan-Turkist nature of the Young Turkish regime. Pan-Turkism that flourished between 1908 and 1918 became the guiding ideological principle of the CUP regime especially during the First World War, *Pan-Turkism: From Irredentism to Cooperation* (Bloomington, IN: Indiana University Press, 1995).

40 Ahmet Yıldız, *Ne Mutlu Türküm Diyebilene?* (How happy he, who can say he is a Turk?) (Istanbul: İletişim, 2001), 30–36, 79–86.

41 However, Kayalı argues that this measure did not necessarily aim at Turkification. When the CUP made Turkish the language of instruction in the Empire's schools, it aimed at "incorporating local groups into the imperial administrative system and at developing an imperial elite." Kayalı, *Arabs and the Young Turks*, 91–92.

42 Yıldız, *Ne Mutlu Türküm*, 80–81.

43 Vahakn Dadrian, *The History of the Armenian Genocide* (Providence: Berghahn Books, 1995), 198.

44 *İskan Tarihçesi* (A History of Resettlement) (Istanbul: Hamit Matbaası, 1932), 5–6.

45 *İskan Tarihçesi*, 8–13. For more on these attempts *vis-à-vis* the Ottoman Bulgars and Greeks, see Ağanoğlu, *Göç*: 119–37.

46 Ahmad, *The Young Turks*: 156–57. For more on economic nationalism in the Young Turk era, see Zafer Toprak, "Nationalism and Economics in the Young Turk Era," in *Industralisation, Communication et Rapports Sociaux*, Varia Turcica XX, ed. Jacques Thobie and Salgur Kançal (Paris: Harmattan, 1994); and Aktar, "Economic Nationalism in Turkey," *Boğaziçi Journal of Economic and Administrative Sciences: passim*.

47 Ziya Gökalp, *The Principles of Turkism*, ed. and trans. Niyazi Berkes (London: George Allen and Unwin, 1959), 67.

48 For a good review on the advent of Turkish nationalism during and after the Balkan Wars, see Mehmet Ö. Alkan, "Resmi İdeolojinin Doğuşu ve Evrimi Üzerine Bir Deneme" (An Essay on the Birth and Development of the Official Ideology) in *Tanzimat ve Meşrutiyetin Birikimi* (The Legacy of the Tanzimat and the Constitutional Monarchy Era), ed. Mehmet Ö. Alkan, Modern Türkiye'de Siyasi Düşünce (Political Thought in Modern Turkey), vol. 1 (Istanbul: İletişim, 2001), 377–408. In this essay, the author uses school curricula and public policy measures as benchmarks with which to account for the rise of nationalism in this era.

49 Mardin, "The Ottoman Empire," in *After Empire*, 118.

50 Yıldız, *Ne Mutlu Türküm*, 84.

51 Mardin, "The Ottoman Empire," in *After Empire*, 115.

52 Ziya Gökalp, *The Principles of Turkism*, ed. and trans. Robert Devereux (Leiden, Brill, 1968), 131.

53 Dadrian, *The History of the Armenian Genocide*, 185; and Ahmad, *The Young Turks*, 134. Taner Akçam, *Türk Ulusal Kimliği ve Ermeni Sorunu* (Turkish National Identity and the Armenian Question) (Istanbul: İletişim, 1992), 36–44, 91–94, 129–30.

54 Smith, *Ethnic Origins of Nations*, 161–65.
55 Keyder, "The Ottoman Empire," in *After Empire*, 36.
56 Feroz Ahmad, "Unionist Relations with the Greek, Armenian and Jewish Communities of the Ottoman Empire, Remembering the Minorities," *Middle Eastern Studies* 21(4) (1985): 416–17.
57 Dadrian, *The History of the Armenian Genocide*, 180.
58 Başbakanlık Cumhuriyet Arşivi (Prime Minister's Republican Archives), BCA 272.11/37.15.8. May 15, 1918.
59 150,000 Greeks left Western Anatolia at this time for Greece. However, about 100,000 of these people returned after the end of the First World War in 1919, when the Greek armies landed in Izmir to start the invasion of Asia Minor. Stephan Ladas, *The Exchange of Minorities—Bulgaria, Greece and Turkey* (New York Macmillan, 1932), 16.
60 For a province-by-province religious breakdown of Anatolia's population in 1912, see McCarthy, *The Arab World Turkey and the Balkans*, 94–102.
61 Robert Melson, *Revolution and Genocide* (Chicago, IL: University of Chicago Press, 1992), 19.
62 Ahmad, "Unionist Relations with the Greek, Armenian and Jewish Communities," 424.
63 For the number of refugees and survivors, see Richard G. Hovannisian, *The Republic of Armenia*, vol. 1 (Berkeley, CA and Los Angeles, CA: University of California Press, 1971), 69.
64 The deportation policies of the CUP represented a continuum with the well-established population engineering policies of the Ottoman Empire. Since its inception in the fourteenth century, the Empire had often resorted to population transfers, colonization, deportations, and mass banishment. The Porte had used these demographic tools to control newly acquired territories, by maintaining a secure network of roads, friendly strategic footholds, and reliable niches. Additionally, Istanbul employed these mechanisms to pacify belligerent groups of the Empire by dispersing them among loyal populations. Fuat Dündar gives a succinct summary of these policies in his work, *İttihat ve Terakki'nin Müslümanları İskan Politikası* (CUP's resettlement policy of the Muslims) (Istanbul: İletişim, 2001), 39–61. Additionally, in a series of brilliantly written articles, Ömer Lütfi Barkan elaborates on the Ottoman population policies within the background of the Empire's monumental expansion. Ömer Lütfi Barkan, "Osmanlı İmparatorluğunda Bir İskan ve Kolonizasyon Metodu Olarak Vakıflar ve Temlikler" (Wakf and Conveyance as a Resettlement and Colonization Policy in the Ottoman Empire) *Vakıflar* 2 (1942); Ömer Lütfi Barkan, "Osmanlı İmparatorluğunda Bir İskan ve Kolonizasyon Metodu Olarak Sürgünler" (Banishment as a Resettlement and Colonization Policy in the Ottoman Empire) *İktisat Fakültesi Mecmuası* 11–15 (1953–55).
65 BCA 272.11/8.10.11. August 23, 1916.
66 BCA 272.11/35.4.6. April 5, 1915.
67 Dündar, *İttihat ve Terakki'nin Müslümanları İskan Politikası*, 108–29.
68 Dündar, *İttihat ve Terakki'nin Müslümanları İskan Politikası*, 247.
69 Dündar, *İttihat ve Terakki'nin Müslümanları İskan Politikası*, 130–57.
70 Dündar, *İttihat ve Terakki'nin Müslümanları İskan Politikası*, 247.
71 McCarthy, *Death and Exile*, 218–30.
72 In his classic work on Turkish nationalism, Hans Kohn chronicles the intellectual and social history of the rise of this from its roots among the Young Ottomanists of 1860s to the Kemalists of 1920s, *Türk Milliyetçiliği* (Turkish Nationalism) trans. Ali Çetinkaya (Istanbul: Hilmi Kitabevi, 1944).
73 For a work which studies this, see Andrew Mango, "Remembering the Minorities," *Middle Eastern Studies* 21(4) (October 1985): 118–40. In this work, Mango empathetically, reminds us of the great diversity of Ottoman Turkey before 1912. Cf. For a recent work by a Turkish scholar that takes pride in ethnic homogenization in this

period, see Coşkun Üçok, "Atatürk ve Türkiye'nin % 99 Müslümanlaşıp Türkleşmesi" (Atatürk and the 99% Turkification and Islamicization of Turkey) in *Atatürk Haftası Armağanı* (Schriftfest for Atatürk week) (Ankara: Genelkurmay Basımevi, 1986), 55–63.

2 Secularism, Kemalist nationalism, Turkishness, and the minorities in the 1920s

1 Erik Jan Zürcher, "Atatürk and the Start of National Resistance Movement," *Anatolica* 7 (1979–80): 101.
2 İhsan Ezherli, *Türkiye Büyük Millet Meclisi (1920–1992) ve Osmanlı Meclisi Mebusanı (1877–1920)* (Turkish Grand National Assembly (1920–1992) and the Ottoman House of Representatives (1877–1920)) TBMM Kültür Sanat ve Yayın Kurulu Yayınları, No. 54 (Ankara: TBMM, 1992), 22–24.
3 Dankwart A. Rustow, "The Army and the Founding of the Turkish Republic," *World Politics* 11(4) (July 1959): 512–52.
4 Yıldız, *Ne Mutlu Türküm*, 89–101.
5 Justin McCarthy, "Foundation of the Turkish Republic: Social and Economic Change," *Middle Eastern Studies* 19(2) (April 1983): 146.
6 McCarthy, *Death and Exile*, 258; and Mardin, "The Ottoman Empire," in *After Empire*, 119.
7 Kitromilides and Alexandris, "Ethnic Survival and Forced Migration," *Deltio Kentrou Mikrasiatikuon Spoduon*: 30. For more on the role played by the Anatolian Greeks in the Turco-Greek War, see Michael Llewellyn Smith, *Ionian Vision* (London: Hurst & Company, 1998), 86–311. For a collection of oral histories gathered among the Anatolian Greeks on their exodus of 1919–23, see *Göç* (The Exodus), Küçük Asya Araştırmalar Merkezi (Centre for Asia Minor Studies), comp. Herkül Millas, (for the Turkish edition) trans. Damla Demirözü (Istanbul: İletişim, 2001). For a first person account by a Turkish journalist of the retreat of the Greek forces from Asia Minor, the burning of the cities by them, the flight of the Ionian Greeks, and the controversial Izmir fire of September 1922, the cause of which is still being debated, see Asım Uz, *Gördüklerim Duyduklarım Duygularım* (Things I Saw, Things I Heard and How I Feel), (Istanbul: Vakit Matbaası, 1964), 50–79.
8 Karamanlıs are Turkish-speaking Orthdodox Christians. For more on the Karamanlıs, see Speros Vryonis, Jr, "Byzantine Legacy and Ottoman Forms," *Dumbarton Oaks Papers* 23–24, (1969–70): 253–08; Speros Vryonis, *The Decline of Medieval Hellenism in Asia Minor and the Process of Islamization from the Eleventh through the Fifteenth Century* (Berkeley, CA: University of California Press, 1971); and Cami [Baykurt], *Osmanlı Ülkesinde Hristiyan Türkler* (Christian Turks in the Ottoman Empire) (Istanbul: 1922).
9 For more on the Turco-Greek population exchange, see Stephan Ladas, *The Exchange of Minorities—Bulgaria, Greece and Turkey*. In this work, in addition to the Turco-Greek exchange of 1924, the author examines the Turco-Bulgarian exchange of 1913, and the Greco-Bulgarian exchange of 1919 to argue that these were political means with which the three states involved homogenized their territories. For a work which studies the economic impact of the exchange on Greece and Turkey, see Mihri Belli, *Türkiye-Yunanistan Nüfus Mübadelesine Ekonomik Açıdan Bir Bakış* (Turkey–Greece Population Exchange from the Economic Perspective) (Istanbul: Belge, 2004). For a treatment of these exchanges from the Greek perspective, see Dimitri Pentzopoulos, *The Balkan Exchange of Minorities and Its Impact on Greece* (Paris: Mouton, 1962). For a work which focuses on the exchange as part of the amelioration of relations between Turkey and Greece during the 1920s, consult John A. Petropoulos, "The Compulsory Exchange of Populations: Greek–Turkish Peacemaking, 1922–1930," *Byzantine and Modern Greek Studies* 2 (1976). Finally, for a review of the history projects on the exchange, consult Georgios A. Yiannakopoulos, "The Reconstruction of Destroyed

Picture: The Oral History Archive of the Center for Asia Minor Studies," *Mediterranean Historical Review* 8(2) (December 1993): 201–17. Among the works produced by the Turkish scholars on the exchange, a rare monograph is by Kemal Arı, *Büyük Mübadele: Türkiye'ye Zorunlu Göç (1923–1925)* (The Great Exchange: Forced Migration to Turkey (1923–1925)), (Istanbul: Tarih Vakfı, 1995). Although the author examines the transfer of populations into Turkey in his study, he does not elaborate on long-term impact of this on Turkey. Other surveys by the Turkish scholars on the exchange are mostly articles. Of these works, Yücel Demirel's collection provides a good narrative of the exchange process: "Mübadele Dosyası" (The Exchange Folder) *Tarih ve Toplum* 123–26 (March–June 1994): 54–58, 54–57, 49–52, and 56–59, respectively. Another informative article is by Mehmet Çanlı, "Yunanistanda'ki Türklerin Anadolu'ya Nakledilmesi" (The Transfer of the Turks in Greece to Anatolia) *Tarih ve Toplum* 130 (October 1994): 51–59. Then Ayhan Aktar's study successfully argues on the economic, political, and ideological ramifications of the exchange. "Nüfusun Homojenleştirilmesi ve Ekonominin Türkleştirilmesi Sürecinde Bir Aşama: Türk-Yunan Nüfus Mübadelesi, 1923–1924" (A Step Toward Homogenizing the Population and Turkifying the Economy: The Turco-Greek Population Exchange, 1923–1924) in *Varlık Vergisi ve 'Türkleştirme' Politikaları* (The Wealth Tax and the 'Turkification' Policies) (Istanbul: İletişim, 2000), 17–70. Finally, for a work, which examines the Turco-Greek exchange within the background of other exchanges in history, see Joseph Schechla, "Ideological Roots of Population Transfer," *Third World Quarterly* 14(2) (1993): 239–75.

10 For the text of this law as well as its discussion minutes in the parliament, see *Türk Parlamento Tarihi: TBMM-II. Dönem* (Turkish Parliamentary History: TBMM—Second Term) comp. Kâzım Öztürk, vol. 1 (Ankara: TBMM Vakfı Yayınları, 1993): 278–352.

11 The CHP, Turkey's ruling party between 1923 and 1950, was rooted in the Anatolian and Rumeliote League for the Defense of Rights (Anadolu ve Rumeli Müdafaa-i Hukuk Cemiyeti—ARMHC). The ARMHC served as a political body for Atatürk during the independence campaign of 1919–22. After Turkey's liberation, this organization rose as the most powerful group within the (Turkish) Grand National Assembly ([Türkiye] Büyük Millet Meclisi—[T]BMM). On September 9, 1923, the ARMHC's name was changed to People's Party (Halk Fırkası—HF). Following the establishment of the Turkish republic, on November 10, 1924, Halk Fırkası became Republican People's Party (Cumhuriyet Halk Fırkası—CHF). Then, during the party's Fourth Congress on May 12, 1935, the CHF's name was made "pure Turkish" in accordance with the language purification movement (see Chapter 3) of the 1930s. (Interestingly, however, the word "fırka" in the party's name (of Arabic origin, meaning party) was dropped in favor of a French word, "parti"). Hence, Cumhuriyet Halk Fırkası (CHF) became Cumhuriyet Halk Partisi (CHP). Throughout this study, I will refer to this party as CHP.

12 For a Kemalist highbrow work from the 1930s, which describes and legitimizes the secularizing reforms, see Mediha Muzaffer, *İnkılâbın Ruhu* (The Spirit of the Revolution) (Istanbul: Devlet Matbaası, 1933).

13 *Türk Parlamento Tarihi: TBMM-II. Dönem*, vol. 1: 258–62.

14 For this law and its discussion minutes in the parliament, see *Türk Parlamento Tarihi: TBMM-II. Dönem*, vol. 1: 266–72.

15 *Türk Parlamento Tarihi: TBMM-II. Dönem*, vol. 1: 273–77.

16 *Türk Parlamento Tarihi: TBMM-II. Dönem* (Turkish Parliamentary History: TBMM—Second Term) comp. Kâzım Öztürk, vol. 2 (Ankara: TBMM Vakfı Yayınları, 1994): 27–44.

17 *Türk Parlamento Tarihi: TBMM-II. Dönem*, vol. 2: 61–101.

18 *Türk Parlamento Tarihi: TBMM-II. Dönem*, vol. 2: 102–16.

19 TBMM Zabıt Ceridesi (Journal of Proceedings of the Turkish Grand National Assembly (TGNA) term II, vol. 22: 334.

20 TBMM Zabıt Ceridesi (Journal of Proceedings of the Turkish Grand National Assembly (TGNA) term III, vol. 3: 115.

21 *Türkiye Cumhuriyeti Tarihi Sözlüğü* (Historical Dictionary of the Turkish Republic), comp. M. Orhan Bayrak (Istanbul: Milenyum, 2000), 353–59; TBMM Zabıt Ceridesi, term III, vol. 5: 7–8.

22 For the sake of this study, I will not go into the details of Turkey's secularization during the 1920s. For a good account of this, see Niyazi Berkes, *The Development of Secularism in Turkey* (New York: Routledge, 1998), 461–503.

23 Yıldız, *Ne Mutlu Türküm*, 139–54.

24 Yıldız, *Ne Mutlu Türküm*, 124–26.

25 Kemal Karpat, "The Republican People's Party," in *Political Parties and Democracy in Turkey*, ed. Metin Heper and Jacob Landau (London: Tauris, 1991), 50. For more on the territorial definition of the nation during the Kemalist-era, see Frank Tachau, "The Search for National Identity Among the Turks," *Die Welt des Islams*, New Series 8, Part 2/3 (1972).

26 Afet İnan, *Medeni Bilgiler ve Atatürk'ün El Yazıları* (Civics and Atatürk's Manuscripts) (Ankara: TTK, 1969), 364.

27 İnan, *Medeni Bilgiler*, 351.

28 İnan, *Medeni Bilgiler*, 379.

29 Rıfat N. Bali reviews such examples of official and semi-official declarations of voluntaristic and territorial understanding of the nation, *Cumhuriyet Yıllarında Türkiye Yahudileri: Bir Türkleştirme Serüveni (1923–1945)* (Turkish Jews under the Turkish Republic: An Episode of Turkification (1923–1945) (Istanbul: İletişim, 1999), 52–102.

30 *Cümhuriyet Halk Fırkası Nizamnamesi* (Statute of Republican People's Party) (Ankara: 1927), 5.

31 Attempts to nationalize citizenship were not unique to Turkey. Roger Brubaker argues for a similar process of nationalization of citizenship in German nationalism, *Citizenship and Nationhood in France and Germany* (Cambridge, MA: Harvard University Press, 1992), 52.

32 *Cümhuriyet Halk Fırkası Nizamnamesi*, 5.

33 *İstatistik Yıllığı Üçüncü Cilt* (Statistics Yearbook, vol. 3) Türkiye Cumhuriyeti Basvekâlet İstatistik Umum Müdürlüğü (Istanbul: Ahmet İhsan Matbaası, 1930), 57.

34 This replaced Turkey's first constitution of 1921. For a text of the 1921 constitution, see eds Suna Kili and Şeref Gözübüyük, *Türk Anayasa Metinleri* (Texts of Turkish Constitutions) second edn (Istanbul: Türkiye İş Bankası Yayınları, 2000), 100–03.

35 TBMM Zabıt Ceridesi, term II, vol. 8/1: 908–11.

36 *Turkey. Constitution. Translation into English of the Turkish Constitution of 1924, embodying such amendments to the text as have been made to date,* typescript (s.n: s.n, 1937?), 9.

37 Hakkı Uyar, *Sol Milliyetçi Bir Türk Aydını: Mahmut Esat Bozkurt (1892–1943)* (A Leftist Nationalist Turkish Intellectual: Mahmut Esat Bozkurt (1892–1943)) (Izmir: Büke, 2000), 117.

38 Fahir Giritlioğlu, *Türk Siyasi Tarihinde CHP'nin Mevki* (The CHP's Position in Turkish Political Past) (Ankara: Ayyıldız, 1965), 83.

39 *Cümhuriyet Halk Fırkası Nizamnamesi*, 5.

40 *Cümhuriyet Halk Fırkası Nizamnamesi*, 6.

41 Ziya Gökalp, *Türkçülüğün Esasları* (The Principles of Turkism) (Istanbul: Türk Tarih Kurumu, 1952), 15.

42 Aktar, *Varlık Vergisi ve 'Türkleştirme' Politikaları*, 103–08; Bali, *Cumhuriyet Yıllarında Türkiye Yahudileri*, 502–03; and Taha Parla, *Kemalist Tek-Parti İdeolojisi ve CHP'nin Altı Ok'u* (The Single Party Ideology of Kemalism and the Six Arrow of the CHP) (Istanbul: İletişim, 1995), 176–221.

43 *İstatistik Yıllığı Üçüncü Cilt* (Statistics Yearbook, vol. 3), 57.

44 "Jewish," Judeo-Spanish is the language of the Sephardic Jews who fled from Spain and Portugal during the late fifteenth and early sixteenth centuries, and settled in various parts of the Ottoman Empire. Judeo-Spanish is essentially medieval Spanish

(and to a much lesser extent medieval Portuguese) with a heavy Hebrew influence in its vocabulary. Over the centuries, it has also been laden with words from Turkish, Greek, Italian, French, Bulgarian, and Arabic.

45 *İstatistik Yıllığı: Üçüncü Cilt*, 45.
46 *İstatistik Yıllığı Üçüncü Cilt*, 57.
47 *İstatistik Yıllığı: İkinci Cilt 1929* (Statistics Yearbook: vol. 2, 1929) TC Basvekâlet İstatistik Umum Müd. (İstanbul: Cumhuriyet Matbaası, 1929): 45; *İstatistik Yıllığı: 1934–35 Cilt 7* (Statistics Yearbook: 1934–35, vol. 7) (Ankara: Başbakanlık İstatistik G.D., 1934–35), 159.
48 Gökalp, *The Principles of Turkism*, ed. Robert Devereux, 15.
49 Gökalp, *The Principles of Turkism*, ed. Robert Devereux, 78.
50 It is interesting to note that this policy is similar to the state-led assimilation efforts in France during the nineteenth century, which Brubaker analyzes in his work, *Citizenship and Nationhood in France and Germany*, xi.
51 Keyder, "The Ottoman Empire," in *After Empire*, 36. Turkish nationalization under Islam's influence is akin to nationalization-through-religion by most Balkan nationalist movements. Kushner, *The Rise of Turkish Nationalism*, 57. For more on nationalization-through-religion among the Turks and the Ottoman Muslims, see the following works by Kemal H. Karpat, *The Politicization of Islam, passim*; "Transformation of the Ottoman State, 1789–1908" *International Journal of Middle East Studies* 3, 243–81; and "An Inquiry into the Social Foundations of Nationalism in the Ottoman State: From Social Estates to Classes, From Millets to Nations," Research Monograph No. 39, typescript (Princeton University, NJ: Center of International Studies, July 1973). Additionally, consult Karpat's other works: "Millets and Nationality," in *Christians and Jews in the Ottoman Empire*, 141–69; "Ethnicity Problem in a Multi-Ethnic Anational Islamic State," "Continuity and Recasting in the Ottoman State," in *Ethnic Groups and the State*, ed. Paul Brass (London: Croom & Helm, 1985), 95–114; and "The Hijra from Russia," in *Muslim Travelers*, 131–52. Furthermore, refer to Todorova for more on this, "The Ottoman Legacy in the Balkans," in *Imperial Legacy*, 44–77.
52 Erik Jan Zürcher, "Young Turks, Ottoman Muslims and Turkish Nationalists," in *Modern Turkey and Ottoman Past*, ed. Kemal Karpat (Leiden: Brill, 2000), 179.
53 Millions of (Turkish and non-Turkish) Muslims immigrated to Anatolia from eighteenth century onwards. According to a conservative estimate, between 1876 and 1927 alone, 1,994,999 Muslim immigrants arrived from the Balkans and the Black Sea basin, *The Population of the Ottoman Empire and Turkey* comp. Behar, 51, 62. Yet, it is difficult to know how many of these people were non-Turkish, since the Ottoman Empire did not keep detailed statistics on the ethnicity of the Muslim immigrants. One of the first data sets that provide detailed information on the ethnicity of the immigrant Muslims is from the 1935 census. This counted 238,901 Muslims in Turkey who spoke non-Anatolian languages, a mere 1.5 percent of the Turkish population of 16,157,450. *İstatistik Yıllığı Cilt 10* (Statistics Yearbook, vol. 10) Başbakanlık İstatistik Umum Müdürlüğü (Ankara: Hüsnütabiat, 1938–39), 64–65.
54 *Atatürk'ün Söylev ve Demeçleri I–III* (Atatürk's Speeches and Declarations I–III), vol. 1 (Ankara: Atatürk Araştırma Merkezi, 1997), 74–75.
55 Ziya Gökalp, "Refah mı, Saadet mi?" (Welfare or Happiness?) *Küçük Mecmua*, quoted in Hilmi Ziya Ülken, *Türkiye'de Çağdaş Düşünce Tarihi* (The History of Contemporary Thought in Turkey) (Konya: Selçuk Yayınları, 1966), 585.
56 Todorova, "The Ottoman Legacy in the Balkans," in *Imperial Legacy*, 66.
57 *İstatistik Yıllığı: İkinci Cilt 1929*, 44.
58 *İstatistik Yıllığı: Üçüncü Cilt*, 45.
59 *İstatistik Yıllığı: 1934–35 Cilt 7*, 160–61.
60 Donald Everett Webster, *The Turkey of Atatürk* (Philadelphia, PA: The American Academy of Political and Social Science, 1939), 48–49.

61 Akşin Somel, "Cumhuriyet Demokrasi ve Kimlik" (The Republic Democracy and Identity), in *75. Yılda Tebaadan Yurttaşa Doğru* (From Subject to Citizen in the 75th Year) (Istanbul: Türk Tarih Vakfı, 1998), 71–74.
62 Robert Olson argues that nationalism had emerged as a potent force among the Kurds at this time. *The Emergence of Kurdish Nationalism and the Sheikh Said Rebellion, 1880–1925* (Austin, TX: University of Texas Press, 1989), 1–25.
63 Somel, "Cumhuriyet Demokrasi ve Kimlik," in *75. Yılda Tebaadan Yurttaşa Doğru*, 151–68. Robert Olson goes as far to claim that, at this time in the 1920s, nationalism was in ascendancy among the Kurds. *The Emergence of Kurdish Nationalism*, 26–51.
64 Great Britain. Foreign Office: Political Departments: General Correspondence from 1906. Turkey. FO 371/14578/E729. Embassy (Constantinople) to the Foreign Office (London) (Hereafter London), February 10, 1930. *Annual Report for 1929*.
65 For works which study Kurdish resistance to assimilation in the 1920s, see Olson, *The Emergence of Kurdish Nationalism*, 91–127; Martin van Bruinessen, *Agha Shaikh and State: On the Social and Political Organization of Kurdistan*, typescript (1978), 353–406; Martin van Bruinessen, *Origins and Development of Kurdish Nationalism in Turkey*, typescript (Berlin: Berliner Institut für Vergleichende Sozialforschung, 1981); Martin van Bruinessen, *Kurdish Ethno-Nationalism versus Nation-Building States*, Analectica Isisiana, XLVII (Istanbul: Isis, 2000), *passim*; and M. Hakan Yavuz, "Five Stages of the Construction of Kurdish Nationalism in Turkey," *Nationalism and Ethnic Politics* 7(3) (Autumn 2001): 1–24. For a treatment of this era from a perspective sympathetic to the Kurds, Cf. Kendal, "Kurdistan in Turkey," in *People Without a Country: The Kurds and Kurdistan*, ed. Gerard Chaliand, trans. Michael Pallis (London: Zed Press, 1980), 54–67; and Emir Kamuran Bedir-Khan, *La Question Kurde* (Paris: Vogue, 1959), 8–12.
66 *Yeni Türk Lûgatı* (New Turkish dictionary), ed. İbrahim Alaettin (Istanbul: Kanaat, 1930), 638.
67 Afet [İnan], *Vatandaşlık İçin Medeni Bilgiler* (Civic Guidelines for Citizenship) (Istanbul: Devlet Matbaası, 1931), 16.
68 The denial of ethnic identity also applied to other groups. A school textbook printed in 1931 argued that the Circassians were the descendants of Turks, who had settled the Northern Caucasus many years ago. *Tarih II Ortazamanlar* (History II, Middle Ages) (Istanbul: Devlet Matbaası, 1931), 72–73.
69 Abdul Rahman Ghassem Lou [Kassem Lou], *Kurdistan and the Kurds* (Prague: Publication House of the Czechoslovak Academy of Sciences, 1965), 57.
70 Mete Tunçay, *Türkiye Cumhuriyeti'nde Tek-Parti Yönetimin Kurulması* (The Establishment of Single Party Rule in Turkey) (Istanbul: Tarih Vakfı, 1999), 134.
71 For the text of this law, see *Türk Parlamento Tarihi: TBMM-II. Dönem*, vol. 2: 1–26. For the discussion minutes of this law in the Turkish parliament, consult İsmail Göldaş, *Takrir-i Sükûn Görüsmeleri: 1923 Seçimleri, Atama Meclis* (The Discussion Minutes of Takrir-i Sükun: 1923 Elections and the Appointed Parliament) (Sultanahmet, Istanbul: Belge Yayinlari, 1997), 357–469.
72 Tunçay, *Türkiye Cumhuriyeti'nde Tek-Parti Yönetiminin Kurulması*, 145–46.
73 For more on the TpCF, see Erik Jan Zürcher, *Political Opposition in the Early Turkish Republic: The Progressive Republican Party 1924–25* (Leiden: Brill, 1991). In this exhaustive study, Zürcher chronicles the rise and fall of the TpCF within the framework of the early republic.
74 Tunçay, *Türkiye Cumhuriyeti'nde Tek-Parti Yönetiminin Kurulması*, 114.
75 For more on the İstiklâl Tribunals, see Ezherli, *Türkiye Büyük Millet Meclisi (1920–1992)*, 65–85.
76 FO 371/14579/E2678. Edmonds (Turkey) to Henderson (London), May 26, 1930. *Tour by Mr. Edmonds.*
77 FO 371/11541/E5564. Embassy (Constantinople) to London, September 29, 1926.

78 For a detailed work on the Şeyh Said uprising, see Olson, *The Emergence of Kurdish Nationalism*, 91–164. For an account on the Şeyh Said uprising that treats British influence as the main cause of the rebellion, see Bilâl Şimşir, *İngiliz Belgeleriyle Türkiye'de "Kürt Sorunu": (1924–1938) Şeyh Sait, Ağrı ve Dersim Ayaklanmaları* ("The Kurdish Question" in Turkey according to British Documents: (1924–1938) Şeyh Sait, Ağri and Dersim Uprisings) (Ankara: TTK Basımevi, 1991). For another study from a Turkish nationalist perspective, see Hüseyin Koca, *Yakın Tarihten Günümüze Hükümetlerin Doğu-Güneydoğu Anadolu Politikaları: Umumi Müfettişliklerinden Olağanüstü Hal Bölge Valiliğine* (The East-Southeast Policies of our Governments from the Recent Times until Today: From the Inspectorates-General to the Extraordinary Regional Governor) (Konya: Mikro Yayınları, 1998), 72–120. On the other hand, for an analysis of the rebellion sympathetic to the Kurds, which treats it as an outburst of Kurdish nationalism, cf. M. A. Hasretyan, *1925 Kürt Ayaklanması: (Şeyh Sait Hareketi)* (1925 Kurdish uprising: (Şeyh Sait's movement)) (Uppsala: Jina Nû, 1985). For another study sympathetic to Kurdish nationalism, see Mehmet Bayrak, *Kürtler ve Ulusal-Demokratik Mücadeleleri* (The Kurds and their National-Democratic Struggles) (Ankara: Özge Yayınları, 1993), 109–411.

79 In addition to the "Report for Reform in the East," two other documents also voiced such expectations vis-à-vis Eastern Turkey. The first of these was written by Mustafa Abdülhalik (Renda), and the second by Cemil (Ubaydın) both of whom were members of the commission that drafted the "Report for Reform in the East." For the full text of these documents, see Bayrak, *Kürtler ve Ulusal-Demokratik Mücadeleleri*, 452–67, and 467–80, respectively.

80 "Report for Reform in the East," quoted in Bayrak, *Kürtler ve Ulusal-Demokratik Mücadeleleri*, 486.

81 "Report for Reform in the East," quoted in Bayrak, *Kürtler ve Ulusal-Demokratik Mücadeleleri*, 485.

82 "Report for Reform in the East," quoted in Bayrak, *Kürtler ve Ulusal-Demokratik Mücadeleleri*, 488.

83 "Report for Reform in the East," quoted in Bayrak, *Kürtler ve Ulusal-Demokratik Mücadeleleri*, 482.

84 Koca, *Yakın Tarihten Günümüze Hükümetlerin Doğu-Güneydoğu Anadolu Politikaları*, 173.

85 FO 371/13096/E906. Embassy (Constantinople) to London, February 9, 1928. *Annual Report for 1927.*

86 For more on the (First) Inspectorate, see *Güney Doğu Birinci Genel Müfettişlik Bölgesi* (The First Inspectorate's Region of the Southeast) (Istanbul: Umumi Müfettişlik Teşkilatı, 1939).

87 Travelers to the area during the late 1920s reported burnt-out towns, poor roads, untilled fields, and wretched poverty. FO 371/13828/E3538. Clerk (Constantinople) to Henderson (London), July 15, 1929. *Enclosure in No. 1, Notes on a Journey from Angora to Aleppo, Diarbekir, Malatia, Sivas, and the Black Sea Coast, June 9–29, 1929.* Mr Edmonds, an English diplomat, who toured Eastern Turkey, noted that Bitlis

> [i]self is a tragic spectacle. For a Whole mile the ruined houses succeed one another on each of the steep sides of the gorge. Along the main street and here and there on the slopes houses have been made habitable. What was once a town of 40,000 is now a village of perhaps 5,000. Here, if anywhere, the expulsion of the Armenians has dealt the life of the place a deadly blow. What this measure did not destroy the Russian occupation finished off.
> (FO, 371/14579/E2678. Edmonds (Turkey) to Henderson (London), May 26, 1930 *Tour by Mr. Edmonds*)

88 For the text of this law as well as its discussion minutes in the parliament, see *Türk Parlamento Tarihi: TBMM-IV. Dönem* (Turkish Parliamentary History: TBMM-Fourth Term) comp. Kâzım Öztürk, vol. 1 (Ankara: TBMM Vakfı Yayınları, 1994): 407–10.

89 FO 371/13089/E5385. Clerk (Constantinople) to Cushendun (London), November 8, 1928.

90 FO 371/13828/E3538. Clerk (Constantinople) to Henderson (London), July 15, 1929. *Enclosure in No. 1, Notes on a Journey from Angora to Aleppo, Diarbekir, Malatia, Sivas and the Black Sea Coast, June 9–29, 1929.*

91 The Turkish Hearths (Türk Ocakları, sing. Türk Ocağı) were the intellectual power-house of Turkish nationalism between 1912 and 1930. For a good account of the Houses, see Füsun Üstel, *Türk Ocakları (1912–1931)* (Turkish Hearths (1912–1931)) (Istanbul: İletişim, 1997). For a treatment of the Hearths from a more nationalist per-spective, cf. Yusuf Sarınay, *Türk Milliyetçiliğinin Tarihi Gelişimi ve Türk Ocakları 1912–1931* (The Historical Development of Turkish Nationalism and the Turkish Hearths 1912–1931) (Istanbul: Ötüken, 1994).

92 FO 371/14579/2678. Embassy (Constantinople) to the London. *Tour by Mr. Edmonds*, May 26, 1930.

93 FO 371/14579/2678. Embassy (Constantinople) to London. *Tour by Mr. Edmonds*, May 26, 1930.

94 FO 371/13089/E5385. Clerk (Constantinople) to Cushendun (London), November 8, 1928.

95 FO 371/13096/E906. Embassy (Constantinople) to London, February 9, 1928. *Annual Report for 1927.*

96 FO 371/13089/E5385. Clerk (Constantinople) to Cushendun (London), November 8, 1928.

97 The former Bayazıt province, whose name was changed to Ağrı in 1938.

98 Koca, *Yakın Tarihten Günümüze Hükümetlerin Doğu-Güneydoğu Anadolu Politikaları*, 175.

99 Somel, "Cumhuriyet Demokrasi ve Kimlik," in *75. Yılda Tebaadan Yurttaşa Doğru*, 151–68.

100 Rıfat N. Bali, *Musa'nın Evlatları Cumhuriyet'in Yurttaşları* (The Children of Moses, the Citizens of the Republic) (Istanbul: İletişim, 2001), 53–76. Moreover, during the last decades of the Empire, the Jews took an active interest in the constitutionalist move-ment. For a work, which focuses on cooperation between Turks and Jews within the CUP during this era, see Elie Kedourie, "Young Turks, Freemasons and Jews," *Middle Eastern Studies* 7(1) (Januray 1971): 89–104. In this rather amusing article, Kedourie uses British diplomatic correspondence to discuss London's anti-Semitism as well as British discomfort toward the presence of Jews within the CUP.

101 N. M. Gelber, "An Attempt to Internationalize Salonika," *Jewish Social Studies* 17 (1955): 105–20; Bali, *Musa'nın Evlatları Cumhuriyet'in Yurttaşları*, 76–81.

102 Yıldız, *Ne Mutlu Türküm*, 265.

103 Salahi Sonyel, "Turco-Jewish Relations During the First World War and Turkey's War of Liberations," in *Turkish-Jewish Encounters: Studies on Turkish-Jewish Relations through the Ages*, ed. Mehmet Tütüncü (Haarlem, the Netherlands: SOTA, 2001), 230–34.

104 For a sympathetic account of the Jews' collaboration with the Turks during the col-lapse of the Ottoman Empire, see Yusuf Besalel, *Osmanlı ve Türk Yahudileri* (Ottoman and Turkish Jews) (Istanbul: Gözlem, 1999), 48–54.

105 Bali, *Cumhuriyet Yıllarında Türkiye Yahudileri*, 34–40; Yıldız, *Ne Mutlu Türküm*, 266; Besalel, *Osmanlı ve Türk Yahudileri*, 54–55; Ali Güler, "Son Osmanlı Hahambaşısı Hayim Nahum Efendi ile İlgili Bazı Arşiv Belgeleri Işığında Türk-Yahudi İlişkileri" (Turkish–Jewish Relations in the Light of some Archival Documents about Hayim Nahum Efendi, the Last Chief Rabbi of the Ottomans) in *Turkish–Jewish Encounters*, 211–13; and Sonyel, "Turco-Jewish Relations," in *Turkish-Jewish Encounters*, 234–38.

106 Irina Livezeanu, *Cultural Politics in Greater Romania* (Ithaca, NY: Cornell University Press, 1995), 11–13; and Volovici, *Nationalist Ideology and Antisemitism*, 22–56, 95–113.

107 BCA 272.11/8.8.18. June 23, 1916.

108 BCA 272.11/35.4.8. May 27, 1915.

109 Levi, *Türkiye Cumhuriyeti'nde Yahudiler*, 24–29; Besalel, *Osmanlı ve Türk Yahudileri*, 58–62.

110 FO 371/11548/E1884. Embassy (Constantinople) to the London, March 20, 1926.

111 For more on the economic aspects of this campaign, see Aktar, *Varlık Vergisi ve 'Türkleştirme' Politikaları*, 49–60; Bali, *Cumhuriyet Yıllarında Türkiye Yahudileri*, 196–206; and Alexis Alexandris, *The Greek Minority of Istanbul and Greek-Turkish Relations 1918–1974* (Athens: Center for Asia Minor Studies, 1983), 105–17.

112 Bali, *Cumhuriyet Yıllarında Türkiye Yahudileri*, 205.

113 Ayhan Aktar, "Cumhuriyet'in İlk Yıllarında Uygulanan Türkleştirme Politikaları" (Turkification Policies during the Early Years of the Republic), *Tarih ve Toplum*, no. 156 (December 1996): 4–18; and Levi, *Türkiye Cumhuriyeti'nde Yahudiler*, 32; and Yıldız, *Ne Mutlu Türküm*, 285–86.

114 Bali, *Cumhuriyet Yıllarında Türkiye Yahudileri*, 40–54. Of these towns, Edirne and Çanakkale were both more than 15 percent Jewish. Izmir was 10.5 percent Jewish, Istanbul 7 percent, Tekirdağ 5 percent, and Bursa 3 percent Jewish. *İstatistik Yıllığı: Üçüncü Cilt*, 53–54; 64–65; 76–77; and *İstatistik Yıllığı: Cilt 11* (Statistics Yearbook: vol. 11) Başbakanlık İstatistik Umum Müdürlüğü (Istanbul: Hüsnütabiat Basımevi, 1940), 76–77.

115 Rıfat N. Bali, foreword to *Vatandaş Türkçe Konuş* (Citizen Speak Turkish), by Avram Galanti (Istanbul: Hüsn-i Tabiat Matbaası, 1928), vi–vii.

116 For more on the Alliance schools, see Aron Rodrigue, *French Jews, Turkish Jews: The Alliance Israélite Universelle and the Politics of Jewish Schooling in Turkey* (Bloomington, IN: Indiana University Press, 1990).

117 Galanti, *Vatandaş Türkçe Konuş*, 6, 34.

118 *Vakit*, April 27, 1927.

119 Yıldız, *Ne Mutlu Türküm*, 287.

120 Bali, *Cumhuriyet Yıllarında Türkiye Yahudileri*, 105–09.

121 Bali, *Cumhuriyet Yıllarında Türkiye Yahudileri*, 108.

122 Levi, *Türkiye Cumhuriyeti'nde Yahudileri*, 81–82.

123 Galanti, *Vatandaş Türkçe Konuş*, 24–39.

124 Galanti, *Vatandaş Türkçe Konuş*, 26.

125 Galanti, *Vatandaş Türkçe Konuş*, 6–8.

126 Germany, Auswärtiges Amt. Records of the German Foreign Office received by the Department of State, 1920–1945. AA T-120 4900. Nadolny (Konstantinopel) to the German Foreign Ministry (Berlin) (Hereafter Berlin), May 10, 1928.

127 Jacob M. Landau, *Tekinalp: Bir Türk Yurtseveri (1883–1961)* (Tekinalp: A Turkish Patriot (1883–1961)) (Istanbul: İletişim, 1996), 19.

128 Tekin Alp. *Türkleştirme* (Turkification) (Resimli Ay Matbaası, Istanbul: 1928), 63–65.

129 Rıfat N. Bali, foreword to *Vatandaş Türkçe Konuş*, viii.

130 For an excellent biography of Tekinalp, see Landau, *Tekinalp: Bir Türk Yurtseveri*. In this work, Landau focuses on Tekinalp's intellectual development from his training as a rabbi in Salonika during the Hamidian era, his becoming an avid Turkish nationalist during the 1908 revolution, and his fall from the spotlight during the republican era. During the 1920s and the 1930s, Tekinalp never gained access to the inner circle of the republican elite despite his works in favor of Kemalism and Turkification. Gradually becoming an outsider to the discussions on nationalism, he left Turkey for Southern France to spend the rest of his life as a disheartened Turk. Landau, *Tekinalp: Bir Türk Yurtseveri*, 13–22.

131 AA T-120 4900. Nadolny (Konstantinopel) to Berlin, May 10, 1928.

132 For more on Eliza Niyego's murder and the following events, see Bali, *Cumhuriyet Yıllarında Türkiye Yahudileri*, 109–30.

133 Besalel, *Osmanlı ve Türk Yahudileri*, 64.

134 For a detailed account of the events in Edirne, see Senem Aslan, " 'Citizen Speak Turkish' The Emergence of Turkish National Identity," unpublished paper.

135 Aslan, "Citizen Speak Turkish," 9.

136 FO 371/13096/E906. Embassy (Constantinople) to the London, February 9, 1928. *Annual Report for 1927*.

137 For an example of this, see *Cumhuriyet*, March 9, 1931; for more on the 1927–28 "Speak Turkish" Campaign, see Aslan, "Citizen Speak Turkish."
138 Somel, "Cumhuriyet Demokrasi ve Kimlik," in *75. Yılda Tebaadan Yurttaşa Doğru*, 151–68.
139 Aktar, "Cumhuriyet'in İlk Yıllarında Uygulanan Türkleştirme Politikaları," *Tarih ve Toplum*, 4.
140 Foreign Office: Confidential Print. FO 434/268/E2118. Knox (Ankara) to Chamberlain (London), April 13, 1928.
141 BCA 030.18.1.2/1.14.10. June 18, 1920.
142 BCA 030.18.1.2/1.19.6. November 14, 1920.
143 BCA 272.12/37.20.1. May 5, 1921.
144 BCA 030.18.1.2/3.19.7. May 11, 1921.
145 BCA 34 SU 187/230.66.38.9. September 14, 1924.
146 BCA 34 SU 190/230.66.28.13. December 28, 1924.
147 BCA 34 E 230.28.22.7. March 3, 1925. For details of the pressure brought by the government against private companies so that they would fire their non-Muslim employees, see Bali, *Cumhuriyet Yıllarında Türkiye Yahudileri*, 206–28; and Alexandris, *The Greek Minority of Istanbul*, 108–12.
148 For more on the Jews' and the Greeks' denunciation of their rights, see respectively, Bali, *Cumhuriyet Yıllarında Türkiye Yahudileri*, 59–77, Levi, *Türkiye Cumhuriyeti'nde Yahudiler*. 66–74; and Alexandris, *The Greek Minority of Istanbul*, 135–39.
149 FO 371/11541/E2055. Hoare (Constantinople) to Chamberlain (London), March 29, 1926.
150 For more on the relations between Ankara and the foreign/Christian schools in this era and later, see Ayten Sezer, *Atatürk Döneminde Yabancı Okullar (1923–1938)* (Foreign Schools under Atatürk's Rule (1923–1938)) (Ankara: Türk Tarih Kurumu, 1999), and Hugh Grayson Johnson, *The American Schools in the Republic of Turkey 1923–1933: A Case Study of Missionary Problems in International Relations*, PhD Dissertation (The American University, 1975), 78–258.
151 For a review of this issue, see Baskın Oran, "Lausanne İhlalleri: Türkiye ile Yunanistan Açısından Karşılaştırmalı Bir İnceleme" (The Lausanne Violations: A Comparative Study of Turkey and Greece), unpublished report, 1999.
152 For more on the conflictual nature of the Turco-Greek negotiations between 1923 and 1930, and the debates on the interpretation of the Turco-Greek exchange treaty, see Alexandris, *The Greek Minority of Istanbul*, 124–29.
153 Yorgo Benlisoy and Elçin Macar, *Fener Patrikhanesi* (The Fener Patriarchate) (Istanbul: Ayraç, 1996), 50.
154 Alexandris, *The Greek Minority of Istanbul*, 155.
155 For more on the controversy involving Constantine VI, see Alexandris, *The Greek Minority of Istanbul*, 159–66.
156 Alexandris, *The Greek Minority of Istanbul*, 131–35.
157 BCA 272.11/ 60.168.19. August 11, 1928.
158 McCarthy, *The Arab World, Turkey and the Balkans*, 75.
159 *LCTS* (Treaty Series 16—Treaty of Lausanne, Cmd), 1929, 223–25. Quoted in Alexis Alexandris, "Imbros and Tenedos: A Study of Turkish Attitudes Toward Two Ethnic Greek Island Communities Since 1923," *Journal of the Hellenic Diaspora* 7(1) (Spring 1980): 5–31.
160 *İstatistik Yıllığı: İkinci Cilt 1929*, 6.
161 Alexandris, "Imbros and Tenedos," in *Journal of the Hellenic Diaspora*: 17.
162 Alexandris, "Imbros and Tenedos," in *Journal of the Hellenic Diaspora*: 16–23.
163 Foreign Office: Consulate and Legation, Greece (formerly Ottoman Empire): General Correspondence. FO 286/11013/220. Loraine (Athens) to Chamberlain, February 11, 1927. *Enclosure in Athens dispatch No. 54 of 11-2-27*, December 15, 1926.

164 FO 286/11013/220. Loraine (Athens) to Chamberlain, February 11, 1927. *Enclosure in Athens dispatch No. 54 of 11-2-27*, December 15, 1926. For a detailed discussion of the events surrounding the conscription of the Greek men on the island, see Hikmet Öksüz, "Lozan Sonrasında Gökçeada (İmroz) ve Bozcaada'da Rumların Askere Alınması" (The Conscription of the Greeks on Gökçeada (İmroz) and Bozcaada in the post–Lausanne period) *Tarih Toplum* 34(200) (August 2000): 41–46.

165 FO 371/13081/1855. Knox (Angora) to Chamberlain (London), April 19, 1928.

166 *Vakit*, March 1, 1929. FO 371/13818/E6101 Clerk (Constantinople) to London, November 25, 1929, and FO 371/13818/E6101. *Minutes by W L. C. Knight*, November 26, 1929.

167 BCA 030.18.1.2/8.6.10. February 5, 1930.

168 Alexandris, *The Greek Minority of Istanbul*, 176–77.

169 FO 371/14576/E6089. Clerk (Constantinople) to Henderson (London), November 4, 1930; State Department—United States of America SD 867.9111/292. Embassy (Istanbul) to the State Department (Washington), (Hereafter Washington), December 1930. *Digest of Turkish News*, October 30–November 12, 1930.

170 FO 371/14576/E5768. Ramsay (Athens) to Clerk (Constantinople), October 25, 1930.

171 FO 371/16091/E222. Clerk (Constantinople) to London, January 14, 1932. *Annual Report for 1931*.

172 SD 867.01/194. Fisher (Athens) to Washington, August 20, 1931.

173 BCA 030.18.1.2/60.91.19. Feburay 19, 1935.

174 FO 424/260/2461. Vaughan-Russell (Aleppo) to MacDonald (London), March 4, 1924.

175 BCA 272.11/17.72.2. January 12, 1924.

176 FO 424/260/2461. Vaughan-Russell (Aleppo) to MacDonald (London), March 4, 1924.

177 Quoted in Bayrak, *Kürtler ve Ulusal-Demokratik Mücadeleleri*, 467–80.

178 Quoted in Bayrak, *Kürtler ve Ulusal-Demokratik Mücadeleleri*, 477.

179 FO 371/14579/2678. Embassy (Constantinople) to London. *Tour by Mr. Edmonds*, May 26, 1930.

180 FO 424/260/2461. Vaughan-Russell (Aleppo) to MacDonald (London), March 4, 1924.

181 FO 371/13090/E3058. Leake (Mersina) to Clerk (Constantinople), January 15, 1928.

182 FO 424/268/E129. Clerk (Constantinople) to Chamberlain (London), January 4, 1928.

183 BCA 272.11/16.70.11. December 15, 1923. BCA 272.11/41.48.22. May 11, 1924.

184 FO 371/13818/E6101. Clerk (Constantinople) to London, November 25, 1929. *Minutes by W. L. C. Knight*, November 26, 1929.

185 FO 424/268/E129. Clerk (Constantinople) to Chamberlain (London), January 4, 1928.

186 FO 371/13818/E6101. Clerk (Constantinople) to London, November 25, 1929. *Enclosure in No. 1*, Catton (Mersina) to Clerk (Constantinople), October 28, 1929.

187 SD 867.4016. Crew (Istanbul) to Washington, February 12, 1930.

188 *İstatistik Yıllığı: İkinci Cilt 1929*, 41–42.

189 FO 371/13097/E3524. Clerk (Constantinople) to Sir Austen Chamberlain (London), July 16, 1928.

190 FO 371/13818/E394, League of Nations (Geneva) to Embassy (Constantinople), January 23, 1929. Addenda, *Petition. A son Excellence Monsieur le Président du Conseil de la Société des* Nations, Patriarcat Arménien Catholique de Cilicie (Rome) to the League of Nations (Geneva), July 2, 1928.

191 FO 371/13818/E5576, League of Nations (Geneva) to Embassy (Constantinople), October 29, 1929. *Minutes by G. W. Rendel* (London), October 31, 1929.

192 FO 371/13818/E5576. League of Nations (Geneva) to Embassy (Constantinople), October 29, 1929. Addenda, *Petition. A son Excellence Monsieur le Président du Conseil de la Société des* Nations, Patriarcat Arménien Catholique de Cilicie (Beyrouth) to the League of Nations (Geneva), June 2, 1929.

193 FO 371/13818/E6101. Clerk (Constantinople) to London, November 25, 1929. *Minutes by W. L. C. Knight*, November 26, 1929.

194 FO 371/14579/2678. Embassy (Constantinople) to London. *Tour by Mr. Edmonds*, May 26, 1930.

195 FO 371/14579/2678. Embassy (Constantinople) to London. *Tour by Mr. Edmonds*, May 26, 1930.

196 FO 371/13818/E6101. Clerk (Constantinople) to London, November 25, 1929. *Enclosure in No. 1*, Catton (Mersina) to Clerk (Constantinople), October 28, 1929.

197 FO 371/13827/6149. Monck-Mason (Aleppo) to Henderson (London), December 10, 1929.

198 FO 371/13827/6149. Monck-Mason (Aleppo) to Henderson (London), December 10, 1929.

199 SD 867.4016. Crew (Istanbul) to Washington, February 12, 1930.

200 FO 371/14567. Gracey (London) to Rendel (London), January 9, 1930. Addenda, *Statement for the Press by Save the Children Fund.*

201 FO 371/14567/E1244. Clerk (Constantinople) to Henderson (London), March 10, 1930.

202 FO 371/13827/6651. London to Embassy (Constantinople), December 21, 1929. addenda, *letter from the Overseas Delegate and Appeal Secretary of the Save the Children's Fund Captain Gracey* (London) to Rendel (London), December 19, 1929.

203 FO 371/14587/E729. Embassy (Constantinople) to London, February 10, 1929; and FO 371/14567/EE886. Henderson (London) to Lord Tyrell (Paris), February 24, 1930. *Annual Report for 1929.*

204 SD 867.4016. Crew (Istanbul) to Washington, February 12, 1930.

205 FO 371/14577/E488. Palmer (Tabriz) to Embassy (Constantinople), January 3, 1930.

206 FO 424/260/2461. Vaughan-Russell (Aleppo) to MacDonald (London), March 4, 1924.

207 FO 371/14567. Gracey (London) to Rendel (London), January 9, 1930. Addenda, *Statement for the Press by Save the Children Fund.*

208 FO 371/13827/6524. (Beyrouth) to London, December 21, 1929. Addenda, *Report from Archdeacon of Cyprus*, Buxton via Save the Children's Fund, December 2, 1929.

209 FO 371/14587/E729. Embassy (Constantinople) to London, February 10, 1929. *Annual Report for 1928.*

210 SD 867.4016. Crew (Istanbul) to Washington, February 12, 1930.

211 Ellen Marie Lust-Okar also argues that the exodus was due to a variety of reasons. "Failure of Collaboration: Armenian refugees in Syria," *Middle Eastern Studies* 32(1) (January 1996): 3–4. Except for this work, there is very little literature on the Armenian exodus of 1929–30. A recent biography is the sole Turkish work that discusses this event. In his memoirs titled, *Mahallemizdeki Ermeniler* (The Armenians in Our Quarter) (Istanbul: İletişim, 2001), İsmail Arıkan vividly describes the peaceful coexistence between the Turks and Armenians in Darende, a small town on the anti-Taurus range, and the Armenian exodus from there during the 1920s. According to the author, this exodus owed itself more to hardships and dispossessed Armenians' search for a new life than to government oppression.

212 FO 371/13827/6149. Monck-Mason (Aleppo) to Henderson (London), December 10, 1929.

213 Dashnaktsutiun or Tashnak, also known as the Armenian Revolutionary Federation, is an Armenian nationalist party with roots in the nineteenth century. Today, Tashnak

is still an active party playing an important role in Armenians politics, both in the diaspora and in Armenia. For Tashnak's history, see Louise Nalbandian, *The Armenian Revolutionary Movement* (Berkeley, CA: University of California Press, 1960), 151–78.

214 Dahiliye Vekâleti (Ministry of Interior), DV "Seyahate Ait Dosya 1929," July 25, 1929. *Telegraf.*

215 "Ermeni Suikast Komiteleri tarafından Şehit Edilen veya Bu Uğurda Suveri Muhtelife ile Düçarı Gadrolan Ricalin Ailelerine Verilecek Emlâk ve Arazi hakkında Kanun" (Law about Immovable Property and Land to be Given to the Families of those Dignitaries, Who were Martyred by Armenian Assassination Committees or were Wrongfully Treated by Various Means Regarding this Matter) Nr. 882, May 31, 1926, *Düstur* (Code of Laws) third set, vol. 7: 1439. For discussion minutes of this law in TBMM, see TBMM Zabıt Ceridesi, term II, vol. 25: 601–05; and *Türk Parlamento Tarihi: TBMM-II. Dönem*, vol. 1: 511–14.

216 TBMM Zabıt Ceridesi, term II, vol. 25, 602.

217 Andrew Mango, *Atatürk* (New York: Overlook Press, 1999), 460; FO 424/268/E128. Clerk (Constantinople) to Chamberlain (London), January 4, 1928.

218 Records of the Department of State Relating to Political Relations of Turkey, Greece, and the Balkan States, 1930–1939. SD N 767.91/42. Grew (Istanbul) to Washington, July 26, 1930.

219 For more on French complicity in the creation of an anti-Kemalist front in Syria during the interwar era, see Koca, *Yakın Tarihten Günümüze Hükümetlerin Doğu-Güneydoğu Anadolu Politikaları*, 235–40, 465, 467–68.

220 For a review of the Franco-Armenian alliance in Syria in the 1920s, see Lust-Okar, "Failure of Collaboration," *Middle Eastern Studies.* The anti-Turkish front in Syria, which used the volatility of the international borders to harass Turkey, is reminiscent of the Macedonian nationalist front lead by Internal Macedonian Nationalist Organization (IMRO/VMRO), which attacked Yugoslav Macedonia from Bulgaria during the 1920s and the early 1930s. For more on interwar Macedonia, see Ivan Katardziev, *Sto Godini od Formiranjeto na VMRO: sto godini revoluiconerna tradicija* (Hundred Years of VMRO's Formation: Hundred Years of Revolutionaries) (Skopje: Misla, 1993), 62–70.

221 DV, "Yevmi Asayiş Dosyası," Correspondence Nr JUK 3/?, *1/7/929 dan 1/8/929 tarihine kadar hudut istihbaratı.*

222 DV, "Yevmi Asayiş Dosyası," Correspondence Nr JUK 3/?, *1/7/929 dan 1/8/929 tarihine kadar hudut istihbaratı.*

223 Despite exhaustive research on Hoybûn and its activities, scholarly community has been unable to agree on the exact national character of this organization. This is largely due to the partisan nature of such studies, which depict Hoybûn either as a heroic Kurdish nationalist organization, or a tool for Armenian aspirations. For studies representing these approaches, see respectively the following works: Rohat Alakom, *Hoybûn Örgütü ve Ağrı Ayaklanması* (Hoybûn Organization and the Ağrı Uprising) (Istanbul: Avesta, 1998); and Koca, *Yakın Tarihten Günümüze Hükümetlerin Doğu-Güneydoğu Anadolu Politikaları.*

224 DV, "Seyahate Ait Dosya 1929," Correspondence Nr JUK 3/9777. From the Ministry of Interior (Ankara) (Hereafter Ankara), to Kaya (Istanbul). Addenda, *Report from the Governor of Mardin Province*, From Mardin Province to the Ministry of Interior, August 2, 1929.

225 SD N 767.91/42. Grew (Istanbul) to Washington, July 26, 1930.

226 For the role played by Tashnak in the uprising, see Koca, *Yakın Tarihten Günümüze Hükümetlerin Doğu-Güneydoğu Anadolu Politikaları*, 247. In this work, Koca gives a Turkish nationalist account of Tashnak's contribution to the events in Ağrı.

227 SD N 767.91/42. Grew (Istanbul) to Washington, July 26, 1930.

228 For a detailed account of these incursions into Turkey, see Koca, *Yakın Tarihten Günümüze Hükümetlerin Doğu-Güneydoğu Anadolu Politikaları*, 257–63. For Hoybûn's role in the Ağrı uprising, see Alakom, *Hoybûn Örgütü, passim.*

229 SD N 767.91/43. Cardashian (New York) to Murray (Washington), August 12, 1930. *Letter from Vahan Cardashian in New York City.*

230 FO 371/14579/E3898. Clerk (Constantinople) to Henderson (London), July 21, 1930.

231 SD N 767.91/42. Grew (Istanbul) to Washington, July 26, 1930.

232 For a detailed account of the Ağrı uprising from a perspective that sympathizes with the Turkish government, see Koca, *Yakın Tarihten Günümüze Hükümetlerin Doğu-Güneydoğu Anadolu Politikaları*, 301–12. Koca paints this rebellion mainly as a work of Armenian nationalists, the Persian government, and a few tribal Kurdish leaders. For an account of this incident by its leader Nuri Paşa, Cf. Général Ihsan Nouri Pasha, *La Révolte de L'Agri Dagh: "Ararat" (1927–1930)* (Geneva: Éditions Kurde, 1985).

233 SD N 767.91/43. Cardashian (New York) to Murray (Washington), August 26, 1930. *Letter from Vahan Cardashian in New York City.*

234 General Directorate of Public Security (Emniyet-i Umumiye Umum Müdiriyeti—EUUM) was the headquarters of the Turkish police in Ankara, under the Ministry of Interior Affairs. In fall 1933, this was renamed Emniyet İşleri Umum Müdiriyeti—EİUM (General Directorate of Public Security).

235 İpsala is a town in Edirne, not far from the Greek frontier.

236 DV "Sadıra 1928 Teşrini Sani, Dahiliye Vekaleti Yazışmalar," Correspondance Nr DV-EUUM 4/5469. File Nr 13308. From Ankara to the Governors of Istanbul and Edirne, November 7, 1928

237 DV "Seyahate Ait Dosya 1929," Correspondence Nr DV-EUM 4/3173. File Nr 1/1564. From Ankara to the Governors of Istanbul, Izmir, Antalya…and the First Inspectorate-General (Diyarbakır), August 8, 1929.

238 DV "Sadıra 1928 Teşrini Sani, Dahiliye Vekaleti Yazışmalar," Correspondance Nr DV-EUUM 4/5827. File Nr. 1/3522. From Ankara to the First Inspectorate-General (Diyarbakır), December 8, 1928.

239 Zürcher, "Young Turks, Ottoman Muslims and Turkish Nationalists," in *Ottoman Past and Today's Turkey*, 179.

240 Irving Louis Horowitz, *Genocide, State Power and Mass Murder* (New Brunswick, NJ: Transaction Books, 1976): 45.

241 Çağlar Keyder, "Consequences of the Exchange of Populations for Turkey," unpublished article.

242 FO 371/13824/E906. Embassy (Constantinople) to London, February 9, 1929. *Annual Report for 1928.*

3 Kemalism par excellence in the 1930s: the rise of Turkish nationalism

1 Tunçay, *Türkiye Cumhuriyeti'nde Tek-Parti Yönetiminin Kurulması*, 247–51.

2 Tunçay *Türkiye Cumhuriyeti'nde Tek-Parti Yönetiminin Kurulması* 259. For more on Atatürk's role in the SCF experience, see Uz, *Gördüklerim Duyduklarım Duygularım*, 127–49.

3 Tunçay, *Türkiye Cumhuriyeti'nde Tek-Parti Yönetiminin Kurulması*, 268.

4 Mango, *Atatürk*, 472.

5 BCA 490.01/1.14.15. September 6, 1930; and BCA 490.01/1.14.16. September 6, 1930.

6 Tunçay, *Türkiye Cumhuriyeti'nde Tek-Parti Yönetiminin Kurulması*, 271–75.

7 Rifat N. Bali, "La Politique Relative aux Minorités sous la République," in *Les Relations entre Turcs et Juifs dans la Turquie Moderne*, ed. Rifat N. Bali (Istanbul: Isis, 2001), 143; and Rifat N. Bali, "1930 yılı Seçimleri ve Serbest Fırka'nın Azınlık Adayları"

(The 1930 Elections and the Minority Candidates of the Free Party) Tarih ve Toplum, no 167 (November 1997): 25–34.

8 SD 867.9111/288. Embassy (Istanbul) to Washington, November 1930. *Digest of Turkish News,* October 2–15, 1930.

9 *Cumhuriyet,* October 5, 6, 9, 14, 1930.

10 Cem Emrence, "1930 Seçimlerinde CHP'nin Baskı ve Propaganda Yöntemleri" (Pressure and Propaganda Methods of the CHP in the 1930 Elections) *Tarih ve Toplum* no. 200 (August 2000).

11 FO 371/14585/E5650. Clerk (Constantinople) to Henderson (London), October 20, 1930.

12 SD 867.9111/288. Embassy (Istanbul) to Washington, November 1930. *Digest of Turkish News,* October 2–15, 1930.

13 Tunçay, *Türkiye Cumhuriyeti'nde Tek-Parti Yönetiminin Kurulması,* 274–77. For more on this, see Fethi Okyar's memoirs, which provide valuable insight into the SCF era. In his biography, compiled by his son, Okyar discusses the extent to which Atatürk controlled the entire SCF. eds Osman Okyar and Mehmet Seyitdanlıoğlu, *Fethi Okyar'ın Anıları* (The Memoirs of Fethi Okyar) (Ankara: Türkiye İş Bankası Yayınları, 1999), 63–190.

14 For more on the Ağrı uprising, see Tunçay, *Türkiye Cumhuriyeti'nde Tek-Parti Yönetiminin Kurulması,* 242–45.

15 The Nakşibendi order had been suppressed on November 30, 1925 in accordance with Law Nr 2/478. "Tekke ve Zaviyeler ile Türbelerin Kapatılmasına ve Türbedarlıklar ile Bir Takım Unvanların Men ve İlgasına dair Kanun" (Law for Closing the Tekkes [Dervish Lodges], Zaviyes [Small Dervish Lodges], Türbes [Saint's Shrines], Banning, and Voiding Various Titles Including Türbedar [Shrine-Keeper]). This legislation had outlawed all Islamic orders, closed their shrines, and made it illegal to participate in their services. For more on this law and its discussion minutes, see *Türk Parlamento Tarihi: TBMM-II. Dönem,* vol. 2: 27–44.

16 Tunçay, *Türkiye Cumhuriyeti'nde Tek-Parti Yönetiminin Kurulması,* 303–05. For a treatment of the Menemen affair from a Kemalist perspective, see Kemal Üstün, *Menemen Olayı ve Kubilay* (The Menemen incident and Kubilay) (Istanbul: Çağdaş, 1981). For an account more sympathetic to the Islamic orders, cf. Mustafa Müftüoğlu, *Yakın Tarihimizden Bir Olay: Menemen Vak'ası* (An Episode from Our Recent History: The Menemen Incident) (Fatih, Istanbul: Risale, 1991).

17 FO 371/16091/E222. Embassy (Stambul) to London, January 14, 1932. *Annual Report for 1931.*

18 *Turbulent Era, A Diplomatic Record of Fifty Years, 1904–1945,* vol. 2, eds Walter Johnson et al. (Boston, MA: Houghton Mifflin, 1952), 880.

19 BCA 490.01/34.142.1. *Atatürk'ün Seyahat Notları* (Atatürk's Travel Notes), November 17, 1930. BCA 490.01/34.141.2. *Atatürk'ün İkinci Seyahat Notları* (Atatürk's Second Travel Notes), November 17, 1930.

20 For this letter, see *Türk Parlamento Tarihi: TBMM-IV. Dönem,* vol. 1: 3.

21 FO 371/16091/E222. Embassy (Stambul) to London, January 14, 1932. *Annual Report for 1931.*

22 The sixth İnönü government stayed in power until the end of TBMM's fourth term on May 1, 1935.

23 *Hükümet Programları 1920–1965* (Government programs, 1920–1965) comp. İsmail Arar (Istanbul: Burçak, 1968), 55.

24 Arar, *Hükümet Programları 1920–1965,* 55.

25 For a work that reviews nationalism in the cabinet programs between 1920 and 1931, see Yalçın Toker, *Milliyetçiliğin Yasal Kaynakları* (The Legal Sources of Nationalism) (Sirkeci, Istanbul: Toker Yayınları, 1979): 385–93. In this highly nationalist work biased against İnönü, the author claims that in his assessment, the 1931 program did not have "any expressions that guard nationalism," 393.

26 Ahmet Makal, *Türkiye'de Tek Partili Dönemde Çalışma İlişkileri: 1920–1946* (Labor Relations in Turkey during the Single Party Era: 1920–1946) (Ankara: İmge, 1999), 169–78.

27 *Atatürk'ün Tamim ve Telgrafları ve Beyannameleri* (Atatürk's Circulars Telegrams and Declarations) vol. IV (Ankara: Atatürk Araştırma Merkezi, 1991), 606. For a high-brow work from the 1930s, which elaborates on the six principles, consult Şeref Aykut, *Kamâlizm* (Kemalism) (İstanbul: Muallim Ahmet Halit Kitap Evi, 1936).

28 Recep [Peker], *CHF Programının İzahı* (Explanation of Republican People's Party's Program) (Ankara: Ulus Matbaası, 1931), 3–16.

29 Baskın Oran argues that nationalism was the central tenet of Kemalism, on which all its other principles hinged, "Altı Ok Arasındaki İlişkiler ya da Milliyetçilik Ekseni Çevresinde Kemalizm" (The Relations among the Six Arrows or Kemalizm around the Axis of Nationalism) in *Uluslararası Atatürk Konferansı* (International Atatürk Conference) vol. 3 (İstanbul: Boğaziçi Üniversitesi, 1981), 1–8.

30 FO 371/16091/E222. Embassy (Stambul) to London, January 14, 1932. *Annual Report for 1931.*

31 BCA 490.01/63.242.6. "Cumhuriyet Halk Partisi Kuruluş ve Yürüyüşü" (The Establishment and Development of the Republican People's Party), typescript, (1939?), 7–8.

32 *Cümhuriyet Halk Fırkası Nizamnamesi*, 3.

33 *Cümhuriyet Halk Fırkası Nizamnamesi ve Programı 1931* (By-laws and Program of Republican People's Party 1931) (Ankara: TBMM Matbaası, 1931), 30.

34 Beşikçi, *Cumhuriyet Halk Fırkası'nın Programı*, 18–19.

35 See the CHP's 1931 program, quoted in Beşikçi, *Cumhuriyet Halk Fırkası'nın Programı*, 18–19. In this work, Beşikçi draws attention to the nationalist orientation of the program.

36 *Cümhuriyet Halk Fırkası Nizamnamesi ve Programı 1931*, 29.

37 *Cümhuriyet Halk Fırkası Nizamnamesi ve Programı 1931*, 4.

38 The word "akalliyet," of Arabic origin, means minority in Turkish. However, it was officially used to refer only to Jews, Armenians, and Greeks, until "azınlık," a pure Turkish word replaced it the mid-1930s. "Azınlık," was also officially used only in reference to the Jews, the Armenians, and the Greeks.

39 *Cumhuriyet Halk Fırkası Katibiumumiliğinin Fırka Teşkilatına Umumi Tebligatı* (General Announcements of the Secretary General of the Republican People's Party to the Party Organization) Mahremdir, Hizmete Mahsustur, vol. 1 (confidential and classified) (Ankara: Hakimiyeti Milliye, 1933), 82.

40 It seems that, even after this memorandum, confusion regarding non-Muslims' membership to the CHP did not disappear. For instance, as late 1946, the CHP once again felt obliged to clarify its position on this issue. It wrote that non-Muslims could be accepted as members to the CHP. BCA 490.01/178.710.1. Secretary General of CHP to Party Branches, October 25, 1946.

41 In their presentations, Bayur focused on Kemalism and foreign policy, Tengirşenk spoke on Kemalist economy, and Bozkurt presented a comparative analysis of the Kemalist and other revolutions. Uyar, *Sol Milliyetçi Bir Türk Aydını*, 68. Bozkurt also wrote in the newspapers to articulate on Kemalism. For some examples of his works, see *Tan*, May 27, 28, 29, 1935.

42 [Peker], *CHF Programının İzahı*, 7.

43 [Peker], *CHF Programının İzahı*, 6.

44 İnan, *Medeni Bilgiler ve Atatürk'ün El Yazıları*, 378.

45 [İnan], *Vatandaşlık İçin Medeni Bilgiler*, 16.

46 The People's Houses were nationalist mass education institutions. Inspired by various nationalist popular education institutions in Central-Eastern Europe at the time, such as the Czechoslovakian Sokóls, the Houses helped spread Kemalism, while functioning as urbane *joie de vivre* machinery. CHP's steadfast commitment helped the Houses

evolve into mass institutions. In 1937, for instance, more than six million people visited the Houses, which sponsored more than 3,000 conferences; 1,164 concerts; 135 art exhibits; 1,164 plays; and 1,549 movie showings. Furthermore, with 130,000 books on their shelves, House libraries recorded 1,598,191 readers. BCA 490.01/63.242.6. "Halkevleri" (The People's Houses), typescript (1938?), 2–4. By 1938, the number of the Houses reached 209, and membership climbed to 136,535. *CHP 1939'da Halkevleri* (CHP People's Houses in 1939) (Ankara: Recep Ulusoğlu Basımevi, 1939), 6–27. For more on the Houses, see Anıl Çeçen, *Atatürk'ün Kültür Kurumu Halkevleri* (A Cultural Institution of Atatürk: The People's Houses) (İstanbul: Cumhuriyet Kitapları, 2000); and Soner Cagaptay, *Crafting the Turkish Nation*, PhD Dissertation, Yale University, 2003. For two works on the Houses written in the 1930s, see *Halkevleri, 1932–1935: 103 Halkevi Geçen Yıllarda Nasıl Çalıştı* (People's Houses, 1932–1935: How did the 103 People's Houses Work in the Recent Years) (Ankara: 1935); and *CHP Halkevleri Öğreneği* (The Regulations of the CHP People's Houses) (Ankara: Ulus Basımevi, 1935).

47 *Hükümet Programları 1920–1965*, pp. 64–66.

48 *CHP Tüzüğü. Partinin Dördüncü Büyük Kurultayı Onaylamıştır* (Republican People's Party's By-Laws. Approved by the Fourth General Congress of the Party) (Ankara: Ulus Basımevi, 1935).

49 *CHP Dördüncü Büyük Kurultayı Tüzük ve Program Komisyonlarınca Onanan Program Taslağı* (Draft Program Approved by the By-Laws and Program Commissions of Republican People's Party's Fourth General Congress) (Ankara: May 12, 1935).

50 *CHP Dördüncü Büyük Kurultayı Görüşmeleri Tutulgası* (Records of Sessions of CHP's Fourth General Congress) (Ankara: May 9–16, 1935), 45.

51 *CHP Büyük Kurultayının Tetkikine Sunulan Program Taslağı* (Draft Program Presented for Approval to the Fourth General Congress of the Republican People's Party) (Ankara: May 9, 1935), 1.

52 Celal Bozkurt, *Cumhuriyet Halk Partisi Dünü, Bugünü, İdeolojisi* (Republican People's Party, Its Past, Present and Ideology) (Ankara: 1967), 147–49; *CHP Dördüncü Büyük Kurultayı Görüşmeleri Tutulgası*, 44–46, 59–60, 61–62.

53 *Türk Parlamento Tarihi: TBMM-IV. Dönem*, vol. 1: 36–41.

54 *Türk Parlamento Tarihi: TBMM-IV. Dönem*, vol. 1: 41–42.

55 *Türk Parlamento Tarihi: TBMM-IV. Dönem*, vol. 1: 42.

56 *CHP Dördüncü Büyük Kurultayı Görüşmeleri Tutulgası*, 44–46. For another speech by Peker in which he elaborates on the six principles along the same lines, see *CHP Genel Sekreteri R. Pekerin*, 9–13.

57 FO 371/17961/E2192. Clerk (Angora) to London, April 9, 1934.

58 Law Nr 2393 and government decree 2–150.

59 FO 371/17961/E2192. Clerk (Angora) to London, April 9, 1934.

60 FO 371/17902/E 4915. Embassy (Angora) to London, July 27, 1934.

61 Goloğlu, *Tek Partili Cumhuriyet*, 161.

62 *İsmet İnönü Defterler 1919–1973* (İsmet İnönü Notebooks 1919–1973), comp. Ahmet Demirel, vol. 1 (İstanbul: Yapı Kredi Yayınları, 2001), 170.

63 This province, which was established in 1936 by the amalgamation of Rize and Artvin provinces, was later on broken down into its former components. However, the Artvin province was called Çoruh until 1956.

64 Koca, *Yakın Tarihten Günümüze Hükümetlerin Doğu-Güneydoğu Anadolu Politikaları*, 175.

65 Records of the Department of State Relating to Political Relations Between Turkey and Other States, 1910–1929. SD 767.00/67. MacMurray (İstanbul) to Washington, May 19, 1937.

66 Walter Johnson *et al.*, eds, *Turbulent Era*, vol. 2, 842.

67 FO 371/20867/E6770. Loraine (Angora) to Eden (London), November 17, 1937.

68 As a result, Soviet support for Turkey diminished after 1934. For example, during the Montreux Conference in 1936 as well as in the Sancak of Alexandratta case

after 1937, Moscow gave Ankara unsatisfactory backing. SD 767.00/67. MacMurray (Istanbul) to Washington, May 19, 1937. Hence, starting with 1935, Ankara proceeded to feel out the possibility of a rapprochement with the United Kingdom to befriend London instead of Moscow for great power support. Accordingly, Anglo-Turkish relations, which had been sour since the beginning of the First World War, and which had been only slightly ameliorated during the term of Ambassador Sir George Clerk between 1929 and 1934, improved significantly after 1934, under the term of Ambassador Loraine. For a review of the improvement in Anglo-Turkish relations after 1934, see Brock Millman, *The Ill-Made Alliance: Anglo-Turkish Relations*, (Montreal: McGill-Queen's University, 1998), 35–104. During Loraine's stay in Ankara, Turkey and Britain moved to a close friendship. This showed itself in King Edward VIII's symbolic visit to Istanbul on September 4, 1936. Gordon Waterfield, *Professional Diplomat: Sir Percy Loraine of Kirkharle Bt. 1880–1961* (London: John Murray, 1962), 208–10. In declaration of this suddenly entrenched friendship, Atatürk is quoted to have said: "I have thrown myself into the arms of England." Waterfield, *Professional Diplomat*, 212.

69 FO 371/20091/E933. Embassy (Angora) to London, February 20, 1936. *Annual Report for 1935*.

70 The name change of the province signaled its Turkification. Dersim is a word of Kurdish/Persian origin likely meaning the "silver gate," while Tunceli is of Turkish word and means the "land of bronze."

71 Current Bingöl province in Turkey has had four names under the republic. The original name of the province, Genç, was changed to Çapakçur in 1936, to Karlıova in 1938, and to Bingöl in 1945. While the former names of this province (Genç and Çapakçur) were not Turkish, the latter two were. Genç, for instance, was a Kurdish word that meant "treasure," while Karlıova and Bingöl were Turkish words, respectively meaning the "snowy plain" and the "thousand lakes."

72 Koca, *Yakın Tarihten Günümüze Hükümetlerin Doğu-Güneydoğu Anadolu Politikaları*, 176.

73 Demirel, *İsmet İnönü Defterler*, 185–86.

74 Koca, *Yakın Tarihten Günümüze Hükümetlerin Doğu-Güneydoğu Anadolu Politikaları*, 57–151, 161–567. In this work, sympathetic toward the Inspectorates Koca argues for their utilitarian value.

75 For more on the Inspectorates, see Koca, *Yakın Tarihten Günümüze Hükümetlerin Doğu-Güneydoğu Anadolu Politikaları*, 57–151, 161–567. The Inspectorates lasted well into the 1940s. On June 27, 1947, the government passed a decree (Nr 3-5899) to establish the Fifth Inspectorate along the Syrian border and the Eastern Mediterranean littoral in Southern Turkey. This Fifth Inspectorate, which included Adana (Seyhan), Hatay, Gaziantep, and Kahramanmaraş provinces, promoted economic development of these provinces while fighting banditry there. Koca, *Yakın Tarihten Günümüze Hükümetlerin Doğu-Güneydoğu Anadolu Politikaları*, 176–77. Like the Houses, the Inspectorates were also abolished after the May 1950 elections, in which the CHP lost to the DP. On January 24, 1952, the DP passed Law Nr 8270 and eliminated the Inspectorates.

76 Afet [İnan] *et al.*, *Türk Tarihinin Ana Hatları* (Main Themes of Turkish history) Türk Ocakları Türk Tarihi Tetkik Heyeti (Turkish Hearths Committee for the Study of Turkish History) (Istanbul: Devlet Matbaası, 1930).

77 Uluğ İğdemir, "Atatürk'ün Emriyle Hazırlanan Program" (A Program Prepared on Atatürk's Orders) *Belleten* 27 (1963): 644.

78 İğdemir, Atatürk'ün Emriyle Hazırlanan Program: 644.

79 İğdemir, Atatürk'ün Emriyle Hazırlanan Program: 646.

80 İğdemir, Atatürk'ün Emriyle Hazırlanan Program: 647.

81 İğdemir, Atatürk'ün Emriyle Hazırlanan Program: 644.

82 *Türk Tarihinin Ana Hatlarına Methal* (Introduction to the Main Themes of Turkish History) ed. by Members of the Society for the Study of Turkish History (Istanbul: Devlet Matbaası, 1930).

83 *Birinci Türk Tarih Kongresi* (First Turkish History Congress) (Ankara: T. C. Maarif Vekâleti, 1933).

84 SD 867.41/11. Allen (Istanbul) to Washington, July 13, 1932.

85 Mustafa Ergün, *Atatürk Devri Türk Eğitimi* (Turkish Education Under Atatürk) (Ankara: DTCF, 1982), 126.

86 *Yeni Türk Lûgatı*, 1152.

87 *Türk Tarihinin Ana Hatlarına Methal*, 26–30.

88 Afet [İnan], "Tarihten Evvel ve Tarih Fecrinde" (In Pre-historic Times and at the Dawn of History) *Birinci Türk Tarih Kongresi* (First Turkish History Congress) (Ankara: T.C. Maarif Velaketi, 1933), 31.

89 *Türk Tarihinin Ana Hatlarına Methal*, 50–58.

90 [İnan], Tarihten Evvel ve Tarih Fecrinde, 34.

91 *Türk Tarihinin Ana Hatlarına Methal*, 8.

92 Reşit Galip, "Türk Irkı ve Medeniyet Tarihine Umumi Bir Bakış" (An Overview of the Racial and Civilizational History of the Turks) *Birinci Türk Tarih Kongresi* (First Turkish History Congress) (Ankara: T.C. Maarif Velaketi, 1933), 159. In recognition of European intellectual influence on the *Turkish History Thesis*, it should be noted that Galip's arguments were in fact based upon the works of European anthropologists, including the following books: Pierre Legendre, "La Race Blanche et La Race Jaune," *Illustration*, (June 27, 1924); Ronald Burrage Dixon, *The Racial History of Men* (New York: C. Scribner's Sons, 1923); and William Zebina Ripley, *Races of Europe, A Sociological Study* (New York: D. Appleton and Company, 1899).

93 Galip, Türk Irkı ve Medeniyet Tarihine Umumi Bir Bakış, 117–24.

94 Galip, Türk Irkı ve Medeniyet Tarihine Umumi Bir Bakış, 109. For more on the *Turkish History Thesis*, see *Birinci Türk Tarih Kongresi*, *Passim*; and İsmail Hakkı Danişmend, *Türklerle Hind-Avrupalıların Menşe Birliği* (Common Origins of the Turks and the Indo-Europeans) (Istanbul: Devlet Matbaası, 1935).

95 For Atatürk's role in the creation of the *Turkish History Thesis*, see Ergün, *Atatürk Devri Türk Eğitimi*, 125–32; and İğdemir, Atatürk'ün Emriyle Hazırlanan Program, 105–08.

96 Étienne Copeaux, *Espaces et Temps de la Nation Turque* (Paris: CNRS, 1997), 52–53.

97 *Türkiye Halkının Antropolojik Karakteri ve Türkiye Tarihi: Türk Irkının Vatanı Anadolu 64,000 kişi üzerinde Anket* (The Anthropological Character of the People of Turkey and Turkish History: Anatolia, the Homeland of the Turkish Race and a Survey Conducted on 64,000 People) (University of Geneva: 1937), and (Ankara: Türk Tarih Kurumu, 1947).

98 Yıldız, *Ne Mutlu Türküm*, 165–66; and Artun Ünsal, "La Bibliothèque Politique Française D'Atatürk," in *La Turquie et la France a L'Époque d'Atatürk: Publié à L'occasion du centenaire de la naissance de Kemal Ataturk*, ed. Irène Mélikoff, Jean-Louis Bacqué-Grammont and Paul Dumont, Collection Turcica 1 (Paris: Association pour le Dévelopment Études Turques, 1981), 42; Copeaux, *Espaces et Temps de la Nation Turque*, 52–53.

99 Eugène Pittard, *Les Races et l'Histoire Introduction Ethnologique à l'Histoire* (Paris: La Renaissance du Livre, 1924).

100 Arthur de Gobineau, *The Inequality of Human Races*, with preface by George L. Mosse, (New York: H. Fertig, 1999).

101 Alfred Cort Haddon, *The Races of Man and Their Distribution* (New York: Gordon Press, 1981).

102 Georges Montandon, *La Race. Les Races. Mise au Point d'ethnologie Somatique* (Paris: Payot, 1933).

103 Jean-Marie Jacques de Morgon, *L'Humanité Préhistorique* (Paris: Renaissance du Livre, 1924).

104 Joseph Deniker, *Essai d'une Classification des Races Humaines* (Paris: Masson, 1889).

105 İnan, *Medeni Bilgiler ve Atatürk'ün El Yazıları*, 352; *Türk Tarihinin Ana Hatlarına Methal*, 38; *Tarih I Tarihten-evvelki Zamanlar ve Eski Zamanlar* (History I pre-historic and ancient ages) (Istanbul: Devlet Matbaası, 1931), 20.

106 İnan, *Medeni Bilgiler ve Atatürk'ün El Yazıları*, 371. [İnan], *Vatandaşlık İçin Medeni Bilgiler*, 13.
107 Yıldız, *Ne Mutlu Türküm*, 159.
108 SD 867.41/10. Sherill (Istanbul) to Washington, July 13, 1932.
109 Şemsettin Günaltay and Reşit Tankut, *Dil ve Tarih Tezlerimiz Üzerine Bazı İzahlar* (Some Reflections on Our Language and History Thesis) (Istanbul: Devlet Basımevi, 1938), 10–17, 21–26.
110 *Tarih I Tarihten-evvelki Zamanlar*, 189.
111 *Tarih İlkmektepler İçin V* (History for Grade Schools: Fifth Grade) (Ankara: T. C. Maarif Vekâleti, 1933), 24–25.
112 İnan and Karal, *Atatürk'ün Tarih Tezi*, 63.
113 Günaltay and Tankut, *Dil ve Tarih Tezlerimiz Üzerine Bazı İzahlar*, 19.
114 İnan and Karal, *Atatürk'ün Tarih Tezi*, 63–64.
115 İnan and Karal, *Atatürk'ün Tarih Tezi*, 57.
116 İnan and Karal, *Atatürk'ün Tarih Tezi*, 57 and [İnan], "Tarihten Evvel ve Tarih Fecrinde," 31–32.
117 İnan and Karal, *Atatürk'ün Tarih Tezi*, 59.
118 SD 867.41/2. Patterson (Ankara) to Washington, June 19, 1930. *Memorandum of Interview with Prof. H. H. van der Osten, University of Chicago Anatolian Expedition.*
119 Suavi Aydın, "Türk Tarih Tezi ve Halkevleri" (The Turkish History Thesis and the People's Houses) *Kebikeç* 2(3) (1996): 107–30.
120 For examples of newspapers articles that seem to have been inspired by the *Thesis*, see *Anadolu*, especially, October 4, 5, 9, 1934, and March 1, 6, 1935.
121 Danişmend, *Türklerle Hind-Avrupalıların Menşe Birliği*, 18–19.
122 Danişmend, *Türklerle Hind-Avrupalıların Menşe Birliği*, 15.
123 Danişmend, *Türklerle Hind-Avrupalıların Menşe Birliği*, 71–75.
124 However, there were also differences between the two congresses, especially *vis-à-vis* the composition of their delegates. First, while the History Congress had only one non-Muslim Turkish representative (Professor Galanti of Darülfünun), the Language Congress had more, including five Armenians (a journalist, a university professor, a schoolteacher, and two without stated professions), three Greeks (a doctor of law, and two ex-Ottoman bureaucrats), and four Jews (two ex-Ottoman bureaucrats, a university professor and a publisher). There was also a Catholic priest, and a teacher from the Italian High School in Istanbul, who may have been Turkish citizens as well. Second, while there had been no foreign delegates at the History Congress, there were two at the Language Congress: Edmund Tilley, a member of the International Phonetics Society, and Louis Mikolco, representing the Hungarian mission in Turkey. The participation of non-Muslims and foreigners at the Language Congress may be taken to hint at its inclusive and international nature. However, one should remember that, while the total number of delegates at this congress was 717, the presence of the two foreigners and fourteen non-Muslims would be a drop in the ocean in this crowd. *Birinci Türk Dil Kurultayı* (First Turkish Language Congress) (Istanbul: Devlet Matbaası, 1933), xi–xxx.
125 Étienne Copeaux, *Türk Tarih Tezinden Türk-İslam Sentezine* (From the Turkish History Thesis to the Turkish-Islamic Synthesis) (Istanbul: Tarih Vakfı Yurt Yayınları, 1998), 45–53.
126 Uriel Heyd, *Language Reform in Turkey* (Jerusalem: Israel Oriental Society, 1954), 25–26.
127 SD 867.402/48. Embassy (Istanbul) to Washington, October 17, 1932.
128 *Birinci Türk Dil Kurultayı*, 389, 401–03.
129 *Birinci Türk Dil Kurultayı*, 249–50.
130 SD 867.402/48, Embassy (Istanbul) to Washington, October 17, 1932.
131 Heyd, *Language Reform in Turkey*, 26.
132 SD 867.9111/383. Embassy (Istanbul) to Washington, November 16, 1932. *Digest of Turkish News*, October 30–November 12, 1932.

133 Heyd, *Language Reform in Turkey*, 29.
134 Heyd, *Language Reform in Turkey*, 30.
135 For a good review of the purification movement, see Geoffrey Lewis, *The Turkish Language Reform* (Oxford: Oxford University Press, 1999).
136 Heyd, *Language Reform in Turkey*, 21.
137 Çeçen, *Atatürk'ün Kültür Kurumu Halkevleri*, 123, 125, 130.
138 SD 867.402/61. Allen (Istanbul) to Washington, April 9, 1933.
139 SD 867.402/61. Allen (Istanbul) to Washington, April 9, 1933.
140 SD 867.402/61. Allen (Istanbul) to Washington, April 9, 1933.
141 Yıldız, *Ne Mutlu Türküm*, 137.
142 DV "24/9/935 ve 3938 18/10/935 4338'e," Correspondance Nr DV-EİUM 1/10096. From Ankara to the Governors of all provinces, October 1935.
143 SD 867.402/61. Allen (Istanbul) to Washington, April 9, 1933. From 1930s onwards, this bank emerged as Turkey's leading industrial and textile conglomerate. For more on it, consult Sait Emin Özbek, *La Sümer Bank et l'industrialisation de la Turquie sous la République* (Lyon: Imprimerie du Salut Public, 1938).
144 For more on the foundation of *Eti Bank*, consult Aslan Tufan Yazman, ed., *Eti Bank*, 1935–1945 (Ankara: 1945).
145 For a first person account of the fast deterioration of Atatürk's health, see the memoirs of his *aide de camp*, İsmail Hakkı Tekçe, *Muhafızı Atatürk'ü Anlatıyor: Emekli General İsmail Hakkı Tekçe'nin Anıları* (His Guard Tells About Atatürk: The Memoirs of Retired General İsmail Hakkı Tekçe) (Istanbul: Kaynak, 2000), 58–61.
146 FO 371/21927/E7381. Camciyan (Istanbul) to Chaplain (London), November 18, 1938.
147 *İstatistik Yıllığı Cilt 10*, 64–65.
148 *İstatistik Yıllığı Cilt 10*, 64–65.
149 Heyd, *Language Reform in Turkey*, 30.
150 SD 867.00/2048. Bursky (Izmir) to Washington, November 1, 1930. *News Of Izmir—* 1930, Nr 2.
151 SD 867.4016 JEWS/3. George (Izmir) to Washington, December 13, 1932.
152 AA T-120 4900. Rosenberg (Ankara) to Berlin, December 20, 1933.
153 TBMM Zabıt Ceridesi, term IV: vol. 23, 70.
154 SD 867.9111/391. Embassy (Istanbul) to Washington, February 21, 1933. *Digest of Turkish Press*, February 5–February 18, 1933.
155 SD 867.9111/392. Embassy (Istanbul) to Washington, March 8, 1933. *Digest of Turkish Press*, February 19–March 4, 1933.
156 Milliyet, July 22, 1933; SD 867.9111/390. Embassy (Istanbul) to Washington, February 1933. *Digest of Turkish Press* January 22–February 4, 1933; and SD 867.9111/405. Embassy (Istanbul) to Washington, August 1933. *Digest of Turkish Press*, July 16–August 11, 1933.
157 SD 867.9111/410. Embassy (Istanbul) to Washington, December 11, 1933. *Digest of Turkish Press*, November 5–December 2, 1933.
158 SD 867.9111/410. Embassy (Istanbul) to Washington, March 5, 1934. *Digest of Turkish Press*, November 5–December 2, 1933.
159 SD 867.9111/414. Embassy (Istanbul) to Washington, December 11, 1933. *Digest of Turkish Press*, January 28–February 24, 1934.
160 Landau, *Tekinalp: Bir Türk Yurtseveri*, 20.
161 FO 371/17958/E4912. Loraine (Angora) to London, July 7, 1934; and FO 371/17958/E6178. Catton (Mersina) to Morgan (Angora), September 17, 1934.
162 FO 371/16985/E2053. Embassy (Constantinople) to London, April 6, 1933.
163 FO 371/17958/E4912. Loraine (Angora) to London, July 27, 1934. *Copy of letter*, Catton (Mersina) to Loraine (Angora), July 7, 1934.
164 FO 371/16985/E2053. Embassy (Angora) to London, April 6, 1934.

165 SD 867.9111/ Embassy (Istanbul) to Washington, January 11, 1933. *Digest of Turkish Press*.
166 FO 371/17958/E4912. Loraine (Angora) to London, July 27, 1934. *Copy of letter*, Catton (Mersina) to Loraine (Angora), July 7, 1934.
167 FO 371/17969/E5028. Davis (Smyrna) to Loraine (Angora), July 19, 1934. FO 371/17969/E5028. Davis (Smyrna) to Loraine (Angora), August 2, 1934.
168 *CHP Dördüncü Büyük Kurultayı Görüşmeleri Tutulgası* (Records of the sessions of CHP's fourth General Congress) (Ankara: May 9–16, 1935), 149.
169 Bali, *Cumhuriyet Yıllarında Türkiye Yahudileri*, 269–72.
170 SD 867.9111/422. Embassy (Istanbul) to Washington, October 3, 1934. *Digest of Turkish Press, August 12–September 22, 1934*.
171 Bali, *Cumhuriyet Yıllarında Türkiye Yahudileri*, 273.
172 Landau, *Tekinalp: Bir Türk Yurtseveri*, 21.
173 Bali, *Cumhuriyet Yıllarında Türkiye Yahudileri*, 275.
174 Bali, *Cumhuriyet Yıllarında Türkiye Yahudileri*, 277.
175 Bali, *Cumhuriyet Yıllarında Türkiye Yahudileri*, 276.
176 Bali, *Cumhuriyet Yıllarında Türkiye Yahudileri*, 281–87.
177 Bali, *Cumhuriyet Yıllarında Türkiye Yahudileri*, 281–82.
178 Mahir Şaul, "The Mother Tongue of the Polyglot: Cosmopolitanism and Nationalism among the Sepharadim of Istanbul," in *Turkish-Jewish Encounters*, 157.
179 Cengiz is a Turkish name, which derives from Genghis Khan's name.
180 For the text of this law, see "Soy Adı Kanunu" (Law on last names) Nr 2525, June 21, 1934, *Düstur*, third set, vol. 15, addenda: 1282–83. For its discussion minutes in the parliament, see *Türk Parlamento Tarihi: TBMM-IV.Dönem*, vol. 1: 180–89.
181 TBMM Zabıt Ceridesi, term IV, vol. 23/1: 249.
182 TBMM Zabıt Ceridesi, term IV, vol. 23/1: 249.
183 Çeçen, *Atatürk'ün Kültür Kurumu Halkevleri*, 120.
184 Minister Kaya told the TBMM that only 3–5 percent of the country's population actually lacked last names. TBMM Zabıt Ceridesi, term IV, vol. 23/1: 223.
185 "Soy Adı Nizamnamesi" (Statue on Last Names) *Resmi Gazete*, Nr 2805, December 20, 1934.
186 Barzilai Guiladi, "Le Judaïsme muet," *Israel*, January 29, 1937 (Alexandria, Egypt). Quoted in Bali, *Cumhuriyet Yıllarında Türkiye Yahudileri*, 289.
187 *Türk Parlamento Tarihi: TBMM-IV.Dönem*, vol. 1: 184–85. For the discussion minutes of this, see TBMM Zabıt Ceridesi, term IV, vol. 25/1: 202–03.
188 Aktar, *Varlık Vergisi ve 'Türkleştirme'*, 60–66, 103–08; Bali, *Cumhuriyet Yıllarında*, 502–03; and Parla, *Kemalist Tek-Parti İdeolojisi*, 176–221.
189 Zürcher, "Young Turks, Ottoman Muslims and Turkish Nationalists," in *Modern Turkey and Ottoman Past*, 179.
190 FO 371/21915/E4624. Loraine (Ankara) to London, August 8, 1938.

4 Who is a Turk? Kemalist citizenship policies

1 For more on this, Stanley G. Payne, *A History of Fascism 1914–1945* (Madison, WI: University of Wisconsin Press, 1955), 129–46, 267–89, 317–27. For nationalism and authoritarianism in interwar Poland, Hungary, Romania, Yugoslavia, and Bulgaria, see ed. Joseph Rothschild, *East Central Europe Between the Two World Wars, A History of East Central Europe*, vol. 9 (Seattle, WA: University of Washington Press, 1998), 3–72, 137–357, 382–96. For the turn to the right in these countries, consult Banac and Verdery, *National Character and National Ideology in Interwar Eastern Europe*; Thomas W. Simmone, Jr, *Eastern Europe in the Postwar Years* (New York: St. Martin's Press, 1993), 17–37; Antony Polonsky, *The Little Dictators: The History of Eastern Europe Since 1918* (London: Routledge, 1975), 1–62, 77–94, 127–56; and Hugh Seton-Watson,

Eastern Europe Between the Wars 1918–1941 (Hamden, CT: Archon Books, 1962), 157–361.

2 For a study on authoritarianism and nationalities policies in Iran during the interwar era, see Ervand Abrahamian, *Iran Between Two Revolutions* (Princeton, NJ: Princeton University Press, 1983).

3 Ivo Banac and Katherine Verdery, *National Character and National Ideology in Interwar Eastern Europe* (New Haven, CT: Yale Center for International and Area Studies, 1995), xx.

4 Banac and Verdery, *National Character and National Ideology*, xxi.

5 For a work that studies the rise of royal dictatorship in Yugoslavia, see Ivo Banac, *The National Question in Yugoslavia* (Ithaca, NY: Cornell University Press, 1994). For studies that examine right-wing interwar Romanian nationalism, consult Volovici, *Nationalist Ideology and Antisemitism*; and Livezeanu, *Cultural Politics in Greater Romania*, passim. For works on Greece, with special emphasis on Metaxas dictatorship, see P. J. Vatikiotis, *Popular Autocracy in Greece 1936–41: A Political Biography of General Metaxas* (London: Frank Cass, 1998); Richard Clogg, *A Concise History of Greece* (Cambridge: Cambridge University Press, 1992), 100–44; and Jon V. Kofas, *Authoritarianism in Greece*, East European Monographs, No. CXXXIII (Boulder, CO and New York: Columbia University Press, 1983). For another work on Greece, which studies the relations between the state and minorities within the background of ethnic homogenization of Greek Macedonia, consult Anastasia N. Karakasidou, *Fields of Wheat, Hills of Blood: Passages to Nationhood in Greek Macedonia, 1870–1990* (Chicago, IL: University of Chicago, 1997), 190–237. Also see George Th. Mavrogordatos, *Stillborn Republic: Social Conditions and Party Strategies in Greece, 1922–1936* (Berkeley, CA: University of California Press, 1983) for state–minority relations in interwar Greece, 226–72. On the other hand, for interwar Bulgaria, consult, R. J. Crampton, *A Short History of Modern Bulgaria* (Cambridge: Cambridge University Press, 1987), 82–123.

6 Such a hardening took place also in the borderlands of Eastern Europe. For instance, between 1919 and 1929, Ukrainian nationalism experienced a "turn to the right," Alexander Motyl, *Turn to the Right*, East European Monographs, No. LXV (Boulder, CO and New York: Columbia University Press, 1980), especially, 129–73. Additionally, for the failure of democracy and the rise of right-wing authoritarianism in Austria and the Baltics, see Polonsky, *The Little Dictators*, 62–77, and 100–02, respectively.

7 David I. Kertzer and Dominique Arel, "Censuses, Identity Formation and the Struggle for Political Power," in *Census and Identity: The Politics of Race, Ethnicity, and Language in National Censuses*, ed. David I. Kertzer and Dominique Arel (Cambridge: Cambridge University Press, 2002), 3.

8 For more on the political uses of censuses, see Kertzer and Arel, "Censuses, Identity Formation," 1–42.

9 McCarthy, *The Arab World, Turkey and the Balkans*, 64–68.

10 Dündar, *İttihat ve Terakki'nin Müslümanları İskân Politikası*, 84–87.

11 *İstatistik Yıllığı İkinci Cilt*, 44.

12 *İstatistik Yıllığı İkinci Cilt*, 51.

13 BCA 272.11/6.5.3. March 23, 1927.

14 BCA 272.11/6.5.6. May 10, 1927.

15 BCA 272.12/59.161.6. June 18, 1928.

16 *İstatistik Yıllığı Cilt 10*, 64.

17 *İstatistik Yıllığı Cilt 10*, 65.

18 DV "Giden Şifreler 1/12/1930 Sayılı Dosya," Correspondence Nr DV-NUM 3/3954/1920. File Nr 1/2831. From Ankara to the Governors of Siirt, Van, and other provinces, December 4, 1930.

19 DV "Şifre Kartunu 1/5/33-14/6/33," Correspondence Nr DV-EUUM ?/5430. File Nr? From Ankara to the Governor of Bayazit, May 3, 1933.

20 DV "Çıkan Şifre 15/6/1933'den 31/7/33 Tarihine Kadar," Correspondence Nr DV-EUUM 6157. File Nr 1/1463. From Ankara to the Governor of Bayazit, June 22, 1933.

21 DV "Şifre Kartunu 1/5/33-14/6/33," Correspondence Nr DV-EUUM 5029. File Nr 1/1099. From Ankara to the Governor of Mardin, May 20, 1933.

22 DV "Özel Kalem Şifreli Yazışma 30/11/1931," Correspondence Nr DV-EUUM 1.B.3/8218. File Nr 1/2462. From Ankara to the First Inspectorate-General (Diyarbakır) and the Provinces, October 25, 1931.

23 DV "Şifre Kartunu 1/5/33-14/6/33," Correspondence Nr DV-4842. File Nr 1/1046. From Ankara to the Governor of Tekirdağ, May 14, 1933.

24 DV "Şifre Kartunu 1/5/33-14/6/33," Correspondence Nr DV-EUUM 1.B/4597 File Nr 1/971. From Ankara to the Governor of Gümüşhane, May 7, 1933.

25 DV "Şifre Kartunu 1/5/33-14/6/33," Correspondence Nr DV-EUUM 4786. File Nr 1/1030. From Ankara to the Governor of Yozgat, May 13, 1933.

26 DV "Giden Şifreler 1/12/1930 Sayılı Dosya," Correspondence Nr DV-NUM 3/3954/1920. File Nr 1/2831. From Ankara to the Governors of Siirt, Van, and other provinces, December 4, 1930.

27 DV "Şifre Kartunu 1/5/33-14/6/33," Correspondence Nr DV-NUM 4/676/1 File Nr 1/1375. From Ankara to the Governor of Antalya, June 14, 1933.

28 DV "Giden Şifreler 1/12/1930 Sayılı Dosya," Correspondence Nr DV-NUM 3/1919/3153. File Nr 1/2828. From Ankara to the Governors of Diyarbekir, Elazız, and other provinces, December 1930.

29 TBMM Zabıt Ceridesi, term II, vol. 5: 149–50. For more on this law titled, "Türkiye Cumhuriyeti Tabiiyetine Haiz Şirketler ile Eşhas tarafından Mubayaa Edilecek Sefainin Gümrük Resminden İstisnasına dair (2/289) Numaralı Teklifi Kanunisi" (bill Nr 2/289 on the exemption of ships bought by companies or persons of Turkish citizenship, from customs duties), see TBMM Zabıt Ceridesi, term II, vol. 5: 146–57.

30 *Düstur*, third set, vol. 9: 527. For more on this law, see "Türkiye'de Gençlik Teşkilâtının Türk Vatandaşlarına Hasrı hakkında Kanun" (Law on the allotment of youth organizations in Turkey to Turkish citizens) Nr 1246, May 12, 1928, *Düstur*, third set, vol. 9: 526–27.

31 "Antalya Mebusu Ahmet Saki Bey ve Rüfekasının Umum Memurin Kanunu Unvanlı (2/376) numaralı Teklifi Kanunisi ile (1/815) Numaralı Memurin Kanunu" (Bill [Nr 2/376] by MP Ahmet Saki Bey [Antalya] and his colleagues on the General Government Employee Law and the Government Employee Law [Nr 1/815]) March 15, 1926, TBMM Zabıt Ceridesi, term II, vol. 23: 18–57, 178–90.

32 TBMM Zabıt Ceridesi, term II, vol. 23: 179.

33 TBMM Zabıt Ceridesi, term II, vol. 23: 186.

34 TBMM Zabıt Ceridesi, term II, vol. 23: 187.

35 "Tababet ve Şuabatı San'atlarının Tarzı İcrasına dair Kanun," (Law on the Execution Methods of Medicinal Science and its Branches) Nr 1214, April 11, 1928, *Kanunlar*, February 1994, addenda 19, 887–98. For the discussions of this law, see TBMM Zabıt Ceridesi, term III, vol. 3: 1–20, 63–77, 99, 101.

36 TBMM Zabıt Ceridesi, term III: vol. 3, 63.

37 TBMM Zabıt Ceridesi, term III, vol. 3: 68, 72, 74.

38 TBMM Zabıt Ceridesi, term III: vol. 3, 65.

39 SD 867.43/5. MacMurray (Istanbul) to Washington, September 15, 1938. For the text of this law in English, see SD 867.43/5. MacMurray (Istanbul) to Washington, September 15, 1938. For the text and discussion minutes of this law, see TBMM Zabıt Ceridesi, term V, vol. 26: 412–17, and addenda 303, 1–21.

40 "Matbuat Kanunu" (The Press Law) Nr 1881, July 25, 1931, *Düstur*, third set, vol. 12: 369. For the full text of this law, consult *Düstur*, third set, vol. 12: 366–80.

41 "Türkiye'de Türk Vatandaşlarına Tahsis Edilen Sanat ve Hizmetler Hakkında Kanun" (Law on Professions and Services Allocated to Turkish Citizens in Turkey)

Nr 2007, June 11, 1932, *Düstur*, third set, vol. 13: 649–50. For the discussion minutes of this law, see TBMM Zabıt Ceridesi, term IV, vol. 9: 64–68, 90.

42 TBMM Zabıt Ceridesi, term IV, vol. 15: 261, 468.

43 Aktar, *Varlık Vergisi ve 'Türkleştirme' Politikaları*, 121–29; Alexandris, *The Greek Minority of Istanbul and Greek–Turkish Relations*, 174–85.

44 SD 867.4016. Greeks/4. Skinner (Istanbul) to the Secretary of State (Washington DC), June 30, 1934.

45 TBMM Zabıt Ceridesi, term V, vol. 26: 468.

46 TBMM Zabıt Ceridesi, term V, vol. 26, addenda: 315, 2.

47 For a detailed list of these laws, see Yıldız, *Ne Mutlu Türküm*, 234–37.

48 DV "1/10.33'den 15/11/33 Tarihine Kadar Şifre," Correspondence Nr DV-EİUM 9999. File Nr 1/2960. From Ankara to the Governor of Bayazit, November 13, 1933.

49 Düstur, third set, vol. 8: 572. For the discussion minutes of this law, see TBMM Zabıt Ceridesi, term II, vol. 32: 169–70.

50 BCA 030.18.1.2/26.19.16. March 24, 1932.

51 BCA 030.18.1.2/78.72.15. August 20, 1937.

52 BCA 030.18.1.2/21.49.01. July 4, 1931.

53 BCA 030.18.1.2/19.29.1. May 16, 1931.

54 BCA 030.18.1.2/18.18.16. March 18, 1931.

55 BCA 030.18.1.2/19.29.2. May 16, 1931.

56 BCA 030.18.1.2/9.19.7. April 9, 1930.

57 BCA 030.18.1.2/18.18.8. March 18, 1931. BCA 030.18.1.2/6.54.8. November 6, 1929. BCA 030.18.1.2/41.19.12. December 3, 1933.

58 BCA 030.18.1.2/80.98.7. December 1, 1937.

59 There are many examples of denaturalization of non-Muslims in accordance with Law Nr 1041. For some of them, see BCA 030.18.1.2/6.56.9. February 20, 1929, BCA 030.18.1.2/5.50.5. October 9, 1929; BCA 030.18.1.2/19.29.13. May 16, 1931; BCA 030.18.1.2/21.49.2. July 1, 1931; BCA 030.18.1.2/25.8.15. January 31, 1932; BCA 030.18.1.2/31.67.20. October 26, 1932; and BCA 030.18.1.2/78.72.15. August 20, 1937.

60 BCA 030.18.1.2/41.84.15. February 26, 1933.

61 For the text of this law, see *Düstur*, third set, vol. 9: 994–98. For discussion minutes of this, consult TBMM Zabıt Ceridesi, term III, vol. 4: 262–63, 295–98.

62 *Düstur*, third set, vol. 9: 996.

63 FO 371/14578/E?. Drummond (Geneva) to Cadogan (London), November 18, 1930. *Note sure un Entretien avec S. E. Tewfik Rouschdy Bey.*

64 BCA 030.18.1.2/82.27.11. April 2, 1936.

65 BCA 030.18.1.2/18.12.4. February 18, 1930.

66 BCA 030.18.1.2/18.12.6. February 18, 1931.

67 BCA 030.18.1.2/34.18.15. March 19, 1933.

68 BCA 030.18.1.2/28.39.15. May 17, 1932.

69 BCA 030.18.1.2/11.36.15. May 22, 1930.

70 BCA 030.18.1.2/23.62.9. August 23, 1931.

71 There are many archival documents on the denaturalization of non-Turks in accordance with Law Nr 1312. For some of them, see BCA 030.18.1.2/5.41.19. August 25, 1929; BCA 030.18.1.2/6.54.8. November 6, 1929; BCA 030.18.1.2/6.55.6. November 11, 1929; BCA 030.18.1.2/14.66.17. October 8, 1930; BCA 030.18.1.2/18.18.14. March 18, 1931; BCA 030.18.1.2/18.18.15. March 18, 1931; BCA 030.18.1.2/22.53.3. July 20, 1931; BCA 030.18.1.2/28.39.15. May 17, 1932; BCA 030.18.1.2/55.51.13. June 17, 1935; and BCA 030.18.1.2/80.124.5. January 8, 1940.

72 BCA 030.18.1.2/34.19.16. March 26, 1933.

73 BCA 030.18.1.2/55.43.1. May 25, 1935.

74 BCA 030.18.1.2/51.18.1. February 4, 1932.

75 BCA 030.18.1.2/13.54.10. July 24, 1930.

76 BCA 030.18.1.2/18.11.7. February 18, 1931.
77 BCA 030.18.1.2/55.43.5. May 23, 1935.
78 BCA 030.18.1.2/51.18.5. February 3, 1935.
79 SD 867.0128/5. Embassy (Istanbul) to Murray (Washington DC), August 16, 1933.
80 SD 867.0128/6. Embassy (Istanbul) to Murray (Washington DC), September 2, 1933.
81 SD 867.0128/6. Embassy (Istanbul) to Murray (Washington DC), September 2, 1933.
82 DV "Şifre Kartunu 1/5/33–14/6/33," Correspondence Nr DV-EUUM B/5031. File Nr 1/1098. From Ankara to the Inspectorates General, the border and coastal provinces, May 20, 1933.
83 This recognition of former Ottoman Jews would later on save their lives in Nazi Europe. During the Holocaust, Turkish diplomats in various European countries interfered with the German authorities to save the lives of hundreds of Ottoman Jews on grounds that they were qualified Turkish citizens. For more on this, see Stanford J. Shaw, *Turkey and the Holocaust: Turkey's Role in Rescuing Turkish and European Jewry from Nazi Persecution, 1933–1945* (London: Macmillan, 1993), 46–249.
84 FO 371/15381/E4093. League of Nations (Geneva) to London, July 30, 1931. *Petition de M. Pachalian (Paris)*, to the League of Nations (Geneva), April 21, 1931.
85 *Düstur*, third set, vol. 19: 740.
86 *Düstur*, third set, vol. 9: 995.
87 BCA 030.18.1.2/48.63.11. September 24, 1934.
88 BCA 030.18.1.2/76.54.6. June 16, 1937.
89 BCA 030.18.1.2/58.80.19. October 25, 1935.
90 BCA 030.18.1.2/85.93.12. November 12, 1938. There are many documents on Greeks, who converted to Islam and received citizenship in the 1930s. For examples, consult, BCA 030.18.1.2/87.55.11. June 14, 1939; and BCA 030.18.1.2/61.8.3. January 29, 1936.
91 BCA 030.18.1.2/58.80.19. October 25, 1935.
92 The incorporation of individual Europeans into the Turkish nation was not a novelty. In the Ottoman era, too, asylum seekers, converts, and many other Christians and Jews from Europe had been given safe haven by Istanbul. For a study on this topic, see Savaş Saim, "Müslüman olan Macar-Leh Mültecileri Meselesi" (The Question of Islamicized Hungarian-Polish Refugees) *Toplumsal Tarih* 16(24) (December 1995).
93 BCA 030.18.1.2/43.19.9. April 5, 1934.
94 BCA 030.18.1.2/53.29.2. April 20, 1935.
95 BCA 030.18.1.2/69.87.7. November 10, 1936.
96 BCA 030.18.1.2/69.85.18. November 2, 1936.
97 BCA 030.18.1.2/74.38.15. May 10, 1937.
98 BCA 030.18.1.2/83.57.3. June 23, 1938.
99 BCA 030.18.1.2/53.26.20. April 15, 1935.
100 BCA 030.18.1.2/66.55.8. June 27, 1936.
101 BCA 030.18.1.2/80.99.19. December 10, 1939.
102 BCA 030.18.1.2/67.70.12. August 19, 1936.
103 BCA 030.18.1.2/37.45.10. June 13, 1933.
104 BCA 030.18.1.2/49.75.9. November 3, 1934.
105 BCA 030.18.1.2/51.9.16. February 11, 1935.
106 BCA 030.18.1.2/49/75.2. November 7, 1934.
107 BCA 030.18.1.2/45.39.1. April 4, 1934.
108 BCA 030.18.1.2/49.74.9. October 31, 1934.
109 There are numerous archival records on this. For cases of East Europeans, who became citizens under Turkish-Muslim names, following conversion, see, for an exemplary year, the records of 1935: BCA 030.18.1.2/53.26.20. April 15, 1935; BCA 030.18.1.2/53.26.20. April 15, 1935; BCA 030.18.1.2/53.30.18. April 25, 1935; BCA 030.18.1.2/55.44.9. May 28, 1935; BCA 030.18.1.2/56.51.10. June 18, 1935; BCA 030.18.1.2/65.58.17. July 15, 1935; BCA 030.18.1.2/56.60.8. July 4, 1935;

BCA 030.18.1.2/57.63.17. July 29, 1935; BCA 030.18.1.2/58.74.8. September 20, 1935; and BCA 030.18.1.2/60.98.12. December 25, 1935.

110 BCA 030.18.1.2/43.14.17. March 18, 1933.

111 BCA 030.18.1.2/58.58.8. October 10, 1935. For other examples of naturalization of East Europeans without mention of conversion, see BCA 030.18.1.2/42.2.10. January 14, 1934; and BCA 030.18.1.2/87.55.11. June 14, 1939.

112 BCA 030.18.1.2/45.39.14. June 4, 1934.

113 SD 867.0128/5. Skinner (Istanbul) to the Secretary of State (Washington DC), November 28, 1934.

114 BCA 030.18.1.2/65.45.8. May 29, 1936.

115 BCA 030.18.1.2/52.15.9. February 28, 1935

116 BCA 030.18.1.2/64.31.13. April 20, 1936.

117 BCA 030.18.1.2/5.50.11. October 17, 1929.

118 BCA 030.18.1.2/6.52.11. October 23, 1929.

119 BCA 030.18.1.2/6.56.3. November 20, 1929.

120 BCA 030.18.1.2/22.15.7. July 12, 1931.

121 BCA 030.18.1.2/31.64.9. September 21, 1932.

122 There are hundreds of records on the naturalization of Muslims from Turkey's vicinity. Some of these include the following documents for 1929: BCA 030.18.1.2/4.35.4. June 12, 1929; BCA 030.18.1.2/4.36.10. June 19, 1929; BCA 030.18.1.2/5.41.17. August 25, 1929; BCA 030.18.1.2/6.53.17. November 6, 1929; BCA 030.18.1.2/6.55.4. November 11, 1929; BCA 030.18.1.2/5.41.8. August 25, 1920; BCA 030.18.1.2/5.47.14. September 16, 1929; and BCA 030.18.1.2/6.52.11. October 23, 1929. On the other hand, for examples of naturalization of Muslims during 1930, 1931 and 1932, see BCA 030.18.1.2/8.1.19. January 8, 1930; BCA 030.18.1.2/10.23.3. April 26, 1930; BCA 030.18.1.2/11.33.10. May 21, 1930; BCA 030.18.1.2/12.45.49. June 21, 1930; BCA 030.18.1.2/12.46.11. July 2, 1930; BCA 030.18.1.2/16.85.17. November 17, 1930; BCA 030.18.1.2/17.1.16. January 7, 1931; BCA 030.18.1.2/18.12.2. February 18, 1931; BCA 030.18.1.2/19.23.8. April 5, 1931; BCA 030.18.1.2/20.18.9. June 7, 1931; BCA 030.18.1.2/22.55.20. August 2, 1931; BCA 030.18.1.2/23.67.17. October 4, 1931; BCA 030.18.1.2/26.15.15. March 10, 1932; BCA 030.18.1.2/27.25.5. April 20, 1932; BCA 030.18.1.2/31.64.9. September 21, 1932; and BCA 030.18.1.2/32.74.8. December 10, 1932.

123 BCA 030.18.1.2/23.61.20. August 17, 1931.

124 BCA 030.18.1.2/34.13.1. April 4, 1933.

125 BCA 030.18.1.2/35.23.18. April 12, 1933.

126 BCA 030.18.1.2/38.55.17. August 5, 1933.

127 There are various documents in the Turkish archives dating between spring 1933 and late 1934, which used the word Turk to identify potential citizens. For some of them, see BCA 030.18.1.2/37.49.4. July 2, 1933; BCA 030.18.1.2/40.72.9. October 19, 1933; and BCA 030.18.1.2/47.60.8. September 4, 1934.

128 BCA 030.18.1.2/39.67.13. August 26, 1933; BCA 030.18.1.2/37.49.7. July 2, 1933.

129 Although rather infrequently, the word "person" had been used to identify immigrants also before 1934. For examples of this, see BCA 030.18.1.2/2.15.9. February 6, 1929, BCA 030.18.1.2/8.3.2. January 15, 1930; and BCA 030.18.1.2/9.18.13. April 2, 1930.

130 BCA 030.18.1.2/47.55.11. August 5, 1934.

131 BCA 030.18.1.2/47.60.13. September 4, 1934.

132 BCA 030.18.1.2/58.79.8. October 17, 1935.

133 BCA 030.18.1.2/59.85.11. November 11, 1935.

134 There are hundreds of documents in the archives from dating after fall 1934, in which the word person identifies the immigrants. Some of them include: BCA 030.18.1.2/47.60.8. September 4, 1934; BCA 030.18.1.2/55.45.16. June 3, 1935;

BCA 030.18.1.2/57.65.2. August 5, 1935; BCA 030.18.1.2/59.85.11. November 11, 1935; BCA 030.18.1.2/62.19.16. March 12, 1936; BCA 030.18.1.2/67.70.12. August 19, 1936; BCA 030.18.1.2/69.84.10. October 22, 1936; BCA 030.18.1.2/74.70.12. May 15, 1937; BCA 030.18.1.2/77.63.18. July 10, 1937; BCA 030.18.1.2/82.5.15. January 15, 1938; and BCA 030.18.1.2/82.30.17. April 13, 1938.

135 Of the 217,528 immigrants that came to Turkey between 1934 and 1945, 208,195 were from these three countries. *Başvekâlet Toprak ve İskân İşleri Genel Müdürlüğü Çalışmaları* (Activities of the Prime Minister's Office of General Directorate of Land and Resettlement) (Ankara, 1952), 56–57.

136 DV "Giden- Birinci Kanun Şubat 1932 Mart 1932 Nisan 1932," Correspondence Nr DV-EUUM 1.B.2/502. File Nr 1/1515. From Ankara to the Governor of Bayazit, April 6, 1932.

137 DV "31/8/935 ve 3391 23/9/935 ve 3927," Correspondence Nr DV-EİUM 1.A/9190. File Nr 1/3850. From Ankara to the Governor of Istanbul, September 20, 1935.

138 There are many archival documents, in which Ankara questions the nationality of suspects. Some of them include, DV "31/8/935 ve 3391 23/9/935 ve 3927," Correspondence Nr DV-EİUM 1.B/9204. File Nr 1/3831. From Ankara to the Governors of Izmir, İçel, Antalya, Muğla, Aydın, September 20, 1935; DV "31/8/935 ve 3391 23/9/935 ve 3927," Correspondence Nr DV-EİUM 1.B/8689. File Nr 1/3599. From Ankara to the Governor of Niğde, September 10, 1935; DV "24/9/935 3939 18/10/935 4338," Correspondence Nr DV-EİUM 1.B/10549. File Nr 1/4418. From Ankara to the Governors of Samsun and Giresun, October 12, 1935; DV "24/9/935 ve 3938 18/10/935 4338," Correspondence Nr DV-EİUM 1.B/10549. File Nr 1/4418. From Ankara to the Governors of Samsun and Giresun, October 12, 1935; DV "6/8/937'den 15/10/937'e Kadar," Correspondence Nr DV-EİUM 1.G.B/11169. File Nr 2389. From Ankara to the Governors of Aydın and Kars, October 6, 1937; DV "1. Kanun 938'den 1 no dan 647 numaraya 7 Şubat 1938'e," Correspondence Nr DV-EUM 1.G.2/4754. File Nr 346. From Ankara to the Governor of Kırklareli, January 31, 1938; DV "1938 1295'den 1980 kadar 16 Mayıs 38'den 18 Temmuz 938'e kadar," Correspondence Nr DV-EUM 1.G.1/32403. File Nr 1793. From Ankara to the First Inspectorate-General (Diyarbakır) June 28, 1938; DV "4/11/938 den 3324 dan 31/12/938 ve 3942," Correspondence Nr DV-EUM 1.G.1/65350. File Nr 3855. From Ankara to the Governor of Kars, December 23, 1938.

139 DV "Gidenler-Mayıs-Haziran-Temmuz-Ağustos 1932," Correspondence Nr DV-EUUM 1/3334. File Nr 1/992. From Ankara to the Governor of Bayazit, July 6, 1932.

140 DV "Gönderilen Şifre 1935 570 Numaraları ve 18-2-935 ve 31-3-935 1071," Correspondence Nr DV-EİUM 1.B/2203. File Nr 1/933. From Ankara to the Governors of Balıkesir, Çanakkale, and Istanbul, March 14, 1935.

141 DV "Gönderilen Şifre 1935 570 Numaraları ve 18–2-935 ve 31–3-935 1071," Correspondence Nr DV-EİUM 1.A/1939. File Nr 1/816. From Ankara to the Governor of Izmir, March 8, 1935.

142 DV "Özel Kalem Şifreli Yazışma 30/11/1931," Correspondence Nr DV-EUUM 1.B.3/8434. File Nr 1/2536. From Ankara to the First Inspectorate-General (Diyarbakır) and the Provinces, November 1, 1931. For another case, in which Ankara inquires about the "race of a suspect," see DV "18/10/935 4339 ve 15/12/935," Correspondence Nr DV-EİUM 1.B/11936. File Nr 1/4806. From Ankara to the Governors of Niğde and Kırşehir, November 9, 1935.

143 DV "24/9/935 ve 3938 18/10/935 4338," Correspondence Nr DV-EİUM 1.B/10096. File Nr 1/4255. From Ankara to the Governor of Aydın, October 5, 1935.

144 DV "18/24/935 3938'den 4338 ve 18/10/935'e," Correspondence Nr DV-EİUM 1.B/10097. File Nr 1/4256. From Ankara to the Governor of Muş, October 5, 1935.

145 DV "24/9/935 ve 3938 18/10/935 4338," Correspondence Nr DV-EİUM 1.A/ 10345. File Nr 1/4364. From Ankara to the Thrace Inspectorate-General (Edirne), October 9, 1935.
146 DV "24/9/935 ve 3938 18/10/935 4338," Correspondence Nr DV-EİUM 1.A/10616. File Nr 1/4451. From Ankara to the Governor of, October 14, 1935.
147 Karakasidou, *Fields of Wheat, Hills of Blood*, 141–89, *passim.*
148 Israel Gershoni and James P. Jankowski, *Redefining the Egyptian Nation, 1930–1945* (Cambridge: Cambridge University Press, 1995), 97–117.

5 Defining the boundaries of Turkishness: Kemalist immigration and resettlement policies

1 For a review of immigration into Turkey in the 1920s and 1930s, see Ağanoğlu, *Göç*: *passim*, 273–345, The Turkish archives hold an extensive collection of documents on Muslim immigration to Turkey in the 1920s, from various parts of the Ottoman Empire and beyond. For instance, BCA 272.11/44.08.10. March 29, 1925; BCA 272.1146.79.3. October 6, 1927; BCA 272.11/49.98.5. August 25, 1926; BCA 272.11/49.97.4. July 3, 1926; BCA 272.11/50.105.13. November 20, 1926; BCA 272.11/54.130.20. July 11, 1927; BCA 030.18.1.2/3.29.6. May 8, 1929; BCA 030.18.1.2/3.29.10. May 8, 1929; BCA 030.18.1.2/3.10.14. May 15, 1929; and BCA 030.18.1.2/4.32.9. May 26, 1929.
2 BCA 272.11/46.79.3. October 6, 1925.
3 FO 371/20091/E1296. Hathorn (Amman) to Thomas (London), March 7, 1936.
4 BCA 272.11/53.124.9. May 12, 1927.
5 *İstatistik Yıllığı İkinci Cilt*, 65–5; *İstatistik Yıllığı Cilt 10*, 89.
6 Gülten Kazgan, "Milli Türk Devletinin Kuruluşu ve Göçler" (The Establishment of the Turkish Nation State and Migrations) *Cumhuriyet Dönemi Türkiye Ansiklopedisi* (Encyclopedia of Turkey of the Republic Era) vol. 6, 1556.
7 İsmail Soysal, *Türkiye'nin Siyasi Antlaşmaları* (Political Treaties of Turkey) (Ankara: Türk Tarih Kurumu, 1983), 21. For the text of this treaty, see Soysal, *Türkiye'nin Siyasi Antlaşmaları*, 19–23.
8 TBMM Zabıt Ceridesi, term II, vol. 2: 136.
9 For the text of this treaty, see TBMM Zabıt Ceridesi, term II, vol. 2: 131–37.
10 For the full text of this agreement, see Soysal, *Türkiye'nin Siyasi Antlaşmaları*, 255–59.
11 Soysal, *Türkiye'nin Siyasi Antlaşmaları*, 236.
12 For the text of the accord with Greece, see *İskân Tarihçesi*: 6, 8–13. For the September 4, 1936 treaty with Romania, consult "Türkiye ile Romanya Arasında Münakid Dobrucadaki Türk Ahalinin Muhaceretini Tanzim Eden Mukavelenamenin Tasdiki Hakkındaki Kanun" (Law to Ratify the Treaty Cosigned by Turkey and Romania to Regulate the Emigration of the Turkish Population in the Dobrudja) Nr 3102, January 25, 1937, *Düstur*, third set, vol. 18: 252–70.
13 *İskân Tarihçesi*, 8.
14 BCA 030.18.1.2/8.49.17. July 22, 1923.
15 BCA 030.18.1.2/8.49.9. January 20, 1924.
16 *Düstur*, third set, vol. 18: 253.
17 Despite the Gagavuzes' exclusion from immigration, there were individual Gagavuzes admitted to Turkey. For example, on April 6, 1936, the NUM wrote to Istanbul that a certain Gagavuz named Vasil could stay in Turkey as an immigrant if he wished to do so. DV "25/3/36'dan 30/5/37'ya kadar Şifre Dosyası," Correspondence Nr DV-NUM 2/1936. File Nr 679. From Ankara to the Governor of Istanbul, April 6, 1936.
18 Yaşar Nabi Nayır, *Balkanlar ve Türklük* (The Balkans and Turkishness) (Ankara: Ulus Basımevi, 1936), 57–106.
19 Nayır, *Balkanlar ve Türklük*, 106–10.

20 FO 424/268/E2218. Knox (Angora) to Chamberlain (London), April 13, 1928.
21 FO 371/17963/E7281. Loraine (Angora) to Simon (London), December 5, 1934; FO 371/13092/E3058. Dodd (Sofia) to Chamberlain (London), June 18, 1928.
22 DV "31/8/935 ve 3391 23/9/935 ve 3927," Correspondence Nr DV-EİUM 1.A/8853. File Nr 1/3693. From Ankara to the Governors of Çanakkale, Balıkesir, and other provinces, September 21, 1935.
23 DV "31/8/935 ve 3391 23/9/935 ve 3927," Correspondence Nr DV-EİUM 1/8587. File Nr 1/3546. From Ankara to the First and Thrace Inspectors-General and the Governors of Siirt, Elâziz, and other provinces, September 7, 1935.
24 DV "6/8/937'den 15/10/937'e Kadar," Correspondence Nr DV-EİUM 7/2273. File Nr 2159. From Ankara to the Governor of İçel, September 14, 1937; and DV "6/8/937'den 15/10/937'e Kadar," Correspondence Nr DV-EİUM 7/2320. File Nr 2193. From Ankara to the Governor of Antalya, September 16, 1937.
25 FO 371/13092/E3058. Dodd (Sofia) to Chamberlain (London), June 18, 1928.
26 TBMM Zabıt Ceridesi, term II, vol. 25: 649–53.
27 "İskân Kanunu" (Resettlement Law) Nr 885, May 31, 1926, *Düstur*, third set, vol. 7: 1441.
28 BCA 272.11/ 15.54.7. January 19, 1929.
29 BCA 272.11/ 46.79.19. October 15, 1925.
30 BCA 272.11/22.113.28. December 26, 1926.
31 DV, "Giden 1929 VII ve IX," Correspondence Nr DV-KM 1/3407. From Ankara to the Governor of Izmir, November 20, 1929.
32 DV "18/10/935 4339 ve 15/12/935," Correspondence Nr DV-NUM 2/29479/6096. File Nr 1/4952. From Ankara to the Thrace Inspectorate-General (Edirne), November 20, 1935.
33 BCA 030.18.1.2/12.65.5. December 28, 1924.
34 BCA 030.18.1.2/11.43.18. September 14, 1924.
35 BCA 272.11/20.99.4. November 9, 1924.
36 BCA 030.18.1.2/13.30.9. May 6, 1925.
37 BCA 272.11/60.171.3. October 8, 1928.
38 "İskân Kanunu," Nr 885, 1441.
39 FO 371/11557/E6677. Clerk (Angora) to Chamberlain (London), December 6, 1926.
40 Yonca Köksal, "Transformation of a Central State: Provincial Administration in the Ottoman Empire, Tanzimat Reform Period (1839–1878)," PhD dissertation in progress, Columbia University, 2001; Dündar, *İttihat ve Terakki'nin Müslümanları İskân Politikası*, 137–54; and Koca, *Yakın Tarihten Günümüze Hükümetlerin Doğu-Güneydoğu Anadolu Politikaları*, 328–30. For more on the Ottoman resettlement policies, including the economic causes and impact of these strategies, see İlhan Tekeli, "Osmanlı İmparatorluğu'ndan Günümüze Nüfüsun Zorunlu Yer Değiştirmesi," *Toplum ve Bilim*, 50 (1990): 49–55.
41 *İskân Tarihçesi*, 137.
42 *İskân Tarihçesi*, 137.
43 "Bazı Eşhasın Şark Menatıkından Garp Vilayetlerine Nakillerine Dair Kanun" (Law on the Transfer of Certain People from Eastern Regions to the Western Provinces) Nr 1097, July 17, 1927, in *Eski ve Yeni Toprak, İskân Hükümleri Uygulaması Kılavuzu* (Guide to the Application of Old and New Land and Resettlement Decisions) ed. Naci Kökdemir (Ankara: 1952), 28–30.
44 BCA 272.11/23.120.18. November 20, 1927. The Turkish archives hold many documents on limited resettlement of Kurds in Western Turkey. For some examples, see BCA 272.11/23.119.34. November 17, 1927; BCA 272.11/23.118.34. November 12, 1927; and BCA 272.11/23.118.37. November 12, 1927.
45 FO 371/14579/E3898. Clerk (Constantinople) to Henderson (London), July 21, 1930.

46 FO 371/13828/E3538. Clerk (Constantinople) to Henderson (London), July 15, 1929. *Enclosure in no. 1, Notes on a Journey from Angora to Aleppo, Diarbekir, Malatia, Sivas and the Black Sea Coast,* June 9–29, 1929.

47 FO 371/13096/E906. Embassy (Constantinople) to London, February 9, 1928. *Annual Report for 1927.*

48 Ankara's benevolence was however shrouded by its claim that the Halikanlıs were Turkish. FO 371/15369/E5131. Clerk (Constantinople) to Marquess of Reading (London), October 31, 1931.

49 For a map showing this border realignment, see FO 371/15359/E5614. Hoare (Teheran) to London.

50 FO 371/16091/E222. Embassy (Constantinople) to London, January 14, 1932. *Annual Report for 1931.*

51 SD 867.9111/340. Embassy (Istanbul) to Washington, December 1, 1931. *Digest of Turkish News,* November 15–30, 1931.

52 BCA 030.18.1.2/27.25.13. April 20, 1932.

53 BCA 272.12/62.185.1. August 31, 1929.

54 FO 371/13090/E129. Clerk (Constantinople) to Chamberlain (London), January 9, 1928.

55 SD 867.00/2047. Buxley (Izmir) to Washington, October 3, 1930, *News of Izmir,* September 1930.

56 FO 371/17958/E4912. Catton (Mersina) to Loraine (Angora), July 7, 1934.

57 "İskân Kanunu" (Resettlement law) Nr 2510, June 13, 1934, *Düstur,* third set, vol. 15, addenda: 1156–1175. For the text and discussions of this law in the TBMM, see TBMM Zabıt Ceridesi, term IV, vol. 23: 67–85, 140–66, 189.

58 TBMM Zabıt Ceridesi, term IV, vol. 23: 67.

59 "İskân Kanunu," Nr 2510, 1156.

60 "İskân Kanunu," Nr 2510, 1156. According to İsmail Beşikçi, the Zone 3 areas included Ağrı, Sason, Tunceli, Zeylan (Van), southern sections of Kars, parts of Diyarbakır, and sections of Bingöl, Bitlis, and Muş, *Kürtlerin 'Mecburi İskan'ı* (The 'Forced Resettlement' of the Kurds) (Istanbul: Komal, 1977), 133.

61 "İskân Kanunu," Nr 2510, 1160.

62 "İskân Kanunu," Nr 2510, 1159–60.

63 "Birinci İskân Mıntıkalarında Toprak Tevziatına," in Kökdemir, *Eski ve Yeni Toprak,* 166–70.

64 "İskân Kanunu," Nr 2510, 1159–60.

65 "İskân Kanununun 12. Maddesini Kısmen Değiştiren ve 17. ve 23. Maddelerine Birer Fıkra Ekleyen Kanun" (Law Adding Additional Paragraph to Articles 17 and 23 and Partially Amending Article 12 of the Resettlement Law) Nr 3667, July 5, 1939, *Düstur,* third set, vol. 20: 1556.

66 DV "Gidenler- Mayıs-Haziran-Temmuz-Ağustos 1932," Correspondence Nr DV 20133. File Nr 1/1010. From Ankara to the First Inspectorate-General (Diyarbakır), July 12, 1932.

67 DV "24/9/935 3938'den 4338 ve 18/10/935'e," Correspondence Nr DV-NUM 2/2636/5.583. File Nr 1/2737. From Ankara to the Governor of Kars, September 30, 1935.

68 "Birinci İskân Mıntıkalarında Toprak Tevziatına," in Kökdemir, *Eski ve Yeni Toprak,* 166–71.

69 In 1934, while the eastern Black Sea littoral had a population density of 68 people per square kilometer, this ratio was 38 for the Aegean littoral, 35 for the Marmara basin, 32 for the western Black Sea littoral, 25 for Thrace, 22 for central Anatolia, and 15 for northeast Anatolia. The population density of the First Inspectorate-General per square kilometer was a dismal people. "İskân Kanunu Muvakkat Encümen Mazbatası" (Official Report by the Temporary Commission for the Law of Resettlement) TBMM Zabıt Ceridesi, term IV, vol. 23, addenda 189: 6.

70 For the text of this report, see "Report for Reform in the East," quoted in Bayrak, *Kürtler ve Ulusal-Demokratik Mücadeleleri*, 481–89.

71 "Report for Reform in the East," quoted in Bayrak, *Kürtler ve Ulusal-Demokratik Mücadeleleri*, 483.

72 BCA 030.18.1.2/40.77.9. November 5, 1933.

73 "İskân Kanunu," Nr 2510, 1158.

74 "İskân Kanunu," Nr 2510, 1165–66.

75 FO 371/16983/E529. Embassy (Constantinople) to London, January 27, 1933. *Annual Report for 1932*. For a detailed study on this, see Beşikçi, *Kürtlerin 'Mecburi İskan'ı*, *passim*. In this work, the author gives a sympathetic account of the Kurds' resettlement in the 1930s.

76 *Başvekâlet Toprak ve İskân İşleri Genel Müdürlüğü Çalışmaları*, 108–09. However, a law passed in 1947 restored the population deported in the 1930s to its original domicile. Then, 22,515 people in 4,128 households returned to their homes.

77 DV "Çıkan Şifre 15/6/1933'den 31/7/33 Tarihine Kadar," Correspondence Nr DV-NUM 1469/747. File Nr 1/1519. From Ankara to the Governor of Kırşehir, June 27, 1933.

78 DV "Çıkan Şifre 15/6/1933'den 31/7/33 Tarihine Kadar," Correspondence Nr DV-NUM 1/2262/1053. File Nr 1/1608. From Ankara to the Governor of Tokat, July 9, 1933.

79 BCA 030.18.1.2/25.2.1. January 3, 1932.

80 "İskân Kanunu," Nr 2510, 1157–58.

81 TBMM Zabıt Ceridesi, term IV, vol. 23: 145.

82 DV "Giden-Birinci Kanun Şubat 1932 Mart 1932 Nisan 1932," Correspondence Nr DV-NUM 17501. File Nr 1/1482. From Ankara to the Governor of Bayazit, April 3, 1932.

83 DV "Giden-Birinci Kanun Şubat 1932 Mart 1932 Nisan 1932," Correspondence Nr DV-EUUM 1.B.2/596/366. File Nr 1/153. From Ankara to the Governor of Bayazit, January 28, 1932.

84 DV "Giden-Birinci Kanun Şubat 1932 Mart 1932 Nisan 1932," Correspondence Nr DV-EUUM 1.B.2/3521. File Nr 1/1056. From Ankara to the Governor of Kars, July 18, 1932.

85 DV "1/10.33'den 15/11/33 Tarihine Kadar Şifre," Correspondence Nr DV-NUM 1/9383/4739. File Nr 1/2754. From Ankara to the Governor of Kars, October 19, 1933.

86 DV "1/10.33'den 15/11/33 Tarihine Kadar Şifre," Correspondence Nr DV-EUUM 1.A/9902. File Nr 1/2925. From Ankara to the Governor of Urfa, November 9, 1933.

87 DV "Çıkan Şifre 15/6/1933'den 31/7/33 Tarihine Kadar," Correspondence Nr DV-NUM 1/3603/1742. File Nr 1/1807. From Ankara to the Governor of Kars, July 25, 1933.

88 DV "24/9/935 3938'den 4338 ve 18/10/935'e," Correspondence Nr DV-EİUM 1.A/10345. File Nr 1/4364. From Ankara to the Thrace Inspectorate-General (Edirne), October 9, 1935.

89 DV "6/8/937'den 15/10/937'e Kadar," Correspondence Nr DV-EİUM 4/? File Nr 2379. From Ankara to the Governor of Ağrı, October 5, 1937.

90 DV "Çıkan Şifre 15/6/1933'den 31/7/33 Tarihine Kadar," Correspondence Nr DV-NUM 1/1816/861. File Nr 1/1561. From Ankara to the First Inspectorate-General (Diyarbakır), July 2, 1933.

91 BCA 030.18.1.2/84.79.8. September 6, 1938.

92 DV "4/11/938 den 3324 dan 31/12/938 ve 3942," Correspondence Nr DV-EUM 1.G.2/60588. File Nr 3599. From Ankara to the Governor of Yozgat, November 29, 1938.

93 DV "4/11/938 den 3324 dan 31/12/938 ve 3942," Correspondence Nr DV-EUM 1.G.3/63309. File Nr? From Ankara to the Governor of Kayseri, December 14, 1938.

94 BCA 030.18.1.2/64.37.9. May 11, 1936.
95 BCA 030.18.1.2/79.89.10. November 2, 1937.
96 The CUP, too, had appreciated Central Anatolia's role in assimilating non-Turks. In the 1910s, the CUP had resettled Albanians, Bosniaks, Kurds, and Arabs in Central Turkey, while relocating ethnic Turks to the Anatolian periphery. Dündar, *İttihat ve Terakki'nin Müslümanları İskân Politikası*, 92–157; and Ağanoğlu, *Göç*: 108–18.
97 BCA 030.18.1.2/86.13.2. February 13, 1939.
98 "İskân Kanunu," Nr 2510, 1157.
99 FO 371/17970/E6434. Morgan (Constantinople) to London, October 13, 1934. *Minutes by C. W. Baxter*, November 3, 1934.
100 *Başvekâlet Toprak ve İskân İşleri Genel Müdürlüğü*, 56–57.
101 FO 371/17963/E7281. Loraine (Angora) to Simon (London), December 5, 1934.
102 TBMM Zabıt Ceridesi, term IV, vol. 23, addenda 189: 1–2.
103 TBMM Zabıt Ceridesi, term IV, vol. 23: 69.
104 TBMM Zabıt Ceridesi, term IV, vol. 23, addenda 189: 6.
105 Confidential Decree of September 1930, quoted in Bayrak, *Kürtler ve Ulusal-Demokratik Mücadeleleri*, 506–09.
106 Bayrak, *Kürtler ve Ulusal-Demokratik Mücadeleleri*, 508.
107 "İskân Kanunu," Nr 2510, 1159.
108 DV "Çıkan Şifre 15/6/1933'den 31/7/33 Tarihine Kadar," Correspondence Nr DV-NUM 1/1595/782. File Nr 1/1534. From Ankara to the First Inspectorate-General (Diyarbakır), June 28, 1933.
109 DV "18/10/935 4339 ve 15/12/935," Correspondence Nr DV-NUM 2/18212/4153. File Nr 1/5012. From Ankara to the Governor of Bursa, November, 1935.
110 BCA 030.18.1.2/50.88.13. December 27, 1934.
111 "İskân Muafiyetleri Nizamnamesi" (Statute on exemptions from resettlement) Nr 2/1777, October 27, 1934, *Düstur*, third set, vol. 16: 523.
112 "İskân Muafiyetleri Nizamnamesi," 521.
113 "İskân ve Nüfus İşlerinin Süratle İkmali Hakkında Tamim" (Circular on the Speedy Disposal of Resettlement and Population Matters) Nr 15035/6599, August 7, 1934, in Kökdemir, *Eski ve Yeni Toprak*, 235–36.
114 "İskân ve Nüfus İşlerinin Süratle İkmali Hakkında Tamim," in Kökdemir, *Eski ve Yeni Toprak*, 235–36.
115 Johnson *et al.*, eds, *Turbulent Era*, vol. 2, 753.
116 DV "Giden- Birinci Kanun Şubat 1932 Mart 1932 Nisan 1932," Correspondence Nr DV-EUUM 1.B.2/1387. File Nr 1/452. From Ankara to the Governors of Artvin, Rize, and other provinces. March 29, 1932.
117 BCA 030.18.1.2/47.52.18. July 14, 1934.
118 BCA 030.18.1.2/79.89.1. November 2, 1937.
119 DV "1/10.33'den 15/11/33 Tarihine Kadar Şifre," Correspondence Nr DV-EUUM 1.A/9472. File Nr 1/2730. From Ankara to the Governors of Çoruh, Kars, and Bayazit, October 18, 1933.
120 DV "1938 1295'den 1980 kadar 16 Mayıs 38'den 18 Temmuz 938'e kadar," Correspondence Nr DV-EUM 1.G.4/30034. File Nr 1951. From Ankara to the First, Second, Third and Fourth Inspectorates-General, the Governors of Ağrı, Kars, and other provinces, July 16, 1938.
121 DV "Vilayetlere ve Umumi Müfettişliklere Yazılan Şifreler," Correspondence Nr DV-NİUM 4/2722. File Nr 649. From Ankara to the Governor of Kars, March 31, 1939.
122 DV "Giden Şifreler 1/12/1930 Sayılı Dosya," Correspondence Nr DV-EUUM 1.K.2/5827/299. File Nr 1/2849. From Ankara to the Governor of Kars, December 8, 1930.
123 DV "Şifre Kartunu 1/5/33–14/6/33," Correspondence Nr DV-EUUM 5345 File Nr 1/1191. From Ankara to the Governor of Bayazıt, May 28, 1933.

124 DV "Çıkan Şifre 15/6/1933'den 31/7/33 Tarihine Kadar," Correspondence Nr DV-EUUM 1.A/7313. File Nr 1/1877. From Ankara to the Governor of Bayazıt, July 31, 1933.

125 DV "Giden- Birinci Kanun Şubat 1932 Mart 1932 Nisan 1932," Correspondence Nr DV-EUUM 1.B.3/1690. File Nr 1/545. From Ankara to the Governors of all Coastal and Border Provinces, April 14, 1932.

126 DV "Şifre Kartunu 1/5/33–14/6/33," Correspondence Nr DV-EUUM 5345. File Nr 1/1191. From Ankara to the Governor of Bayazit, May 28, 1933.

127 DV "Çıkan Şifre 15/6/1933'den 31/7/33 Tarihine Kadar," Correspondence Nr DV-EUUM 1.A/7313. File Nr 1/1877. From Ankara to the Governor of Bayazit, July 31, 1933.

128 DV "Çıkan-Hususi Kalem Dosyası," Correspondence Nr DV-HKM File Nr 5.298. From Ankara to Secretary General of the President's Office, June 10, 1933.

129 Ahmet Demirel, *Birinci Mecliste Muhalefet: İkinci Grup* (Opposition in the First Assembly: The Second Group) (Istanbul: İletişim, 1994), 492–95, 500.

130 Kemal H. Karpat, *Türk Demokrasi Tarihi* (History of the Turkish Democracy) (Istanbul: Afa Yayınları, 1996), 95, fn. 37.

131 DV "Çıkan Şifre 15/6/1933'den 31/7/33 Tarihine Kadar," Correspondence Nr DV-EUUM 1.A/7121. File Nr 1/1796. From Ankara to the Governor of Gaziantep, July 25, 1933.

132 "İskân Kanunu," Nr 2510, 1157.

133 For more on prejudice against the Roma, see Angus Fraser, *The Gypsies* (Oxford: Blackwell, 1992), 123–90.

134 For examples of correspondence in which the provinces provided detailed figures on the Roma, see DV "Çıkan Şifre 15/6/1933'den 31/7/33 Tarihine Kadar," Correspondence Nr DV-NUM 4/4140/185. File Nr 1/1892. From Ankara to the Governor of Diyarbakır, September 3, 1933; DV "Çıkan Şifre 15/6/1933'den 31/7/33 Tarihine Kadar," Correspondence Nr DV-NUM 4/4136/181. File Nr 1/1888. From Ankara to the Governor of Balıkesir, July 3, 1933; and DV "Çıkan Şifre 15/6/1933'den 31/7/33 Tarihine Kadar," Correspondence Nr DV-NUM 4/3265/85. File Nr 1/1758. From Ankara to the Governor of Kütahya, July 22, 1933.

135 DV "Şifre Kartunu 1/5/33–14/6/33," Correspondence Nr DV-NUM 1/29732/75. File Nr 1/1051. From Ankara to the Governor of Hakkâri, May 15, 1933.

136 BCA 272.11/63.190.15. March 7, 1933.

137 BCA 272.12/63.190.5. March 7, 1933.

138 DV "Çıkan Şifre 15/6/1933'den 31/7/33 Tarihine Kadar," Correspondence Nr DV-NUM 3760/1827. File Nr 1/1833. From Ankara to the Governor of Van and the First Inspectorate-General (Diyarbakır), July 26, 1933.

139 DV "Giden Şifreler 1/12/1930 Sayılı Dosya," Correspondence Nr DV-EİUM 1.B.2/98.4732. File Nr 1/2768. From Ankara to the Governor of Artvin, December 2, 1931.

140 DV "Giden-Birinci Kanun Şubat 1932 Mart 1932 Nisan 1932," Correspondence Nr DV-EUUM 1/833. File Nr 1/264. From Ankara to the Governor of Artvin, February 25, 1932.

141 DV "1938 1295'den 1980 kadar 16 Mayıs 38'den 18 Temmuz 938'e kadar," Correspondence Nr DV-EUM 7/31746. File Nr 1744. From Ankara to the First Inspectorate-General (Diyarbakır) and the Governor of Hakkâri, June 22, 1938.

142 DV "Çıkan Şifre 15/6/1933'den 31/7/33 Tarihine Kadar," Correspondence Nr DV-NUM 2127/1002. File Nr 1/1590. From Ankara to the Governor of Bayazit, July 6, 1933.

143 DV "Çıkan Şifre 15/6/1933'den 31/7/33 Tarihine Kadar," Correspondence Nr DV-NUM 2584/1212. File Nr 1/1662. From Ankara to the Governor of Bayazit, July 13, 1933.

144 Demirel, *İsmet İnönü Defterler*, 168. For other references by İnönü to the non-Turkish character of different regions of the country, see Demirel, *İsmet İnönü Defterler*, 167, 172, 179.
145 Demirel, *İsmet İnönü Defterler*, 168.
146 Demirel, *İsmet İnönü Defterler*, 171.
147 FO 371/17970/E5167. Loraine (Angora) to London, August 4, 1934. *Minutes by A. K. Haddon*, August 16, 1934.
148 FO 371/17970/E5161. Loraine (Constantinople) to London, August 4, 1934. *Minutes by A. K. Haddon*, August 16, 1934.
149 TBMM Zabıt Ceridesi, term V, vol. 6: 78.
150 TBMM Zabıt Ceridesi, term V, vol. 6: 77.

6 Secularized Islam defines Turkishness: Kurds and other Muslims as Turks

1 Şevket Süreyya [Aydemir], "Derebeyi ve Dersim" (The Feudal Lord and Dersim) *Kadro* 6 (1932), 41.
2 There were also individual attempts at theorizing Kemalism. Among them, Mahmut Esat Bozkurt, who defined Kemalism as a *sui generis* movement, was notable. For more on him, see Hakkı Uyar, "Türk Devrimini Teorileştirme Çabaları: Mahmut Esat Bozkurt Örneği-I" (Attempts to Theorize on the Kemalist Revolution: The Example of Mahmut Esat Bozkurt-I) *Tarih ve Toplum*, 119 (November 1993): 9–15; Hakkı Uyar, "Türk Devrimini Teorileştirme Çabaları: Mahmut Esat Bozkurt Örneği-II" (Attempts to Theorize on the Kemalist Revolution: The Example of Mahmut Esat Bozkurt-II) *Tarih ve Toplum*, 120 (December 1993): 9–16. For more on Bozkurt, see his biography, *Mahmut Esat Bozkurt (1892–1943)* (İstanbul: Büke, 2000).
3 For the Kadroists' leftist past, see Mustafa Türkeş, *Kadro Hareketi* (The Kadro Movement) (Ankara: İmge, 1999), 69–97.
4 For an elaboration of these views by Aydemir, see his following articles, Şevket Süreyya [Aydemir], "Fikir Hareketleri arasında Türk Nasyonalizmi. I. Faşizm" (Turkish Nationalism Among Ideological Movements. I. Fascism) *Kadro* 18 (1933), 5–14; Şevket Süreyya [Aydemir], "Fikir Hareketleri arasında Türk Nasyonalizmi. II. Marksizm" (Turkish Nationalism Among Ideological Movements. II. Marxism) *Kadro* 19 (1933), 6–16; Şevket Süreyya [Aydemir], "Beynelmilel Fikir Hareketleri arasında Türk Nasyonalizmi. III. Türk Nasyonalizmi" (Turkish Nationalism Among International Ideological Movements. III. Turkish Nationalism) *Kadro* 20 (1933), 4–11; Şevket Süreyya [Aydemir], "Beynelmilel Fikir Hareketleri arasında Türk Nasyonalizmi. IV. Türk Nasyonalizmi" (Turkish Nationalism Among International Ideological Movements. IV. Turkish Nationalism) *Kadro* 21 (1933), 5–14.
5 [Aydemir], "Beynelmilel Fikir Hareketleri arasında Türk Nasyonalizmi. IV. Türk Nasyonalizmi," *Kadro*, 7.
6 [Aydemir], "Fikir Hareketleri arasında Türk Nasyonalizmi. I. Faşizm," *Kadro*, 5, 18; [Aydemir], "Beynelmilel Fikir Hareketleri arasında Türk Nasyonalizmi. III. Türk Nasyonalizmi," *Kadro*, 4–6.
7 [Aydemir], "Beynelmilel Fikir Hareketleri arasında Türk Nasyonalizmi. IV. Türk Nasyonalizmi," *Kadro*, 8.
8 [Aydemir], "Beynelmilel Fikir Hareketleri arasında Türk Nasyonalizmi. III. Türk Nasyonalizmi," *Kadro*, 4–6.
9 "Ulusal Ökonomya Kurumlu Ökonomyadır" (National economy is institutionalized economy) *Kadro* 35–36, (1934), 3–4.
10 Türkeş, *Kadro Hareketi*, 104.
11 Türkeş, *Kadro Hareketi*, 12.
12 [Aydemir], "Beynelmilel Fikir Hareketleri arasında Türk Nasyonalizmi. III. Türk Nasyonalizmi," *Kadro*, 8.

13 Türkeş, *Kadro Hareketi*, 203.
14 For more on the Kadro movement, and brief biographies of the Kadroists, see Türkeş, *Kadro Hareketi*. For a critical work, Cf. Beşikçi, *Cumhuriyet Halk Fırkası'nın Programı*, 37–105. In this work, the author links the ideological roots of Kemalism's maltreatment of the Kurds to the Kadroists. Thus, instead of seeing this as a fringe movement inspired by Kemalism, Beşikçi portrays the Kadroists as a mentor to the regime.
15 İsmail Hüsrev [Tökin], "Şark Vilâyetlerinde Derebeylik I" (Feudalism in the Eastern Provinces I) *Kadro* 11, 22–29.
16 [Aydemir], "Derebeyi ve Dersim," *Kadro*, 6, 42.
17 [Aydemir], "Derebeyi ve Dersim," *Kadro*, 6, 43.
18 [Aydemir], "Derebeyi ve Dersim," *Kadro*, 6, 42.
19 [Aydemir], "Derebeyi ve Dersim," *Kadro*, 6, 43.
20 [Aydemir], "Derebeyi ve Dersim," *Kadro*, 6, 44.
21 [Aydemir], "Derebeyi ve Dersim," *Kadro*, 6, 44.
22 [Aydemir], "Derebeyi ve Dersim," *Kadro*, 6, 45.
23 İsmail Hüsrev [Tökin], "Şark Vilâyetlerinde Derebeylik II" (Feudalism in the Eastern Provinces II) *Kadro* 12, 21.
24 [Tökin], "Şark Vilâyetlerinde Derebeylik," *Kadro*, 11, 21.
25 [Tökin], "Şark Vilâyetlerinde Derebeylik," *Kadro*, 11, 23.
26 Bayrak, *Kürtler ve Ulusal-Demokratik Mücadeleleri*, 446–49.
27 However, there had been a Kurdish uprising even in this period. The Koçgiri rebellion of 1920 represented an effort by the tribal, Alevi Kurdish notables of Western Dersim to capitalize on the initial weakness of the Kemalist campaign. These people hoped to gain certain concessions from Ankara in return for their support for the Kemalist cause. When such expectations did not materialize, they rebelled. However, Kemalist forces crushed the uprising swiftly. Bruinessen, *Agha Shaikh and State*, 374; Bruinessen, *Origins and Development of Kurdish Nationalism*, 101. For more on the Koçgiri uprising, see Kâzım Karabekir, *Kürt Meselesi* (The Kurdish Question), ed. Prof. Dr Faruk Özerengin (Istanbul: Emre Yayınları, 1994), 79–108.
28 Bruinessen, *Agha Shaikh and State*, 372.
29 Ergun Özbudun, "Milli Mücadele ve Cumhuriyet'in Resmi Belgelerinde Yurttaşlık Sorunu" (The Question of Citizenship in the Main Documents of the National Liberation and Republic), in *75. Yılda Tebaadan Yurttaşa Doğru*, 63–70.
30 Mango, *Atatürk*, 428.
31 Bruinessen, *Origins and Development of Kurdish Nationalism*, 1, 13.
32 Bruinessen, *Origins and Development of Kurdish Nationalism*, 10, 12–13.
33 For a detailed account of these incidents throughout the 1920s, see Koca, *Yakın Tarihten Günümüze Hükümetlerin Doğu-Güneydoğu Anadolu Politikaları*, 120–43, 146–51, 280–85, 289–91, 297–301; and Bruinessen, *Agha Shaikh and State*, 393.
34 For more on the First and Second Ağrı rebellions, see Koca, *Yakın Tarihten Günümüze Hükümetlerin Doğu-Güneydoğu Anadolu Politikaları*, 143–46.
35 For more on the Tendürek and Zeylân incidents see Koca, *Yakın Tarihten Günümüze Hükümetlerin Doğu-Güneydoğu Anadolu Politikaları*, respectively, 287–88, 292–97.
36 Tekeli, "Osmanlı İmparatorluğu'ndan Günümüze Nüfusun Zorunlu Yer Değiştirmesi," *Toplum ve Bilim*, 62.
37 FO 371/13828/E3538. Clerk (Constantinople) to Henderson (London), July 15, 1929. *Enclosure in No. 1, Notes on a Journey from Angora to Aleppo, Diarbekir, Malatia, Sivas and the Black Sea Coast, June 9–29, 1929.*
38 FO 371/13828/E3538. Clerk (Constantinople) to Henderson (London), July 15, 1929. *Enclosure in No. 1, Notes on a Journey from Angora to Aleppo, Diarbekir, Malatia, Sivas and the Black Sea Coast, June 9–29, 1929.*
39 FO 371/ 14579/E1511. Embassy (Angora) to Henderson (London), March 17, 1930.

40 DV "18/10/935 4339 ve 15/12/935," Correspondence Nr DV-EİUM 1.B/12087. File Nr 1/4897. From Ankara to the Governors of Afyon, Eskişehir, and other provinces, November 14, 1935.

41 DV "Giden Şifreler 1/12/1930 Sayılı Dosya," Correspondence Nr DV-VİUM 1/6539. File Nr 1/2910. From Ankara to the Governors of Erzincan, December 22, 1930.

42 FO 371/15369/E68. Clerk (Constantinople) to Henderson (London), January 5, 1931. Interview between Major O'Leary and Nuri Bey, December 22, 1930, *Some Observations on Kurdistan by Colonel Nuri Bey, General Staff.*

43 BCA 030.18.1.1/47.54.16. August 1, 1934.

44 BCA 030.18.1.1/88.83.20. August 31, 1939.

45 BCA 030.18.1.1/85.101.14. December 3, 1938.

46 FO 371/16983/E529. Embassy (Constantinople) to London, January 27, 1933. *Annual Report for 1932.*

47 FO 371/13828/E3538. Clerk (Constantinople) to Henderson (London), July 15, 1929. *Enclosure in No. 1, Notes on a Journey from Angora to Aleppo, Diarbekir, Malatia, Sivas and the Black Sea Coast, June 9–29, 1929.*

48 FO 371/14579/E2678. Embassy (Constantinople) to London, May 26, 1930. *Tour by Mr. Edmonds.*

49 DV "Çıkan Şifre 15/6/1933'den 31/7/33 Tarihine Kadar," Correspondence Nr DV-EUUM 4/3204. File Nr 1/1405. From Ankara to the Governor of Urfa, June 1933.

50 DV "24/9/935 3938'den 4338 ve 18/10/935'e," Correspondence Nr DV-EİUM 4/6978. File Nr 1/4085. From Ankara to the Governor of Urfa, September 28, 1935.

51 Bruinessen, *Agha Shaikh and State*, 393; Koca, *Yakın Tarihten Günümüze Hükümetlerin Doğu-Güneydoğu Anadolu Politikaları*, 411, 457. For the developments in Sason, as well as the 1935 uprising there, see Koca, *Yakın Tarihten Günümüze Hükümetlerin Doğu-Güneydoğu Anadolu Politikaları*, 381–82, 457.

52 Koca, *Yakın Tarihten Günümüze Hükümetlerin Doğu-Güneydoğu Anadolu Politikaları*, 411.

53 Bruinessen, *Kurdish Ethno-Nationalism*, 101.

54 Bruinessen, *Agha Shaikh and State*, 399; Bruinessen, *Origins and Development of Kurdish Nationalism*, 13–14.

55 Yet, although Kurmançi speakers do not necessarily understand Zaza, Zaza speakers do comprehend Kurmançi.

56 Şükrü Sökmen Süer, *Umumi Müfettişler Konferansı'nda Görüşülen ve Dahiliye Vekâleti'ni İlgilendiren İşlere Dair Toplantı Zabıtları ile Rapor ve Hülâsası 1936* (1936 Report, Summary, and Minutes about the Matters of Relevance to the Ministry of Interior Reviewed at the Conference of the Inspectorates-General) (Ankara: Başvekâlet Matbaası, 1936), 22, quoted in Koca, *Yakın Tarihten Günümüze Hükümetlerin Doğu-Güneydoğu Anadolu Politikaları*, 447–52.

57 Sökmen Süer, 22, *Umumi Müfettişler Konferansı'nda Görüşülen*, quoted in Koca, *Yakın Tarihten Günümüze Hükümetlerin Doğu-Güneydoğu Anadolu Politikaları*, 448–49.

58 For this report, see Bayrak, *Kürtler ve Ulusal-Demokratik Mücadeleleri*, 452–67.

59 Bayrak, *Kürtler ve Ulusal-Demokratik Mücadeleleri*, 453, 460.

60 Karabekir, *Kürt Meselesi*, 87.

61 SD 867.9111/337. Embassy (Istanbul) to Washington, December 1931. *Digest of Turkish News*, November 12–25, 1930.

62 BCA, KL 69 D 457 EN, 25, quoted in Koca, *Yakın Tarihten Günümüze Hükümetlerin Doğu-Güneydoğu Anadolu Politikaları*, 373–89.

63 Saygı Öztürk, "21 Ağustos 1935, İsmet Paşa'nın Kürt Raporu" (The Kurdish Report of İsmet Paşa, August 21, 1935) *Hürriyet*, September 7, 1992, quoted in Koca, *Yakın Tarihten Günümüze Hükümetlerin Doğu-Güneydoğu Anadolu Politikaları*, 426–39.

64 For the text and discussion minutes of this law, see İsmail Beşikçi, *Tunceli Kanunu (1935) ve Dersim Jenosidi* (The Tunceli Law (1935) and the Dersim Genocide) (Istanbul: Belge, 1990), 9–24.

65 Koca, *Yakın Tarihten Günümüze Hükümetlerin Doğu-Güneydoğu Anadolu Politikaları*, 176.

66 FO 371/20087/E129. Loraine (Angora) to London, January 9, 1936.

67 DV "25/3/36'dan 30/5/37'ya kadar Şifre Dosyası," Correspondence Nr VİUM 2/?. File Nr 640. From Ankara to the Third Inspectorate-General (Trabzon), March 28, 1936.

68 DV "1937," Correspondence Nr DV-HKM 1254. File Nr 2881. From the Fourth Inspector-General (Elaziz) to Ankara, May 2, 1937.

69 SD 867.00/3039. Williamson (Istanbul) to Washington, June 25, 1937. *Revolt of Kurdish Tribes in the Vilayet of Tunceli, formerly called Dersim*; FO 371/20084/E2291. Loraine (Angora) to London, May 17, 1937.

70 SD 867.00/3039. Williamson (Istanbul) to Washington, June 25, 1937. *Revolt of Kurdish Tribes in the Vilayet of Tunceli, formerly called Dersim*; FO 371/20084/E2291. Loraine (Angora) to London, May 17, 1937.

71 FO 371/20084/E4238. Loraine (Istanbul) to London, July 18, 1937.

72 DV "1937," Correspondence Nr DV-HKM 1254. File Nr 2881. From the Fourth Inspector-General (Elaziz) to Ankara, May 2, 1937.

73 DV "Hususi Kalem Harekât Dosyası-1933," in DV "1937," Correspondence Nr DV-HKM 12/1409. File Nr? From the First Inspector-General (Diyarbakır) to Ankara, September 6, 1933.

74 DV "1937," Correspondence Nr DV-HKM 3699. File Nr 7296. From the Fourth Inspector-General (Elaziz) to Ankara, September 4, 1937.

75 AA T-120 4365/K-219967. Keller (Tarabya–Istanbul) to Berlin, June 21, 1937.

76 FO 371/21925/E5961. Matthews (Trabeizond) to Loraine (Ankara), September 27, 1938. For details of this from a perspective sympathetic to the Dersimlis, see Beşikçi, *Tunceli Kanunu*, 65–76. For a literary account of the events of 1938, also from a sympathetic view, see the novel by Barbaros Baykara, *Tunceli 1938* (Istanbul: Akyar, 1975).

77 AA T-120 4365/K220072. Consulate (Trabzon) to Berlin, October 3, 1938.

78 *Cumhuriyet Halk Partisi Üsnomal Büyük Kurultayının Zabıtları 26. XII. 1938* (Records of the Extraordinary General Congress of the CHP 26. XII. 1938) (Ankara: Recep Ulusoğlu Basimevi, 1938), 8–29.

79 BCA 030.18.1.1/29.44.16. June 9, 1932.

80 BCA 030.18.1.1/81.105.16. December 27, 1937.

81 Erik Jan Zürcher, *Turkey: A Modern History*, (London: I.B. Tauris, 1998), 164.

82 İsmail Soysal, *150'likler* (The 150 [Exiles]) (Istanbul: Gür, 1985), 61.

83 For a 1920s account of these efforts, see Arnold J. Toynbee, *The Western Question in Greece and Turkey* (London: Constable and Company, 1922), 281–82.

84 For more on this rebellion, see TBMM Zabıt Ceridesi, term I, vol. 9: 375.

85 For an example of a 1930 police document, in which the EUUM inquired about a Circassian, assumed to be collaborating with Armenian nationalists, see DV "Giden Şifreler 1/12/1930 Sayılı Dosya," Correspondence Nr DV-EUUM 1.B.3/. File Nr 1/2643. From the Ministry of Interior (Ankara) to the First Inspectorate-General (Diyarbakır), coastal and border provinces, November 15, 1930.

86 FO 371/19041/E4965. From London to Loraine (Constantinople), August 14, 1936.

87 DV "31-8-935 ve 3351 23-9-935 3927," Correspondence Nr DV-EİUM File Nr 1/3767. From Ankara to all the Provinces and the Inspectorate, August 16, 1935.

88 For some examples of this, see DV "31-8-935 ve 3351 23-9-935 3927," Correspondence Nr DV-EİUM 1.B/9306. File Nr 1/3895. From Ankara to all the Provinces and Inspectorates General, September 21, 1935; DV "31-8-935 ve 3351 23-9-935 3927," *Confidential Letter*. From Ankara to Kaya (Istanbul), September 16, 1935.

89 DV "31-8-935 ve 3351 23-9-935 3927," Correspondence Nr DV-EİUM 1.B/8863. File Nr 1/3733. From Ankara to the Governors of Ankara, Istanbul, and other provinces, September 15, 1935.

90 DV "31-8-935 ve 3351 23-9-935 3927," Correspondence Nr DV-EİUM 1.B/9203. File Nr 1/3845. From Ankara to the Governors of Istanbul and Bolu, August 20, 1935.

91 DV "Giden-Birinci Kanun Şubat 1932 Mart 1932 Nisan 1932," Correspondence Nr DV-EUUM 1.B.3/1417. File Nr 1/1456. From Ankara to the Governor of Maraş, March 29, 1932.

92 DV "1938 2630 no dan 15/9/938 tarihinden 3323 4/11/938 tarihine kadar," Correspondence Nr DV-EUM 1.G.8/56637. File Nr 3293. From Ankara to the Governor of Izmir, November 12, 1938.

93 For some examples of such reports, see DV "31-8-935 ve 3351 23-9-935 3927," Correspondence Nr DV-UM 8788. File Nr 1/3634. From Ankara to the Governor of Kayseri, September 12, 1935; DV "24/9/935 3938'den 4338 ve 18/10/935'e," Correspondence Nr DV-EİUM 1.A/10345. File Nr 1.B/10451. From Ankara to the Governors of İçel and Istanbul, October 10, 1935; DV "18/10/935 4339 ve 15/12/935," Correspondence Nr DV-EİUM 2/11977. File Nr 1/4782. From Ankara to the Governors of Malatya, Sivas, and Tokat, November 4, 1935; DV "18/10/935 4339 ve 15/12/935," Correspondence Nr DV-EİUM 1.B/11924. File Nr 1/4854. From Ankara to the Thrace Inspectorate-General (Edirne), Governors of Çanakkale and Istanbul, November 8, 1935; DV "18/10/935 4339 ve 15/12/935," Correspondence Nr DV-EİUM 1.B/13272. File Nr 1/5852. From Ankara to the Governors of Kocaeli, Bursa, and other provinces, December 9, 1935.

94 DV "31-8-935 ve 3351 23-9-935 3927," Correspondence Nr DV-EİUM 1.B/8818. File Nr 1/3668. From Ankara to the Governor of Çanakkale, September 13, 1935.

95 DV "24/9/935 3938'den 4338 ve 18/10/935'e," Correspondence Nr DV-EİUM 1/9896. File Nr 1/4146. From Ankara to all the provinces and Inspectorates-General, October 2, 1935.

96 DV "18/10/935 4339 ve 15/12/935," Correspondence Nr DV-EİUM 1.B/11128. File Nr 1/4115. From Ankara to all the provinces and Inspectorates-General, October 22, 1935; DV "18/10/935 4339 ve 15/12/935," Correspondence Nr DV-EİUM 1.B/11662. File Nr 1/4770. From Ankara to the Governor of Istanbul, November 7, 1935.

97 DV "24/9/935 3938'den 4338 ve 18/10/935'e," Correspondence Nr DV-EİUM 1.B/10527. File Nr 1/4426. From Ankara to the Governors of Afyon and Antalya, October 12, 1935.

98 DV "24/9/935 3938'den 4338 ve 18/10/935'e," Correspondence Nr DV-EİUM 1.A/10811. File Nr 1/4471. From Ankara to all the provinces and Inspectorates-General, October 15, 1935.

99 DV "Giden 12/7/935-31/7/935," Correspondence Nr DV-EİUM 6766. File Nr 1/2579. From Ankara to the Governor of Çoruh, July 17, 1935.

100 For some examples of such documents, see DV "31-8-935 ve 3351 23-9-935 3927," Correspondence Nr DV-EİUM 9300. File Nr 1/3893. From Ankara to the Governors of Çoruh, Trabzon, and other provinces, September 21, 1935; DV "24/9/935 3938'den 4338 ve 18/10/935'e," Correspondence Nr DV-EİUM 1.B/10082. File Nr 1/4268. From Ankara to the Thrace Inspectorate-General (Edirne) and the Governors of Çoruh, Trabzon, and other provinces, October 5, 1935.

101 It is interesting to note, in regard to Ankara's qualms about the Georgians and the Lazes, and perhaps explaining the recent historical roots of such aversion, that the two organizers of the famous 1926 attempt on Atatürk's life had been a Laze, Ziya Hurşit, and a Georgian, Yusuf. Mango, *Atatürk*, 445.

102 DV "31-8-935 ve 3351 23-9-935 3927," Correspondence Nr DV-EİUM 1/8499. File Nr 1/2493. From Ankara to the Governor of Çoruh, September 15, 1935. For some other examples of documents that implicated the Turkish Georgians, or held them suspects, see DV "24/9/935 3938'den 4338 ve 18/10/935'e," Correspondence

Nr DV-EİUM 1.B/10182. File Nr 1/4289. From Ankara to the Thrace Inspectorate-General (Edirne), October 7, 1935.

103 DV "31-8-935 ve 3351 23-9-935 3927," Correspondence Nr DV-EİUM 1/8866. File Nr 1/3729. From Ankara to the Governor of İstanbul, August 14, 1935.

104 DV "18/10/935 4339 ve 15/12/935," Correspondence Nr DV- EİUM 1.B/11128. File Nr 1/4115. From Ankara to all the provinces and Inspectorates-General, October 22, 1935.

105 DV "31-8-935 ve 3351 23-9-935 3927," Correspondence Nr DV-EİUM 6/2201. File Nr 1/3500. From the Ankara to the Governors of Kocaeli, Balıkesirand other provinces, September 5, 1935.

106 DV "31-8-935 ve 3351 23-9-935 3927," Correspondence Nr DV-EİUM 1/9207. File Nr 1/3835. From Ankara to the Governor of İzmir, September 20, 1935.

107 DV "31-8-935 ve 3351 23-9-935 3927," Correspondence Nr DV-EİUM 1/8813. File Nr 1/3677. From Ankara to the Governors of İzmir, Manisa, and other provinces, September 13, 1935.

108 FO 371/20864/E1790. Matthews (Mersin) to Loraine (Ankara), March 2, 1937.

109 For a map showing the Franco-Turkish armistice line in the Sancak, see Stéphane Yerasimos, "Le Sanjak D'Alexandrette: formation et intégration d'un territoire," *La Revue du Monde Musulman et de la Méditerranée*, no. 27, (1988): 199.

110 For a map showing the 1921 Franco-Turkish armistice line in the Sancak, see Yerasimos, "Le Sanjak D'Alexandratte," 199.

111 For the text of the Franklin–Bouillon treaty, see Michel Gilquin, *D'Antioche au Hatay: l'histoire oubliée du Sandjak a'Alexandratte* (Paris: Harmattan, 2000), 171–82.

112 Philip K. Khory, *Syria and the French Mandate: The Politics of Arab Nationalism 1920, 1945,* (Princeton, NJ: Princeton University Press, 1987), 496.

113 Khory, *Syria and the French Mandate*, 496.

114 Yücel Güçlü, *The Sanjak of Alexandratta, a study in Turkish–French–Syrian Relations,* (Ankara: Turkish Historical Society, 2001), 334–41.

115 FO 371/196/E 20845, Ward (London), *Memo,* January 11, 1937, quoted in Khory, *Syria and the French Mandate*, 496.

116 SD 767.90d/15 Keely (Beirut) to Washington, June 6, 1930. Nevertheless, in a later report from Beirut in 1931, Consul General Keely wrote: "There is little justification for believing that the French have any thought of creating an Armenian state, as such, in Northern Syria." SD 767.90d/16 Keely (Beirut) to Washington, February 20, 1931.

117 Khory, *Syria and the French Mandate*, 499. For a copy of this treaty, see Güçlü, *The Sanjak of Alexandratta*, 344–7.

118 Gologlu, *Tek Partili Cumhuriyet*, 198.

119 Gologlu, *Tek Partili Cumhuriyet*, 199.

120 For the full text of this treaty titled, "Traité D'Amitié Et D'Alliance Entre La France Et La Syrie," see Lucien Bitterlin, *Alexandrette: le "Munich" d'Orient ou quand la France capitulait* (Paris: Jean Piccolec, 1999), 343–52.

121 Bitterlin, *Alexandrette: le "Munich" d'Orient*, 352.

122 Khory, *Syria and the French Mandate*, 500.

123 Khory, *Syria and the French Mandate*, 495. For a detailed break down of this population, as well as a map showing different ethnicities in the Sancak, see Bitterlin, *Alexandrette: le "Munich" d'Orient*, 187–89.

124 DV "23/3/937'den 1/6/937'e kadar Şifre Dosyası," Correspondence Nr DV-EİUM 1.B/5589. File Nr 1177. From Ankara to the Governor of Seyhan, May 31, 1937; and FO 371/20864/E1790. Matthews (Mersin) to Loraine (Ankara), March 2, 1937.

125 Agop Dilaçar, *Alpin Irk, Türk Etnisi, ve Hatay Halkı* (The Alpine Race, Turkish Ethnie and the People of Hatay) (Ankara: Türk Tarih Kurumu, 1939).

126 Dilaçar, *Alpin Irk, Türk Etnisi, ve Hatay Halkı,* 14–15.

127 Dilaçar, *Alpin Irk, Türk Etnisi, ve Hatay Halkı,* 16–17.

128 Hasan Reşit Tankut, *Nusayriler ve Nusayrilik Hakkında* (About the Nusayris and Nusayrism) (Ankara: Ulus Basımevi, 1938).
129 Tankut, *Nusayriler ve Nusayrilik Hakkında*, 12–22.
130 Tankut, *Nusayriler ve Nusayrilik Hakkında*, 5–7.
131 Tankut, *Nusayriler ve Nusayrilik Hakkında*, 19–20.
132 BCA 490.01/4.17.23.
133 Fore the text of the Turkish Memorandum, see Gilquin, *D'Antioche au Hatay*, 187–89.
134 For a copy of the reply letter sent by Leon Blum, see Gilquin, *D'Antioche au Hatay*, 191–93.
135 For a copy of this resolution, see Güçlü, *The Sanjak of Alexandratta*, VII, 350–52.
136 Güçlü, *The Sanjak of Alexandratta*, VII, 350.
137 Güçlü, *The Sanjak of Alexandratta*, VII, 351.
138 For more on the competition between Turkish and Arab nationalisms in Hatay at this time, see Khory, *Syria and the French Mandate*, 499–511.
139 For nationalist accounts of Turkish support for the Hatay cause, see Gologlu, *Tek Partili Cumhuriyet*, 197–302; Hamdi Selçuk, *Hatay'ın O Günleri* (Those Days of Hatay) (Istanbul: 1972), 68–142. For a review of nationalist activities in Hatay by the local Turks in the 1930s, consult Nuri Aydın Konuralp, *Hatay'da Kurtuluş ve Kurtarış Mücadelesi Tarihi* (The History of Salvation and Liberation Struggle in Hatay) (İskenderun: Hatay Postası, 1970), 139–59. For an assessment of collaboration between Turkey and the Turks in Hatay in this period, consult Tayfur Sökmen, *Hatay'ın Kurtuluşu İçin Harcanan Çabalar* (Efforts for the Liberation of Hatay) (Ankara: Türk Tarih Kurumu, 1978), 73–117 For a collection of editorials in the daily *Vakit*, reflecting the nationalist sentiments in the country during the late 1930s, see Uz, *Gördüklerim Duyduklarım Duygularım*, 153–61.
140 SD 867.014/71. MacMurray (Istanbul) to Washington, October 5, 1936.
141 Selçuk, *Hatay'ın O Günleri*, 89.
142 Ahmet Halaçoğlu, *Hatay'ın Anavatana Katılmasında Dörtyol'un Yeri* (Dörtyol's Role in Hatay's Annexation to the Motherland) (Ankara: Türk Tarih Kurumu, 1995), 12–13.
143 For the text of this treaty titled, "Traité De Garantie De L'Intégrité Territoriale Du Sanjak," see Gilquin, *D'Antioche au Hatay*, 195–200.
144 For the text of Hatay's constitution, see Jean Elie Barbaro, *La Question du Sandjak D'Alexandrette* (Alep: Imprimerie Rotos, 1941), 55–74.
145 Halaçoğlu, *Hatay'ın Anavatana Katılmasında*, 13.
146 For the text of the Franco-Turkish treaty, to which the UK, also acceded, see Barbaro, *La Question du Sandjak D'Alexandrette*, 103–09.
147 For more on Paris' pusillanimity toward Turkey on the Hatay issue, see the following works that are critical of French policy, Gilquin, *D'Antioche au Hatay; and* Bitterlin, *Alexandrette: le "Munich" d'Orient.*
148 DV "23/3/937'den 1/6/937'e kadar Şifre Dosyası," Correspondence Nr DV-UM. File Nr 1173. From Ankara to the Governors of Istanbul, Izmir, and Adana, May 30, 1937.
149 *League of Nations Publications, General 1938*, 1–6, "Question of Alexandratta. Final Regulations for the First Elections in the Sanjak of Alexandratta," 6.
150 *League of Nations Publications, General 1938*, 8.
151 DV "23/3/937'den 1/6/937'e kadar Şifre Dosyası," Correspondence Nr DV-EİUM 1.B/5582. File Nr 1172. From Ankara to the Governor of Seyhan, May 29, 1937; DV "23/3/937'den 1/6/937'e kadar Şifre Dosyası," Correspondence Nr DV-EİUM 1.B/ 5442. File Nr 11405. From Ankara to the District Governor of Kilis, May 26, 1937.
152 DV "CHP Dosyası 1936," Correspondence Nr DV-HKM 1.G.3/? File Nr? From Ankara to the Secretary General of the CHP, June 16, 1936.
153 DV "1. Kanun 938'den 1 no dan 647 numaraya 7 Şubat 1938'e," Correspondence Nr DV-EUM 1.B/5712. File Nr 416. From Ankara to the MP Tayfur Sökmen, via the Directorate of Security (Dörtyol), February 5, 1938.

154 DV "1. Kanun 938'den 1 no dan 647 numaraya 7 Şubat 1938'e," Correspondence Nr DV-EUM 1.B/5702. File Nr 422. From Ankara to the District Governor of Dörtyol, February 5, 1937.

155 DV "1. Kanun 938'den 1 no dan 647 numaraya 7 Şubat 1938'e," Correspondence Nr DV-EUM 1.B/5698. File Nr 408. From Ankara to MP Tayfur Sökmen, via the Directorate of Security (Dörtyol)? 1938.

156 DV "1. Kanun 938'den 1 no dan 647 numaraya 7 Şubat 1938'e," Correspondence Nr DV-EUM 1.B/814. File Nr 62. From Ankara to the MP Tayfur Sökmen, via the Directorate of Security (Dörtyol), January 5, 1938.

157 DV "6/8/937'den 15/10/937'e Kadar," Correspondence Nr DV-EİUM 1.G.4/9116. File Nr 1862. From Ankara to all the provinces and Inspectorates-General, August 13, 1937.

158 DV "1. Kanun 938'den 1 no dan 647 numaraya 7 Şubat 1938'e," Correspondence Nr DV-EUM 1.B/268. File Nr 20. From Ankara to MP Tayfur Sökmen, via the Directorate of Security (Dörtyol), January 4, 1938.

159 DV "1. Kanun 938'den 1 no dan 647 numaraya 7 Şubat 1938'e," Correspondence Nr DV-EUM 1.B/3835. File Nr 288. From Ankara to MP Tayfur Sökmen, via the Directorate of Security (Dörtyol), January 25, 1938.

160 DV "23/3/937'den 1/6/937'e kadar Şifre Dosyası," Correspondence Nr DV-UM. File Nr 1173. From Ankara to the Governors of Istanbul, Izmir, and Adana, May 30, 1937.

161 DV "23/3/937'den 1/6/937'e kadar Şifre Dosyası," Correspondence Nr DV-EİUM 1.B/5582. File Nr 1172. From Ankara to the Governor of Seyhan, May 29, 1937.

162 DV "23/3/937'den 1/6/937'e kadar Şifre Dosyası," Correspondence Nr DV-EİUM 1.B/5442. File Nr 11405. From Ankara to the District Governor of Kilis, May 26, 1937.

163 DV "1937, Vasıtamızla Gelen Şifreler Dosyası" Correspondence Nr DV-UM 10137. File Nr? From Ankara to the Governor of Seyhan, January 10, 1937.

164 DV "1937, Vasıtamızla Gelen Şifreler Dosyası" Correspondence Nr? File Nr? From Hadi Baysal (Seyhan) to Şükrü Kaya (Ankara), January 14, 1937.

165 DV "1938 1295'den 1980 kadar 16 Mayıs 38'den 18 Temmuz 938'e kadar," Correspondence Nr DV-EUM 1.B/23681. File Nr 1310. From Ankara to MP Tayfur Sökmen, via the Directorate of Security (Dörtyol), May 17, 1938.

166 DV "1938 1295'den 1980 kadar 16 Mayıs 38'den 18 Temmuz 938'e kadar," Correspondence Nr DV-EUM 1.B/25043. File Nr 1404. From Ankara to the Governor of Seyhan, May 24, 1938.

167 Konuralp, *Hatay'da Kurtuluş ve Kurtarış*, 151–52.

168 Halaçoğlu, *Hatay'ın Anavatana Katılmasında*, 13.

169 For a good summary of the events surrounding Hatay, from 1920 until 1938, see Majid Khadduri, "The Alexandratta Dispute," *The American Journal of International Law* (1945): 406–25.

170 DV "1938 2630 no dan 15/9/938 tarihinden 3323 4/11/938 tarihine kadar," Correspondence Nr DV-EUM 1.B/53266. File Nr 2985. From Ankara to Mr Tayfur Sökmen, the president of the State of Hatay, via the telegram house of Payas, October 15, 1938.

171 DV "4/11/938 den 3324 dan 31/12/938 ve 3942," Correspondence Nr DV-EUM 1/67307. File Nr 3942. From Ankara to Mr Tayfur Sökmen, the president of the State of Hatay, via the telegram house of Payas, December 31, 1938.

172 SD 767.90D/36. MacMurray (Istanbul) to Washington, March 13, 1939.

173 For the text of this agreement titled, "Arrangement Portant Règlement Définitive des Questions Territoriales entre la Turquie et la Syrie," see Barbaro, *La Question du Sandjak D'Alexandrette*, 94–102.

174 For more on Hatay, for a recent and very detailed work, which gives a thorough analysis of the events from the 1920s until 1939, see Güçlü, *The Sanjak of Alexandratta*.

This work, somewhat favorable to the Turkish side, makes extensive use of British and French diplomatic records. Alternatively, for another recent study, which uses French diplomatic records to compile a brief account of the events, sympathetic to the Syrian side, see Peter A. Shambrook, *French Imperialism in Syria* (London: Ithaca Press, 1998), 291–97.

175 DV "1938 2630 no dan 15/9/938 tarihinden 3323 4/11/938 tarihine kadar," Correspondence Nr DV-EUM 1.B/56022. File Nr 3218. From Ankara to Cevat Açıkalın, extraordinary plenipotentiary in Hatay, via Payas, October 31, 1938.

176 Khory, *Syria and the French Mandate*, 513. For some British diplomatic documents, recording this exodus, and implying Turkish complicity in it, see FO 371/21915/ E5045. Davis (Aleppo) to Halifax (London), August 6, 1938; FO 371/23302/E5610; FO 371/23302/E5132. Davis (Aleppo) to the Principal Secretary of State (London), July 10, 1939; FO 371/25015/E1601. Davis (Aleppo) to the Principal Secretary of State (London), August 4, 1939; and FO 371/25015/E1601. Davis (Aleppo) to Halifax (London), February 3, 1940.

177 DV "4/11/938 den 3324 dan 31/12/938 ve 3942," Correspondence Nr DV-EUM 1/67312. File Nr 3941. From Ankara to Mr Tayfur Sökmen, the president of the State of Hatay, via the telegram house of Payas, December 31, 1938.

178 BCA 030.18.1.1/84.68.11. July 26, 1938.

179 BCA 030.18.1.1/88.77.16. August 5, 1939.

180 DV "24/9/935 3938'den 4338 ve 18/10/935'e," Correspondence Nr DV-EİUM 1.A/10614. File Nr 1/4458. From Ankara to the Governor of Seyhan, October 14, 1935.

181 DV "CHP Dosyası 1937," Correspondence Nr DV-HKM 3/126. File Nr? From Ankara to the Secretary General of the CHP? 1936.

182 DV "Giden Şifreler 1/12/1930 Sayılı Dosya," Correspondence Nr DV-EİUM 1.G.3/11040. File Nr 2351. From Ankara to the Governors of First Inspectorate-General (Diyarbakır) and the Governors of Urfa and Mardin, October 1, 1937.

183 DV "25/3/36'dan 30/5/36'ya kadar Şifre Dosyası," Correspondence Nr DV- EİUM 1/5362. File Nr 897. From Ankara to the Inspectorates-General and all the provinces, May 13, 1936.

184 DV "CHP Dosyası 1936," Correspondence Nr DV-HKM 3/261. File Nr? From Ankara to the Secretary General of the CHP, November 6, 1936.

7 Ethno-religious limits of Turkishness: Christians excluded from the nation

1   BCA 030. 18. 1.2/3.29.3. May 8, 1929.

2   SD 867.9111/337. Embassy (Istanbul) to Washington, December 2, 1930. *Digest of Turkish News*, November 13–20, 1930.

3   FO 371/16091/E1246. Morgan (Angora) to Simon (London), March 11, 1932.

4   *İstatistik Yıllığı: 1934–5 Cilt 7*, 159.

5   *İstatistik Yıllığı Cilt 10*, 65.

6   *İstatistik Yıllığı: 1934–5 Cilt 7*, 159.

7   *İstatistik Yıllığı Cilt 10*, 65.

8   This law titled, "Bazı Kisvelerin Geyilmeyeceğine dair Kanun" (Law Stipulating that Certain Garbs May not be Worn, was passed on December 3, 1934. For the discussion minutes and text of this, see TBMM Zabıt Ceridesi, term IV, vol. 25, 75–78; and addenda 22: 1–3.

9   FO 371/19040/E4264. Morgan (Constantinople) to Hoare (London), July 11, 1935.

10 DV "6/8/937'den 15/10/937'e kadar," Correspondence Nr DV-EİUM 1.G.7/ 11015. File Nr 2346. From Ankara to the Inspectorates-General and all the provinces, October 1, 1937; and BCA 030.18.1.2/79.83.14. October 5, 1937.

11 *İstatistik Yıllığı Cilt 10*, 65.
12 These people kept their anti-Turkish activities in the 1930s, when Ankara was monitoring them. "CHP Dosyası 1937 3/000," Correspondence Nr DV-HKM 1.G.5/3/3. File Nr? From Ankara to the Secretary General of the CHP, January 4, 1937. Then, on October 25, 1935, the Ankara warned about the assassination attempts by these. DV "18/10/935 4339 ve 15/12/935," Correspondence Nr DV-EİUM 1.B/11128. File Nr 1/4615. From Ankara to the Inspectorates-General and all the provinces, October 22, 1935.
13 Alexandris, *The Greek Minority of Istanbul*, 187.
14 SD 867.911/294. Embassy (Istanbul) to Washington, December 2, 1930. *Digest of Turkish News*, November 12–30, 1930.
15 DV "Giden- Birinci Kanun Şubat 1932 Mart 1932 Nisan 1932," Correspondence Nr DV-EUUM 4.B.2/920. File Nr 1/522. From Ankara to the Governor of Izmir, April 11, 1932.
16 Alexandris, *The Greek Minority of Istanbul*, 180.
17 DV "Çıkan Şifre 15/6/1933'den 31/7/33 Tarihine Kadar," Correspondence Nr DV-HKM 5/353. File Nr 1/1756. From the Ankara to the Governor of, Balıkesir, July 22, 1933.
18 FO 371/16091/E1246. Morgan (Angora) to Simon (London), March 11, 1932.
19 Alexandris, *The Greek Minority of Istanbul*, 179.
20 SD 867.9111/380. Embassy (Istanbul) to Washington, September 1932. *Digest of Turkish News*, August 21–September 24, 1931.
21 Alexandris, *The Greek Minority of Istanbul*, 180.
22 DV "Şifre Kartunu 1/5/33-14/6/33," Correspondence Nr DV-EUUM 4/2336. File Nr 1/1066. From Ankara to the Governors of Trabzon and Erzurum, May 10, 1933.
23 Alexandris, *The Greek Minority of Istanbul*, 180.
24 Alexandris, "Imbros and Tenedos," in *Journal of the Hellenic Diaspora*: 23.
25 Alexandris, "Imbros and Tenedos," in *Journal of the Hellenic Diaspora*: 23–24.
26 The Turkish-Orthodox Church was born out of a failed attempt in the early 1920s, sponsored by the Kemalist movement, to set up an autonomous church for Turkish-speaking Orthodox Christians in Turkey. For more on this, see Jäschke von Gottard, "Die Türkisch-Orthodoxe Kirche," *Der Islam* 39 (1964): 96–129; and Hakan Alkan, *Türk Ortodoks Patrikhanesi* (The Turkish-Orthodox Patriarchate) (Ankara: Günce, 2000).
27 "İdari ve Siyasi Müsteşarlıklar Muhaberelerine ait Dosya," Correspondence Nr DV-HKM? File Nr? Report by MP Özdamar? 1936.
28 Quoted in SD 867.42/79. Embassy (Istanbul) to Washington, April 22, 1931.
29 Alexandris, *The Greek Minority of Istanbul*, 184.
30 DV "Giden Birinci-Kanun, Şubat, Mart, Nisan 1932," Correspondence Nr DV-MİUM 1/47. File Nr 98/1. From Ankara to Governor of Istanbul, January 9, 1932.
31 SD 867.9111/287. Embassy (Istanbul) to Washington, October 7, 1930. *Digest of Turkish News*, September 1932.
32 SD 867.402/61. Allen (Istanbul) to Washington, April 19, 1933.
33 DV "18/10/935 4339 ve 15/12/935," Correspondence Nr DV-EİUM 4/7693. File Nr 1/4704. From Ankara to the Governor of Istanbul, October 28, 1935.
34 DV "Giden-Birinci Kanun Şubat 1932 Mart 1932 Nisan 1932," Correspondence Nr DV-MİUM 480/11. File Nr 1/449. From Ankara to the Governor of Izmir, March 29, 1932.
35 DV "Giden-Birinci Kanun Şubat 1932 Mart 1932 Nisan 1932," Correspondence Nr DV-MİUM 480/33. File Nr 1/503. From Ankara to the Governor of Izmir, April 6, 1932.
36 DV "Giden-Birinci Kanun Şubat 1932 Mart 1932 Nisan 1932," Correspondence Nr DV-MİUM 480/38. File Nr 1/531. From Ankara to the Governor of Izmir, April 12, 1932.

37 DV "1. Kanun 938'den 1 no dan 647 numaraya 7 Şubat 1938'e," Correspondence Nr DV-EİUM 4.B/5006. File Nr 368. From Ankara to the Governor of Çoruh, November 2, 1938.

38 "CHP Dosyası 1937 3/000," Correspondence Nr DV-HKM 1/3/49. File Nr? From Ankara to the Secretary General of the CHP, March 15, 1937.

39 DV "24/9/935 ve 3938 18/10/935 4338," Correspondence Nr DV-EİUM 1.B/10090. File Nr 1/4275. From Ankara to the Governors of Malatya, Seyhan, and other provinces, October 5, 1935.

40 DV "Giden Şifreler 20/2/939'dan 3/6/939'a kadar" Correspondence Nr DV-HKM 2300. File Nr Em.681. From the Governor of Mardin to Ankara, March 26, 1939.

41 For accounts of these events that describe the fight between the Assyrian tribes and the Ottoman armies as genocide of the Assyrians, see Gabriele Yonan, *Ein Vergessener Holocaust: die Vernichtung der Christlichen Assyrer in der Türkei* (Göttingen: Gesellschaft für Bedrohte Völker, 1989); Joseph Yacoub, *The Assyrian Question*, second edn (Chicago, IL: Alpha Graphic, 1993), 57–120; and Joseph Yacoub, *La Question Assyro-Chaldéenne: les Puissance Européennes et la Société des Nations (1908–1936)*, PhD dissertation, 4 vols, (University of Lyon, 1984), especially vol. 1, 70–126, and vol. 2, 235–277. For another evaluation of these events, sympathetic toward the Assyrians, consult the following work by a British Anglican churchman, F. N. Heazell, *The Woes of a Distressed Nation: an account of the Assyrian people from 1914 to 1934* (London: The Faith Books, 1934). On the other hand, for a review of the same events that treats them as a by-product of an alliance between the Russians and the Assyrians against the Ottoman during the First World War, Cf. W. A. Wigram, *The Assyrians and Their Neighbors* (London: G. Bell & Sons, 1929), 211–39.

42 For an evaluation of the events in 1923–25, see Yacoub, *La Question Assyro-Chaldéenne*, vol. 2, 235–277.

43 For the resettlement of the Assyrians in Northern Iraq during the 1920s and the 1930s, see R. S. Stafford, *The Tragedy of the Assyrians* (London: George Allen & Unwin, 1935), 44–62.

44 FO 371/16036/E4981. Hall (Geneva) to Rendell (London), September 26, 1932.

45 FO 371/16036/E4981. Hall (Geneva) to Rendell (London), September 26, 1932. *Letter from Rendell (London) to Clerk (Constantinople)*, November 8, 1932.

46 DV "Özel Kalem Şifreli Yazışma 30/11/1931," Correspondence Nr DV-JUK 3.1/36774. File Nr 1/2561. From Ankara to the First Inspectorate-General (Diyarbakır), November?, 1931.

47 DV "1938 1295'den 1980 kadar 16 Mayıs 38'den 18 Temmuz 938'e kadar," Correspondence Nr DV-EUM 7/35160. File Nr 1915. From Ankara to the First Inspectorate-General (Diyarbakır) and the Governor of Hakkâri, July 12, 1938.

48 FO 371/19040/E4264. Morgan (Constantinople) to Hoare (London), July 11, 1935.

49 DV "Giden-Birinci Kanun Şubat 1932 Mart 1932 Nisan 1932," Correspondence Nr DV-EUUM 4.B.2/535. File Nr 1/317. From Ankara to the First Inspectorate-General (Diyarbakır), March 6, 1932.

50 BCA 030.18.1.2/74.35.5. April 28, 1937.

51 BCA 030.18.1.2/75.50.1. June 7, 1937.

52 FO 371/15381/E4093. League of Nations (Geneva) to London, July 30, 1931. *Petition de M. Pachalian (Paris)*, to the League of Nations (Geneva), April 21, 1931.

53 SD 867.9111/380. Embassy (Istanbul) to Washington, September 1932. *Digest of Turkish News*, August 21–September 24, 1932.

54 FO 371/16982/E323. League of Nations (Geneva) to London. *Petition by Mr. Essayan (Paris)*, to the League of Nations (Geneva), October 7, 1931.

55 FO 371/16982/E323. League of Nations (Geneva) to London. *Observations du Gouvernement Turc*, Aras (Ankara) to the League of Nations (Geneva), December 11, 1931.

56 FO 371/20093/E4405. Essayan (Athens) to London. July 14, 1936.

57 DV "25/3/36'dan 30/5/37'ya kadar Şifre Dosyası," Correspondence Nr DV-EİUM 1.G.3/6125. File Nr ? From Ankara to the Governor of Istanbul, May 29, 1936.

58 DV "25/3/36'dan 30/5/37'ya kadar Şifre Dosyası," Correspondence Nr DV- EİUM 1.G.3/5498. File Nr 932. From Ankara to the Governor of Istanbul, May 18, 1936. Many other records document Ankara's suspicion toward the entry of suspicious Armenians into Turkey. For some of them, see DV "Şifre Kartunu 1/5/33-14/6/33," Correspondence Nr DV-EUUM?/5031. File Nr 1/1098. From Ankara to First Inspectorate-General (Diyarbakır), the border and coastal provinces, May 20, 1933; DV "Şifre Kartunu 1/5/33-14/6/33," Correspondence Nr DV-EUUM 1.B/5231 File Nr 1/1158. From Ankara to the Governors of Antalya and Mersin, May 24, 1933; DV "Çıkan Şifre 15/6/1933'den 31/7/33 Tarihine Kadar," Correspondence Nr DV-EUUM 1/6853. File Nr 1/1671. From Ankara to the First Inspectorate-General (Diyarbakır), July 15, 1933; DV "Çıkan Şifre 15/6/1933'den 31/7/33 Tarihine Kadar," Correspondence Nr DV-EUUM 1/6948. File Nr 1/1711. From Ankara to the Governors of Erzincan and Elâziz, July 18, 1933.

59 DV "Giden Şifreler 1/12/1930 Sayılı Dosya," Correspondence Nr DV- EİUM 1.B.3/8760. File Nr 1/2643. From Ankara to the First Inspector-General (Diyarbakır), the border and coastal provinces, November 15, 1931.

60 DV "Giden Şifreler 1/12/1930 Sayılı Dosya," Correspondence Nr DV-EİUM 1.B.3/8157. File Nr 1/2446. From Ankara to the Governor of Istanbul, October 24, 1931.

61 DV "Giden Şifreler 1/12/1930 Sayılı Dosya," Correspondence Nr DV-EİUM 1.B.3/8528. File Nr 1/2559. From Ankara to the First Inspectorate-General, the coastal and border provinces and the Governors of Erzurum and Elaziz, November 4, 1930.

62 SD 867.9111/334. Embassy (Istanbul) to Washington, November 1930. *Digest of Turkish News*, October 29–November 11, 1931; SD 867.9111/331. Embassy (Istanbul) to Washington, October 1930. *Digest of Turkish News*, October 15–28, 1931.

63 FO 371/16091/E222. Morgan (Angora) to Simon (London), March 11, 1932. Embassy (Constantinople) to London, January 14, 1932. *Annual Report for 1931*.

64 FO 371/15370/E5133. Clerk (Constantinople) to the Marquess of Reading (London), October 8, 1931.

65 DV "Giden Şifreler 1/12/1930 Sayılı Dosya," Correspondence Nr DV-EİUM 1.B.3/8619. File Nr 1/2577. From Ankara to the First Inspector-General (Diyarbakır), the border and coastal provinces, November 8, 1931.

66 DV "Giden Şifreler 1/12/1930 Sayılı Dosya," Correspondence Nr DV-EİUM 1.B.3/8764. File Nr 1/2645. From Ankara to Şükrü Kaya (Ankara), November 16, 1931.

67 For some of them, see DV "Giden Şifreler 1/12/1930 Sayılı Dosya," Correspondence Nr DV-EİUM 1.B.3/8716. File Nr 1/2627. Ankara to the First Inspector-General (Diyarbakır), the border and coastal provinces, November 12, 1931; DV "Özel Kalem Şifreli Yazışma 30/11/1931," Correspondence Nr DV-EUUM 1.B.3/9077. File Nr 1/2712. From Ankara to the border and coastal provinces, November 24, 1931; DV "Giden-Birinci Kanun Şubat 1932 Mart 1932 Nisan 1932," Correspondence Nr DV-EUUM 1.B.3/280. File Nr 1/89. From Ankara to the First Inspectorate-General (Diyarbakır), the border and coastal provinces, January 17, 1932; DV "Giden- Birinci Kanun Şubat 1932 Mart 1932 Nisan 1932," Correspondence Nr DV-EUUM 1.B.3/1607. File Nr 1/515. From the Ankara to the border and coastal provinces, April 9, 1932; DV "Özel Kalem Şifreli Yazışma 30/11/1931," Correspondence Nr DV-EUUM 3.1/8744. File Nr 1/2637. From Ankara to the First Inspectorate-General (Diyarbakır), the border and coastal provinces, November 1931.

68 DV "Gidenler-Mayıs-Haziran-Temmuz-Ağustos 1932," Correspondence Nr DV-EUUM 1.B/3008. File Nr 1/1280. From Ankara to the First Inspectorate-General (Diyarbakır), the border and coastal provinces, August 21, 1932.

69 FO 371/16095/E4067. Clerk (Angora) to Simon (London), August 2, 1932.
70 DV "Gidenler-Mayıs-Haziran-Temmuz-Ağustos 1932," Correspondence Nr DV-EUUM 1B.3/3339. File Nr 1/1130. From Ankara to the First Inspectorate-General (Diyarbakır), the border and coastal provinces, July 3, 1932.
71 DV "Gönderilen Şifre 1935 570 Numaraları ve 18-2-935 ve 31-3-935 1071," Correspondence Nr DV-EİUM 1.B/? File Nr 1/946. From Ankara to the First Inspectorate-General (Diyarbakır), the border and coastal provinces, March 21, 1935.
72 DV "31/8/935 ve 3391 23/9/935 ve 3927," Correspondence Nr DV-EİUM ?. File Nr 1/3767. From Ankara to the Inspectorates-General, and all the provinces, September 16, 1935.
73 FO 371/19041/E6245. Morgan (Constantinople) to London, October 19, 1935. DV "24/9/935 ve 3938 18/10/935 4338," Correspondence Nr DV-EİUM 1.B/11255. File Nr 1/4655. From Ankara to the First Inspectorate-General (Diyarbakır), and the Governors of Seyhan, Antep, and other provinces, October 25, 1935.
74 DV "Gidenler-Mayıs-Haziran-Temmuz-Ağustos 1932," Correspondence Nr DV-EUUM 1.B.3/2856. File Nr 1/980. From Ankara to the First Inspectorate-General (Diyarbakır), July 4, 1932.
75 Quoted in FO 371/19041/E16470. Embassy (Angora) to Hoare (London), October 26, 1935.
76 FO 371/19041/E16470. Embassy (Angora) to Hoare (London), October 26, 1935.
77 DV "23/3/937'den 1/6/937'e kadar Şifre Dosyası," Correspondence Nr DV-EİUM 4.A/4939. File Nr? From Ankara to the Governor of Kocaeli, April 6, 1937.
78 DV "Giden Şifreler 1/12/1930 Sayılı Dosya," Correspondence Nr DV-EİUM 1.B.3/8788. File Nr 1/2650. From Ankara to the Governors of Adana and Cebelibereket, November 16, 1931.
79 DV "Giden Şifreler 1/12/1931'e kadar," Correspondence Nr DV-HKM 20147. File Nr 3288. From the Governor of (Diyarbakır) to Şükrü Kaya, Ankara, December 19, 1931. Many other records document Ankara's scrutiny of people, whom it suspected were involved in the Tashnak Party or Armenian nationalism. For some of them, see DV "Özel Kalem Şifreli Yazışma 30/11/1931," Correspondence Nr DV-HKM 18546. File Nr 17210. From EUUM to the Private Secretary of the Ministry of Interior (Ankara), November 22, 1931; DV "Giden Şifreler 20/2/939'dan 3/6/939'a kadar" Correspondence Nr DV-HKM 1612. File Nr Em. 233. From the Governor of Sivas to Ankara, February 28, 1939.
80 DV "Özel Kalem Şifreli Yazışma 30/11/1931," Correspondence Nr DV-EUUM 1.B.3/8499. File Nr 1/2551. From Ankara to the Governor of Erzincan, November 3, 1931.
81 DV "Giden Şifreler 1/12/1930 Sayılı Dosya," Correspondence Nr DV-EİUM 1.B.3/8560. File Nr 1/2568. From Ankara to First Inspectorate-General (Diyarbakır), and all the provinces, November 5, 1931.
82 DV "Giden Şifreler 1/12/1930 Sayılı Dosya," Correspondence Nr DV-EİUM 1.B.3/8223. File Nr 1/2467. From Ankara to the Governor of Istanbul, October 25, 1931.
83 DV "Giden Şifreler 1/12/1930 Sayılı Dosya," Correspondence Nr DV-EİUM 1.B.3/8289. File Nr 1/2505. From Ankara to the Governor of Istanbul, October 27, 1931. Many other records document government's wariness toward Armenians, who took trips within the country, traveled often, or went abroad frequently. For some of them, see DV "Özel Kalem Şifreli Yazışma 30/11/1931," Correspondence Nr DV-EUUM 1.B.3/8039. File Nr 1/2397. From Ankara to the Governors of Konya, Afyonkarahisar, Kütahya, Eskişehir, Bilecik, Kocaeli, October 18, 1931; DV "Gidenler-Mayıs-Haziran-Temmuz-Ağustos 1932," Correspondence Nr DV-EUUM 1.B.3/2857. File Nr 1/979. From Ankara to the Governor of Edirne, July 4, 1932; DV "Şifre Kartunu 1/5/33-14/6/33," Correspondence Nr DV-EUUM 1.A/4846. File Nr 1/1047. From Ankara to the Governors of Sivas, Istanbul and Diyarıbekir, May 14, 1933; DV "31-8-935 ve 3351 23-9-935 3927," Correspondence

Nr DV-EİUM 1.B/8319. File Nr 1/3416. From Ankara to the Governor of Kayseri, August 2, 1935; DV "24/9/935 ve 3938 18/10/935 4338," Correspondence Nr DV-EİUM 1.B/10166. File Nr 1/4319. From Ankara to the Governor of Istanbul, October 7, 1935; DV "1938 2630 no dan 15/9/938 tarihinden 3323 4/11/938 tarihine kadar," Correspondence Nr DV-EUM 1.G.8/59577. File Nr 3480. From Ankara to the Governors of Istanbul, Izmir, and Kütahya, November 17, 1938; DV "Giden Şifreler 20/2/939'dan 3/6/939'a kadar," Correspondence Nr DV-HKM 1740. File Nr Em. 1/256. From the Governor of Sivas to Ankara, March 7, 1939.

84 DV "31-8-935 ve 3351 23-9-935 3927," Correspondence Nr DV-EİUM 1/8583. File Nr 1/3557. From Ankara to the Governors and Inspectorates-General, August 7, 1935.

85 Ankara's alertness on conversions to Islam extended to other Christians, too. For example, on June 22, 1933, the EUUM asked the Ağrı province about Armenians, Assyrians, Jacobites, and Chaldeans, who had recently converted to Islam. Ankara wanted to know their exact numbers. DV "Çıkan Şifre 15/6/1933'den 31/7/33 Tarihine Kadar," Correspondence Nr DV-EUUM 1.B/6157. File Nr 1/1403. From Ankara to the Governor of Bayezit, June 22, 1933.

86 DV "Giden-Birinci Kanun Şubat 1932 Mart 1932 Nisan 1932," Correspondence Nr DV-EUUM 1.B.3/1769. File Nr 1/592. From Ankara to the Governor of Istanbul, April 28, 1932.

87 DV "24/9/935 ve 3938 18/10/935 4338," Correspondence Nr DV-EİUM 1.B/9763. File Nr 1/4115. From Ankara to the First Inspectorate-General (Diyarbakır), September 30, 1935.

88 "CHP Dosyası 1936 3," Correspondence Nr DV-HKM 3/260. File Nr? From Ankara to the Secretary General of the CHP, November 6, 1936. For other examples of government caution toward Armenian converts, see DV "31/8/935 ve 3391 23/9/935 ve 3927," Correspondence Nr DV-EİUM 1.B/9022. File Nr 1/3768. From Ankara to the Governor of Antalya, September 16, 1935; DV "24/9/935 ve 3938 18/10/935 4338," Correspondence Nr DV-EİUM 1.B/9981. File Nr 1/4206. From Ankara to the Governor of Istanbul, October 4, 1935; DV "24/9/935 ve 3938 18/10/935 4338," Correspondence Nr DV-EİUM 1.B/10160. File Nr 1/4313. From Ankara to the Governors of Erzurum, Kastamonu, and other provinces, October 7, 1935; DV "4/11/938 den 3324 dan 31/12/938 ve 3942," Correspondence Nr DV-EUM 1/57518. File Nr 3345. From Ankara to the Governor of Malatya, November 7, 1938; DV "Giden Şifreler 20/2/939'dan 3/6/939'a kadar," Correspondence Nr DV-HKM 2336. File Nr Em. 517. From the Governor of Bilecik to Ankara, March 28, 1939; DV "Giden Şifreler 20/2/939'dan 3/6/939'a kadar" Correspondence Nr DV-HKM 2266. File Nr Em. 30. From the Governor Of Konya to Ankara, March 25, 1939.

89 DV "23/3/937'den 1/6/937'e kadar Şifre Dosyası," Correspondence Nr DV-EİUM 1.G.2/2996. File Nr 650. From Ankara to the Governor of Balıkesir, March 30, 1937.

90 DV "1938 2630 no dan 15/9/938 tarihinden 3323 4/11/938 tarihine kadar," Correspondence Nr DV-EUM 1.G.2/47019. File Nr 2657. From Ankara to the Governor of Kırşehir, September 15, 1938.

91 DV "1938 2630 no dan 15/9/938 tarihinden 3323 4/11/938 tarihine kadar," Correspondence Nr DV-JGK 49041. File Nr 2742. From Ankara to the First Inspectorate-General (Diyarbakır), September 23, 1938.

92 SD 867.9111/307. Embassy (Istanbul) to Washington, March 31, 1932. *Digest of Turkish News*, March 5–18, 1932. SD 867.9111/308. Embassy (Istanbul) to Washington, April 1932. *Digest of Turkish News*, March 19–April 31, 1932.

93 SD 867.4016-ARMENIANS/4. Allen (Istanbul) to Washington, July 27, 1932.

94 SD 867.4061-Musa Dagh/17. Skinner (Istanbul) to Washington, June 4, 1935; and SD 867.4061-MOTION PICTURES/38. Murray (Istanbul) to Washington, June 18, 1935.

95 FO 371/19039/E5667. Morgan (Istanbul) to Hoare (London), September 14, 1935.
96 Bali, *Musa'nın Evlatları Cumhuriyet'in Yurttaşları*, 124–25.
97 FO 371/19039/E5667. Morgan (Istanbul) to Hoare (London), September 14, 1935.
98 FO 371/19039/E7518. Loraine (Angora) to the Secretary of State (London), December 20, 1935.
99 For more on the controversy surrounding Werfel's work and the plans by Metro Goldwyn Mayer to turn it into a movie, see Bali, *Musa'nın Evlatları Cumhuriyet'in Yurttaşları*, 116–34.
100 BCA 030.18.1.2/35.30.3. April 26, 1933.
101 BCA 030.18.1.2/46.49.5. July 10, 1934.
102 BCA 030.18.1.2/49.77.15. November 17, 1934.
103 BCA 030.18.1.2/50.89.17. December 30, 1934.
104 BCA 030.18.1.2/79.82.14. September 28, 1937. DV "6/8/937'den 15/10/937'e kadar," Correspondence Nr DV-EİUM 1.G.3/9919. File Nr 2041. From Ankara to Şükrü Kaya (Istanbul), the Inspectorates-General and all the provinces, September 3, 1937.
105 BCA 030.18.1.2/82.24.8. March 31, 1938.
106 BCA 030.18.1.2/84.64.5. July 7, 1938.
107 BCA 030.18.1.2/86.40.18. May 11, 1939.
108 BCA 030.18.1.2/88.81.1. August 25, 1939.
109 TBMM Zabıt Ceridesi, term V, vol. 26: 414.
110 TBMM Zabıt Ceridesi, term V, vol. 26, addenda 303: 2.
111 TBMM Zabıt Ceridesi, term V, vol. 26: 412.
112 It appears that the case of Keresteciyan being chosen as an MP to propose a new law detrimental to his group interests was not unique. For example, in 1924, the offer to abolish the Shariat "had been made in the name of a cleric, Halil Hulki, a deputy for the conservative town of Siirt in eastern Anatolia." Likewise, "a cleric, Şeyh Safvet, deputy for Urfa, a conservative town, known to Muslims as the city of Abraham, was chosen to present the bill putting an end to the caliphate and exiling the Ottoman dynasty." Mango, *Atatürk*, 404. The strategy here was to give legitimacy to the proposed laws by having people, on whom such laws would have an immediate impact, propose them.
113 TBMM Zabıt Ceridesi, term V, vol. 26: 412.
114 TBMM Zabıt Ceridesi, term V, vol. 26: 417.
115 For a Turkish appraisal of the missionary activities of the Western Churches in the Ottoman Empire, and the conflicts between them and the Ottomans, see İlknur Polat Haydaroğlu, *Osmanlı İmparatorluğu'nda Yabancı Okullar* (Foreign Schools in the Ottoman Empire) (Ankara: Kültür Bakanlığı, 1990), 192–225. For an American account of the same, Cf. Johnson, *The American Schools in the Republic of Turkey*, 8–77.
116 SD 867.404 /208. Sherill (Istanbul) to Washington, July 20, 1932.
117 For an evaluation of the relations between Ankara and foreign/missionary schools in this regard, see Sezer, *Atatürk Döneminde Yabancı Okullar*, 36–54. For the same on American schools, consult Johnson, *The American Schools in the Republic of Turkey*, 78–258.
118 DV "1. Kanun 938'den 1 no dan 647 numaraya 7 Şubat 1938'e," Correspondence Nr DV-EUM 1.G.2/2814. File Nr 205. From Ankara to the First Inspectorate-General (Diyarbakır) and the Governor of Muş, January 19, 1938.
119 "CHP Dosyası 1936 3," Correspondence Nr DV-HKM 3/98. File Nr? From Ankara to the Secretary General of the CHP, April 1936.
120 DV "31/8/935 ve 3391 23/9/935 ve 3927," Correspondence Nr DV-EİUM 1.B/8864. File Nr 1/3733. From Ankara to the Inspectorates-General and all the provinces, September 24, 1935.
121 SD 867.404 /208. Sherill (Istanbul) to Washington, July 20, 1932.
122 DV "Çıkan Şifre 15/6/1933'den 31/7/33 Tarihine Kadar," Correspondence Nr DV-EUUM 1.A/6934. File Nr 1/1705. From Ankara to the Governor of, Maraş, July 17, 1933.

123 FO 371/16986/E4960. Clerk (Angora) to Simon (London), August 20, 1933.
124 FO 371/16985/E1151. Monck-Mason (Aleppo) to Embassy (Ankara), February 1, 1933.
125 DV "Gönderilen Şifre 1935 570 Numaraları ve 18-2-935 ve 31-3-935 1071," Correspondence Nr DV-EİUM 1/2306. File Nr 1/949. From Ankara to the Governor of Istanbul, March 22, 1935.
126 DV "Giden 12/7/935-31/7/935," Correspondence Nr DV-EİUM 1.A/6699. File Nr? From Ankara to the Governor of Istanbul, July 15, 1935.
127 BCA 030.18.1.2/51.7.3. February 4, 1935.
128 BCA 030.18.1.2/76.57.16. June 22, 1937.
129 BCA 030.18.1.2/85.101.16. December 3, 1938.
130 DV "25/3/36'dan 30/5/37'ya kadar Şifre Dosyası," Correspondence Nr DV-BGM 1086. File Nr 743. From Ankara to the Governor of Istanbul, ? 1936.
131 Johnson *et al.*, eds, *Turbulent Era*, vol. 2, 781.

8 Jews in the 1930s: Turks or not?

1 *İstatistik Yıllığı 1934–5 Cilt 7*, 159.
2 *İstatistik Yıllığı Cilt 10*, 65.
3 Bali, *Musa'nın Evlatları Cumhuriyet'in Yurttaşları*, 176.
4 *İstatistik Yıllığı: Üçüncü Cilt, 53–54; 64–65; 76–77*; and *İstatistik Yıllığı: Cilt 11* (Statistics Yearbook: vol. 11) Başbakanlık İstatistik Umum Müdürlüğü (Istanbul: Hüsnütabiat Basımevi, 1940), 76–77.
5 Maxwell H. H. Macartney and Paul Cremona, *Italy's Foreign and Colonial Policy 1914–1937* (London: Oxford University Press, 1938), 211.
6 FO 1011/178. Loraine (Angora) to C. H. Bentnick (Sofia), March 7, 1935. Turkey was apprehensive of Italy also due to Rome's expansionism in the Mediterranean. At this time, Italy controlled the Dodecanese Islands, and was Turkey's maritime neighbor. In 1934, contrary to her treaty obligations, Italy started to fortify the Dodecanese. Millman, *The Ill-Made Alliance*, 27. In this regard, the government was especially concerned about Italian fortification of Levyos (Leros), a small island in the Dodecanese archipelago, right across the Turkish coast. Ankara saw this as a "gun pointed at Turkey." On its behalf, Italy argued, "Leros was principally a defensive measure against France." Its fortification was necessary "to keep open, in case of a war with France, Italy's line of supplies from the Black Sea and the Suez." FO 371/19037/E854. Embassy (Constantinople) to London, February 7, 1935. *Annual Report for 1934*. Ankara found these arguments unconvincing. In addition, Rome's aggressive foreign policy led Ankara to believe that "Italy had territorial ambitions in Anatolia." SD 867.00/49. Shaw (Istanbul) to Washington, September 1, 1934. On March 18, 1934, Mussolini noted in a fiery speech, that Italian expansionism would be directed towards Africa and Asia. Macartney and Cremona, *Italy's Foreign and Colonial Policy*, 7. This increased Ankara's fears about Italian designs *vis-à-vis* Turkey. In early April, the Turkish Ambassador in Rome requested a private audition with Mussolini to discuss this. Although, the Duce assured the Turkish diplomat that he considered Turkey to be a European country, this did not alleviate Ankara's fears about official Italian expansionism in Africa and Asia. Ankara was not persuaded and maintained a strong "fear and distrust of Italy." SD 767.00/64. Shaw (Istanbul) to Washington, March 8, 1936. In view of this, during the spring of 1934, Turkish battle ships staged war games in the Aegean, near the Dodecanese. Then, Atatürk took a trip along this coastline, traveling from Çeşme on the Aegean to Silifke on the Mediterranean, aboard the Turkish battle ship, *Yavuz*. Additionally, Minister Kaya warned: while Turkey has cordial relations with all its neighbors, the army, "which is under the command of the *greatest Captain in history* [*sic*] guarantees our security on that side." He added, "if in spite of this, anyone should seek to attack Turkey, this attack

will break itself against the hard and sharp rocks of our frontiers." SD 767.00/64. Shaw (Istanbul) to Washington, March 8, 1936. At this stage, Rome avoided any more demarches towards Turkey. As a result, Ankara toned down its rhetoric towards Italy and the two countries developed better terms. For instance, in 1937, Aras visited his Italian counterpart Ciano in Milan. At this meeting, while Aras agreed to "support Italy's claim of recognition of Ethiopian annexation at Geneva," Ciano recognized that "Turkey's desire to fortify the Straits was natural and proper." SD 767.00/67. MacMurray (Istanbul) to Washington, May 19, 1937.

7 FO 371/17964/E4780. Sargent (London) to Embassy (Angora), July 23, 1934; FO 371/17964/E3073. Loraine (Angora) to London, May 10, 1934. For more on Bulgaria's revisionism, and Sofia's alliance with Rome, see Barlas, *Etatism and Diplomacy in Turkey*, 141–45.
8 SD 767.00/54. Skinner (Istanbul) to Washington, June 1, 1934.
9 SD 767.74/641. Shaw (Istanbul) to Washington, September 28, 1932.
10 SD 767.74/42. Barnes (Sofia) to Washington, October 14, 1933. For more on the establishment of the Balkan Pact and the efforts to include Bulgaria into it, see Macartney and Paul Cremona, *Italy's Foreign and Colonial Policy*, 209–13.
11 SD 767.74/31. Shoemaker (Sofia) to Washington, April 26, 1933.
12 SD 767.74/61. Shaw (Istanbul) to Washington, August 27, 1935.
13 Records of the Department of State Relating to Internal Affairs of Greece, 1910–1929. SD 868.00/6817. Sterling (Sofia) to Washington, March 12, 1935.
14 SD 767.74/51. Gray (Geneva) to Washington, March 9, 1935. *Telegram*.
15 SD 867.4016.JEWS/2. Sherill (Istanbul) to Washington, September 20, 1932.
16 FO 371/17902/E 4915. Embassy (Angora) to London, July 27, 1934.
17 "İskân Kanununun Bazı Maddelerinin Değiştirilmesine ve İskân İşlerinin Sıhhat ve İçtimai Muavenet Vekâletine Devrine ve Ayrı Bütçe ile İdare Olunan Bir İskân Umum Müdürlüğü Teşkiline Dair Kanun Layihası" (Bill to Amend Some Articles of the Resettlement Law, Transfer the Responsibility on Resettlement Matters to the Ministry of Health and Social Solidarity, and Establish a General Directorate of Resettlement with an Independent Budget), TBMM Zabıt Ceridesi, term V, vol. 6: 78.
18 [Nihal] Atsız, "Komünist, Yahudi ve Dalkavuk" (The Communist, the Jew and the Sycophant) *Orhun*, 5 (March 21, 1934): 93.
19 [Nihal] Atsız, "Musa'nın Necip (!) Evlatları Bilsinler ki:," (The Noble (!) Sons of Moses Should Know That:) Orhun 7 (May 25, 1934): 140.
20 For good reviews of Atilhan's life and works, see by Rifat N. Bali, "Cevat Rıfat Atilhan I-II," *Tarih ve Toplum*, 175–76 (July–August 1998): 15–24, 21–30. For the same article in French, consult "Cevat Rıfat Atilhan," in *Les Relations entre Turcs et Juifs*, 75–106.
21 Shaw, *Turkey and the Holocaust*, 14.
22 "Yahudiler Kıpırdandı" (The Jews are Acting Up) *İnkılâp* 2, (May 1933), 4.
23 [Atilhan], Cevat Rıfat, "L'Antisémitisme!" *İnkılâp* 4, (July 1, 1933): 2.
24 "Alman Müesseseleri ve Yahudiler" (German Corporations and the Jews) *Milli İnkılâp* 1, (May 1934): 4–5.
25 *Milli İnkılâp* 1, (May 1934): 5.
26 Aktar, *Varlık Vergisi ve 'Türkleştirme' Politikaları*, 80–82, 89–99.
27 Levi, *Türkiye Cumhuriyeti'nde Yahudiler*, 111–12.
28 FO 371/17970/E 5155. Hugh (Constantinople) to London, August 10, 1934.
29 SD 867.4016.JEWS/10. Skinner (Istanbul) to Washington, July 8, 1934.
30 Levi, *Türkiye Cumhuriyeti'nde Yahudiler*, 15.
31 For a personal account on the Kırklareli events, written by a native Jew, describing both government aloofness toward the Exodus, as well as benevolent acts of individual government officials and Muslim Turks to protect the Jews, see Erol Haker, *Bir Zamanlar Kırklareli'nde Yahudiler Yaşardı* (Once Upon a Time, Jews Lived Used to Live in Kırklareli) (Istanbul: İletişim, 2002): 249–68.

32 SD 767.4016.JEWS/8. Skinner (Istanbul) to Washington, July 27, 1934. "*Turkish Government Sanctioned Thrace Pogroms Report Hints*," Article from "Jewish Telegraphic Agency," July 24, 1934.
33 FO 371/17969/E4916. Loraine (Constantinople) to Simon (London), July 27, 1934.
34 FO 371/17969/E4633. Loraine (Constantinople) to Simon (London), July 18, 1934.
35 "İskân Kanunu," Nr 2510, 1158.
36 SD 867.9111/422. Embassy (Istanbul) to Washington, October 1934. *Digest of Turkish News*, August 12–September 12, 1930.
37 SD 867.9111/419. Embassy (Istanbul) to Washington, July 28, 1934. *Digest of Turkish News*, June 17–July 17, 1934. *Report on "The Minorities" by Charles E. Allen.*
38 SD 867.9111/419. Embassy (Istanbul) to Washington, July 28, 1934. *Digest of Turkish News*, June 17–July 17, 1934. *Report on "The Minorities" by Charles E. Allen.*
39 SD 867.4016.JEWS/14. Shaw (Istanbul) to Washington, August 21, 1934.
40 SD 867.9111/419. Embassy (Istanbul) to Washington, July 28, 1934. *Digest of Turkish News*, June 17–July 17, 1934. *Report on "The Minorities" by Charles E. Allen.*
41 SD 867.4016.JEWS/10. Skinner (Istanbul) to Washington, July 8, 1934.
42 FO 371/17969/E5123. McPherson (Constantinople) to the Secretary of State (London), August 3, 1934.
43 SD 767.4016.JEWS/9. Skinner (Istanbul) to Washington, June 29, 1934.
44 SD 867.4016.JEWS/14. Shaw (Istanbul) to Washington, August 21, 1934.
45 FO 371/17969/E4633. Loraine (Constantinople) to Simon (London), July 18, 1934.
46 SD 867.20/48 McArdle (Sofia) to Washington, July 20, 1934.
47 SD 767.4016.JEWS/9. Skinner (Istanbul) to Washington, June 29, 1934.
48 FO 1011/174. Loraine (Constantinople) to Rendel (London), July 22, 1934.
49 Levi, *Türkiye Cumhuriyeti'nde Yahudiler*, 113–14, 116.
50 Levi, *Türkiye Cumhuriyeti'nde Yahudiler*, 116.
51 Levi, *Türkiye Cumhuriyeti'nde Yahudiler*, 114.
52 Levi, *Türkiye Cumhuriyeti'nde Yahudiler*, 115.
53 Levi, *Türkiye Cumhuriyeti'nde Yahudiler*, 120.
54 Shaw, *Turkey and the Holocaust*, 15–20.
55 Haluk Karabatak, "1934 Trakya Olayları ve Yahudiler" (The 1934 Thracian Incidents and the Jews) *Tarih ve Toplum* 146 (February 1996): 4–16.
56 Bali, *Cumhuriyet Yıllarında Türkiye Yahudileri*, 254.
57 Bali, *Cumhuriyet Yıllarında Türkiye Yahudileri*, 260–61.
58 Bali, *Cumhuriyet Yıllarında Türkiye Yahudileri*, 253–56.
59 Zafer Toprak, "1934 Trakya Olaylarında Hükümetin ve CHF'nin Sorumluluğu" (The Responsibility of the Government and the CHF in the 1934 Thracian Incidents) *Toplumsal Tarih* 34 (October 1996): 19–33.
60 Aktar, *Varlık Vergisi ve 'Türkleştirme' Politikaları*, 82–84.
61 Aktar, *Varlık Vergisi ve 'Türkleştirme' Politikaları*, 89–99.
62 Aktar, *Varlık Vergisi ve 'Türkleştirme' Politikaları*, 84–88.
63 *Cumhuriyet Halk Firkası Genel Katibliğinin Fırka Teşkilatına Umumi Tebligatı Temmuz 1934'den*, 37–38. Quoted and translated in Shaw, *Turkey and the Holocaust*, 18.
64 *Cumhuriyet Halk Firkası Genel Katibliğinin Fırka Teşkilatına Umumi Tebligatı Temmuz 1934'den*, 41. Quoted and translated in Shaw, *Turkey and the Holocaust*, 18.
65 *Cumhuriyet Halk Firkası Genel Katibliğinin Fırka Teşkilatına Umumi Tebligatı Temmuz 1934'den*, 41. Quoted and translated in Shaw, *Turkey and the Holocaust*, 19.
66 SD 867.9111/419. Embassy (Istanbul) to Washington, July 28, 1934. *Digest of Turkish News*, June 17–July 17, 1934. *Report on "The Minorities" by Charles E. Allen.*
67 Levi, *Türkiye Cumhuriyeti'nde Yahudiler*, 126.
68 *İstatistik Yıllığı: 1934–5 Cilt 7*, 159; and *İstatistik Yıllığı Cilt 10*, 65.
69 FO 371/17969/E5406. Loraine (Constantinople) to Simon (London), August 9, 1934.
70 SD 867.9111/420. Embassy (Istanbul) to Washington, August 25, 1934. Digest of Turkish News, July 15–August 11, 1934.

71 Bali, *Cumhuriyet Yıllarında Türkiye Yahudileri*, 262.

72 Bali, *Musa'nın Evlatları Cumhuriyet'in Yurttaşları*, 172.

73 Bali, *Musa'nın Evlatları Cumhuriyet'in Yurttaşları*, 265.

74 [Nihal] Atsız, "Yirminci Asırda Türk Meselesi II: Türk Irkı = Türk Milleti" (The Turkish Question in the Twentieth Century: Turkish Race = Turkish Nation) Orhun, 6 (July 16, 1934): 157.

75 Shaw, *Turkey and the Holocaust*, 15.

76 For a later edition of this work, see Cevat Rıfat Atilhan, *Yahudi Dünyayı Nasıl İstila Ediyor* (How the Jew Invades the World) (Istanbul: Aykurt, 1962).

77 Cevat Rıfat Atilhan, *Sina Cephesinde Yahudi Casuslar* (Jewish Spies on the Sinai Front) (Izmir: Meşher, 1933).

78 For a later edition of this, see Cevat Rıfat Atilhan, *İğneli Fıçı* (The Needled Barrel) (Istanbul: Kitsan, 1979).

79 For a later edition of this title, see Cevat Rıfat Atilhan, *see Suzi Liberman'ın Hatıra Defteri* (The Diary of Suzi Liberman) (Istanbul: Sinan Yayınları, 1995).

80 DV "1938 2630 no dan 15/9/938 tarihinden 3323 4/11/938 tarihine kadar," Correspondence Nr DV-EUM 1.G.A/66268. File Nr 3908. From Ankara to the Governor of Istanbul, December 28, 1938.

81 BCA 030.18.1.2/68.77.19. September 17, 1936.

82 For more on *Karikatür* and its anti-semitism, see Lauren Mallet, "*Karikatür Dergisinde Yahudilerle İlgili Karikatürler (1936–1948)* (Caricatures on Jews in the Journal *Karikatür* (1936–1948)) *Toplumsal Tarih* 34 (October 1996): 26–33.

83 Rıza Çavdarlı, *Tarihte Yahudiler ve Düşmanlık Sebepleri* (Jews in History and the Reasons for Animosity Toward Them) (Galata, Istanbul: Rizzo, 1939).

84 BCA 030.18.1.2/66.53.7. June 19, 1936.

85 BCA 030.18.1.2/85.111.12. January 6, 1939.

86 DV "CHP Dosyası 1936," Correspondence Nr DV-HKM 3/227. File Nr? From Ankara to the Secretary General of the CHP, September 30, 1936.

87 DV "Vılayetlere ve Umumi Müfettişliklere Yazılan Şifreler," Correspondence Nr DV-BGD. 6034/3/I/B. File Nr 3. From Ankara to the Governors of Istanbul, Izmir and Seyhan, January 2, 1939.

88 Shaw, *Turkey and the Holocaust*, 23.

89 SD 867.4016.JEWS/27. Murray (Istanbul) to Washington, August 6, 1938.

90 SD 867.4016.JEWS/29. Embassy (Istanbul) to Washington, August 27, 1938.

91 Shaw, *Turkey and the Holocaust*, 22.

92 Shaw, *Turkey and the Holocaust*, 23.

93 DV "1938 2630 no dan 15/9/938 tarihinden 3323 4/11/938 tarihine kadar," Correspondence Nr DV-EUM 1.G.2/49587. File Nr 2812. From Ankara to the Governor of Edirne, September 27, 1938.

94 DV "1938 2630 no dan 15/9/938 tarihinden 3323 4/11/938 tarihine kadar," Correspondence Nr DV-EUM 1.G.2/60950. File Nr 3635. From Ankara to the Governor of Bursa, December 1, 1938.

95 DV "1938 2630 no dan 15/9/938 tarihinden 3323 4/11/938 tarihine kadar," Correspondence Nr DV-EUM 1.G.2/10588. File Nr 3599. From Ankara to the Governor of Istanbul, November 29, 1938.

96 DV "Vılayetlere ve Umumi Müfettişliklere Yazılan Şifreler," Correspondence Nr DV-EUM. 4/05385. File Nr 214. From Ankara to the Inspectors-General and the Governors, January 28, 1939.

97 SD 867.4016/JEWS/16. Embassy (Istanbul) to Washington, November 16, 1933.

98 Fritz Neumark, *Zuflucht am Bosporus: Deutsche Gelehrte, Politiker und Künstler in Deutscher Emigration: 1933–1953* (Frankfurt am Main: Knecht, 1980), 23–27.

99 SD 867.4016/JEWS/15. Skinner (Istanbul) to Washington, November 16, 1834.

100 For more on these people, see Horst Widmann, *Atatürk Üniversite Reformu, passim*; Fritz Neumark, *Zuflucht am Bosporus, passim*; Shaw, *Turkey and the Holocaust*, 4–14. For short

biographies of the refugee Germans and Austrians, see Neumark, *Zuflucht am Bosporus*, 72–123; and Shaw, *Turkey and the Holocaust*: appendix 8, 353–369

101 SD 867.4016.JEWS/30. Newbegin (Istanbul) to Washington, February 20, 1939. *Memorandum of Conversation*, February 6, 1939.
102 TBMM Zabıt Ceridesi, term V, vol. 26, addenda 206: 1–3.
103 SD 867.4016.JEWS/25. Kelley (Istanbul) to Washington, January 13, 1938.
104 For the discussion minutes of this law, see TBMM Zabıt Ceridesi, term V, vol. 26: 3–10.
105 FO 371/21925/E376. Scrivener (Angora) to Eden (London), January 20, 1938. Letter from Scrivener, January 12, 1938.
106 FO 371/23290/E150. Loraine (Angora) to Halifax (London), December 31, 1938.
107 SD 867.4016.JEWS/26. Murray (Istanbul) to Washington, February 15, 1938.
108 SD 867.4016.JEWS/32. Murray (Istanbul) to Washington, March 15, 1939.
109 FO 1011/191. Baxter (London) to Loraine (Angora), November 7, 1938.
110 SD 867.4016.JEWS/32. Murray (Istanbul) to Washington, March 15, 1939.
111 FO 1011/193. Loraine (Istanbul) to Rothschild (London), July 16, 1938.
112 SD 867.4016.JEWS/27. Murray (Istanbul) to Washington, August 6, 1938; SD 867.4016.JEWS/32. Embassy (Istanbul) to the Washington, August 27, 1938.
113 *Cumhuriyet*, January 11, 1938. Quoted and translated in Shaw, *Turkey and the Holocaust*, 25.
114 Bali, *Musa'nın Evlatları Cumhuriyet'in Yurttaşları*, 322–26.
115 Shaw, *Turkey and the Holocaust*, 25.
116 FO 371/23290/E150. Loraine (Angora) to Halifax (London), December 31, 1938.
117 *Sabah*, January 27, 1939, and *Journal D'Orient*, January 29, 1939. Quoted and translated in Shaw, *Turkey and the Holocaust*, 26.
118 Bali, *Musa'nın Evlatları Cumhuriyet'in Yurttaşları*, 327.
119 *Sabah*, January 27, 1939, and *Journal D'Orient*, January 29, 1939. Quoted and translated in Shaw, *Turkey and the Holocaust*, 26.
120 SD 867.4016.JEWS/30. Newbegin (Istanbul) to Washington, February 20, 1939.
121 SD 867.4016.JEWS/30. Newbegin (Istanbul) to Washington, February 20, 1939.
122 FO 371/23290/E150. Loraine (Angora) to Halifax (London), December 31, 1938.
123 SD 867.4016.JEWS/29. Pool (Sephardic Refugee Committee) to Washington, January 27, 1939.
124 BCA 030.18.1.2/85.113.12. January 6, 1939.
125 BCA 030.18.1.2/85.113.11. January 6, 1939.
126 BCA 030.18.1.2/86.19.10. March 6, 1939.
127 BCA 030.18.1.2/86.19.7. March 6, 1939.

Conclusion: understanding Turkish nationalism in modern Turkey—the Kemalist legacy

1 Karabatak, "1934 Trakya Olaylarıve Yahudiler" *Tarih ve Toplum*: 5.
2 DV "1939 Vilayetlere ve Umumi Müfettişliklere Yazılan Şifereler 1/1/939 dan 31/3/939 1-654," Correspondence Nr DV-EUM 7/13563. File Nr 547. From Ankara to the First Inspectorate-General (Diyarbakır) and the Governors of Urfa and Gaziantep, March 16, 1939.
3 DV "Giden Şifreler 20/2/939 dan 3/6/939 a kadar," Correspondence Nr DV-HKM 2111. Telegram Nr 606. From the Governor of Hakkâri to Ankara, March 18, 1939.
4 DV "4/11/938 den 3324 dan 31/12/938 ve 3942," Correspondence Nr DV-EUM 1.G.8/65627. File Nr 3876. From the Ankara to the Inspectorate-General and the provinces, December 24, 1938.
5 FO 371/23290/E150. Loraine (Angora) to Halifax (London), December 31, 1938.
6 In my studies of High Kemalist works, I have come across two rare references to the destruction of Armenians: the first in a work on education and the second in an aforementioned history textbook. The first one writes: "Having been abused by the

European diplomats, this industrious [Armenian] nation behaved so poorly that while causing us great harm, it bid farewell to its existence in Anatolia and Thrace" Osman Ergin, *Türkiye Maarif Tarihi* (History of Turkish Education), vol. 2 (Istanbul: Osmanbey Matbaası, 1940), 663. The second work refers to "Armenians massacres" by the Committee of Union and Progress as a result of the Committee's violent action against the Armenians, *Tarih III Yeni ve Yakın Zamanlar*, 303.

7 DV "Çıkan Şifre 15/6/1933'den 31/7/33 Tarihine Kadar," Correspondence Nr DV-NUM 1/1343/678. File Nr 1/1496. From Ankara to the Governors of Kars and Çoruh, June 25, 1933.

8 Kemal Kirişçi, "Disaggregating Turkish Citizenship and Immigration Practices," *Middle Eastern Studies* 36(3) (July 2000): 1–2.

9 Rothschild, *East Central Europe Between the Two World Wars*, 289.

10 Hugh Poulton, *Balkanlar: Çatışan Azınlıklar, Çatışan Devletler* (Balkan Minorities and States in Conflict) (Istanbul: Sarmal, 1993), 220–27; and Mavrogordatos, *Stillborn Republic*, 242–46, 252–55, 264–65.

11 Mavrogordatos, *Stillborn* Republic, 241, 253–62, 265–68; Esther Benbassa and Aron Rodrigue, *Sephardi Jewry: A History of the Judeo-Spanish Community, 14th to 20th Centuries* (Berkeley, CA: University of California Press, 1999), 134–43, 161.

12 Paschalis M. Kitromilides, " 'Imagined Communities' and the Origins of the National Question in the Balkans," *European History Quarterly* 19(2): 157.

13 Karakasidou, *Fields of Wheat, Hills of Blood*, 218–37. Poulton, *Balkanlar*, 210–16, 228–31. Mavrogordatos, *Stillborn Republic*, 226–29, 242–65.

14 Mavrogordatos, *Stillborn Republic*, 228.

15 Andrew Rossos, "Macedonianism and Macedonian Nationalism on the Left," in eds Banac and Verdery, *National Character and National Ideology in Interwar Eastern Europe*, 233.

16 Mavrogordatos, *Stillborn Republic*, 249.

17 Mavrogordatos, *Stillborn Republic*, 227.

18 Mavrogordatos, *Stillborn Republic*, 229, 247, 254–55.

19 Mavrogordatos, *Stillborn Republic*, 226; Clogg, *A Concise History*, 105–06.

20 Poulton, *Balkanlar*, 214–19, 221–28, 229–31.

21 Even if the Kemalist notion of Turkishness is sturdy, the EU process may yet become the biggest likely recalibration of Turkish nationalism since the 1930s. Since 1999, significant reforms Turkey has carried out toward EU accession have started a debate on the relationship between Ankara, the non-Muslim communities and the Kurds. For more on this, see Soner Cagaptay, "Where Goes the U.S.–Turkish Relationship?" *Middle East Quarterly* XI, no. 4 (fall 2004): 44–45.

22 Yavuz, "Five Stages of the Construction of Kurdish Nationalism," *Nationalism and Ethnic Politics*; and Kemal Kirişçi and Gareth M. Winrow, *The Kurdish Question and Turkey: An Example of a Trans-State Ethnic Conflict* (London: Frank Cass, 1997).

23 For a first person account on this, see Bali, *Musa'nın Evlatları Cumhuriyet'in Yurttaşları*, 25–50. In his work, Bali describes the fluctuating fortunes of a Jewish family in Turkey from the 1930s until the present.

Bibliography

Archives

The following is a list of the sources and catalogue numbers of archival documents used in this research:

AA   Auswärtiges Amt—Germany

T-120 4900   Germany. Auswärtiges Amt. Records of the German Foreign Office received by the Department of State, 1920–45.

BCA   Başbakanlık Cumhuriyet Arşivi
(Prime Minister's Republican Archives)—Turkey

0.51	Diyanet İşleri (Directorate of Religious Affairs)
030.1	Başbakanlık Özel Kalem Müdürlüğü (Private Secretary of the Prime Minister's Office)
030.18.1.2	Bakanlar Kurulu (Cabinet of Ministers)
230	Bayındırlık Bakanlığı (Ministry of Public Works)
272	Toprak-İskan Genel Müdürlüğü (General Directorate of Land and Resettlement)
34	Istanbul Belediyesi (Municipality of Istanbul)
490.1	Cumhuriyet Halk Partisi (Republican People's Party)

DV   Dahiliye Vekâleti—İçişleri Bakanlığı
(Ministry of Interior)—Turkey

I used many individual files from the 1920s and the 1930s in this archive. However, since the documents at this depository were not catalogued, I developed my own system of reference, giving as much information about these documents as possible. (See examples in the notes.)

FO   Foreign Office—Great Britain

286   Foreign Office: Consulate and Legation, Greece (formerly Ottoman Empire), General Correspondence 1813–1969.

371 Great Britain. Foreign Office: Political Departments, General Correspondence from 1906. Turkey.
424 Foreign Office: Confidential Print Turkey.
434 Foreign Office: Confidential Print.
1011 Great Britain. Foreign Office: Loraine Papers.

SD State Department—United States of America

767 Records of the Department of State Relating to Political Relations Between Turkey and Other States, 1910–29.
867 Records of the Department of State Relating to the Internal Affairs of Turkey 1930–44.
868 Records of the Department of State Relating to Internal Affairs of Greece, 1910–29.
N 767 Records of the Department of State Relating to Political Relations of Turkey, Greece, and the Balkan States, 1930–39.

Books and articles

Abrahamian, Ervand. *Iran Between Two Revolutions*. Princeton, NJ: Princeton University Press, 1983.
Ağanoğlu, H. Yıldırım. *Göç: Osmanlı'dan Cumhuriyet'e Balkanlar'ın Makûs Talihi* (Migration, the Unhappy History of the Balkans from the Ottomans through the Republic). Istanbul: Kum Saati, 2001.
Ahmad, Feroz. *The Young Turks: The CUP in Turkish Politics, 1908–1914*. Oxford: Oxford University Press, 1969.
———. "Unionist Relations with the Greek, Armenian and Jewish Communities of the Ottoman Empire, Remembering the Minorities." *Middle Eastern Studies* 21(4) (1985): 416–17.
Akçam, Taner. *Türk Ulusal Kimliği ve Ermeni Sorunu* (Turkish National Identity and the Armenian Question). Istanbul: İletişim, 1992.
Aktar, Ayhan. "Nüfusun Homojenleştirilmesi ve Ekonominin Türkleştirilmesi Sürecinde Bir Aşama: Türk-Yunan Nüfus Mübadelesi, 1923–1924" (A Step Towards Homogenizing the Population and Turkifying the Economy: The Turco-Greek Population Exchange, 1923–1924). In *Varlık Vergisi ve "Türkleştirme" Politikaları* (The Wealth Tax and the "Turkification" Policies). Ed. Ayhan Aktar, 17–70. Istanbul: İletişim, 2000.
———. "Cumhuriyet'in İlk Yıllarında Uygulanan Türkleştirme Politikaları" (Turkification Policies during the Early Years of the Republic). *Tarih ve Toplum*, no. 156 (December 1996): 4–18.
———. "Economic Nationalism in Turkey. The Formative Years, 1912–1925." *Boğaziçi Journal of Economic and Administrative Sciences* 10(1–2) (1996): 263–90.
Alakom, Rohat. *Hoybûn Örgütü ve Ağrı Ayaklanması* (Hoybûn Organization and the Ağrı Uprising). Istanbul: Avesta, 1998.
Alexandris, Alexis. "The Greek Census of Anatolia and Thrace (1910–1912): A Contribution to Ottoman Historical Demography." In *Ottoman Greeks in the Age of Nationalism*. Eds Dimitri Goncidas and Charles Issawi. Princeton, NJ: Darwin Press, 1999.
———. *The Greek Minority of Istanbul and Greek-Turkish Relations 1918–1974*. Athens: Center for Asia Minor Studies, 1983.

Alkan, Mehmet Ö. "Resmi İdeolojinin Doğuşu ve Evrimi Üzerine Bir Deneme" (An Essay on the Birth and Development of the Official Ideology). In *Tanzimat ve Meşrutiyetin Birikimi* (The Legacy of the Tanzimat and the Constitutional Monarchy Era). Ed. Mehmet Ö. Alkan. Modern Türkiye'de Siyasi Düşünce, Vol. 1. (Political Thought in Modern Turkey), 377–408. Istanbul: İletişim, 2001.

"Alman Müesseseleri ve Yahudiler" (German Corporations and the Jews). *Milli İnkılâp* 1 (May 1934): 4–5.

Andrews, Peter Alford. "Tatars." In *Ethnic Groups in the Republic of Turkey*. Ed. and Comp. Peter Alford Andrews and Rüdiger Benninghaus, 442–53. Wiesbaden: Dr Ludwig Reichert Verlag, 1989.

Arai, Masami. *Turkish Nationalism in the Young Turk Era*. Leiden: Brill, 1992.

Arar, İsmail. "Atatürk'ün Günümüz Olaylarına Işık Tutan Bazı Konuşmaları" (Some Homilies by Atatürk that Shed Light on Our Era). *Belleten* 45–46(177) (1981): 23–24.

Arı, Kemal. *Büyük Mübadele: Türkiye'ye Zorunlu Göç (1923–1925)* (The Great Exchange: Forced Migration to Turkey (1923–1925)). Istanbul: Tarih Vakfı, 1995.

Arıkan, İsmail. *Mahallemizdeki Ermeniler* (The Armenians in Our Quarter). Istanbul: İletişim, 2001.

Asım, Necib. *Türk Tarihi* (Turkish History). Istanbul: Dar al-Matba'ah al-'Amirah, 1316 (1898 or 1899).

Atatürk'ün Söylev ve Demeçleri I–III (Atatürk's Speeches and Declarations I–III). Vol. 1. Ankara: Atatürk Araştırma Merkezi, 1997.

Atatürk'ün Tamim ve Telgrafları ve Beyannameleri (Atatürk's Circulars Telegrams and Declarations). Vol. IV. Ankara: Atatürk Araştırma Merkezi, 1991.

Atilhan, Cevat Rıfat. *İğneli Fıçı* (The Needled Barrel). Istanbul: Kitsan, 1979.

———. *Suzi Liberman'ın Hatıra Defteri* (The Diary of Suzi Liberman). Istanbul: Sinan Yayınları, 1995.

———. *Yahudi Dünyayı Nasıl İstila Ediyor* (How the Jew Invades the World). Istanbul: Aykurt, 1962.

———. *Sina Cephesinde Yahudi Casuslar* (Jewish Spies on the Sinai Front). Izmir: Meşher, 1933.

———. "L'Antisémitisme!" *İnkılâp* 4 (July 1, 1933): 2.

Atsız, [Nihal]. "Komünist, Yahudi ve Dalkavuk" (The Communist, the Jew and the Sycophant). *Orhun* 5 (March 21, 1934): 93.

———. "Musa'nın Necip (!) Evlatları Bilsinler ki:" (The Noble (!) Sons of Moses Should Know That:). *Orhun* 7 (May 25, 1934): 140.

———. "Yirminci Asırda Türk Meselesi II: Türk Irkı = Türk Milleti" (The Turkish Question in the Twentieth Century: Turkish Race = Turkish Race) *Orhun* 6 (July 16, 1934): 157.

Avtorkhanov, Abdurrahman. "The Chechens and Ingush during the Soviet Period and Its Antecedents." In *The North Caucasus Barrier: The Russian Advance Towards the Muslim World*. Ed. Marie Bennigsen Broxup, 146–94. London: Hurst & Company, 1992.

[Aydemir], Şevket Süreyya. "Beynelmilel Fikir Hareketleri arasında Türk Nasyonalizmi. III. Türk Nasyonalizmi" (Turkish Nationalism among International Ideological Movements. III. Turkish Nationalism). *Kadro* 20 (1933): 4–11.

———. "Beynelmilel Fikir Hareketleri arasında Türk Nasyonalizmi. IV. Türk Nasyonalizmi" (Turkish Nationalism among International Ideological Movements. IV. Turkish Nationalism). *Kadro* 21 (1933): 5–14.

———. "Fikir Hareketleri arasında Türk Nasyonalizmi. I. Faşizm" (Turkish Nationalism among Ideological Movements. I. Fascism). *Kadro* 18 (1933): 5–14.

[Aydemir], Şevket Süreyya. "Fikir Hareketleri arasında Türk Nasyonalizmi. II. Marksizm" (Turkish Nationalism among Ideological Movements. II. Marxism). *Kadro* 19 (1933): 6–16.

[Aydemir], Şevket Süreyya. "Derebeyi ve Dersim" (The Feudal Lord and Dersim). *Kadro* 6 (1932): 41.

Aydın, Suavi. "Türk Tarih Tezi ve Halkevleri" (The Turkish History Thesis and the People's Houses). *Kebikeç* 2(3) (1996): 107–30.

Aykut, Şeref. *Kamâlizm* (Kemalism). Istanbul: Muallim Ahmet Halit Kitap Evi, 1936.

Bali, Rifat N. "Cevat Rıfat Atilhan." In *Les Relations entre Turcs et Juifs dans la Turquie Moderne.* Ed. Rifat N. Bali, 75–106. Istanbul: Isis, 2001.

——. "La Politique Relative aux Minorités sous la République." In *Les Relations entre Turcs et Juifs dans la Turquie Moderne.* Ed. Rifat N. Bali. Istanbul: Isis, 2001.

——. *Musa'nın Evlatları Cumhuriyet'in Yurttaşları* (The Children of Moses, the Citizens of the Republic). Istanbul: İletişim, 2001.

——. *Cumhuriyet Yıllarında Türkiye Yahudileri: Bir Türkleştirme Serüveni (1923–1945)* (Turkish Jews under the Turkish Republic: An Episode of Turkification (1923–1945). Istanbul: İletişim, 1999.

——. "Cevat Rıfat Atilhan I–II" *Tarih ve Toplum*, 175–76 (July–August 1998): 15–24,21–30.

——. "1930 yılı Seçimleri ve Serbest Fırka'nın Azınlık Adayları" (The 1930 Elections and the Minority Candidates of the Free Party). *Tarih ve Toplum*, no. 167 (November 1997): 25–34.

——. Foreword to *Vatandaş Türkçe Konuş* (Citizen Speak Turkish), by Avram Galanti. Istanbul: Hüsn-i Tabiat Matbaası, 1928.

Banac, Ivo. "Bosnian Muslims: From Religious Community to Socialist Nationhood and Postcommunist Statehood, 1918–1992." In *The Muslims of Bosnia–Herzegovina: Their Historic Development from the Middle Ages to the Dissolution of Yugoslavia.* Ed. Mark Pinson, 129–53. Cambridge, MA: Harvard University Press, 1996.

——. *The National Question in Yugoslavia.* Ithaca, NY: Cornell University Press, 1994.

Banac, Ivo and Katherine, Verdery. *National Character and National Ideology in Interwar Eastern Europe* (New Haven, CT: Yale Center for International and Area Studies, 1995), xx.

Barbaro, Jean Elie. *La Question du Sandjak D'Alexandrette.* Alep: Imprimerie Rotos, 1941.

Barkan, Ömer Lütfi. "Osmanlı İmparatorluğunda Bir İskan ve Kolonizasyon Metodu Olarak Vakıflar ve Temlikler" (Vakifs and Conveyances as a Resettlement and Colonization Policy in the Ottoman Empire). *Vakıflar* 2 (1942).

Baykara, Barbaros. *Tunceli 1938.* Istanbul: Akyar, 1975.

[Baykurt], Cami. *Osmanlı Ülkesinde Hristiyan Türkler* (Christian Turks in the Ottoman Empire). Istanbul: s.n., 1922.

Bayrak, Mehmet. *Kürtler ve Ulusal-Demokratik Mücadeleleri* (The Kurds and their National-Democratic Struggles). Ankara: Özge Yayınları, 1993.

Bedir-Khan, Emir Kamuran. *La Question Kurde.* Paris: Vogue, 1959.

Belli, Mihri. *Türkiye-Yunanistan Nüfus Mübadelesine Ekonomik Açıdan Bir Bakış* (Turkey–Greece Population Exchange from the Economic Perspective). Istanbul: Belge, 2004.

Benbassa, Esther and Aron Rodrigue. *Sephardi Jewry: A History of the Judeo-Spanish Community, 14th to 20th Centuries.* Berkeley, CA: University of California Press, 1999.

Benlisoy, Yorgo and Elçin Macar. *Fener Patrikhanesi* (The Fener Patriarchate). Istanbul: Ayraç, 1996.

Benninghaus, Rüdiger. "The Laz: An Example of Multiple Identification." In *Ethnic Groups in the Republic of Turkey.* Ed. and Comp. Peter Alford Andrews and Rüdiger Benninghaus, 497–502. Wiesbaden: Dr. Ludwig Reichert Verlag, 1989.

Berkes, Niyazi. *The Development of Secularism in Turkey.* New York: Routledge, 1998.

Besalel, Yusuf. *Osmanlı ve Türk Yahudileri* (Ottoman and Turkish Jews). Istanbul: Gözlem, 1999.

Beşikçi İsmail. *Tunceli Kanunu (1935) ve Dersim Jenosidi* (The Tunceli Law (1935) and the Dersim Genocide). Istanbul: Belge, 1990.

——. *Cumhuriyet Halk Fırkası Tüzüğü (1927) ve Kürt Sorunu* (The Statute of the Republican People's Party (1927) and the Kurdish Question). Istanbul: Komal, 1978.

——. *Kürtlerin 'Mecburi İskan'ı* (The 'Forced Resettlement' of the Kurds). Istanbul: Komal, 1977.

Birinci Türk Dil Kurultayı (First Turkish Language Congress). Istanbul: Devlet Matbaası, 1933.

Birinci Türk Tarih Kongresi (First Turkish History Congress). Ankara: T. C. Maarif Vekaleti, 1933.

Bitterlin, Lucien. *Alexandrette: le "Munich" d'Orient ou quand la France capitulait* (Paris: Jean Piccolec, 1999), 343–52.

Bozkurt, Celal. *Cumhuriyet Halk Partisi Dünü, Bugünü, İdeolojisi* (Republican People's Party, Its Past, Present and Ideology). Ankara: s.n., 1967.

Bozkurt, Mahmut Esat. *Atatürk İhtilâli* (Ataturk's Revolution). Istanbul: Altın Kitaplar, 1967.

Brubaker, Roger. *Citizenship and Nationhood in France and Germany*. Cambridge, MA: Harvard University Press, 1992.

van Bruinessen, Martin. *Kurdish Ethno-Nationalism versus Nation-Building States*. Analectica Isisiana, XLVII. Istanbul: Isis, 2000.

——. *Origins and Development of Kurdish Nationalism in Turkey*. Typescript. Berlin: Berliner Institut für Vergleichende Sozialforschung, 1981.

——. *Agha Shaikh and State: On The Social and Political Organization of Kurdistan*. Typescript. 1978.

Cagaptay, Soner. "European Union Reforms Diminish the Role of the Turkish Military: Ankara Knocking on Brussels' Door," *Policywatch*, no. 781, The Washington Institute for Near East Policy, August 12, 2003.

——. "Where Goes the U.S.–Turkish Relationship?" *Middle East Quarterly* XI, no. 4 (fall 2004): 43–52.

Çanlı, Mehmet. "Yunanistanda'ki Türklerin Anadolu'ya Nakledilmesi" (The Transfer of the Turks in Greece to Anatolia). *Tarih ve Toplum* 130 (October 1994): 51–59.

Çavdarlı, Rıza. *Tarihte Yahudiler ve Düşmanlık Sebepleri* (Jews in History and the Reasons for Animosity Toward Them). Galata, Istanbul: Rizzo, 1939.

Çeçen, Anıl. *Atatürk'ün Kültür Kurumu Halkevleri* (A Cultural Institution of Atatürk: The People's Houses). Istanbul: Cumhuriyet Kitapları, 2000.

CHP Büyük Kurultayının Tetkikine Sunulan Program Taslağı (Draft Program Presented for Approval to the Fourth General Congress of the Republican People's Party). Ankara: May 9, 1935.

CHP Dördüncü Büyük Kurultayı Görüşmeleri Tutulgası (Records of Sessions of CHP's Fourth General Congress). Ankara: May 9–16, 1935.

CHP Dördüncü Büyük Kurultayı Tüzük ve Program Komisyonlarınca Onanan Program Taslağı (Draft Program Approved by the By-Laws and Program Commissions of Republican People's Party's Fourth General Congress). Ankara: May 12, 1935.

CHP Genel Sekreteri R. Pekerin Söylevleri (Speeches of R. Peker, Secretary General of the CHP). Ankara: s.n., 1933.

CHP 1939'da Halkevleri (CHP People's Houses in 1939). Ankara: Recep Ulusoğlu Basımevi, 1939.

CHP Halkevleri Öğreneği (The Regulations of the CHP People's Houses). Ankara: Ulus Basımevi, 1935.

CHP Tüzüğü. Partinin Dördüncü Büyük Kurultayı Onaylamıştır (Republican People's Party's By-laws. Approved by the Fourth General Congress of the Party). Ankara: Ulus Basımevi, 1935.

Clogg, Richard. *A Concise History of Greece*. Cambridge: Cambridge University Press, 1992.

Copeaux, Étienne. *Türk Tarih Tezinden Türk-İslam Sentezine* (From the Turkish History Thesis to the Turkish–Islamic Synthesis). Istanbul: Tarih Vakfı Yurt Yayınları, 1998.

——. *Espaces et Temps de la Nation Turque*. Paris: CNRS, 1997.

Crampton, R. J. *A Short History of Modern Bulgaria*. Cambridge: Cambridge University Press, 1987.

Cumhuriyet Halk Fırkası Genel Katibliğinin Fırka Teşkilatına Umumi Tebligatı Temmuz 1934'den Birincikânun 1934 sonuna kadar (General Announcements of the Secretary General of the Republican People's Party to the Party Organization from July 1934 until the end of December 1934). Mahremdir, Hizmete Mahsustur (Confidential and classified). Vol. 5. Ankara: Hakimiyeti Milliye, 1933. Quoted and translated in Shaw, Stanford J. *Turkey and the Holocaust: Turkey's Role in Rescuing Turkish and European Jewry from Nazi Persecution, 1933–1945*. London: Macmillan, 1993, 17–19, 25–27.

Cumhuriyet Halk Fırkası Katibiumumiliğinin Fırka Teşkilatına Umumi Tebligatı (General Announcements of the Secretary General of the Republican People's Party to the Party Organization). Mahremdir, Hizmete Mahsustur (Confidential and classified). Vol. 1. Ankara: Hakimiyeti Milliye, 1933.

Cumhuriyet Halk Fırkası Katibiumumiliğinin Fırka Teşkilatına Umumi Tebligatı Mayıs 1931'den Birincikanun 1932 Nihayetine Kadar (General Announcements of the General Secretariat of the CHF: From May 1931 until the end of December 1932). Vol. 1. Ankara: Hakimiyeti Milliye, 1933.

Cümhuriyet Halk Fırkası Nizamnamesi (Statute of Republican People's Party). Ankara: s.n., 1927.

Cümhuriyet Halk Fırkası Nizamnamesi ve Programı 1931 (By-Laws and Program of Republican People's Party 1931). Ankara: TBMM Matbaası, 1931.

Cumhuriyet Halk Partisi Üsnomal Büyük Kurultayının Zabıtları 26. XII. 1938 (Records of the Extraordinary General Congress of the CHP 26. XII. 1938). Ankara: Recep Ulusoğlu Basimevi, 1938.

Dadrian, Vahakn. *The History of the Armenian Genocide*. Providence: Berghahn Books, 1995.

Danişmend, İsmail Hakkı. *Türklerle Hind-Avrupalıların Menşe Birliği* (Common Origins of the Turks and the Indo-Europeans). Istanbul: Devlet Matbaası, 1935.

Demirel, Ahmet. *Birinci Mecliste Muhalefet: İkinci Grup* (Opposition in the First Assembly: The Second Group). Istanbul: İletişim, 1994.

Demirel, Yücel. "Mübadele Dosyası" (The Exchange Folder). *Tarih ve Toplum* 123–26 (March–June 1994): 54–58, 54–57, 49–52, and 56–59.

Deniker, Joseph. *Essai d'une Classification des Races Humaines*. Paris: Masson, 1889.

Deringil, Selim. "The Ottoman Origins of Kemalist Nationalism: Namık Kemal's and Mustafa Kemal." *European History Quarterly* 23(2) (1993): 165–91.

Dilaçar, Agop. *Alpin Irk, Türk Etnisi, ve Hatay Halkı* (The Alpine Race, Turkish Ethnie and the People of Hatay). Ankara: Türk Tarih Kurumu, 1939.

Dixon, Ronald Burrage. *The Racial History of Men*. New York: C. Scribner's Sons, 1923.

Dündar, Fuat. *İttihat ve Terakki'nin Müslümanları İskan Politikası* (CUP's Resettlement Policy of the Muslims). Istanbul: İletişim, 2001.

Emrence, Cem. "1930 Seçimlerinde CHP'nin Baskı ve Propoganda Yöntemleri" (Pressure and Propaganda Methods of the CHP in the 1930 Elections). *Tarih ve Toplum* no. 200, (August 2000).

Ergin, Osman. *Türkiye Maarif Tarihi* (History of Turkish Education). Vol. 2. Istanbul: Osmanbey Matbaası, 1940.

Ergün, Mustafa. *Atatürk Devri Türk Eğitimi* (Turkish Education Under Atatürk). Ankara: DTCF, 1982.

Ersanlı Behar, Büşra. *İktidar ve Tarih: Türkiye'de "Resmi Tarih" Tezinin Oluşumu, 1929–1937* (Hegemony and History: The Formation of the Official History Thesis in Turkey, 1929–1937). Istanbul: Afa, 1992.

Ezherli, İhsan. *Türkiye Büyük Millet Meclisi (1920–1992) ve Osmanlı Meclisi Mebusanı (1877–1920)* (Turkish Grand National Assembly (1920–1992) and the Ottoman House of Representatives (1877–1920)). TBMM Kültür Sanat ve Yayın Kurulu Yayınları, no. 54. Ankara: TBMM, 1992.

Fraser, Angus. *The Gypsies*. Oxford: Blackwell, 1992.

Galip, Reşit. "Türk Irkı ve Medeniyet Tarihine Umumi Bir Bakış" (An Overview of the Racial and Civilizational History of the Turks). In *Birinci Türk Tarih Kongresi* (First Turkish History Congress). Ankara: T.C. Maarif Vekaleti, 1933.

Gelber, N. M. "An Attempt to Internationalize Salonika." *Jewish Social Studies* 17 (1955): 105–20.

Gellner, Ernest. *Nations and Nationalism*. Ithaca, NY: Cornell University Press, 1983.

Gershoni, Israel and James P. Jankowski. *Redefining the Egyptian Nation, 1930–1945*. Cambridge: Cambridge University Press, 1995.

Ghassem Lou [Kassem Lou], Abdul Rahman. *Kurdistan and the Kurds*. Prague: Publication House of the Czechoslovak Academy of Sciences, 1965.

Gilquin, Michel. *D'Antioche au Hatay: l'histiore oubliée du Sandjak a'Alexandratte*. Paris: Harmattan, 2000.

Giritlioğlu, Fahir. *Türk Siyasi Tarihinde CHP'nin Mevki* (The CHP's Position in Turkish Political Past). Ankara: Ayyıldız, 1965.

de Gobineau, Arthur. *The Inequality of Human Races*. With preface by George L. Mosse. New York: H. Fertig, 1999.

Göç (The Exodus). Küçük Asya Araştırmalar Merkezi (Centre for Asia Minor Studies). Comp. Herkül Millas. (for the Turkish edition). Trans. Damla Demirözü. Istanbul: İletişim, 2001.

Gökalp Ziya. *The Principles of Turkism*. Ed. and Trans. Robert Devereux. Leiden: Brill, 1968.

———. "Refah mı, Saadet mi?" (Welfare or Happiness?). *Küçük Mecmua*. Quoted in Hilmi Ziya Ülken, *Türkiye'de Çağdaş Düşünce Tarihi* (The History of Contemporary Thought in Turkey), 585. Konya: Selçuk Yayınları, 1966.

———. *The Principles of Turkism*. Ed. and Trans. Niyazi Berkes. London: George Allen & Unwin, 1959.

———. *Türkçülüğün Esasları* (The Principles of Turkism). Istanbul: Türk Tarih Kurumu, 1952.

Göldaş, İsmail. *Takrir-i Sükûn Görüsmeleri: 1923 Seçimleri, Atama Meclis* (The Discussion Minutes of Takrir-i Sükun: 1923 Elections and the Appointed Parliament). Sultanahmet, Istanbul: Belge Yayınları, 1997.

Gologlu, Mahmut. *Tek Partili Cumhuriyet 1931–1938* (Single Party Republic 1931–1938). Ankara: Kalite, 1974.

von Gottard, Jäschke. "Die Türkisch-Orthodoxe Kirche." *Der Islam* 39 (1964): 96–129.

Güçlü, Yücel. "The Nyon Arrangement of 1937 and Turkey." *Middle Eastern Studies* 38(1) (January 2002): 53–70.

———. *The Sanjak of Alexandratta, a study in Turkish-French-Syrian Relations*. Ankara: Turkish Historical Society, 2001.

Guiladi, Barzilai. "Le Judaïsme muet" *Israel*, January 29, 1937 (Alexandria, Egypt). Quoted in Bali, Rıfat N. *Cumhuriyet Yıllarında Türkiye Yahudileri: Bir Türkleştirme Serüveni (1923–1945)* (Turkish Jews Under the Turkish Republic: An Episode of Turkification (1923–1945)), 289. Istanbul: İletişim, 1999.

Güler, Ali. "Son Osmanlı Hahambaşısı Hayim Nahum Efendi ile İlgili Bazı Arşiv Belgeleri Işığında Türk-Yahudi İlişkileri" (Turkish-Jewish Relations in the Light of Some Archival

Documents about Hayim Nahum Efendi, the Last Chief Rabbi of the Ottomans). In *Turkish-Jewish Encounters: Studies on Turkish-Jewish Relations through the Ages*. Ed. Mehmet Tütüncü. Haarlem, the Netherlands: SOTA, 2001.

Günaltay Şemsettin and Reşit Tankut. *Dil ve Tarih Tezlerimiz Üzerine Bazı İzahlar* (Some Reflections on Our Language and History Thesis). Istanbul: Devlet Basımevi, 1938.

Güney Doğu Birinci Genel Müfettişlik Bölgesi (The First Inspectorate's Region of the Southeast). Istanbul: Umumi Müfettişlik Teşkilatı, 1939.

Haddon, Alfred Cort. *The Races of Man and Their Distribution*. New York: Gordon Press, 1981.

Haker, Erol. *Bir Zamanlar Kırklareli'nde Yahudiler Yaşardı* (Once upon a Time, Jews used to live in Kırklareli). Istanbul: İletişim, 2002.

Halaçoğlu, Ahmet. *Hatay'ın Anavatana Katılmasında Dörtyol'un Yeri* (Dörtyol's Role in Hatay's Annexation to the Motherland). Ankara: Türk Tarih Kurumu, 1995.

Halkevleri, 1932–1935: 103 Halkevi Geçen Yıllarda Nasıl Çalıştı (People's Houses, 1932–1935: How did the 103 People's Houses work in the recent years). Ankara: 1935.

Hanioğlu, Şükrü. *The Young Turks in Opposition*. Oxford: Oxford University Press, 1994.

Hasretyan, M. A. *1925 Kürt Ayaklanması: (Şeyh Sait Hareketi)* (1925 Kurdish Uprising: [Şeyh Sait's Movement]). Uppsala: Jina Nû, 1985.

Haydaroğlu, İlknur Polat. *Osmanlı İmparatorluğu'nda Yabancı Okullar* (Foreign Schools in the Ottoman Empire). Ankara: Kültür Bakanlığı, 1990.

Heazell, F. N. *The Woes of a Distressed Nation: An account of the Assyrian People from 1914 to 1934*. London: The Faith Books, 1934.

Henze, Paul B. "Circassian Resistance to Russia" In *The North Caucasus Barrier: The Russian Advance Towards the Muslim World*. Ed. Marie Bennigsen Broxup, 62–111. London: Hurst & Company, 1992.

Heper, Metin. *İsmet İnönü, Yeni Bir Yorum Denemesi* (İsmet İnönü, an Attempt at a New Interpretation). Istanbul: Tarih Vakfı Yurt Yayınları, 1999.

Heyd, Uriel. *Language Reform in Turkey*. Jerusalem: Israel Oriental Society, 1954.

Hirsch, Ernst. *Dünya Üniversiteleri ve Türkiye'de Üniversitelerin Gelişmesi* (World Universities and the Development of Universities in Turkey). 2 vols. Istanbul: s.n., 1950.

Horowitz, Irving Louis. *Genocide, State Power and Mass Murder*. New Brunswick, NJ: Transaction Books, 1976.

Hovannisian, Richard G. *The Republic of Armenia*. Vol. 1. Berkeley, CA and Los Angeles, CA: University of California Press, 1971.

Hroch, Miroslav. *Social Preconditions of National Revival in Europe*. New York, NY: Columbia University Press, 2000.

Hükümet Programları 1920–1965 (Government Programs, 1920–1965). Comp. İsmail Arar. Istanbul: Burçak, 1968.

İğdemir, Uluğ. "Atatürk'ün Emriyle Hazırlanan Program" (A Program Prepared on Atatürk's Orders). *Belleten* 27 (1963): 644.

Imamović, Mustafa. *Historija Bošnjaka* (History of the Bosniaks). Sarajevo: Bošnjaka Zajednica Kulture Sarajevo, 1997.

İnan, Afet. *Medeni Bilgiler ve Atatürk'ün El Yazıları* (Civics and Atatürk's Manuscripts). Ankara: TTK, 1969.

—— and Enver Ziya Karal. *Atatürk'ün Tarih Tezi* (Atatürk's History Thesis). Ankara: Türk Tarih Kurumu, 1956.

[İnan], Afet. "Tarihten Evvel ve Tarih Fecrinde" (In Pre-historic Times and at the Dawn of History). In *Birinci Türk Tarih Kongresi* (First Turkish History Congress). Ankara: T.C. Maarif Vekaleti, 1933.

——. *Vatandaşlık İçin Medeni Bilgiler* (Civic Guidelines for Citizenship) (Istanbul: Devlet Matbaası, 1931), 16.

—— et al., *Türk Tarihinin Ana Hatları* (Main Themes of Turkish History). Türk Ocakları Türk Tarihi Tetkik Heyeti (Turkish Hearths' Committee for the Study of Turkish History). Istanbul: Devlet Matbaası, 1930.

İpek, Nedim. *Rumeli'den Anadolu'ya Türk Göçleri 1871–1890* (Turkish Migrations from Rumelia to Anatolia 1871–1890). Ankara: Türk Tarih Kurumu, 1994.

İskan Tarihçesi (A History of Resettlement). Istanbul: Hamit Matbaası, 1932.

İsmet İnönü Defterler 1919–1973 (İsmet İnönü Notebooks 1919–1973). Comp. Ahmet Demirel. Vol. 1. Istanbul: Yapı Kredi Yayınları, 2001.

Istorija Naroda Jugoslavije: početka XVI do kraja XVIII veka (History of the Yugoslav Peoples: From the Beginning of Sixteenth Century to the End of Eighteenth Century). Eds Bogo Grafenauer, Jorjo Tadič, and Branislav Čurčić. Vol. 2. Belgrade: Prosveta, 1960.

Jedlicki, Jerzy. "Polish Concepts of Native Culture." In *National Character and National Ideology in Interwar Eastern Europe*. Eds Ivo Banac and Katherine Verdery. New Haven, CT: Yale Center for International and Area Studies, 1995.

Johnson, Walter *et al.*, eds, *Turbulent Era, A Diplomatic Record of Fifty Years, 1904–1945*. Vol. 2. Boston, MA: Houghton Mifflin, 1952.

Karabatak, Haluk. "1934 Trakya Olayları ve Yahudiler" (The 1934 Thracian Incidents and the Jews). *Tarih ve Toplum* 146 (February 1996): 4–16.

Karabekir, Kâzım. *Kürt Meselesi* (The Kurdish Question). Ed. Prof. Dr Faruk Özerengin. Istanbul: Emre Yayınları, 1994.

Karakasidou, Anastasia N. *Fields of Wheat, Hills of Blood: Passages to Nationhood in Greek Macedonia, 1870–1990*. Chicago, IL: University of Chicago, 1997.

Karpat, Kemal H. "Ottomanism, Fatherland and the 'Turkishness' of the State." In *The Politicization of Islam: Reconstructing Identity, State, Faith, and Community in the Late Ottoman State*. Ed. Kemal H. Karpat. Oxford: Oxford University Press, 2001.

——. "Historical Continuity and Identity Change." In *Ottoman Past and Today's Turkey*. Ed. Kemal H. Karpat. Leiden: Brill, 2000.

——. "The Republican People's Party." In *Political Parties and Democracy in Turkey*. Eds Metin Heper and Jacob Landau. London: Tauris, 1991.

——. "The Hijra from Russia and the Balkans: The Process of Self-Determination in the Late Ottoman State." In *Muslim Travelers: Pilgrimage, Migration, and the Religious Imagination*. Eds Dale F. Eickelman and James Piscatore. London: Routledge, 1990.

——. *Türk Demokrasi Tarihi* (History of the Turkish Democracy). Istanbul: Afa Yayınları, 1996.

——. "Ethnicity Problem in a Multi-Ethnic Anational Islamic State: Continuity and Recasting in the Ottoman State." In *Ethnic Groups and the State*. Ed. Paul Brass, 95–114. London: Croom & Helm, 1985.

——. "Millets and Nationality: The Roots of Incongruity of Nation and State in the Post-Ottoman Era." In *Christians and Jews in the Ottoman Empire*. Eds Benjamin Braude and Bernard Lewis. New York: Holmes and Meier, 1982.

——. "An Inquiry into the Social Foundations of Nationalism in the Ottoman State: From Social Estates to Classes, From Millets to Nations." Research Monograph No. 39. Typescript. Princeton University, NJ: Center of International Studies, July 1973.

——. "Transformation of the Ottoman State: 1789–1908." *International Journal of Middle East Studies* 3 (1972).

Katardziev, Ivan. *Sto Godini od Formiranjeto na VMRO: sto godini revoluiconerna tradicija* (Hundred Years of VMRO's Formation: Hundred years of Revolutionaries). Skopje: Misla, 1993.

Kayalı, Hasan. *Arabs and the Young Turks: Ottomanism, Arabs, and Islamism in the Ottoman Empire, 1908–1918*. Berkeley, CA: University of California Press, 1997.

Kedourie, Elie. "Young Turks, Freemasons and Jews." *Middle Eastern Studies* 7(1) (January 1971): 89–104.

Kemal, Namık. *Vatan yahut Silistre* (The Homeland or Silistre). Ed. Kenan Akyüz. Ankara: Kültür ve Turizm Bakanlığı, 1988.

Kendal. "Kurdistan in Turkey." In *People Without a Country: The Kurds and Kurdistan*. Ed. Gerard Chaliand. Trans. Michael Pallis. London: Zed Press, 1980.

Kerem, Yitzchak. "Jewish-Turkish Relations in the Greek Peninsula during the Nineteenth and Early Twentieth Centuries." In *Turkish-Jewish Encounters: Studies on Turkish-Jewish Relations through the Ages*. Ed. Mehmet Tütüncü. Haarlem, the Netherlands: SOTA, 2001.

Kertzer, David I. and Dominique Arel. "Censuses, Identity Formation and the Struggle for Political Power." In *Census and Identity: The Politics of Race, Ethnicity, and Language in National Censuses*. Eds David I. Kertzer and Dominique Arel. Cambridge: Cambridge University Press, 2002.

Kevorkian, Raymond H. and Paul B. Paboudjian, Eds, *Les Arméniens*. Paris: Editions d'art et l'Histoire, 1992.

Khadduri, Majid. "The Alexandratta Dispute." *The American Journal of International Law* (1945): 406–25.

Khory, Philip K. *Syria and the French Mandate: The Politics of Arab nationalism 1920, 1945*. Princeton, NJ: Princeton University Press, 1987.

Kili, Suna and Şeref Gözübüyük, Eds, *Türk Anayasa Metinleri* (Texts of Turkish Constitutions). Second edn. Istanbul: Türkiye İş Bankası Yayınları, 2000.

Kirişçi, Kemal. "Disaggregating Turkish Citizenship and Immigration Practices." *Middle Eastern Studies* 36(3) (July 2000).

Kirişçi, Kemal and Gareth M. Winrow, *The Kurdish Question and Turkey: An Example of a Trans-State Ethnic Conflict*. London: Frank Cass, 1997.

Kitromilides, Paschalis M. " 'Imagined Communities' and the Origins of the National Question in the Balkans." *European History Quarterly* 19(2) (1989): 149–92.

——. and Alexis Alexandris. "Ethnic Survival and Forced Migration." *Deltio Kentrou Mikrasiatikuon Spoduon* 5 (1977): 9–44.

Kläy, Johannes. "Endstation 'Islambol'. Die Türkei als Assyland für muslimische Glaubensflüchtlinge und Rückwanderer *(muhacir)* im 19. und 20. Jahrhundert." In *Migrations en Asie: Migrants, Personnes Déplacées et Réfugiés*. Ed. Micheline Cetlivres-Demont. Berne: Société Suisse d'Ethnologie, 1983.

Koca, Hüseyin. *Yakın Tarihten Günümüze Hükümetlerin Doğu-Güneydoğu Anadolu Politikaları: Umumi Müfettişliklerinden Olağanüstü Hal Bölge Valiliğine* (The East-Southeast Policies of Our Governments from the Recent Times until Today: From the Inspectorates-General to the Extraordinary Regional Governor). Konya: Mikro Yayınları, 1998.

Kocatürk, Utkan. *Atatürk ve Türkiye Cumhuriyeti Tarihi Kronolojisi* (A Chronology of Atatürk and the Turkish Republic). Ankara: Türk Tarih Kurumu Basımevi, 1988.

Kofas, Jon V. *Authoritarianism in Greece*. East European Monographs, No. CXXXIII, Boulder, CO and New York: Columbia University Press, 1983.

Kohn, Hans. *Türk Milliyetçiliği* (Turkish Nationalism). Trans. Ali Çetinkaya. Istanbul: Hilmi Kitabevi, 1944.

Konstantinov, Yulian. "Strategies for Sustaining a Vulnerable Identity: The Case of the Bulgarian Pomaks." In *Muslim Identity and the Balkan State*. Eds Hugh Poulton and Suha Taji-Farouki, 33–53. New York: New York University Press, 1997.

Konuralp, Nuri Aydın. *Hatay'da Kurtuluş ve Kurtarış Mücadelesi Tarihi* (The History of Salvation and Liberation Struggle in Hatay). İskenderun: Hatay Postası, 1970.

Kuran, Ercümend. "The Impact of Nationalism on the Turkish Elite in the Nineteenth Century." In *Beginnings of Modernization in the Middle East*. Eds William R. Polk and Richard L. Chambers. Chicago, IL: University of Chicago, 1968.

Kushner, David. *The Rise of Turkish Nationalism*. London: Frank Cass, 1977.

Ladas, Stephan. *The Exchange of Minorities—Bulgaria, Greece and Turkey*. New York, NY: Macmillan, 1932.

Landau, Jacob M. *Tekinalp: Bir Türk Yurtseveri (1883–1961)* (Tekinalp: A Turkish Patriot (1883–1961)). Istanbul: İletişim, 1996.

——. *Pan-Turkism: From Irredentism to Cooperation*. Bloomington, IN: Indiana University Press, 1995.

Legendre, Pierre. "La Race Blanche et La Race Jaune." *Illustration* (June 27, 1924).

Lemercier–Quelguejay, Chantal. "Co-Optation of the Elites of Kabarda and Daghestan in the Sixteenth Century." In *The North Caucasus Barrier: The Russian Advance Towards the Muslim World*. Ed. Marie Bennigsen Broxup, 18–44. London: Hurst & Company, 1992.

Lewis, Bernard. "History Writing and National Revival in Turkey." *Middle Eastern Affairs* 4(6–7) (1953): 218–29.

Lewis, Geoffrey. *The Turkish Language Reform*. Oxford: Oxford University Press, 1999.

Livezeanu, Irina. *Cultural Politics in Greater Romania*. Ithaca, NY: Cornell University Press, 1995.

Lust-Okar, Ellen Marie. "Failure of Collaboration: Armenian Refugees in Syria." *Middle Eastern Studies* 32(1) (January 1996).

Macartney, Maxwell H. H. and Paul Cremona. *Italy's Foreign and Colonial Policy 1914–1937*. London: Oxford University Press, 1938.

McCarthy, Justin. *Death and Exile: The Ethnic Cleansing of the Ottoman Muslims, 1821–1922*. Princeton, NJ: Darwin Press, 1995.

——. "Muslim Refugees in Turkey: The Balkan Wars, World War I and the Turkish War of Independence." In *Humanist and Scholar: Essays in Honor of Andreas Tietze*. Eds Heath Lowry and Donald Quataert. Istanbul: Isis Press, 1993.

——. "Foundation of the Turkish Republic: Social and Economic Change." *Middle Eastern Studies* 19(2) (April 1983).

——. *The Arab World, Turkey and the Balkans (1878–1914): A Handbook of Historical Statistics*. Boston, MA: G. K. Hall, 1982.

Macfie, Alec L. *The End of the Ottoman Empire 1908–1923*. London: Longmont, 1998.

Mahmut Esat Bozkurt (1892–1943). Istanbul: Büke, 2000.

Makal, Ahmet. *Türkiye'de Tek Partili Dönemde Çalışma İlişkileri: 1920–1946* (Labor Relations in Turkey during the Single Party Era: 1920–1946). Ankara: İmge, 1999.

Malcolm, Noel. *Bosnia: A Short History*. New York, NY: New York University Press, 1996.

Mallet, Lauren. "*Karikatür Dergisinde Yahudilerle İlgili Karikatürler (1936–1948)* (Caricatures on Jews in the Journal *Karikatür* (1936–1948)). *Toplumsal Tarih* 34 (October 1996): 26–33.

Mango, Andrew. *Atatürk*. New York, NY: Overlook Press, 1999.

——. "Remembering the Minorities." *Middle Eastern Studies* 21(4) (October 1985): 118–40.

Mardin, Şerif. "The Ottoman Empire." In *After Empire*. Eds Mark von Hagen and Karen Barkey. Boulder, CO: University of Colorado, 1997.

——. *The Genesis of Young Ottoman Thought: A Study in the Modernization of Turkish Political Ideas*. Princeton, NJ: Princeton University Press, 1962.

Mark Pinson, "Ottoman Colonization of the Circassians in Rumili after the Crimean War." *Etudes Balkaniques* 8(3) (1972).

Mavrogordatos, George Th. *Stillborn Republic: Social Conditions and Party Strategies in Greece, 1922–1936.* Berkeley, CA: University of California Press, 1983.

"Megilat Oven" la meghilla di Buda (1986) trans. with a preface by Paolo Agostini, *Testimonianze sull'ebraismo*, 13 (Rome: Carucci, 1982).

Melson, Robert. *Revolution and Genocide.* Chicago, IL: University of Chicago Press, 1992.

Millman, Brock. *The Ill-Made Alliance: Anglo-Turkish Relations* (Montreal: McGill-Queen's University, 1998), 35–104.

Montandon, Georges. *La Race. Les Races. Mise au Point d'ethnologie Somatique.* Paris: Payot, 1933.

de Morgon, Jean-Marie Jacques. *L'Humanité Préhistorique.* Paris: Renaissance du Livre, 1924.

Motyl, Alexander. *Turn to the Right.* East European Monographs, No. LXV, Boulder, CO and New York: Columbia University Press, 1980.

Müftüoğlu, Mustafa. *Yakın Tarihimizden Bir Olay: Menemen Vak'ası* (An Episode from Our Recent History: The Menemen Incident). Fatih, Istanbul: Risale, 1991.

Muzaffer, Mediha. *İnkılâbın Ruhu* (The Spirit of the Revolution). Istanbul: Devlet Matbaası, 1933.

Nabi, Yaşar. *Mete.* Istanbul: Muallim Ahmet Halit Kütüphanesi, 1932.

Nalbandian, Louise. *The Armenian Revolutionary Movement.* Berkeley, CA: University of California Press, 1960.

Nayır, Yaşar Nabi. *Balkanlar ve Türklük* (The Balkans and Turkishness). Ankara: Ulus Basımevi, 1936.

Nouri Pasha, Général Ihsan. *La Revolte de L'Agri Dagh: "Ararat" (1927–1930).* Geneva: Éditions Kurde, 1985.

Öksüz, Hikmet. "Lozan Sonrasında Gökçeada (İmroz) ve Bozcaada'da Rumların Askere Alınması" (The Conscription of the Greeks on Gökçeada (İmroz) and Bozcaada in the post-Lausanne period). *Tarih Toplum* 34(200) (August 2000): 41–46.

Okyar, Osman and Mehmet Seyitdanlıoğlu, eds. *Fethi Okyar'ın Anıları* (The Memoirs of Fethi Okyar). Ankara: Türkiye İş Bankası Yayınları, 1999.

Olson, Robert. "The Kurdish Question and Turkey's Foreign Policy towards Syria, Iran, Russia, and Iraq since the Gulf War." In *The Kurdish Nationalist Movement in the 1990s.* Ed. Robert Olson. Lexington, KY: University Press of Kentucky, 1996.

——. *The Emergence of Kurdish Nationalism and the Sheikh Said Rebellion, 1880–1925.* Austin, TX: University of Texas Press, 1989.

Oran, Baskın. "Altı Ok Arasındaki İlişkiler ya da Milliyetçilik Ekseni Çevresinde Kemalizm" (The Relations Among the Six Arrows or Kemalism around the Axis of Nationalism). In *Uluslararası Atatürk Konferansı* (International Atatürk Conference). Vol. 3. Istanbul: Boğaziçi Üniversitesi, 1981.

Özbek, Batıray. "Tscherkessen in der Türkei." In *Ethnic Groups in the Republic of Turkey.* Ed. and Comp. Peter Alford Andrews and Rüdiger Benninghaus, 581–90. Wiesbaden: Dr. Ludwig Reichert Verlag, 1989.

Özbek, Sait Emin. *La Sümer Bank et l'industrialisation de la Turquie sous la République.* Lyon: Imprimerie du Salut Public, 1938.

Özbudun, Ergun. "Milli Mücadele ve Cumhuriyet'in Resmi Belgelerinde Yurttaşlık Sorunu" (The Question of Citizenship in the Main Documents of the National Liberation and Republic). In *75. Yılda Tebaadan Yurttaşa Doğru* (From Subject to Citizen in the 75th year), 63–70. Istanbul: Türk Tarih Vakfı, 1998.

Öztürkmen, Arzu. *Türkiye'de Folklor ve Milliyetçilik* (Folklore and Nationalism in Turkey). Istanbul: İletişim, 2001.

Parla, Taha. *Kemalist Tek-Parti İdeolojisi ve CHP'nin Altı Ok'u* (The Single Party Ideology of Kemalism and the Six Arrow of the CHP). Istanbul: İletişim, 1995.

Payne, Stanley G. *A History of Fascism 1914–1945*. Madison, WI: University of Wisconsin Press, 1995.

Peckham, Robert Shannon. "Frontier Fictions." In *National Histories, Natural States Nationalism and the Politics of Place in Greece*. Ed. Robert Shannan Peckham. London: I. B. Tauris, 2001.

[Peker], Recep. *CHF Katibiumumisi Recep Beyin bir İntihap Nutku* (An Election Speech by Recep [Peker], the Secretary General of the Republican People's Party). Ankara: Hakimiyeti Milliye Matbaası, 1933.

——. *CHF Programının İzahı* (Explanation of Republican People's Party's Program). Ankara: Ulus Matbaası, 1931.

Pentzopoulos, Dimitri. *The Balkan Exchange of Minorities and Its Impact on Greece*. Paris: Mouton, 1962.

Petropoulos, John A. "The Compulsory Exchange of Populations: Greek-Turkish Peacemaking, 1922–1930." *Byzantine and Modern Greek Studies* 2 (1976).

Pittard, Eugène. *Les Races et l'Histoire Introduction Ethnologique à l'Histoire*. Paris: Le Renaissance du Livre, 1924.

Polonsky, Antony. *The Little Dictators: The History of Eastern Europe since 1918*. London: Routledge, 1975.

Popović, Alexandre. *L'Islam Balkanique*. Berlin: In Komission bei Otto Harassowitz-Wiesbaden, 1986.

Poulton, Hugh. "Changing Notions of National Identity among Muslims in Thrace and Macedonia: Turks, Pomaks and Roma." In *Muslim Identity and the Balkan State*. Eds Hugh Poulton and Suha Taji-Farouki. New York: New York University Press, 1997.

——. *Who are the Macedonians*, London: Hurst and Company, 1995.

——. *Balkanlar: Çatışan Azınlıklar, Çatışan Devletler* (Balkan Minorities and States in Conflict). Istanbul: Sarmal, 1993.

Ripley, William Zebina. *Races of Europe, A Sociological Study*. New York: D. Appleton and Company, 1899.

Rodrigue, Aron. *French Jews, Turkish Jews: The Alliance Israélite Universelle and the Politics of Jewish Schooling in Turkey*. Bloomington, IN: Indiana University Press, 1990.

Rossos, Andrew. "Macedonianism and Macedonian Nationalism on the Left." In *National Character and National Ideology in Interwar Eastern Europe*. Eds Ivo Banac and Katherine Verdery. New Haven, CT: Yale Center for International and Area Studies, 1995.

Rothschild, Joseph, Ed. *East Central Europe Between the Two World Wars, A History of East Central Europe*. Vol. 9. Seattle, WA: University of Washington Press, 1998.

Rustow, Dankwart A. "The Army and the Founding of the Turkish Republic." *World Politics* 11(4) (July 1959).

Saim, Savaş. "Müslüman olan Macar-Leh Mültecileri Meselesi" (The Question of Islamicized Hungarian-Polish Refugees). *Toplumsal Tarih* 16(24) (December 1995).

Samardžić, Radovan. "Srbi u Turksom Čarstvu" (Serbs in the Turkish Empire). Vol. 4, part 1. *Istorija Srpskog Naroda* (History of the Serb Nation). Beograd: Srpska Književna Zadruga, 1981–1993.

Sarınay, Yusuf. *Türk Milliyetçiliğinin Tarihi Gelişimi ve Türk Ocakları 1912–1931* (The Historical Development of Turkish Nationalism and the Turkish Hearths 1912–1931). Istanbul: Ötüken, 1994.

Şaul, Mahir. "The Mother Tongue of the Polyglot: Cosmopolitanism and Nationalism among the Sepharadim of Istanbul." In *Turkish-Jewish Encounters: Studies on Turkish-Jewish Relations through the Ages*. Ed. Mehmet Tütüncü. Haarlem, the Netherlands: SOTA, 2001.

Schechla, Joseph. "Ideological Roots of Population Transfer." *Third World Quarterly* 14(2) (1993): 239–75.

Schulhof, Isaac. "Megilat Oven" (La meghilla di Buda [1686]). Trans. with a preface by Paolo Agostini. In *Testimonianze sull'ebraismo*, 13. Rome: Carucci, 1982.

Selçuk, Hamdi. *Hatay'ın O Günleri* (Those Days of Hatay). Istanbul: s.n., 1972.

Seton-Watson, Hugh. *Eastern Europe Between the Wars 1918–1941*. Hamden, CT: Archon Books, 1962.

Seyfettin, Ömer. *Kızılelma Neresi* (Where is Red Apple). Istanbul: Nurdoğan Matbaası, 1976.

Sezer, Ayten. *Atatürk Döneminde Yabancı Okullar (1923–1938)* (Foreign Schools Under Atatürk's Rule (1923–1938)). Ankara: Türk Tarih Kurumu, 1999.

Shambrook, Peter A. *French Imperialism in Syria*. London: Ithaca Press, 1998.

Shaw, Stanford J. *Turkey and the Holocaust: Turkey's Role in Rescuing Turkish and European Jewry from Nazi Persecution, 1933–1945*. London: Macmillan, 1993.

Simmons Jr, Thomas W. *Eastern Europe in the Postwar Years*. New York: St. Martin's Press, 1993.

Şimşir, Bilâl. *İngiliz Belgeleriyle Türkiye'de "Kürt Sorunu": (1924–1938) Şeyh Sait, Ağrı ve Dersim Ayaklanmaları* ("The Kurdish Question" in Turkey According to British Documents: (1924–1938) Şeyh Sait, Ağri and Dersim Uprisings). Ankara: TTK Basımevi, 1991.

Smith, Anthony. *Nations and Nationalism in the Global Era*. Cambridge: Polity Press, 1995.

——. *Ethnic Origins of Nations*. Oxford: Basil Blackwell, 1986.

Smith, Michael Llewellyn. *Ionian Vision*, London: Hurst & Company, 1998.

Sökmen, Tayfur. *Hatay'ın Kurtuluşu İçin Harcanan Çabalar* (Efforts for the Liberation of Hatay). Ankara: Türk Tarih Kurumu, 1978.

Somel, Akşin. "Cumhuriyet Demokrasi ve Kimlik" (The Republic Democracy and Identity). In *75. Yılda Tebaadan Yurttaşa Doğru* (From Subject to Citizen in the 75th Year). Istanbul: Türk Tarih Vakfı, 1998.

Sonyel, Salahi. "Turco-Jewish Relations," in *Turkish-Jewish Encounters: Studies on Turkish-Jewish Relations through the Ages*. Ed. Mehmet Tütüncü. Haarlem, the Netherlands: SOTA, 2001.

Soysal, İsmail. *150'likler* (The 150 (exiles)). Istanbul: Gür, 1985.

——. *Türkiye'nin Siyasi Antlaşmaları* (Political Treaties of Turkey). Ankara: Türk Tarih Kurumu, 1983.

Stafford, R. S. *The Tragedy of the Assyrians*. London: George Allen & Unwin, 1935.

Tachau, Frank. "The Search for National Identity Among the Turks." *Die Welt des Islams*, New Series 8, Part 2/3 (1972): 165–76.

Tankut, Hasan Reşit. *Nusayriler ve Nusayrilik Hakkında* (About the Nusayris and Nusayrism). Ankara: Ulus Basımevi, 1938.

Tekçe, İsmail Hakkı. *Muhafızı Atatürk'ü Anlatıyor: Emekli General İsmail Hakkı Tekçe'nin Anıları* (His Guard Tells About Atatürk: The Memoirs of Retired General İsmail Hakkı Tekçe). Istanbul: Kaynak, 2000.

Tekeli, İlhan. "Osmanlı İmparatorluğu'ndan Günümüze Nüfusun Zorunlu Yer Değiştirmesi." *Toplum ve Bilim*, 50 (1990): 49–55.

The North Caucasus Barrier: The Russian Advance Towards the Muslim World. Ed. Marie Bennigsen Broxup. London: Hurst & Company, 1992.

The Other Balkan Wars: A 1913 Carnegie Endowment Inquiry in Retrospect. With a new introduction and reflections by George F. Kennan. Washington, DC: Carnegie Endowment for International Peace, Brookings Institute Publications, 1993.

The Population of the Ottoman Empire and Turkey. Comp. Cem Behar, Historical Statistics Series, Vol. 2. Ankara: State Institute of Statistics, 1996, 51.

The Tatars of Crimea Return to the Homeland: Studies and Documents. Ed. Edward A. Allworth. Durham, NC: Duke University Press, 1998.

Todorova, Maria. "The Ottoman Legacy in the Balkans." In *Imperial Legacy*. Ed. Carl Brown. New York: Columbia University Press, 1996.

Toker, Yalçın. *Milliyetçiliğin Yasal Kaynakları* (The Legal Sources of Nationalism). Sirkeci, Istanbul: Toker Yayınları, 1979.

[Tökin], Hüsrev. "Şark Vilâyetlerinde Derebeylik I" (Feudalism in the Eastern Provinces I). *Kadro* 11: 22–29.

———. "Şark Vilâyetlerinde Derebeylik II" (Feudalism in the Eastern Provinces II). *Kadro* 12: 12–21.

Toprak, Zafer. "1934 Trakya Olaylarında Hükümetin ve CHF'nin Sorumluluğu" (The Responsibility of the Government and the CHF in the 1934 Thracian Incidents). *Toplumsal Tarih* 34 (October 1996): 19–33.

———. "Nationalism and Economics in the Young Turk Era." In *Industralisation, Communication et Rapports Sociaux*. Eds Jacques Thobie and Salgur Kançal. Varia Turcica XX. Paris: Harmottan, 1994.

Toumarkine, Alexandre. *Les Migrations des Musulmanes Balkaniques en Anatolie (1876–1913)*. Istanbul: Isis, 1995.

Toynbee, Arnold J. *The Western Question in Greece and Turkey*. London: Constable and Company, 1922.

Tunçay, Mete. *Türkiye Cumhuriyeti'nde Tek-Parti Yönetimin Kurulması* (The Establishment of Single Party Rule in Turkey). Istanbul: Tarih Vakfı, 1999.

Türk Tarihinin Ana Hatlarına Methal (Introduction to the Main Themes of Turkish History). Ed. Members of the Society for the Study of Turkish History. Istanbul: Devlet Matbaası, 1930.

Türkeş, Mustafa. *Kadro Hareketi* (The Kadro Movement). Ankara: İmge, 1999.

Üçok, Coşkun. "Atatürk ve Türkiye'nin % 99 Müslümanlaşıp Türkleşmesi" (Atatürk and the 99% Turkification and Islamicization of Turkey). In *Atatürk Haftası Armağanı* (Schriftfest for Atatürk Week). Ankara: Genelkurmay Basımevi, 1986.

"Ulusal Ökonomya Kurumlu Ökonomyadır" (National Economy is Institutionalized Economy). *Kadro* 35–36 (1934): 3–4.

Ünsal, Artun. "La Bibliothèque Politique Française D'Atatürk." In *La Turquie et la France a L'Époque d'Atatürk: publié à L'occasion du centenaire de la naissance de Kemal Ataturk*. Eds Irène Mélikoff, Jean-Louis Bacqué-Grammont and Paul Dumont. Collection Turcica 1. Paris: Association pour le Dévelopment Études Turques, 1981.

Üstel, Füsun. *Türk Ocakları (1912–1931)* (Turkish Hearths (1912–1931)). Istanbul: İletişim, 1997.

Üstün, Kemal. *Menemen Olayı ve Kubilay* (The Menemen Incident and Kubilay). Istanbul: Çağdaş, 1981.

Uyar, Hakkı. *Sol Milliyetçi Bir Türk Aydını: Mahmut Esat Bozkurt (1892–1943)* (A Leftist Nationalist Turkish Intellectual: Mahmut Esat Bozkurt (1892–1943)). Izmir: Büke, 2000.

———. "Türk Devrimini Teorileştirme Çabaları: Mahmut Esat Bozkurt Örneği-II" (Attempts to Theorize on the Kemalist Revolution: The Example of Mahmut Esat Bozkurt-II). *Tarih ve Toplum*, no. 120 (December 1993): 9–16.

———. "Türk Devrimini Teorileştirme Çabaları: Mahmut Esat Bozkurt Örneği-I" (Attempts to Theorize on the Kemalist Revolution: The Example of Mahmut Esat Bozkurt-I). *Tarih ve Toplum*, no. 119 (November 1993): 9–15.

Uz, Asım. *Gördüklerim Duyduklarım Duygularım* (Things I Saw, Things I Heard and How I Feel). Istanbul: Vakit Matbaası, 1964.

Vatikiotis, P. J. *Popular Autocracy in Greece 1936–41: A Political Biography of General Metaxas.* London: Frank Cass, 1998.

Volovici, Leon. *Nationalist Ideology and Antisemitism: The Case of Romanian Intellectuals in the 1930s.* Oxford: Pergamon Press, 1991.

Vryonis Jr, Speros. *The Decline of Medieval Hellenism in Asia Minor and the Process of Islamicization from the Eleventh through the Fifteenth Century.* Berkeley, CA: University of California Press, 1971.

——. "Byzantine Legacy and Ottoman Forms." *Dumbarton Oaks Papers* 23–24, (1969–70): 253–308.

Waterfield, Gordon. *Professional Diplomat: Sir Percy Loraine of Kirkharle Bt. 1880–1961.* London: John Murray, 1962.

Webster, Donald Everett. *The Turkey of Atatürk.* Philadelphia, PA: The American Academy of Political and Social Science, 1939.

Wigram, W. A. *The Assyrians and Their Neighbors.* London: G. Bell & Sons, 1929.

Yacoub, Joseph. *The Assyrian Question.* Second edn. Chicago, IL: Alpha Graphic, 1993.

"Yahudiler Kıpırdandı" (The Jews are Acting Up). *İnkılâp* 2, (May 1933): 4.

Yavuz, M. Hakan. "Five Stages of the Construction of Kurdish Nationalism in Turkey." *Nationalism and Ethnic Politics.* 7(3) (Autumn 2001): 1–24.

——. "The Patterns of Islamic Identity: Dynamics of National and Transnational Loyalties and Identities." *Central Asian Survey* 14(3) (1995): 360.

——. "Islam and Nationalism: Yusuf Akçura, Üç Tarz-i Siyaset." *Oxford Journal of Islamic Studies* 4(2) (1993): 175–207.

Yazman, Aslan Tufan, ed. *Eti Bank, 1935–1945.* Ankara: s.n., 1945.

Yerasimos, Stéphane. "Le Sanjak D'Alexandrette: Formation et Integration d'un Territoire." *La Revue du Monde Musulman et de la Méditerranée,* no. 27 (1988).

Yeşilkaya, Neşe G. *Halkevleri: İdeoloji ve Mimarlık* (The People's Houses: Ideology and Architecture). Istanbul: İletişim, 1999.

Yiannakopoulos, Georgios A. "The Reconstruction of Destroyed Picture: The Oral History Archive of the Center for Asia Minor Studies." *Mediterranean Historical Review* 8(2) (December 1993): 201–17.

Yıldız, Ahmet. *Ne Mutlu Türküm Diyebilene* (How Happy He, Who Can Say He is a Turk). Istanbul: İletişim, 2001.

Yonan, Gabriele. *Ein Vergessener Holocaust: Die Vernichtung der Christlichen Assyrer in der Türkei.* Göttingen: Gesellschaft für Bedrohte Völker, 1989.

Zürcher, Erik Jan. "Young Turks, Ottoman Muslims and Turkish Nationalists." In *Modern Turkey and Ottoman Past.* Ed. Kemal Karpat. Leiden: Brill, 2000.

——. *Turkey: A Modern History.* London: I. B. Tauris, 1998.

——. *Political Opposition in the Early Turkish Republic: The Progressive Republican Party 1924–5.* Leiden: Brill, 1991.

——. "Atatürk and the Start of National Resistance Movement." *Anatolica* 7 (1979–80).

Textbooks

[Bozkurt], Mahmut Esat, Recep [Peker], and Yusuf Kemal [Tengirşenk]. *1933 Yılında Istanbul Ünıversitesinde Başlayan İlk İnkılâp Tarihi Ders Notları* (Lecture Notes of the First Course on Revolution at Istanbul University in 1933). Comp. Oktay Aslanapa. Istanbul: Türk Dünyası Araştırmaları Vakfı, 1997.

Peker, Recep. *İnkılâb Tarihi Dersleri* (Lessons on the History of Revolution). Ankara: Ulus Basımevi, 1936.

———. *İnkılâb Dersleri Notları* (Notes for Classes on Revolution). First edn. Ankara: Ulus Matbaası, 1935.

———. *Deux Discours de Recep Peker, Secrétaire Général du Parti Républicain de Peuple*. Ankara: s.n., 1935.

Tarih İlkmektep Kitapları IV. Sınıf (History Primary Schoolbooks: Fourth Grade). Istanbul: Maarif Vekâleti, 1933.

Tarih İlkmektepler İçin V (History for Grade Schools: Fifth Grade). Ankara: Maarif Vekâleti, 1933.

Manuscripts, unpublished papers, PhD dissertations

Aslan, Senem. " 'Citizen Speak Turkish' The Emergence of Turkish National Identity" Unpublished paper.

Cagaptay, Soner. *Crafting the Turkish Nation*, PhD disseration, Yale University, 2003.

[İnan, Afet]. *Türkiye Halkının Antropolojik Karakteri ve Türkiye Tarihi: Türk Irkının Vatanı Anadolu 64,000 kişi üzerinde Anket* (The Anthropological Character of the People of Turkey and Turkish History: Anatolia, the Homeland of the Turkish Race and a Survey Conducted on 64,000 People). PhD dissertation. University of Geneva, 1937. Also present at Ankara: Türk Tarih Kurumu, 1947.

Johnson, Hugh Grayson. *The American Schools in the Republic of Turkey 1923–1933: A Case Study of Missionary Problems International Relations*. PhD dissertation. The American University, 1975.

Keyder, Çağlar. "Consequences of the Exchange of Populations for Turkey." Unpublished article.

Köksal, Yonca. "Transformation of a Central State: Provincial Administration in the Ottoman Empire, Tanzimat Reform Period (1839–1878)." PhD dissertation in progress. Columbia University, 2001.

Oran, Baskın. "Lausanne İhlalleri: Türkiye ile Yunanistan Açısından Karşılaştırmalı Bir İnceleme" (The Lausanne Violations: A Comparative Study of Turkey and Greece). Unpublished report. 1999.

Yacoub, Joseph. *La Question Assyro-Chaldéenne: Les Puissance Europennes et la Société des Nations (1908–1936)*, PhD dissertation. 4 vols, University of Lyon, 1984.

Government reports and statistics

Başvekâlet Toprak ve İskân İşleri Genel Müdürlüğü Çalışmaları (Activities of the Prime Minister's Office of General Directorate of Land and Resettlement). Ankara: s.n, 1952.

"Cumhuriyet Halk Partisi Kuruluş ve Yürüyüşü" (The Establishment and Development of the Republican People's Party). Typescript. 1939? In BCA 490.01/63.242.6.

"Halkevleri" (The People's Houses). Typescript. 1938? In BCA 490.01/63.242.6.

İstatistik Yıllığı Cilt 10 (Statistics Yearbook, Vol. 10). Başbakanlık İstatistik Umum Müdürlüğü. Ankara: Hüsnütabiat, 1938–39.

İstatistik Yıllığı Üçüncü Cilt (Statistics Yearbook: Vol. 3). Türkiye Cumhuriyeti Basvekâlet İstatistik Umum Müdürlüğü. Istanbul: Ahmet İhsan Matbaası, 1930.

İstatistik Yıllığı: 1934–5 Cilt 7 (Statistics Yearbook: 1934–5, Vol. 7). Ankara: Başbakanlık İstatistik G.D, 1934–35.

İstatistik Yıllığı: Cilt 11 (Statistics Yearbook: Vol. 11). Başbakanlık İstatistik Umum Müdürlüğü. Istanbul: Hüsnütabiat Basımevi, 1940.

İstatistik Yıllığı: İkinci Cilt 1929 (Statistics Yearbook: Vol. 2, 1929). TC Basvekâlet İstatistik Umum Müd. Istanbul: Cumhuriyet Matbaası, 1929.

Öztürk, Saygı. "21 Ağustos 1935, İsmet Paşa'nın Kürt Raporu" (The Kurdish Report of İsmet Paşa, August 21, 1935). *Hürriyet*, September 7, 1992. Quoted in Koca, Hüseyin. *Yakın Tarihten Günümüze Hükümetlerin Doğu-Güneydoğu Anadolu Politikaları: Umumi Müfettişliklerinden Olağanüstü Hal Bölge Valiliğine* (The East-Southeast Policies of Our Governments from the Recent Times until Today: From the Inspectorates-General to the Extraordinary Regional Governor). Konya: Mikro Yayınları, 1998, 426–39.

"Şark Islahat Raporu" (Report for Reform in the East). Quoted in Bayrak, Mehmet. *Kürtler ve Ulusal-Demokratik Mücadeleleri* (The Kurds and their National-Democratic Struggles). Ankara: Özge Yayınları, 1993, 452–67.

Sökmen Süer, Şükrü. *Umumi Müfettişler Konferansı'nda Görüşülen ve Dahiliye Vekâleti'ni İlgilendiren İşlere Dair Toplantı Zabıtları ile Rapor ve Hülâsası 1936* (1936 Report, Summary, and Minutes about the Matters of Relevance to the Ministry of Interior Reviewed at the Conference of the Inspectorates-General). Ankara: Başvekâlet Matbaası, 1936, 22. Quoted in Koca, Hüseyin. *Yakın Tarihten Günümüze Hükümetlerin Doğu-Güneydoğu Anadolu Politikaları: Umumi Müfettişliklerinden Olağanüstü Hal Bölge Valiliğine* (The East-Southeast Policies of our Governments from the Recent Times until Today: From the Inspectorates-General to the Extraordinary Regional Governor). Konya: Mikro Yayınları, 1998, 447–52.

The Other Balkan Wars: A 1913 Carnegie Endowment inquiry in retrospect, with a new introduction and reflections by George F. Kennan (Washington, DC: Carnegie Endownment for International Peace: Brookings Institute Publications, 1993).

International treaties and agreements

Akdenizde Korsanlık Ef'aline Karşı İttihaz Edilecek Müşterek Tedbirler Hakkindaki Nyon Anlaşmasının ve Zeylinin Tastikine dair Kanun (Law for the Approval of the Nyon Treaty and its Supplement on Joint Measures to be Taken Against Acts of Piracy in the Mediterranean). Ankara: Başvekâlet Neşriyat ve Müdeverrat Dairesi, 1937.

"Arrangement Portant Règlement Definitive des Questions Territoriales entre la Turquie et la Syrie." Quoted in Barbaro, Jean Elie. *La Question du Sandjak D'Alexandrette.* Alep: Imprimerie Rotos, 1941, 94–102.

LCTS (Treaty Series 16—Treaty of Lausanne, Cmd). 1929. Quoted in Alexis Alexandris, "Imbros and Tenedos: A Study of Turkish Attitudes Toward Two Ethnic Greek Island Communities Since 1923." *Journal of the Hellenic Diaspora* 7(1) (Spring 1980): 5–31.

League of Nations Publications, General 1938. 1–6. "Question of Alexandratta. Final Regulations for the First Elections in the Sanjak of Alexandratta." (s.n: s.n.,1938).

"Traité D'Amitié Et D'Alliance Entre La France Et La Syrie." Quoted in Bitterlin, Lucien. *Alexandrette: le "Munich" d'Orient ou quand la France capitulait.* Paris: Jean Piccolec, 1999, 343–52.

"Traite De Garantie De L'Integrite Territoriale Du Sanjak." Quoted in Gilquin, Michel. *D'Antioche au Hatay: l'histiore oubliée du Sandjak a'Alexandratte.* Paris: Harmattan, 2000, 195–200.

"Türkiye ile Romanya Arasında Münakid Dobrucadaki Türk Ahalinin Muhaceretini Tanzim Eden Mukavelenamenin Tasdiki Hakkındaki Kanun" (Law to Ratify the Treaty Cosigned by Turkey and Romania to Regulate the Emigration of the Turkish Population in the Dobrudja). Nr 3102, January 25, 1937. In *Düstur* (Code of Laws). Third set. Vol. 18. Ankara: Türkiye Büyük Millet Meclisi: 252–70.

Laws, regulations, statues, codices, and parliamentary records

"Antalya Mebusu Ahmet Saki Bey ve Rüfekasının Umum Memurin Kanunu Unvanlı (2/376) numaralı Teklifi Kanunisi ile (1/815) Numaralı Memurin Kanunu" (Bill [Nr 2/376] by MP Ahmet Saki Bey [Antalya] and his colleagues on the General Government Employee Law and the Government Employee Law [Nr 1/815]). March 15, 1926. TBMM Zabıt Ceridesi, (Journal of Proceedings of the Turkish Grand National Assembly [TGNA]). Term II. Vol. 23. Ankara: Türkiye Büyük Millet Meclisi, 1983, 18–57, 178–90.

"Bazı Eşhasın Şark Menatıkından Garp Vilayetlerine Nakillerine Dair Kanun" (Law on the Transfer of Certain People from Eastern Regions to the Western Provinces). Nr 1097. July 17, 1927. In *Eski ve Yeni Toprak, İskân Hükümleri Uygulaması Kılavuzu* (Guide to the Application of Old and New Land and Resettlement Decisions). Ed. Naci Kökdemir, 28–30. Ankara: 1952.

"Bazı Kisvelerin Geyilmeyeceğine dair Kanun" (Law Stipulating that Certain Garbs May Not Be Worn). December 3, 1934. TBMM Zabıt Ceridesi (Journal of Proceedings of the Turkish Grand National Assembly [TGNA]). Term IV. Vol. 25, addenda. Ankara: Türkiye Büyük Millet Meclisi, 1983, 1–3, 22.

"Birinci İskân Mıntıkalarında Toprak Tevziatına dair olan Talimatnamenin Kabulü hakkında Kararname" (Decree Concerning the Adoption of the Executive Act on Land Distribution in the First Resettlement Zones). Nr 2/12374. November 24, 1939. In *Eski ve Yeni Toprak, İskân Hükümleri Uygulaması Kılavuzu* (Guide to the Application of Old and New Land and Resettlement Decisions). Ed. Naci Kökdemir, 166–70. Ankara: 1952.

Düstur (Code of Laws) (Hereafter *Düstur*). Third set. Vol. 12. Ankara: Türkiye Büyük Millet Meclisi.

Düstur. Third set. Vol. 15, addenda. Ankara: Türkiye Büyük Millet Meclisi.

Düstur. Third set. Vol. 7. Ankara: Türkiye Büyük Millet Meclisi.

Düstur. Third set. Vol. 8. Ankara: Türkiye Büyük Millet Meclisi.

Düstur. Third set. Vol. 9. Ankara: Türkiye Büyük Millet Meclisi.

Düstur. Third set. Vol. 13. Ankara: Türkiye Büyük Millet Meclisi.

Düstur. Third set. Vol. 14. Ankara: Türkiye Büyük Millet Meclisi.

Düstur. Third set. Vol. 15, addenda. Ankara: Türkiye Büyük Millet Meclisi.

Düstur. Third set. Vol. 16. Ankara: Türkiye Büyük Millet Meclisi.

Düstur. Third set. Vol. 18. Ankara: Türkiye Büyük Millet Meclisi.

Düstur. Third set. Vol. 19. Ankara: Türkiye Büyük Millet Meclisi.

Düstur. Third set. Vol. 20. Ankara: Türkiye Büyük Millet Meclisi.

"Ermeni Suikast Komiteleri tarafından Şehit Edilen veya Bu Uğurda Suveri Muhtelife ile Düçarı Gadrolan Ricalin Ailelerine Verilecek Emlâk ve Arazi hakkında Kanun" (Law about Immovable Property and Land to be Given to the Families of Those Dignitaries, Who Were Martyred by Armenian Assassination Committees or were Wrongfully Treated by Various Means Regarding This Matter). Nr 882. May 31, 1926. *Düstur* (Code of Laws). Third set. Vol. 7. Ankara: Türkiye Büyük Millet Meclisi: 1439.

"İskân Kanunu Muvakkat Encümen Mazbatası" (Official Report by the Temporary Commission for the Law of Resettlement). TBMM Zabıt Ceridesi (Journal of Proceedings of the Turkish Grand National Assembly (TGNA). Term IV. Vol. 23, addenda. Ankara: Türkiye Büyük Millet Meclisi, 1983: 6.

"İskân Kanunu" (Resettlement Law). Nr 2510. June 13, 1934. *Düstur* (Code of Laws). Third set. Vol. 15, addenda. Ankara: Türkiye Büyük Millet Meclisi: 1156–75.

"İskân Kanunu" (Resettlement Law). Nr 885. May 31, 1926. *Düstur* (Code of Laws). Third set. Vol. 7. Ankara: Türkiye Büyük Millet Meclisi: 1441.

"İskân Kanununun 12. Maddesini Kısmen Değiştiren ve 17. ve 23. Maddelerine Birer Fıkra Ekleyen Kanun" (Law Adding Additional Paragraph to Articles 17 and 23 and Partially Amending Article 12 of the Resettlement Law). Nr 3667. July 5, 1939. *Düstur* (Code of Laws). Third set. Vol. 20. Ankara: Türkiye Büyük Millet Meclisi: 1556.

"İskân Kanununun Bazı Maddelerinin Değiştirilmesine ve İskân İşlerinin Sıhhat ve İçtimai Muavenet Vekâletine Devrine ve Ayrı Bütçe ile İdare Olunan Bir İskân Umum Müdürlüğü Teşkiline Dair Kanun Layihası" (Bill to Amend some Articles of Resettlement Law, Transfer the Responsibility on Resettlement Matters to the Ministry of Health and Social Solidarity, and Establish a General Directorate of Resettlement with an Independent Budget). TBMM Zabıt Ceridesi (Journal of Proceedings of the Turkish Grand National Assembly [TGNA]). Term V. Vol. 6. Ankara: Türkiye Büyük Millet Meclisi, 1983: 78.

"İskân Muafiyetleri Nizamnamesi" (Statute on Exemptions from Resettlement). Nr 2/1777. October 27, 1934. *Düstur* (Code of Laws). Third set. Vol. 16. Ankara: Türkiye Büyük Millet Meclisi: 523.

"İskân ve Nüfus İşlerinin Süratle İkmali Hakkında Tamim" (Circular on the Speedy Disposal of Resettlement and Population Matters). Nr 15035/6599. August 7, 1934. In *Eski ve Yeni Toprak, İskân Hükümleri Uygulaması Kılavuzu* (Guide to the Application of Old and New Land and Resettlement Decisions). Ed. Naci Kökdemir, 235–36. Ankara: 1952.

"Matbuat Kanunu" (The Press Law). Nr 1881. July 25, 1931. *Düstur* (Code of Laws). Third set. Vol. 12. Ankara: Türkiye Büyük Millet Meclisi: 369, 366–380.

"Soy Adı Kanunu" (Law on Last Names). Nr 2525. June 21, 1934. *Düstur* (Code of Laws). Third set. Vol. 15, addenda. Ankara: Türkiye Büyük Millet Meclis: 1282–83.

"Soy Adı Nizamnamesi" (Statue on Last Names). *Resmi Gazete*. Nr 2805. December 20, 1934.

"Tababet ve Şuabatı San'atlarının Tarzı İcrasına dair Kanun" (Law on the Execution Methods of Medicinal Science and its Branches). Nr 1214. April 11, 1928. *Kanunlar* (The Laws). February 1994. addenda 19. Ankara: Türkiye Büyük Millet Meclisi: 887–98; and TBMM Zabıt Ceridesi (Journal of Proceedings of the Turkish Grand National Assembly [TGNA]). Term III. Vol. 3. Ankara: Türkiye Büyük Millet Meclisi, 1983: 1–20, 63–77, 99, 101.

TBMM Zabıt Ceridesi (Journal of Proceedings of the Turkish Grand National Assembly [TGNA]) (Hereafter TBMM Zabıt Ceridesi). Term I. Vol. 9. Ankara: Türkiye Büyük Millet Meclisi, 1983.

TBMM Zabıt Ceridesi. Term II. Vol. 2. Ankara: Türkiye Büyük Millet Meclisi, 1983.

TBMM Zabıt Ceridesi. Term II. Vol. 5. Ankara: Türkiye Büyük Millet Meclisi, 1983.

TBMM Zabıt Ceridesi. Term II. Vol. 8/1. Ankara: Türkiye Büyük Millet Meclisi, 1983.

TBMM Zabıt Ceridesi. Term II. Vol. 22. Ankara: Türkiye Büyük Millet Meclisi, 1983.

TBMM Zabıt Ceridesi. Term II. Vol. 23. Ankara: Türkiye Büyük Millet Meclisi, 1983.

TBMM Zabıt Ceridesi. Term II. Vol. 25. Ankara: Türkiye Büyük Millet Meclisi, 1983.

TBMM Zabıt Ceridesi. Term II. Vol. 32. Ankara: Türkiye Büyük Millet Meclisi, 1983.

TBMM Zabıt Ceridesi. Term III. Vol. 3. Ankara: Türkiye Büyük Millet Meclisi, 1983.

TBMM Zabıt Ceridesi. Term III. Vol. 4. Ankara: Türkiye Büyük Millet Meclisi, 1983.

TBMM Zabıt Ceridesi. Term III. Vol. 5. Ankara: Türkiye Büyük Millet Meclisi, 1983.

TBMM Zabıt Ceridesi. Term IV. Vol. 9. Ankara: Türkiye Büyük Millet Meclisi, 1983.

TBMM Zabıt Ceridesi. Term IV. Vol. 15. Ankara: Türkiye Büyük Millet Meclisi, 1983.

TBMM Zabıt Ceridesi. Term IV. Vol. 23. Ankara: Türkiye Büyük Millet Meclisi, 1983.

TBMM Zabıt Ceridesi. Term IV. Vol. 23/1. Ankara: Türkiye Büyük Millet Meclisi, 1983.

TBMM Zabıt Ceridesi. Term IV. Vol. 25, addenda. Ankara: Türkiye Büyük Millet Meclisi, 1983.

TBMM Zabıt Ceridesi. Term IV. Vol. 25/1. Ankara: Türkiye Büyük Millet Meclisi, 1983.

TBMM Zabıt Ceridesi. Term V. Vol. 6. Ankara: Türkiye Büyük Millet Meclisi, 1983.

TBMM Zabıt Ceridesi. Term V. Vol. 26. Ankara: Türkiye Büyük Millet Meclisi, 1983.

"Tekke ve Zaviyeler ile Türbelerin Kapatılmasına ve Türbedarlıklar ile Bir Takım Unvanların Men ve İlgasına dair Kanun" (Law for Closing the Tekkes [Dervish Lodges], Zaviyes [Small Dervish Lodges], Türbes [Saint's Shrines], Banning, and Voiding Various Titles including Türbedar [Shrine-Keeper]). Law Nr 2/478. *Türk Parlamento Tarihi: TBMM-II. Dönem* (Turkish Parliamentary History: TGNA—Second term). Vol 2. Comp. Kâzım Öztürk. Ankara: TBMM Vakfı Yayınları, 1994: 27–44.

"Türkiye Cumhuriyeti Tabiiyetine Haiz Şirketler ile Eşhas tarafından Mubayaa Edilecek Sefainin Gümrük Resminden İstisnasına dair (2/289) Numaralı Teklifi Kanunisi" (bill Nr 2/289 on the exemption of ships bought by companies or persons of Turkish citizenship, from customs duties). TBMM Zabıt Ceridesi (Journal of Proceedings of the Turkish Grand National Assembly [TGNA]). Term II. Vol. 5. Ankara: Türkiye Büyük Millet Meclisi, 1983: 146–57.

"Türkiye'de Gençlik Teşkilâtının Türk Vatandaşlarına Hasrı hakkında Kanun" (Law on the Allotment of Youth Organizations in Turkey to Turkish Citizens). Nr 1246. May 12, 1928. *Düstur* (Code of Laws). Third set. Vol. 9. Ankara: Türkiye Büyük Millet Meclisi: 526–27.

"Türkiye'de Türk Vatandaşlarına Tahsis Edilen Sanat ve Hizmetler Hakkında Kanun" (Law on Professions and Services Allocated to Turkish Citizens in Turkey). Nr 2007. June 11, 1932. *Düstur* (Code of Laws). Third set. Vol. 13. Ankara: Türkiye Büyük Millet Meclisi: 649–50; and TBMM Zabıt Ceridesi (Journal of Proceedings of the Turkish Grand National Assembly [TGNA]). Term IV. Vol. 9. Ankara: Türkiye Büyük Millet Meclisi, 1983: 64–8, 90.

Türk Parlamento Tarihi: TBMM-II. Dönem (Turkish Parliamentary History: TBMM—Second Term). Comp. Kâzım Öztürk. Vol. 1. Ankara: TBMM Vakfı Yayınları, 1993.

Türk Parlamento Tarihi: TBMM-II. Dönem (Turkish Parliamentary History: TBMM—Second Term). Comp. Kâzım Öztürk. Vol. 2. Ankara: TBMM Vakfı Yayınları, 1994.

Türk Parlamento Tarihi: TBMM-IV. Dönem (Turkish Parliamentary History: TBMM—Fourth Term). Comp. Kâzım Öztürk. Vol. 1. Ankara: TBMM Vakfı Yayınları, 1996.

Turkey. Constitution. Translation into English of the Turkish Constitution of 1924, Embodying Such Amendments to the Text as have been made to date. typescript. s.n: s.n., 1937?

Encyclopedias and dictionaries

Cumhuriyet Dönemi Türkiye Ansiklopedisi (Encyclopedia of Turkey of the Republic Era). Istanbul: İletişim, 1983.

Türkiye Cumhuriyeti Tarihi Sözlüğü (Historical Dictionary of the Turkish Republic). Comp. M. Orhan Bayrak. Istanbul: Milenyum, 2000.

Yeni Türk Lûgatı (New Turkish Dictionary). Ed. İbrahim Alaettin. Istanbul: Kanaat, 1930.

Newspapers and periodicals

Anadolu (Ankara)
Cumhuriyet (Istanbul)
Hürriyet (Istanbul)
İnkılâp (Izmir)
Kadro (Ankara)
Kültür (Izmir)
La République (Ankara)
Milli İnkılâp (Istanbul)
Milliyet (Istanbul)
Orhun (Edirne)
Radikal (Istanbul)
Resmi Gazete (Official Gazette) (Ankara)
Sabah (Istanbul)
Tan (Istanbul)
Vakit (Istanbul)
Yeni Kültür (Izmir)

Index